FORGOTTEN VOICES

John McManners,
Adjutant, 1st Battalion, the Royal Northumberland Fusiliers,
1942 to 1944

FORGOTTEN VOICES

OF THE
FALKLANDS

IN ASSOCIATION WITH THE
IMPERIAL WAR MUSEUM

HUGH McMANNERS

EBURY
PRESS

5 7 9 10 8 6 4

Published in 2007 by Ebury Press, an imprint of Ebury Publishing

Ebury Publishing is a division of the Random House Group

Introduction © Max Hastings 2007
Text © Hugh McManners and the Imperial War Museum 2007
Photographs © Imperial War Museum 2007

Bill Belcher and Jim Mitchell material taken from interviews performed for the television
programmes *Splendid Hearts* and *Battlecries*, and used by kind permission of the BBC

The author is most grateful to fellow author and Falkland Islander Graham Bound for
permitting use of his personal collection

Hugh McManners has asserted his right to be identified as the author of this work under the
Copyright, Designs and Patents Act 1988

The Random House Group Limited Reg. No. 954009

Addresses for companies within the Random House Group can be found at
www.randomhouse.co.uk

A CIP catalogue record for this book is available from the British Library

The Random House Group Limited makes every effort to ensure that the papers used in our
books are made from trees that have been legally sourced from well-managed and credibly
certified forests. Our paper procurement policy can be found on www.randomhouse.co.uk

Printed and bound in Great Britain by Clays of St Ives PLC

ISBN 9780091908805

Contents

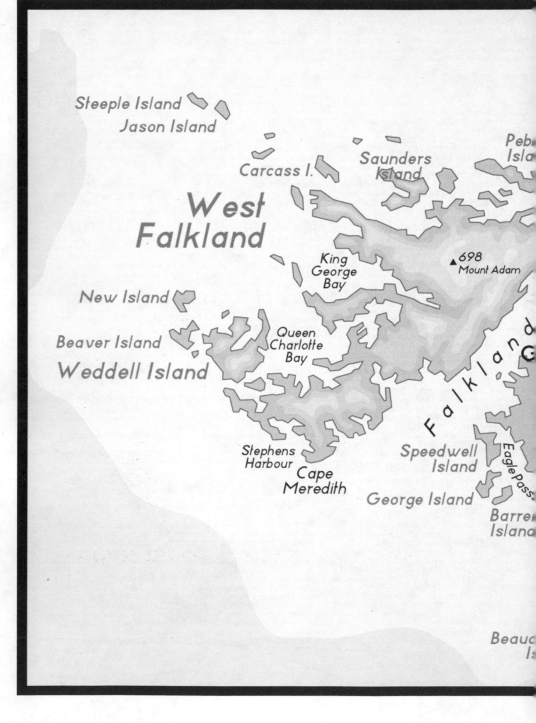

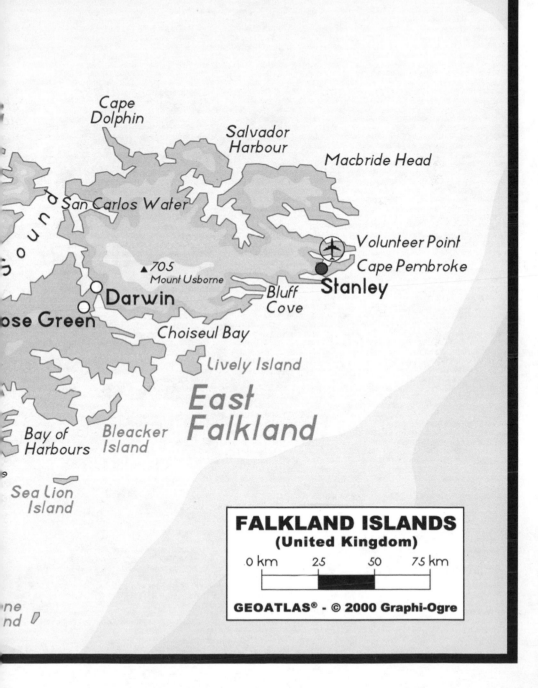

Cape
Dolphin

Salvador
Harbour

Macbride Head

San Carlos Water

Sound

Volunteer Point

Cape Pembroke

▲705
Mount Usborne

Stanley

Darwin

Bluff
Cove

ose Green

Choiseul Bay

Lively Island

Bay of
Harbours

Bleacker
Island

East
Falkland

Sea Lion
Island

ne
nd

FALKLAND ISLANDS
(United Kingdom)

0 km   25   50   75 km

GEOATLAS® - © 2000 Graphi-Ogre

Author's Preface

It has been strangely rewarding to research and write a history book of events in which I took part. I was a naval gunfire forward observer, working with my five-man team as part of the Special Boat Squadron, sometimes on low-key reconnaissance missions, and other times on offensive raids that, once launched, were very high profile indeed. Listening to the testimonies of other people involved in these missions, the thought processes of senior commanders and, in one particularly poignant and upsetting interview, the tragic results of one of my operations, was strange to say the least.

This experience also underlined one of the fundamental truths of war experience, that the memories of one person will be completely different to others, even those closely involved in the same operations or incidents. One interviewee says, after his ship was attacked by Argentine aircraft: 'I was shocked to see just what a difference being a few feet away could make.' A bomb blast can singe one person's eyebrows, whilst dismembering others. Cannon fire can miss the people being aimed at, whilst steel splinters from the riccochets kill and mutilate others close by. There is no common experience, and in any case, people are different, and are very differently affected by their experiences. And as military analysts and historians sometimes forget, it is the sum total of these very different personal experiences that constitute the reality of military operations, not the regimental histories, medal citations and senior commanders' *mémoires*.

This book tells a very wide-ranging and complicated story using nothing but the testimonies of the people who carried out the operation. It is, therefore, a primary historical source, which allows the reader to evaluate what is being said, and make judgements as to why various things happened, and ultimately make their own view of the essential nature of this most unusual war. My father, the late Rev Prof John McManners FBA, an historian of eighteenth and nineteenth-century France, talked with me about the restricted primary sources available to him, and the difficulties of making the actual people come to life just through letters, official records and so on. For twentieth-century historians, access to the less deliberate and unedited verbal accounts of combatants provides often startling revelations, especially when different accounts of the same incidents are cut together, as I have done throughout this book. By listening to the actual voices, one swiftly understands the personal motives of people, especially those attempting to influence posterity with an overly idiosyncratic version of events. Pomposity, arrogance, false self-deprecation and aggrandisement are easily identified, and make tremendous listening, particularly as there are plenty of other more rational, modest interviewees to put the record straight. These verbal accounts are far more valuable than official reports and memoirs. The new problem for historians is one of coping with their sheer volume, a difficulty requiring countless hours of listening and transcribing.

Future military historians will conclude that the British Falkland recovery, Operation Corporate, was a unique, unrepeatable feat of arms over lines of communication that could not be more extreme. The serious failings that led to the war were by politicians and diplomats on both sides, not to be confused with the military disputes and confusion I have chronicled in this book, which were all part of the *ad lib* process of succeeding in something desperate and unprecedented. Some military commanders richly deserve praise, some did not rise to the occasion, a few failed, and others have tried to claim more glory than they deserve, some even attempting to denigrate the efforts of others. 'Twas ever thus, and examples of all these are revealed in this book.

The Falklands War was also the first high-tech war, in which conventional fighting took place using the land, sea and air all at the same time, with units interconnected by radio and radar, very much a precursor to the 'digital battlefield', rather than a continuation of World War Two 'all-arms' tactics. (A friend of my father, the late historian A.L. Rowse, told me he regarded the Falklands War as being in the same tradition as Drake and Raleigh, as Britain's last truly 'Elizabethan' enterprise.) I've included several blow-by-blow accounts of land, sea and air perspectives on the same battle, including some where the witnesses were connected to each other by radio, like Harrier pilots bombing land targets, and naval gunfire forward observers like me in land battles, calling in fire from ships fighting a naval battle at the same time.

It is also very interesting to compare the capabilities of modern weapons with those of the Korean and Second World Wars, which were the last occasions in which British forces had taken part in full-scale conventional battles. In reality, there is no comparison, the weapons of today being so enormously powerful, rapid-firing and accurate, dictating radical changes in battle tactics, as well as creating an illogical but very noticeable reduction in battle casualties, through the necessity of greatly increased battle craft skills. Battles can now be fought exclusively at night, which was the only way Brigadier Julian Thompson, as the senior commander on land until June 1, could work out to overcome the huge numerical superiority of the Argentine Army, thereby maximising the psychological and moral effect of his better-trained and more highly motivated troops, and avoiding a daylight slaughter by the longer-ranging Argentine direct-fire infantry weapons.

The experiences of the Second Battalion of the Parachute Regiment are of particular interest, as they are the only unit to have taken part in two consecutive conventional war battles in the same campaign, certainly since Korea, and probably since the Second World War. Even against the yardstick of the Second World War, 2 Paras' second battle at Wireless Ridge was only a few days separated from their first at Darwin Goose Green, with no reinforcements and very few battle casualty replacements, the most uniquely notable being their Commanding Officer, Lieutenant Colonel David Chaundler, who, upon arrival in theatre from the UK after parachuting into the sea, was told by both his general and the commander 5 Infantry Brigade that he was not needed. 2 Paras' first battle at Goose Green was the crucial test to establish moral domination over a vastly superior enemy, and was very nearly a defeat. I have split this story into two chapters, one covering the intended plan up until the death of the Commanding Officer H Jones, the second showing how his small team of pragmatic, battle-hardened officers and cheerfully ruthless paratroopers turned defeat into the most astonishing victory. 2 Paras' second battle was a very different affair, their having very rapidly learned the lessons that had so nearly led to their defeat first time round.

On land, the man who got us all ashore safely, then planned and fought the key battles, was Brigadier Julian Thompson, who I am proud to say was also my boss for the critical landings. He comes over on tape as he is in real life, modest, clear thinking, amusing and self critical. He insists that he was the architect of 2 Paras' near disaster at Goose Green, and that he should have resisted London's calls for an immediate attack and gone down there himself with an additional Commando, armoured cars being used as light tanks, with full artillery and naval gunfire support, and fought a brigade battle. Of course, this would have delayed the rest of the operation for a week at least, which could have proved disastrous, and London was emphatic in its demands for some immediate good news from the task force. In any case, with his general incommunicado on the liner QE2 for the critical eight days, there was nobody senior enough prepared to tell London where to sling their hook.

The Royal Navy was at odds, not only with its own Fleet Air Arm, but also with its amphibious command and the land forces themselves. The MoD had not appointed an overall commander, and there were serious misunderstandings which were never resolved. The carrier force stayed safely so far north-east of the Islands as to be known as the 'South African Navy', and some thought that its admiral and staff never understood what the amphibious ships commanded by the Commodore Amphibious Warfare (COMMAW) inshore were doing, or the nature of operations ashore. The complications and disasters created by all this are well described by the officers and other ranks affected by the situation, revealing the depth of knowledge and involvement required of every participant in modern, computer-driven warfare.

It has also been a privilege to include not only the Falkland Islanders and their perspective, but also to tell the Argentine story as well. It is clear that the garrison commander, Brigadier General Menendez, and his staff meant well in a very peculiar sort of fashion, but that by virtue of the regime under which they lived, they were incapable of understanding the feelings of the islanders, and were teetering on the brink of their benign 'occupation' turning nasty. It is to their credit that, despite the enormous pressures of the situation, there were no really serious abuses of human rights. I save all my brickbats for the civil servants, politicians and diplomats of the governments of both the Argentine Republic and the United Kingdom – very much in that order. As the Special Boat Squadron sergeant major observed at one point during my initial Falklands operation, the Fanning Head raid: 'This, gentlemen, is not the way to do business.'

Hugh McManners
February 2007

Author's Acknowledgements

The first people I must thank are the interviewees who took the trouble to be so frank and interesting with the Imperial War Museum tape machine running, recounting incidents that many of them will have hidden away in their minds for years, rather than risking the unpleasant memories they can conjure up. It's vital that politicians, voters and historians understand the reality of war, but even though the actual experience is simply too intense to describe, we must all persevere in explaining, lest our leaders be inclined to enter wars without proper and serious consideration . . .

I must thank all my friends on the Falkland Islands for their hospitality and understanding towards my son William and me when we visited in 2005: to Gary Clements and the excellent SAMA82 organisation on the Islands, to Norma and Roger Edwards for a cracking wedding, everyone at Fox Bay and Hill Cove for our hangovers, John Birmingham, Simon Goss, and the team at Sea Lion Island for accommodation and hospitality, to Sharon Halford, Tony Smith, Gerald Cheek and our other many and expert guides and drivers (you have to be able to drive a Land Rover very seriously to get around the Falklands). And Steven Luxton for a tremendous day of wildlife appreciation.

I would also like to thank His Excellency Ambassador Federico Mirré for his kindness, and for recounting the extraordinary scenes in the Foreign Ministry and elsewhere inside Argentina, to his Political Minister Maria Fernada Canas, and his Naval Attaché Captain Carlos Castro Madero for reliving the harrowing memories of the sinking of his ship, *Belgrano*.

In the preparation of this book, many people gave me invaluable help: to Jake Lingwood at Ebury for his calm understanding of my difficulties with deadlines and for his enthusiastic support, and Ken Barlow my long-suffering but equally encouraging editor. My father the Rev Prof John McManners FBA read various sections, but sadly will never see the finished article. His last piece of professional analysis is preserved on a single sheet of A4, advising a more structured approach to my chapter *Vida En Las Islas Malvinas:* it has been rewritten according to his sub-headings.

The Imperial War Museum's Elizabeth Bowers has been a great supporter of this project from inception, and with Gemma Maclagan has solved various difficulties along the way for which many thanks. Margaret Brooks' team in the Sound Archive have been equally supportive, with special thanks to John Stopford-Pickering and Richard McDonough for expert advice and moral support, and to Robert White for so cheerfully shipping out tapes to keep me going during a very long, hot summer of transcribing. I am also most grateful to the Imperial War Museum's historian Terry Charman for verifying the historical accuracy of my manuscript.

My copy editor Bernice Davison was accuracy epitomised, more than countering my inclination toward variation and literary anarchy; and I am also grateful to Ebury's publicity manager Caroline Newbury. And finally, for the unwavering support, encouragement and frank advice of my literary agent and friend of over twenty years, Barbara Levy, very many thanks.

Introduction
by Sir Max Hastings

On a spring morning twenty-five years ago, I was sitting in my study deep in the English countryside, staring intently at a computer screen. Writing history, as I was doing, requires a leap of imagination, to think oneself back into a period. That day, I was trying to picture how it felt to be crouched in a landing craft approaching a hostile shore under naval support bombardment, on June 6, 1944.

Suddenly the phone rang, and a friend said: 'Isn't it amazing, about the Argentine landing in the Falklands?' In the days which followed, I abandoned my D-Day book to hover beside radio, TV and phone, as an extraordinary political drama unfolded. At first, like many others, I was disbelieving when the government announced the dispatch of a naval task force to reoccupy the islands, if the Argentines refused to withdraw. These were the last years of the twentieth century, for heaven's sake. It seemed fantastic to imagine that we might fight a colonial war against a Latin-American nation, for a waterlogged fragment of real estate eight thousand miles down the Atlantic.

Yet as Britain's preparations for battle intensified, I was swept away by the thrill and emotion of the moment. If indeed the prime minister, Margaret Thatcher, was to launch a military expedition to recapture the Falklands, the nearest possible modern equivalent to Kitchener's 1898 descent of the Nile to fight the Khalifa forces, I felt passionately eager to witness it. Thus it was that a few weeks later I found myself crouched in a landing craft amid a company of Royal Marines, approaching the shore of San Carlos amid the distant concussions of the naval support bombardment.

Hugh McManners, who has here assembled a remarkable collection of narratives, recounting participants' memories of the Falklands war, played a much more distinguished personal role than my own. As a forward observer for the Royal Navy's warship guns, he himself experienced all manner of dramas, which he has recounted elsewhere. His own close involvement in the saga makes him ideally suited to orchestrate this symphony of other people's reminiscences. It is so easy, in the rosy evening light of afterwards, to suppose that British victory in the South Atlantic was a foregone conclusion. Hugh knows better. It was a fantastically close-run thing. If the Royal Navy had lost an aircraft carrier, or more Argentine bombs had exploded, what became a national triumph could have been a national tragedy.

Almost all those who participated in the campaign on the British side found the experience profoundly moving. The preceding decades had not been happy ones for our country. The memory of humiliation at Suez in 1956 overhung its foreign policy. Closer to home, economic and industrial failure were pervasive themes of all our lives in the 1960s and 1970s. Most of us were resigned to a belief that national decline was irreversible. We grew accustomed to expecting anything 'Made in Britain' not to work.

Then, in the South Atlantic, we watched the British armed forces display courage, competence and commitment of the highest order. It seemed a joy and privilege suddenly to see our soldiers, sailors and Royal Marines doing something immensely well. For those of us accustomed to existing amid the selfishness, jealousy and pettiness of daily peacetime life, the brotherhood of war seemed real and inspiring.

Of course, one should not idealise this too far. The war was landmarked by plenty of squabbles and dissensions, especially between higher commanders. Rows are inseparable from any conflict, because life and death depend on the issues in dispute. Almost all battles are fought by people who are very tired, and in the Falklands often cold, wet and hungry as well. The cliché is true, that war enables us to see mankind at both his finest and basest. The finest of the South Atlantic task force was very fine indeed. Hugh McManners has gathered in these pages many tales which make the point.

I have reported a good many wars, but there is none of which the scenes and memories remain more vivid than that of 1982: warships listing and sinking at San Carlos as Argentine jets streaked overhead; long columns of filthy, bedraggled, impossibly burdened men trudging across the peat; ponchos stretched for shelter flapping in a wind that never stilled; brilliant flashes of gunfire, lighting up craggy battlefields; the exultant laughter of success overcoming clogging weariness, as at last we glimpsed the low tin roofs of Port Stanley. All the sights and sounds of that extraordinary campaign are here, recalled by the men who did so many remarkable things during its course. No one is better fitted to present the words of the participants than Hugh McManners. His book represents a worthy tribute both to those who died, and to those who survived this freak of history and played their parts in creating a national legend.

Part One

FATAL
MISCALCULATIONS

The causes of the Falklands War of 1982 stem from events as far back as anybody cares to remember, with a great deal for highly paid international lawyers to argue over, but nothing definitive to allow a clear solution to be agreed. The arguments are also rather confusing. Argentina's heartfelt claim is that the British seized the islands from them by force in 1833. Britain says that in this critical incident no shots were fired and only few Argentine officials were told to leave, and in any case the Englishman, Captain John Strong, had already landed, named and claimed the islands in 1690. Further, a British expedition in 1765 claimed sovereignty of all the islands, establishing a settlement the following year.

The background to the key incident of 1833 is equally indistinct. Argentina says Magellan discovered the islands in 1522, whereas the Italian Amerigo Vespucci said he did so in 1502. The first undisputed sighting was by Dutchman Sebald van Weert, circa 1600. Ninety years later Captain Strong landed and named the islands after Viscount Falkland, then First Lord of the Admiralty. Seal-hunting fishermen from St Malo referred to the islands as *Iles Malouines*, from which the Spanish name *Malvinas* is derived. The French founded the first settlement in 1764–5, at Port Louis. In 1764, Port Louis was bought by Spain for £24,000 and renamed Puerto de la Soledad. In 1765 the British were the first to settle in West Falkland.

The sovereignty dispute started in 1770, when a Spanish flotilla forced the British settlers to leave, who returned the following year after threats of war, but withdrew in 1774 for economic reasons. Argentina declared independence from Spain in 1816, but was not recognised by Britain or any other foreign power. An American, Colonel Daniel Jowett, claimed the islands for the Buenos Aires government in 1820, but stayed only a few days. The first Argentine settlement took place in 1828, and the following June, the still unrecognised Argentina placed the islands under its governance – which was disputed by Britain as an infringement of its sovereignty claim from 1690. There is some irony in an American having first claimed the islands for Argentina, and the United States warship *Lexington* then destroying Argentina's Puerto de la Soledad settlement in 1831 as retribution for the arrest of three US seal-hunting ships – nearly leading to war between the two countries.

In 1832 Argentina appointed a Malvinas governor, Mestevier, who was murdered by rebellious Argentine soldiers and settlers. The British 'invasion' of 1833 was made in response to the murder of Mathew Brisbane and others at Port Louis by gauchos led by Antonio Rivera. Brisbane, who was administrating the settlement on behalf of Vernet, was killed by having each limb lassoed to a horse, then being dragged apart, probably because he was paying the gauchos in promissory notes rather than hard cash. Some say that the Argentines' Vice Royalty of the River Plate invited the British to establish control in order to prevent the US from taking over the Falklands. HMS *Clio* arrived and rescued the survivors of Rivera's uprising, who had fled to the neighbouring Tussock Islands, restoring order and British sovereignty, sending the remaining Argentines home. By 1855, eighteen hundred British people were permanently established in a self-supporting community, from which many of today's Falkland Islanders are directly descended.

When the sovereignty of the Falkland Islands was debated in the UN in 1964, Argentina based its claim on its 'inheritance' from Spain, of the division of the New World between Spain and Portugal in 1494, Papal bulls of 1493, and the need to end what it described as the 'colonial occupation' of the islands by the British. Britain argued on the basis of continuous effective possession, occupation and administration, and that Argentine rule would in effect be another form of colonial rule, but against the will of the islanders.

There are two irrefutable and opposing truths: that Argentina desperately wants to possess the islands; and that the people who live there, the majority for five generations and many for much longer, are passionately British and, particularly after the Argentine invasion of 1982, have no desire to be made part of Argentina. The Falkland Islands are described by the British Government as 'a United Kingdom Overseas Territory by choice'. They are, in effect, their own country, with an elected legislative council, and could achieve complete independence from Britain if they so desired. There is, therefore, no question of Argentina being in any sort of conflict or dispute with Britain, but with a very small independent country of four thousand seven hundred square miles and a population of less than three thousand, whose defence and foreign policy is underwritten by the British government.

There is an obvious geopolitical dimension to the Falklands/Malvinas dispute. At their closest to Argentina, the Falklands are some two hundred and fifty miles from the tip of Tierra del Fuego, and over three hundred and fifty miles from the nearest Patagonian coast, and are not considered to be joined to South America's continental shelf; Argentines talk of 'the continent' as separate to the 'the Malvinas'. International law regards various offshore distances as being of significance to territorial disputes: three miles, seven miles and twenty-one miles, with two hundred miles as an absolute limit. Territorial contiguity (via an undersea continental shelf) does not seem to have much force in international law; otherwise presumably the Canaries would belong to Morocco. Argentina also has territorial disputes with neighbouring Chile over ownership of the Beagle Channel, which nearly led her to further war just a few months after the end of her Malvinas War with Britain.

Argentina's belligerence is based upon the logic of considerable self-interest; the Falklands are the gateway to Antarctica and have the highest average per capita income in South America, plus the strong likelihood of oil and precious minerals. Whereas Argentina was once prosperous, now she is not, and it is hard to see how the Falkland Islanders could come to accept being taken over by her.

Since the end of World War Two, the United Nations has given precedence to the desires and needs of people, over the territorial aspirations of nation states. Argentina is in this sense being very old fashioned, pursuing a purely territorial claim that is so clearly against the wishes and interests of the indigenous inhabitants of the Falkland Islands. However, many would argue that for Britain to have ignored both its own responsibilities and the Argentine desire for the Malvinas, to the extent of permitting their invasion of 1982 through the incompetence of the Foreign Office and the negligence of ministers, is rather worse than old fashioned.

1

Mixed Messages and Wishful Thinking

*General Galtieri . . . played the Malvinas card at the insistence
of the Argentine Navy as a way of stifling internal opposition . . .
his actions gave Mrs Thatcher the opportunity to display very considerable
powers of resolution and leadership. It was inevitable that neither
was going to back down.*

Captain Carlos B. Castro Madero
Weapons Officer 5-Inch Anti-Aircraft Batteries,
Warship Belgrano
Like most people in Argentina I think the Malvinas are part of our country,
but separated for reasons we do not accept. I always had mixed feelings about
Great Britain; I admire their history, and the times I've been in Britain people
have always been very respectful, and I really like their way of life. We have
very many things in common, and should always have been in the same team.
But this problem of the Malvinas is putting great difficulty into our relations.
I am convinced that sooner or later the Malvinas must become Argentinian.

Gerald Cheek
Director of Civil Aviation, Falkland Islands
In the 1920s they said every young islander was an Argentine citizen and must
do national service in the Argentine army. Links were then cut with
Argentina, leaving us with no mail and a monthly shipping link with
Uruguay, a four-day voyage. In 1966 a group of Argentines hijacked a DC-4
airliner and landed on Stanley racecourse, and there were a couple of similar

incursions until the Argentines stopped the Falkland Islands Company shipping link with Uruguay, in 1971.

Maria Fernada Canas (Head of Political Section, Argentine Embassy, 2006)
Argentine school teacher
At school in the late Sixties, in geography and history lessons we had some special classes on the Malvinas, presented to us as an Argentine territory that was seized from Argentina by Great Britain using force, in 1833. Britain was at that time a strong power, so it was impossible for us to stand against it.

Captain Barry Hussey
Administrator of Health, Social Services and Education, Islas Malvinas
Las Malvinas Argentinas . . . We used to have it in the reading books for children. I always felt that there would be stronger attachments between the islands and Argentina as time passed, but that it was better to wait.

Maria Fernada Canas (Head of Political Section, Argentine Embassy, 2006)
Argentine school teacher
In 1974, my sister worked in the British secondary school in Buenos Aires and was asked to go to the Malvinas to teach Spanish – good English required. I asked if I could go as well, so after being interviewed by the Argentine Foreign Office and the head of the school in Stanley who had flown to Buenos Aires, we were both chosen. I remember the crosswind when we landed. I could hardly keep myself standing up. It was somewhere strange but very attractive, a curious place I wanted to find out more about. I was in the islands for a year, flying back to Buenos Aires in the holidays. We did evening classes for adults, radio lesson sessions, and a radio programme for the camp. The wife of the governor had private lessons at Government House. The islanders were travelling regularly to Argentina, Uruguay and Chile. Their children got scholarships to schools and went to hospitals in Buenos Aires, where they had to speak Spanish.

Gerald Cheek
Director of Civil Aviation, Falkland Islands
In 1976, the British government thought the Argentines might invade and so a top-secret GCHQ station was built at Feltham Stream, west of Stanley. You couldn't get near to it. One of the Royal Signals guys married a Falkland girl. But we never knew what they were up to: I imagine it was monitoring Argentine signals traffic.

Then in 1977, I guess from the GCHQ intelligence, British Prime Minister Callaghan learned the Argentines were about to invade and sent down a small task force of frigates, an oil tanker and submarines. We discovered this only after the 1982 war. The British government built a permanent airfield, which opened in November 1977, with Argentine air force aircraft coming in twice a week.

Maria Fernada Canas (Head of Political Section, Argentine Embassy, 2006)
Argentine school teacher
There were some difficult moments, and very pleasant moments too. The way of life was very different; kneading your own bread, spinning the wool and making garments with the ladies group, growing tomatoes in a winter house, chopping your own peat and burning it. In our house we had a cooker plus heating and hot water, but most of the houses were heated solely using peat, which is very hard work to keep going. Sometimes the Rayburn stove would go out, which was frustrating.

It was picturesque, a slowed-down rhythm of life, very orderly with a routine for everything: and for just a year it was wonderful, but I did note the lack of entertainment and general development. They might show a movie in the church, and there was the *Calling the Falklands* radio show once a week. A weekly aeroplane brought fresh fruit and vegetables. I thought the situation out in the Camp was precarious. By my standards of that time, their lives seemed bare and basic.

Trudi McPhee
Brookfields, North Camp
I live at Brookfields, thirty-one miles as the crow flies from Stanley, which in 1982, before they put in the roads, took us between three and twenty-seven hours to get there, depending on the state of the ground. If the Camp is wet, you spend hours bogged in. My dad was lucky enough to buy this section when the Falkland Islands Company sub-divided land for ordinary people to buy. An old chimney base was already here, but we had to cut everything else in half and drag it three miles down the track from Green Patch. We lived a year in a caravan, then after cutting the house in half, we nearly wrecked it by dragging it through some balsom bogs which nearly tipped the house off the sleigh.

We didn't have any money and there were no grants, so we had to wait until we received that year's wool clip share before we could buy bricks and cement. People who live on the farms can turn their hands to most things, so we did the building work ourselves.

General Mario Benjamin Menendez
Military Governor, Islas Malvinas
The UN Resolution said England and Argentina should take into account the *interests* of the inhabitants of the Malvinas, something Argentina was always willing to do. But the government of Mrs Thatcher introduced the word 'wishes'. I am sure that the people of the Malvinas did not wish to stop being English subjects, but judging by the conditions in which they lived in the Malvinas, they were second-class subjects.

Maria Fernada Canas (Head of Political Section, Argentine Embassy, 2006)
Argentine school teacher
We saw two distinct and different groups of people: the islanders, and the British people who'd been sent over to do various jobs, with more money and better houses. Being from Great Britain, they also had more education. The local school was old fashioned, like lectures with children listening then repeating things. It was two different worlds.

Neil Watson
Long Island, East Falklands
The Argentine military junta government consisted of the president General Galtieri, and an admiral and an air force general who swapped around as presidents. They lost patience with diplomatic negotiations. As they were also having troubles within Argentina, these three needed to divert attention from the internal troubles, so decided to invade the Falklands. They wanted it done before the 150th anniversary of what they call the British takeover of the Falklands, when the British established their right to the Islands in 1833.

Rear Admiral Anthony John Whetstone
Deputy Chief of Naval Staff (Operations), MoD Whitehall
General Galtieri was very worried about criticism and opposition to his government, and had played the Malvinas card at the insistence of the Argentine Navy as a way of stifling internal opposition, while doing something very dear and deeply rooted in the Argentine psyche. Conversely, his actions gave Mrs Thatcher the opportunity to display very considerable powers of resolution and leadership, and dampen down a lot of the criticism of her domestic policy. It was inevitable that neither of them was going to back down.

General Mario Benjamin Menendez
Military Governor, Islas Malvinas
I think Mrs Thatcher accepted the opportunity that Argentina presented to strengthen her government, prolonging her term as Prime Minister by defending the rights of the inhabitants of the Malvinas. This was hypocrisy; it was no trouble for the British to remove the population of the Diego Garcia island in the Indian Ocean so the United States could set up a military base. I call that a double standard: respecting people's rights when it suits you, but ignoring them when it is not convenient.

Maria Fernada Canas (Head of Political Section, Argentine Embassy, 2006)
Argentine school teacher
A small group of islanders had political concerns about us. Sometimes people turned their heads away when they saw us on the street, crossed to the other side of the road, or wrote things about us. You could tell how the parents thought about us through their children, who would say things spontaneously to us. The parents would smile at us outside, but we knew what they really thought. I suppose it was necessary for them to keep good relations going; they might need to use links with Argentina. At school they did practice exercises for an Argentine invasion: the Defence Group would be running, cars driving about and the children shouting and yelling. I could see there were some strong feelings about this.

Neil Watson
Long Island, East Falkland
As chairman of a group of Falklands people and business friends in London called the Falkland Islands Association, I was involved with the politics. Negotiations took place all through the 1970s. We could see the Argentines getting more and more frustrated. They'd thought that once the communications agreement had been signed in 1971, it would only be a matter of time. A lot of people didn't see it coming – but I did.

Gerald Cheek
Director of Civil Aviation, Falkland Islands
The pressure on us started in earnest when the Argentines took over supplying all our fuel. The Falkland Island Government Colonial Secretary and Chief Executive, both British civil servants, told us that no other companies would supply us with fuel, which wasn't true as they hadn't bothered to ask any other companies. This gave the Argentines a monopoly

on both fuel and our transportation links with the outside world. Next, the Argentines refused to recognise our British passports, and issued us with white Argentine identification cards.

Maria Fernada Canas (Head of Political Section, Argentine Embassy, 2006)
Argentine school teacher
Sometimes the airline company's office windows would be smashed, but there was no personal aggression towards us. At the personal level, life goes on. My sister married an Englishman who was in the islands building the airfield. She moved with him to live in England, so I came many times to visit them. Even with the people who turned their face away, we did normal things like exchange recipes. Afterwards we discovered people thought we were spies!

Major Simon Ewen Southby-Tailyour
Royal Marines
I was the most senior captain in both the Royal Marines and in the landing craft branch of the Royal Marines, and in 1979, I'd been asked by the Foreign Office and Ministry of Defence to rewrite the concept of operations and standard operating procedures for the defence of the Falklands, which was approved at Cabinet level.

However, the Foreign Office representative on the islands tried to prevent us from doing the surveying, and the Foreign Office in London were not actually interested in the defence of the Falklands. Mr Parker also wanted my wife to spy on the social side of the civil population in Stanley, which she refused to do.

The subject of imminent Argentine invasion was the topic of conversation in the Falklands every single day; not 'If' but 'When' and 'How'. The Falklanders' fear was regarded by London as paranoia, but was real and constant.

Neil Watson
Long Island, East Falkland
I was absolutely certain there would be an invasion, and so were a lot of other people, including the governor, Rex Hunt, and the captain of HMS *Endurance*, Nick Barker.

In December 1979 I sent some wool, our main product, to the UK. In February 1980, I telephoned my agent in London and told him not to send the cheque to me, as I thought we'd be likely to need the money in UK, not here. The warnings were there for all to see, but were ignored by the British Government, Foreign Office and the Ministry of Defence.

Major Simon Ewen Southby-Tailyour
Royal Marines

The Argentines had sent a task force in 1977, and after invading South Thule, they'd removed their ambassador from London. They were sending aircraft to the islands containing fifteen pilots, who would then practise landings and gain intelligence, which I reported back. Our new instructions were to have a bloody fight with the invaders, but we had no equipment for this. We couldn't even communicate with UK from eight o'clock in the evening until the next morning, apart from via radio hams. Realistically, with the UK's response at least three weeks away, if we fought we would end up with forty-two dead Royal Marines.

John Fowler
Superintendent of Education, Stanley

In 1980, Nicholas Ridley [British Miniter of State], the British Minister of State, Nicholas Ridley, came down here and spoke to a packed audience in the town hall, probably with a few gins under his belt. He offered us the options: to remain as we were, which he said wouldn't work; Condominium, Shared Sovereignty, or the favoured option – a Hong Kong-style leaseback arrangement with Argentina. After some barracking and a lot of perceptive questioning, Ridley lost his rag, and said things like: 'On your own heads be it, if you continue with this intransigence. This isn't the Victorian era. We're not going to send a gunboat down to save you if you get yourselves into trouble.' Had Mr Ridley looked down to his left beside the fire exit, he would have seen a group of Argentine air force officers from the airline company who were immediately on the phone back to the Casa Rosada in Argentina saying, 'There it is. The British Minister says it's OK. It would appear that if we invade, the British Army won't do anything.'

General Mario Benjamin Menendez
Military Governor, Islas Malvinas

In February 1982 after a series of talks in New York, Argentina observed that England did not wish to discuss sovereignty, when really it was the main subject. I had no knowledge that Argentina had started to think of the military option. A very small commission had worked that out in a completely secret manner.

Neil Watson
Long Island, East Falkland
Despite being worried about this in 1980, we were very proud to buy our own farm, and establish our own part of the world down here. My worries about the future didn't affect this.

Glenda Watson
Long Island, East Falkland
Life had to go on . . . it didn't matter how worried you were. You can't just stand still and do nothing because you think something's going to happen. When we first came out here to Long Island, from Stanley in 1980, I was so frightened, particularly at night time, as I was convinced something bad was going to happen. With other people in Stanley it didn't seem so bad, but when Neil had to go away at night to work, I'd sleep with a gun under my bed.

Rear Admiral Anthony John Whetstone
Deputy Chief of Naval Staff (Operations), MoD Whitehall
I was appointed Chief of Naval Staff (Operations) in 1980, and discovered Mrs Thatcher was looking to make some serious defence cuts. At that stage, she did not regard the armed forces as the saviours of the nation, let alone of the Conservative Party, but as a rather expensive drain on the public finances. Mr Keith Speed was sacked after making a rather good speech in support of the Navy, to be succeeded by another defence minister who was accused of going native, after which John Nott was sent in to 'put the rebellious priests' in order and make some economies.

Commander Robert Denton Green
Intelligence Staff Officer to Commander-in-Chief, Fleet HQ, Northwood
I ran the joint intelligence centre from the bunker at Northwood. I had a team of forty Wrens working round the clock, focused on the Soviets, plotting their deployments and passing out regular reports to the Polaris nuclear submarine office, which was right next door. I also had a communications centre, which had the highest level of security, for getting information from GCHQ and the Americans. The Falklands War was a complete aberration, and very strange.

In December 1981, the government announced the Nott Defence Review, named after the Secretary of State for Defence John Nott, which was going to be very severe.

Air Marshal Joseph Alfred Gilbert
Assistant Chief of Defence Staff (Policy), MoD, Whitehall
I was trying to take up bird watching, and had just booked into a hotel in Scotland, with my wife. I returned to Whitehall to find my horizons radically restricted, from ten years into the future of defence policy planning, to between twenty-four hours and maybe a week ahead, as the Falklands crisis unfolded. My staff were determining what we could do and how. The operators were already loading ships, to be ready to do whatever we decided.

Commander Robert Denton Green
Intelligence Staff Officer to Commander-in-Chief, Fleet HQ, Northwood
Admiral Fieldhouse took over as Commander-in-Chief Fleet in August 1981. He told me he'd attended a meeting in the MoD with Foreign & Commonwealth Office officials, going through all the contingency plans for Britain's remaining dependencies. He told me he had asked specifically for the Falklands contingency plan, and discovered there wasn't one. He'd asked why not, because he knew that if ever there was going to be a plan put into action, this one was going to be his baby. The FCO officials told him that it was all in hand, that they were negotiating it and could handle it, and not to worry. So he let it go.

Rear Admiral Anthony John Whetstone
Deputy Chief of Naval Staff (Operations), MoD Whitehall
When the crisis blew up in the South Atlantic, we were still fighting off Nott's proposals to sell carrier HMS *Invincible* to the Australians, carrier HMS *Hermes* to India, and pay off both amphibious vessels *Fearless* and *Intrepid*. He was also proposing to make corresponding cuts in the navy's manpower levels, and had carried forward the earlier proposal to scrap naval icebreaker HMS *Endurance*.

Commander Robert Denton Green
Intelligence Staff Officer to Commander-in-Chief, Fleet HQ, Northwood
I understand Lord Carrington went personally to plead with Mrs Thatcher for *Endurance* to be excluded because of the appalling signal it would send to General Galtieri about our lack of commitment to the Falklands, but she overruled him. I believe this was the root of that war.

Endurance made its last patrol at Christmas 1981. I knew her captain Nick Barker, and briefed him before he left. He was extremely concerned, especially when it was revealed that getting rid of the ship was only going to save £3m. Directly Captain Barker got to Buenos Aires, he sent back his first report. He was very experienced and had been down there before, where he always held a big cocktail party and social gathering. His report said, 'Things have changed, we are being cold-shouldered, something is going on . . .' But in London he was assumed to be lobbying for his ship, and his reports were ignored.

But Admiral Fieldhouse knew his man and took the reports very seriously. He asked the FCO and MoD yet again for a Falklands contingency plan, but still wasn't given one. By the end of January 1982 Admiral Fieldhouse told us to write a Falklands contingency plan for him, which we finished as *Davidoff*, the 'try-on' scrap metal merchant sent by the Argentines to test our will, arrived in South Georgia. This is why we were able to react so quickly.

General Mario Benjamin Menendez
Military Governor, Islas Malvinas
I first realised I was going to be involved in a Malvinas operation in the first week of March of 1982, during a meeting with General Galtieri. I was Major General of the Army, an important position. When I had completed making my report and we were alone, General Galtieri said to me, 'Now I have to say something.' He then told me that the Argentine government, or rather the military junta, were considering taking military action in the Malvinas if they did not achieve any headway in the conversations they were having with the English, in particular with regard to sovereignty. General Galtieri told me that depending on how things developed, there would be military action, and I would be designated Military Governor: 'Start to revise your English, and prepare yourself to see what you can do in the Malvinas.'

Commander Robert Denton Green
Intelligence Staff Officer to Commander-in-Chief, Fleet HQ, Northwood
I remember writing the 'threat' part of the Falklands contingency plan a month earlier, and realising that because the Argentines were our friends, we knew nothing about their weapon systems and equipment. I'd had to use open sources to get information.

Rear Admiral Anthony John Whetstone
Deputy Chief of Naval Staff (Operations), MoD Whitehall
I was on leave mowing the lawn when C-in-C Fleet Admiral Sir John Fieldhouse came on the phone: 'Tony, we've got these Argentinian scrap metal merchants landed in South Georgia. What are we going to do about it?'

I telephoned First Sea Lord, and we decided to send HMS *Endurance* down with some marines to sort it out. I then packed my razor and returned to London, where very few people took this thing at all seriously.

The First Sea Lord, Sir Henry Leach, and I were very concerned, but other people thought we were exaggerating. A third group thought there was very little we could do about it anyway. Our ambassador in Buenos Aires spoke to the Argentine foreign minister, who assured him they had no intention of doing anything, that they were only scrap metal merchants, nothing to do with the military. The ambassador told us we were overreacting by sending *Endurance*, and to calm things down. The chief of the defence staff, Admiral Terry Lewin, was in New Zealand and the chief of the general staff, General Dwin Bramall, was on leave.

We requested a meeting with Lord Carrington, asking for permission to send two nuclear submarines down to the South Atlantic. During the Callaghan prime ministership, Britain had sent HMS *Dreadnought* into the South Atlantic after rumours of an Argentine attack on the Falklands, preventing further action. Lord Carrington asked how long it would take for nuclear submarines to be on station down there, to which I said ten days.

'We appear to be in a no-win situation, Admiral,' he said.

'That's true at the moment,' I replied.

Defence Secretary John Nott asked us how long it would take to get ships into the area of the Falklands. We pointed out that the islands were seven thousand miles from Gibraltar and five thousand from the West Indies, but only two hundred miles from the Argentine naval bases, so no matter how quickly we might move, we'd never get there in time to prevent an invasion. We also told him that the forces we had permanently in the Falklands were not sufficient to defend them. If the Falklands were attacked and captured, we could either accept it, or mount a considerable force to reoccupy.

Commander Robert Denton Green
Intelligence Staff Officer to Commander-in-Chief, Fleet HQ, Northwood
There were rumours of a Polaris submarine being moved south. Their office was next door to ours, but whenever I went in, they'd pull large blinds down over the charts showing the submarine positions. However, knowing the captains of the Polaris submarines, I felt they would realise they were being retargeted simply through being moved out of range of Moscow into range of Buenos Aires, and would know what they were being lined up for. I just hope and pray that had they ever been given the signal to fire, they would have reported a 'malfunction', then come back to face the court martial. I cannot

believe that any of those commanding officers would have released a Polaris missile against Buenos Aires.

But it really did get me thinking about the nature of Polaris's ability to deter. Our homeland wasn't being threatened, but the entire future of our armed forces was at stake, apart of course from Mrs Thatcher being flung out of power. I really felt that the whole situation of Polaris was destabilising and useless, and what was coming next? Trident . . .

Rear Admiral Anthony John Whetstone
Deputy Chief of Naval Staff (Operations), MoD Whitehall
Sending two submarines meant disrupting the whole submarine operations programme. One submarine had been called home from Gibraltar after reports of Russian submarines operating in the North Sea. The press knew she'd sailed from Gibraltar, assuming to the South Atlantic, an error that nobody bothered to correct, while in the meantime we prepared two other submarines, which left soon after.

Air Marshal John Bagot Curtiss
Air Commander, Northwood
Our nuclear attack submarines sat off the Argentine coast, for which we had to rely on American satellite communications – which they gave us without any problems at all. A similar thing had been done ten years earlier in a previous Falklands crisis.

Rear Admiral Anthony John Whetstone
Deputy Chief of Naval Staff (Operations), MoD Whitehall
On the Wednesday or Thursday before the Argentine invasion, I was at a meeting with the Secretary of State and some Foreign Office people, about the deployment of our submarines to the South Atlantic, when the division bell sounded and off the Secretary of State dashed. A telephone rang, and the private secretary handed me the receiver. It was the Whips Office; First Sea Lord was in full uniform demanding to see the Prime Minister, would I 'rescue' him? He did get to see Mrs Thatcher, and asked her to agree to send a task force if an invasion took place.

We cancelled the Royal Marine Commandos' leave, telling them, plus *Fearless* and *Intrepid*, to get ready for operations. We also stopped the sales of *Invincible* to the Australians and *Hermes* to India, and focused our intelligence on Argentina. The Argentines were revealed to be serious in their intention, but it was now too late to stop them.

Endurance's captain was doing a great job reporting Argentine ship movements, at considerable risk to himself. He would have liked to start the war personally, but we persuaded him he was more valuable gathering intelligence than as a dead hero. At one point I was having trouble getting through to *Endurance* to transmit the new rules of engagement to them, when the captain of an Argentine polar survey ship came up on the radio in my naval ops room offering to forward any message to *Endurance* – which I thought very surrealistic at the time.

General Mario Benjamin Menendez
Military Governor, Islas Malvinas
The order was to maintain secrecy. I was not allowed to talk to other people. I did not talk, not even with my wife. I even said to General Galtieri: 'With whom can I speak?' and he said, 'With nobody.' I asked: 'Can I be informed of the plans?' 'No, you cannot.' It was very difficult to do this alone, but finally there was another person, a general who was more important than I, with whom I could talk, and he said to me: 'Well, so you know?' I said: 'Of course I know this. What do you know?' 'Not much more,' he told me.

Air Marshal Joseph Alfred Gilbert
Assistant Chief of Defence Staff (Policy), MoD, Whitehall
After a special meeting of the defence operations executive, my staff wrote a paper for the chiefs of staff committee, defining fourteen possible military options, ranging from 'Roll over and do nothing', to actions very much worse than sinking the *Belgrano*. We had to think laterally, and I'm not prepared to say how laterally, and seven of the options were used up in the ensuing military actions. There was no time to consult the Foreign and Commonwealth Office properly, so I wrote what I considered the political implications of each option. As the FCO sat on the committee that would consider my paper, there was no danger of the military running out of control on this one.

Commander Nigel David 'Sharkey' Ward
Officer Commanding 801 Squadron, Fleet Air Arm, HMS Invincible
My first indication that something might happen was a round robin letter from Admiral Sir Henry Leach around March 17, two weeks before the April 2 invasion, to unit commanders, saying that everyone going on leave had to be available for rapid recall, and that we had to be ready to get on to an operational footing very quickly. Putting this together with the media reports

of events in the South Atlantic indicated to me that the Falklands would be why we'd get mobilised.

General Mario Benjamin Menendez
Military Governor, Islas Malvinas

There were two or three elements that I thought might stop us from proceeding, so I consulted General Galtieri. He told me to think as a governor and nothing more, and that the military junta would resolve any other problem that occurred with regards to the Malvinas, through the Chancellor. Normally, resolving military problems would involve all the military commanders, so I understood that the Malvinas operation was political rather than military, with only the military junta working with the Chancellor. There was a great lack of knowledge of what England would do, particularly militarily. But I was not going as military commander but as a governor, and my responsibility was as governor.

Captain Carlos B. Castro Madero
Weapons Officer 5-Inch Anti-Aircraft Batteries,
Warship Belgrano

I was sent to the warship *Belgrano* in January 1982. We were in refit when there was this problem with UK because of South Georgia. We followed this in the media, but although we knew there was something going on, we knew nothing specific. All the Malvinas planning was done totally in secret, so we were really surprised by what happened. I met Lieutenant Garcia Quiroga, a diver, Special Forces like a SEAL, one of those who landed in the Malvinas and tried to take Government House. I was saying to him that all this training seemed strange, and he said to me, 'You will hear of us . . . you will hear about us.' So when we recover our islands in April, I was very frustrated, as I wanted to be involved in this very important moment for my country.

2

Liberation Day

*We were listening to the BBC announcer saying, 'There are
unconfirmed reports that the Argentines have invaded the Falkland Islands,'
as we watched the troops marching past our house. My father had turned
on his ham radio and spoke to a contact in Brazil, saying: 'Tell the BBC it
isn't an unconfirmed report. I can see them coming down the bloody road.'*

Air Vice Commodore Carlos Bloomer-Reeve
Secretary General, Islas Malvinas
I had left the islands in 1975, so landing there again in 1982 after almost ten
years, I was afraid to find the friends I had left; I was uncomfortable, an
administrator not a conqueror. We had the idealistic concept to help the
Malvinas people without altering the way of life. But we were coming after a
military action, by very courageous people who fought under orders to avoid
harm to the British, losing three men.

Captain Barry Hussey
Administrator of Health, Social Services and Education, Islas Malvinas
When I heard I was going to the islands, it was the saddest day of my life. We
were pursuing a national ambition to have these islands annexed to
Argentina but nobody really cared a shit about the islands themselves.
Politically, the islands were used very frequently as an idea, but really they
meant nothing to Argentina. I was put in charge of education, social benefits,
social needs and health because I spoke English and had the necessary rank.
Dorrego was an army engineer, so went to public works. He also spoke very
good English having been in the States, and was an intelligent man. But we
both were not designed for the job.

Colonel Manuel Dorrego
Head of Public Works Department, Islas Malvinas

I knew two days before the landing and it was a great surprise. We knew when we were going but not when we were coming back. Two days later we embarked. It was very disconcerting, but we had great expectations because, I have to say it, from a young age we thought those islands belonged to us, and now we had the opportunity to reclaim them and I felt a pride in having been chosen to play a main part in an event so significant and so important for our country to reclaim the Islas Malvinas. It never passed through my mind that this could become a war; it seemed more like an occupation. But when we left Argentina, they were preparing us for this possibility. But we did not go with any aggressive intentions. We all shared the idea of treating the islanders with respect and consideration, and were there as administrators, not soldiers or airmen.

General Mario Benjamin Menendez
Military Governor, Islas Malvinas

I had been given very little time to prepare the means of government, but my directive was very clear and complied with all our planning over a period of seventeen years; that we had to respect the people of the Malvinas, their private property, their religious freedom, and, as far as it was possible, all their customs and way of life. If possible, we were also to implement some measures that would improve their lives. We knew the islands had hardly any roads. Our idea was to make roads and improve communications and supplies to the Malvinas in every way possible. If any citizen wanted to leave the Malvinas, they would be free to go. We did not want anyone to imagine they were hostages.

Air Vice Commodore Carlos Bloomer-Reeve
Secretary General, Islas Malvinas

When I heard that the invasion was taking place I was confused rather than shocked. It was very strange for us to have invaded. Argentina and UK have been partners for a long time. We owe a lot to the British, and they owe a lot to us because they really made money in Argentina. Besides, both of us were committed anti-communists. So why should we be trying to compete for these islands? And besides, there was a very good relationship between the islanders and Argentina, so there was no reason to do this. But orders are orders. But I thought the Argentine government would reach some type of agreement that meant none of the two countries lost face.

Maria Fernada Canas (Head of Political Section, Argentine Embassy, 2006)
Argentine school teacher
I decided to write a social history thesis about the people on the islands. Before the invasion, I knew I would be welcome to go to the islands and do the work. But after the occupation, I realised I would never be able to enter the islands again. I thought of all the people I knew, worrying about how they might react, hoping that nothing would happen to them in the military action.

Air Vice Commodore Carlos Bloomer-Reeve
Secretary General, Islas Malvinas
I was stationed in Germany in as air attaché and was told to come immediately to Buenos Aires to sign a contract with Dornier, but as soon as I got to BA on March 27, Brigadier Siegfriedo Glessen told me: 'We're taking the islands.' With Barry Hussey, a navy captain, we had two days to plan the administration. We asked for the help of Gonzalez Valcarse, a retired colonel. We couldn't tell him what we were doing, or why we needed his help. He suspected, of course. He's not an idiot.

Private Jose Omar Ojeda
Compania Comando Servicios, 3rd Brigade
I had a girlfriend before I went away on obligatory military service, from the age of sixteen. We had argued over silly things, and I left without saying goodbye to her. The painful part was when I went to the Malvinas; I went without saying anything to her. Not even my family knew that I was going to war.

John Fowler
Superintendent of Education, Stanley
The Falkland Government heads of department were called into Government House at the end of the working day. We sat in the big room there for a long time, then finally the governor came in, sat down on a pouffe at the end of the room and, unusually for him, put his head in his hands for a while. We looked at each other rather anxiously, then he said he'd just received a signal from the FCO that we were to be invaded by the Argentinians at dawn the following day. It was just too melodramatic, particularly as the signal finished with a typical meaningless Foreign Office sentence: 'We would urge you to make your dispositions accordingly.' In other words: 'You're on your own mate.'

Gerald Cheek
Director of Civil Aviation, Falkland Islands

We discussed measures we could take. I agreed to block the airport runway with vehicles, and we closed the schools and the Falkland Island Defence Force – FIDF – was called out. The Royal Marines were already out preparing positions down at York Bay near the airport. Their detachment was changing over, so we had double the normal number, with some seventy marines here and others sent to South Georgia. A long signal from the FCO arrived, telling us more about the Argentine force: their deputy commander had been here for a week or so already, under the cover of building a gas storage facility.

John Pole Evans
Falkland Islander

At the time of the invasion I was eleven and living in Stanley with my mother and father and my sister. We also had an aunt and uncle staying with us – just a normal family really. My dad was a mechanic, with me and my sister both at school. There'd been radio broadcasts about the Argentine activity down in South Georgia, which was all we knew about what was going on.

John Fowler
Superintendent of Education, Stanley

The two Royal Marine Majors, Noot and Norman, briefed us on what to expect, telling us definitively that the Argentines would be landing over the beaches to the east of Stanley. It was therefore a great surprise when they came pouring in from the south.

Ailsa Heathman
Estancia Farm, North Camp

My husband Tony was in Stanley on April 1 and heard of the Governor's meeting that afternoon, so we knew something was on. The Governor made his announcement on the radio that evening, then the next morning they were here. We felt pretty gutted.

John Fowler
Superintendent of Education, Stanley

Rex Hunt told us not to tell anyone until he'd made some sort of announcement, but I'm afraid I rushed out and told a few people immediately – including one of my teachers, who lived at the east end of town near the beaches Majors Noot and Norman were planning to defend. We collected their two-week-old twin daughters and luggage, and came to my house. The twins had been born in Buenos Aires where there were more incubators, and were registered as Argentinian. Afterwards, their house was totally riddled with shrapnel. It would have been a serious disaster for the Argentines to start off by killing two newly born Argentine citizens.

The Deputy Colonial Secretary, the Financial Secretary Harold Rolands and I were the keyholders to the government vaults. Harold decided he should lock the government savings bank records in the vault, so later that afternoon we were all three walking down the long drive to Government House on a beautiful evening, peat smoke rising above people's houses, thinking that this was all completely wrong – how could anybody invade this tranquillity?

Gerald Cheek
Director of Civil Aviation, Falkland Islands
I went home for a meal. I was a sergeant in the FIDF so after changing into combat uniform I reported to the drill hall at seven-thirty that evening. I was ordered to take my section on a patrol to the racecourse where we kept the FIGAS Norman Islander aircraft, with a view to doing a dawn flight to observe the Argentine ships. After an uneventful night, we heard some gunfire from Moody Brook, with grenades going off and a few bursts of machine-gun fire. This stopped very quickly after a few minutes, as the buildings were empty.

Private Alejandro Ramon Cano
Grupo Artilleria de Aerotransportada
I joined the military service on February 1, 1982, did a military parachutist course, and joined the parachute unit. On the day before April 2, they made me return to my military base. We were expecting problems in the country from April 2 onwards, so I manned military posts at strategic points in the city . . . but we didn't think that the Islas Malvinas were going to be taken.

Lieutenant Commander Peter Walpole
Signal Communications Officer, HMS Sheffield
One of the modules I'd studied at university was conflict analysis. A classic political strategy for a country having problems at home domestically is diverting the attention of people to some unifying just cause abroad. We'd studied the Falkland Islands so I was well aware of what the Argentines were doing.

John Pole Evans
Falkland Islander

The first we heard of the actual invasion was a broadcast announcement in the evening by the governor telling us that the Argentines were expected by the morning, and that we were all to stay indoors. He said that although they didn't know what was going to happen, we were going to be taken the next day. We had to try to stay calm and not to cause trouble as we were heavily outnumbered, so this would only make it worse for everybody. We were to stay inside and listen to the radio for what was happening.

Private Alejandro Ramon Cano
Grupo Artilleria de Aerotransportada

When our forces take the Islas Malvinas, we were almost a little happy because we had wanted those islands for a long time and we thought that they would once again be ours. But never for one moment did we think that we would have to go to the island.

Maria Fernada Canas (Head of Political Section, Argentine Embassy, 2006)
Argentine school teacher

When the fighting started, I was worried for the islanders I knew, and for the conscripts who were going there. It was devastating and very hard. We wanted to believe that we had some chance, but even the good things that happened were through very sad means. When you sink a ship or put down an airplane, it's good, but it's also very bad. You are achieving something, but it's all very bad really. And the government that was heading all this was not sympathetic at all.

John Pole Evans
Falkland Islander

That night everybody was tensed up. We went to bed, but didn't sleep very much. We had the radio on and listened through the night. We knew they were killing their own people and all that sort of stuff; so we were scared and numb and simply didn't know what might happen by the next morning.

John Fowler
Superintendent of Education, Stanley

We had this odd radio phone-in, with people ringing from the eastern end of town as the armoured personnel carriers came in, reporting to the presenter Patrick Watts who broadcast the details as he received them. It was clear that

A member of the elite Marine *Compania de Commañdos Anfibios*, who spearheaded the Argentine assault on Port Stanley after being landed from the destroyer ARA *Santissima Trinidad* at 2130 hours on April 1, 1982.

whoever was firing and banging at the western side of town was going to have to pass our house to get to the centre of town. We spent the night with the family from across the road sitting on the floor in the passage in the centre of the house, getting up occasionally to make tea. We saw tracer bullets flying across the garden and up and down the harbour, but didn't really see anything more until the morning.

John Smith
Falkland Islander
We woke up the next morning hearing shooting and went upstairs so we could see better, watching as retreating Royal Marines jumped a fence beside the children's playing field and returned fire at advancing Argentines. We only realised how silly we'd been much later.

John Pole Evans
Falkland Islander
Whilst the shooting was going on, we lay on the floor in the centre of the house, the safest place. Tanks came in along the road at the back of the town. We were in the second row of houses back down the hill from the road. Some of them fired into the town through the houses, and pieces of house landed on our roof. We could hear helicopters and planes overhead, but didn't get up to look out the windows.

Commander Robert Denton Green
Intelligence Staff Officer to Commander-in-Chief, Fleet HQ, Northwood
I didn't sleep for thirty-six hours after the Argentine invasion. We were really struggling. There was a complete panic. I was briefing the Admiral, plus we had to keep the Soviet threat monitoring going as well. We asked all the companies who'd supplied the Argentines with ships and weapons systems to come clean on exactly what they'd provided, which versions and modifications. Our dossier on their order of battle started with data from the publication *Jane's Fighting Ships*, and all the aviation weeklies and magazines.

John Pole Evans
Falkland Islander
The first lot of Argentines came banging on our house door and my dad got up and opened it. They only came into the back porch and didn't search the house at that stage, but wanted to know who we were and what we were doing.

Commander Robert Denton Green
Intelligence Staff Officer to Commander-in-Chief, Fleet HQ, Northwood
I never worked so hard in my life. All my friends were down south, risking getting hurt. I was very highly motivated, putting into practice all my experience and training. Being at the nerve centre to a war I'd seen coming was fascinating.

John Fowler
Superintendent of Education, Stanley
There was a lull, then quite a big firefight around Government House. It was still going on when their air force vice commodore arrived, who'd been in the Falklands before. He met up with Dick Baker and they went to the secretariat together, after which the negotiations for the surrender took place. The ladies said the vice commodore looked like Gregory Peck.

Gerald Cheek
Director of Civil Aviation, Falkland Islands
Governor Rex Hunt telephoned round where all the defence force people were deployed, telling us to put down our weapons. Argentine Hercules aircraft landed at the airport, and then around seven-thirty a.m. some Argentine troops walked down the road from Moody Brook. We came out and attracted their attention. They took our weapons and marched us back to the drill hall. Along Ross Road, toward Government House, there were armoured personnel carriers and a World War Two DUKW amphibious vehicle. The Royal Marines were captured at the end of Government House. They told us to go home and take off our uniforms, stay there and not get involved in anything silly.

I'd been up for over twenty-four hours, and found all this very traumatic and upsetting. We were wondering what the hell Britain was up to, getting us into this situation. One of the Argentines had been killed and some injured in the action around Government House that lasted around an hour. I think more were killed, but they kept quiet about that. It had been a long strange night – a lovely night too – not at all cold. I got home about ten o'clock, and found armoured personnel carriers lined up beside my house and lots of Argentine troops.

My Argentine air traffic controller came to my house and told me to go with him to the airport. Their pilots pretended they couldn't speak English. They'd smashed a window in the control tower to get in. They were operating Hercules, Fokker Friendships and Fellowships, and troops from their ice-

British Royal Marine Commandos, members of Naval Party 8901, after surrendering to Argentine forces on April 2, 1982.

Members of Naval Party 8901 outside Government House in Port Stanley, guarded by members of *Compañia de Commandos Anfibios*.

breaker ship off the south coast were landing in Sea Kings. I saw several Argentines I'd met before. There were a lot of troops on the ground with more flying in all the time. One of the Cable and Wireless technicians told me very quietly he'd heard on the World Service that Maggie Thatcher was organising a British task force to retake the islands. That was really good news, as we hadn't been sure how Britain was going to respond.

Stephen Luxton
Falkland Islander
I was aged nine, living in Stanley House – the boarding school for the Camp children where we lived in term time. My parents happened to be in town from Chartres on West Falkland where we lived, so I was out on leave staying with them. On April 2, we were woken up at about five a.m. when the Argentines sneaked up on the marine barracks at Moody Brook and tried to blow it all to smithereens while the Royal Marines were in bed. These explosions were the first indication of the hollowness of their promises not to hurt anybody. Thankfully they missed the marines by many hours.

Our house was the second one from the west end of Stanley at that time, so the Argentines came to us first as they marched into the town from the west, which was unnerving. We were listening to the BBC announcer saying, 'There are unconfirmed reports that the Argentines have invaded the Falkland Islands,' as we watched the troops marching past our house. My father had turned on his ham radio and spoke to a contact in Brazil, saying: 'Tell the BBC it isn't an unconfirmed report. I can see them coming down the bloody road.'

3

Immediate Action

*For the first week I was doing what I'd been doing for the past few years,
mounting an amphibious task force. The only difference was that this time,
instead of sailing from Plymouth and turning right to Norway, the force
was turning left, and they had a heck of a lot further to go.*

Captain Carlos B. Castro Madero
Weapons Officer 5-Inch Anti-Aircraft Batteries,
Warship Belgrano
Of course I don't like to talk about 'invasion', because you don't invade
something that is yours. So after we recover our islands, we knew that we have
to train and prepare very hard, as we were sure that things would get very
complicated.

Lieutenant Commander Peter Walpole
Signal Communications Officer, HMS Sheffield
We were in Gibraltar when the scrap metal merchants went to South
Georgia. It looked like another diplomatic problem, not a war. We'd been
away for five months and were convinced that we were going home in a few
days, but that all changed.

Captain Michael Ernest Barrow
HMS Glamorgan
We were in Portsmouth dockyard, and knew from the media all was not well
in the South Atlantic. There were also 'buzzes' from one's friends working in
the MoD. When we sailed on March 17 on Exercise Spring Train, I had
expected to hear more.

Chief Petty Officer Lionel Norman Kurn
HMS Antrim, Helicopter artificer

I was chief petty officer working as the Number Two airframes fitter on HMS *Antrim*. I had expected there to be trouble in the Falklands, so I knew I was going to miss my birthday back at home.

Lieutenant Commander Graham John Edmonds
Operations Officer and Squadron Warfare Officer, HMS Broadsword

We were in Gibraltar on rest and recreation with fourteen other ships and submarines when the news of the Argentine invasion took place, which was a surprise. But as we were due to go to the Far East with *Yarmouth*, we didn't think it was going to affect us very much.

Chief Petty Officer Terence Bullingham
Fleet Air Arm, HMS Antrim

I'd been a chief petty officer since the end of the 1960s, looking after flight control and armament electronic systems of the Wessex 2 anti-submarine helicopter. We'd been off the coast of Madeira on our spring exercise, and were in Gibraltar for the social part of the exercise, to visit friends on the other ships – with the aim of getting into their bar before they could get into ours.

Lieutenant Commander Raymond John Adams
Signals Officer, HMS Coventry

To me the Falklands were only a hazy memory from school geography, a sea battle in 1914, and a calling station somewhere in the South Atlantic.

Captain Michael Ernest Barrow
HMS Glamorgan

We were under the command of Admiral Sandy Woodward who was a very good friend of mine. He was flying his flag in HMS *Antrim*. Our Commander-in-Chief Admiral Fieldhouse came aboard on Friday evening for some shore activities in Gibraltar over the weekend. But while he was on board, we received a continuous flow of signals from the MoD, Foreign Office and his headquarters, which made it quite clear things were brewing up.

Radio Supervisor Stewart Anthony MacFarlane
HMS Coventry

We'd put into Gibraltar to await spares for a problem with our starboard shaft, and were in a bar on Main Street, Gibraltar when somebody asked if we'd heard of the troubles in the South Atlantic. We didn't really know what or where the Falklands were, so it didn't concern us. We were in the middle of this major naval exercise, which as far we were concerned at the time, is the sort of thing we do.

Chief Petty Officer Terence Bullingham
Fleet Air Arm, HMS Antrim

While we visited colleagues on *Sheffield* and *Coventry*, the nuclear submarine HMS *Spartan* disappeared from along the Gibraltar dockyard wall. We didn't pay attention to world news, which you don't when on a run ashore.

Lieutenant Commander Graham John Edmonds
Operations Officer and Squadron Warfare Officer, HMS Broadsword

We almost made it to Naples at the start of our Far East trip before being recalled. Wives and girlfriends were already there, and we'd booked family holidays in Penang and Malaysia, so we felt disappointment and some dismay at the prospect of an extended but, we thought, futile deployment, leading eventually to an Argentine climbdown.

Lieutenant Commander Raymond John Adams
Signals Officer, HMS Coventry

Around two a.m., we picked up a signal saying the Argentines had invaded the Falklands. Only a disconcertingly small circle of people on board knew: the radio operators on watch at the time, myself, and then, after I'd shaken him, the captain. The signal wasn't addressed to us; we were keeping our ear to the ground.

Captain Michael Ernest Barrow
HMS Glamorgan

I'd held a party in *Glamorgan* for all the captains of the other ships, so we could get to know each other under informal conditions. On sailing from Gibraltar on Monday morning, we were to exercise with the Portuguese Navy with Admiral Fieldhouse on board, but he left us later that day. At 0400 I had to signal them to say had to sail south – for reasons that would become obvious when they listened to the news later in the morning.

Lieutenant Commander Raymond John Adams
Signals Officer, HMS Coventry
The exercise was curtailed and we received an order to sail south, followed by a considerable administrative reordering of things. There was no signal formally sending us off to war and we picked things up as we went along. Other ships were not suitable, or not loaded with the right things, and were to return home, so the major effort of the day was to swap resources round the fleet.

Captain Michael Ernest Barrow
HMS Glamorgan
I didn't know much about the Argentines or their armed forces, as previously I'd always thought of them as our friends and allies. During the early months of 1982, my ship had been host for an Argentine destroyer the *Hercules*, during its post-build work-up in the UK. I'd become friendly with their commanding officer and a number of his officers during the many occasions we spent lying together alongside in Portsmouth dockyard. I thought taking on the *Hercules* would be quite difficult, with people I knew personally.

Commander Ian Inskip
HMS Glamorgan
Having more recent communications equipment, the flag transferred into us, so I became the flag navigator and in a very privileged position to know what was going on. My initial reactions were a mixture of elation, at doing all the things I'd been trained for twenty years to do, and horror at the likelihood of a shooting war.

I went down to the ops room and got out Jane's *All the World's Aircraft*, opening it at 'A' for Argentina, to note that they'd got some two hundred front-line aircraft. With six ships going south, and on a good day we shot down ten each, that left only one hundred and forty aircraft . . . We had to take this very seriously. I felt that we would fight.

Lieutenant Commander Raymond John Adams
Signals Officer, HMS Coventry
The ships not going south were told to hand over everything they'd got, reducing their food supplies to about three days' fresh and frozen, while handing over all their lavatory paper, beer, nutty – chocolate, sweets and so on – medical stores, and live ammunition. We took stores from HMS *Aurora*, using a heavy wire and a pulley between the two ships. Teams of men on two winches pulled stores across for over two hours.

HMS *Glamorgan* – a county-class guided-missile destroyer.

Commander Ian Inskip
HMS Glamorgan

I'd realised we didn't have the charts for Ascension Island let alone further south, so I signalled Flag Officer Gibraltar asking for the requisite chart folios. We were the only ship in the task force to have the right charts. As the invasion of South Georgia was taking place, we were told to hand them over to the flag in *HMS Antrim*, so they would know where Grytviken and Leith were.

Chief Petty Officer Terence Bullingham
Fleet Air Arm, HMS Antrim

We took all HMS *Ariadne*'s war stores: torpedoes, depth charges, detonators, live 4.5-inch ammunition, all the sort of things you don't usually handle – hey, we're in the navy. We don't do all this sort of stuff . . . Then we transited south very quickly, to relieve the 'Red Plum', as we call HMS *Endurance*, which had sprinted south into the ice to hide from the Argentine Navy.

Radio Supervisor Stewart Anthony MacFarlane
HMS Coventry

Everyone on the ship was allowed to send one telegram home, which the radio office had to write out, then transmit by Morse or teletype – two hundred and ninety-four telegrams. But as soon as we'd got them all prepared, we were told to go to radio silence for the run south. I sent them by helicopter in a parcel across to *Hermione*, which was returning to UK and transmitted them a few days later.

Lieutenant Commander Raymond John Adams
Signals Officer, HMS Coventry

We borrowed people from other ships to fill in the gaps; it's possible to be short-staffed on a peacetime exercise, but not in war. *Sheffield* had been away for several months, so there were quite a few people with good reasons for needing to get home, but nobody left for compassionate reasons. We encouraged our sailors to make a will and take out life insurance.

Captain Michael Ernest Barrow
HMS Glamorgan

While we held the Flag, we commanded fifty-three ships. We converted the admiral's quarters into a Flag Ops room where all the detailed planning took place, and he moved into mine, creating space for the enormous amount of signal traffic and paperwork involved. Additional senior officers embarked at Gibraltar to help in the planning phase, including a former captain of *Endurance*, plus two duty captains to enable the admiral to sleep.

There were people on board my ship who questioned whether military means should be used in the Falklands. I was at pains to point out my views on this, during informal discussions on the bridge or around the hearth in the wardroom, that the military must always carry out the wishes of the government when diplomatic means fail. We were given orders, which we had to carry out. My personal view on the politics of this crisis was that it's reasonable to defend people who have been invaded by another power against their wishes, irrespective of who might own the real estate.

Commander Ian Inskip
HMS *Glamorgan*

There were a number of people who didn't want to go, which got the admiral really shirty; and there were other people who didn't feel good about it, saying this wasn't what they joined for; some five per cent of the crew. I said to them, 'Excuse me, but this *is* what you joined for, and there's no way off. The best way of ensuring that you come back is to get stuck in and do the job.'

Captain Michael Ernest Barrow
HMS *Glamorgan*

We were thinking and planning from ignorance, as we had hardly any charts of the area and my ship did not carry any details of Argentine forces. MoD calculated we would lose eleven ships during the course of the operation, a pessimistic estimate, with very few left at the end.

Commander Ian Inskip
HMS *Glamorgan*

On the way south we painted ourselves grey, turning into a business-like fighting machine. Morphine was issued, and Formica removed from everywhere except the sickbay and the galley; the sickbay for hygiene reasons, and the galley as we thought no one would be there at action stations. Formica splinters cause very serious injuries.

Rear Admiral Anthony John Whetstone
Deputy Chief of Naval Staff (Operations), MoD Whitehall

As the previous Flag Officer, sea training, I had tested every ship to ensure it had reached the required level of expertise and ability. But looking back, I don't think I did all I could have done to train the navy properly. We were thinking of blue water fighting against Russia in the Atlantic and the Norwegian Sea with American cooperation; and all our operational training was done with that in mind. Our only air attack defence training was flying civilian aircraft at the ships as they left harbour – purely to make sure the ships' companies were alert. Our short-range air defence weapons were out-dated Oerlikon cannons. We were caught in an anti-Soviet mindset, and very few people were concerned about this. We hadn't given our ships the defences they should have had. I should have taken this more seriously.

Lieutenant Commander Graham John Edmonds
Operations Officer and Squadron Warfare Officer, HMS Broadsword
We had no gun crews, and nobody did any training. We started from scratch, and chose our Royal Marines to man the Bofors guns. We were otherwise very experienced. We'd trialled our Sea Wolf system extensively, and I'd fired over ninety missiles, and, after several exercises, we were at very high peak of capability.

Captain Carlos B. Castro Madero
Weapons Officer 5-Inch Anti-Aircraft Batteries,
Warship Belgrano
We believed that, navy against navy, we had a good chance. But we knew we could do nothing about nuclear submarines. Our sonar had very short range. They could detect us far away, then throw the torpedoes from beyond the range at which we can detect them. So, we *could* have said that the navy can't go out . . . But the navy said, 'We must go out.' Although we knew it was a very risky operation, everybody was convinced that we had to take the risk. Malvinas was an island in the maritime environment and the navy had to take part in its defence, no matter the danger.

Commander Robert Denton Green
Intelligence Staff Officer to Commander-in-Chief, Fleet HQ, Northwood
We were never sure about their submarines, but thought some of them were unserviceable and couldn't go to sea. We spent our time trying to keep tabs on the Argentine fleet, which seemed to remain in port, or sneak out and go down the coast.

Major General (John) Jeremy Moore
Commander, British Land Forces

We had a meeting on April 1 at which Argentine invasion of the Falklands was discussed as a possibility. We were asked, 'Could we provide a unit to go south?' 'Yes, of course we could. That's our business.' One suggestion was to recall a Commando from leave – but nobody must know about it. How do you recall six hundred and fifty chaps from leave without their wives and the local police knowing? Another ridiculous suggestion was to send our air defence troops to Stanley. Buenos Aires airport was the only air link to the islands. Imagine the Argentine reaction to fifty-four young men with short haircuts and big boots, each checking in a double bass?

Federico Mirré (Argentine Ambassador, 2006)
Foreign Office, Buenos Aires

I was Consul General to Germany in Frankfurt-am-Main. I read in the morning headlines 'Falkland War' – and was stunned. After a few days, the under secretary for Foreign Affairs phoned to tell me that I had forty-eight hours to return to Buenos Aires to join the diplomatic War Cabinet with him. I was put in charge of an information-gathering unit. We worked twenty-hour days, gathering from our embassies throughout the world, writing briefs and summaries, issuing press bulletins from the Foreign Ministry, and feeding back further instructions to our embassies – all for the under secretary. I had hectic meetings with the Foreign Minister himself.

Major General (John) Jeremy Moore
Commander British Land Forces

For the first week I was doing what I'd been doing for the past few years, mounting an amphibious task force. The only difference was that this time, instead of sailing from Plymouth and turning right to Norway, the force was turning left, and they had a heck of a lot further to go.

Federico Mirré (Argentine Ambassador, 2006)
Foreign Office, Buenos Aires

There were some very important diplomatic staff in the Argentine Foreign Ministry who regarded the decision of the military junta – General Galtieri specifically – with a high degree of criticism. As good, loyal Argentinians and members of the Foreign Service, we backed the Argentine government whether we liked the military or not. But privately, I knew some very highly considered senior and junior diplomats who could not see a positive end of this war for Argentina. Rapidly, I became very critical of the way the last rounds of the diplomatic efforts were being handled. I was surprised that some of the people I considered most highly had, in my view, a blurred, and in some cases totally distorted, vision of the likely outcome. I become more and more anxious, from both a professional and an Argentine point of view.

Captain Jeremy Edmund Larken
HMS Fearless

We'd come back from a deployment in Norway, and were into a maintenance period with the ship taken to bits and nothing put back together again. On the Thursday we went home aware that things were not right, and on Friday morning at six I was phoned at home by my commander, John Kelly, to say the ship had been placed first in priority for stores above Polaris, and that we should prepare for war. I aroused myself very rapidly and returned to Fountain Lake Jetty where the ship was berthed.

Petty Officer Brandon Smith
HMS Fearless

Fearless was a very happy ship, and we always spent January to March in Norway with the commandos. There was a bad feeling in the dockyard as a lot of men were about to be made redundant, and we felt there was going to be a big strike. Police were hanging around the dockyard when I left on Friday evening. I heard about the Argentine invasion over the weekend, but nobody phoned me. I came back to the ship on the Monday to be told we were sailing next day.

Captain (John) Jeremy Black
HMS Invincible

I was woken at 0400 hours at home in bed; my duty officer from the ship to say I had to be ready to sail by midday the following day – Saturday. Half my ship's company were on leave; several hundreds, one in Canada.

I was giving an eighteenth birthday party on the ship for my daughter and one hundred of her closer friends. Throughout the forenoon I held to the principle that if Drake had played bowls, and Wellington attended a ball on the eve of Waterloo, why shouldn't I have a dance? But we were ammunitioning all night. Sailors humping ammunition surrounded by the blades of Hampshire in their dinner jackets wouldn't look appropriate in the next day's *Daily Mirror*. We still had the party, but not in the ship.

Commander Nigel David 'Sharkey' Ward
Officer Commanding 801 Squadron, Fleet Air Arm, HMS Invincible
801 Naval Air Squadron was based at Yeovilton. HMS *Invincible* was our home deck. I made a long drive back from Leicestershire through thick fog, to find most of the lads were already in, getting the aircraft ready. I felt very excited. We needed to get rid of the white bellies which can be seen too easily in air combat, and to expedite an order of Sidewinder AIM L missiles from America, which were better for combat than the missiles we already had in stock.

Commander Ralph John Wykes-Sneyd
Officer Commanding 820 Sea King Squadron, Fleet Air Arm,
HMS Invincible
I was in command of a squadron of Mark 5 Sea King helicopters, a very sophisticated aircraft for use against nuclear submarines, based on board *Invincible* at Portsmouth. I was at home following an exercise in Norway. My squadron was already embarked in *Invincible*, so all we had to do was get everyone back from leave and take on the stores we needed. I decided early on that we were going to have to fight, and viewed it all with a certain amount of apprehension, whereas I think a lot of others did not.

Captain Jeremy Edmund Larken
HMS Fearless
We filled the ship with every consumable victual we could lay our hands on. The decks and corridors were literally paved with tins of food, including the inevitable Argentine bully beef. There are never plans for an actual crisis, so we used our Norway plans as a point of departure, and then threw the details out of the window.

Commander Nigel David 'Sharkey' Ward
Officer Commanding 801 Squadron, Fleet Air Arm, HMS Invincible
It was big task getting ready, as the aircraft were new and had not completed test-pilot trials of their weapon systems, which we would have to do ourselves, dropping live thousand-pound bombs in various modes: high angle, low level, tossing; leaflet delivery, firing Sidewinders, and firing two-inch rockets.

Mr Hatcher
Air Engineer Mechanic First Class, 801 Harrier Squadron,
HMS Invincible
I was called off Easter leave. Flying in that helicopter towards the *Invincible*, I

remember wondering where the Falklands were and what I was doing. Most of us thought they were islands somewhere off the coast of Land's End, so all this crisis sounded a bit close to home. My father had warned me that I might have to go to war, and I told him that I thought of it as being part of the job. But once you get used to the services as a peacetime job, having to go to war comes as a shock. It was quite frightening. But once I was back on board *Invincible* and started working, we got over the shock.

Air Marshal Joseph Alfred Gilbert
Assistant Chief of Defence Staff (Policy), MoD, Whitehall

MoD decisions are always made by agreement of the chiefs of staff committee, comprising the heads of the three armed forces and other senior officers, chaired by the chief of the defence staff, CDS. They would always finish each meeting by 'inviting' me to write papers on what they'd discussed. These were pretty profound issues, and they would then 'take' these papers the next day, or possibly the day after that, once their staffs had read them carefully and made suggestions.

If the conclusions of a paper could not be agreed, the chiefs of staff would 'invite' me to revise the paper in the light of their discussions, and would take it again in four hours' time. At that time, the only word processor in the Ministry of Defence was in the chiefs of staff secretariat, and the only way for me to get these papers amended in time was to type in the corrections myself. My staff provided the ancillary papers and annexes. So these papers are not very well written. When they are released in thirty years' time, researchers will have a field day.

Air Marshal John Bagot Curtiss
Air Commander, Northwood

The navy was facing severe cutbacks, so some naval officers thought the Falklands should be a purely naval affair in order to vindicate the navy's position. There had been plenty of previous inter-service rivalry, with battles over fixed-wing aircraft carriers and different projects. But there was no inter-service rivalry at the top level during the Falklands campaign, thanks to Admiral Fieldhouse, who was the most inter-service officer you could ask for.

I was the only navigator air marshal in the RAF, commanding aircraft from all over the air force, so I was the envy of many of my colleagues. However, I have to admit that I was under continual pressure from the Chief of the Air Staff to make sure the RAF got its fair share of the action. I had to report to him once a week to be harangued.

Air Marshal Joseph Alfred Gilbert
Assistant Chief of Defence Staff (Policy), MoD, Whitehall

The RAF was peripheral to the Falklands, even though there were to be Vulcan bomber raids against the Argentines. There were also some RAF Harriers on the aircraft carrier *Hermes* for ground attack missions supporting the land forces once they got ashore, and Puma helicopters operating at Ascension alongside the Hercules transport fleet. But initially, our main effort was the air bridge to Ascension Island.

Commander Nigel David 'Sharkey' Ward
Officer Commanding 801 Squadron, Fleet Air Arm, HMS Invincible

I'd never been in combat, and early that year I'd been thinking that my time flying was coming to an end, but wouldn't it be nice if we could somehow prove all this training. It's not very nice to want to go to war, because war means people getting killed. But I was very keen to demonstrate, to a lot of doubters around the three services, the true worth of the Harrier.

Captain (John) Jeremy Black
HMS Invincible

The normal red tape disappeared, and people really galvanised themselves with unusual urgency. We did usually forbidden things like simultaneous fuelling and ammunitioning, and aircraft flying on board while we were still in harbour. *Hermes* had much more of a problem as she was still in refit, whereas I was up and running. We achieved readiness to sail by Saturday lunchtime, but as we didn't sail till Monday, spent the weekend storing everything away.

Mr Hatcher
Air Engineer Mechanic First Class, 801 Harrier Squadron,
HMS Invincible

The accommodation on board *Invincible* was more comfortable than we had ashore. We were quite surprised, as we expected it to be an all-metal tin tub. The junior rates had their own lounge with television and coffee-making facilities – a real home-from-home.

Commander Nigel David 'Sharkey' Ward
Officer Commanding 801 Squadron, Fleet Air Arm, HMS Invincible

There was a hell of a lot of confidence in the squadron but, interestingly, the two pilots I sadly lost, John Heaton Jones and Alan Curtis, were the only ones who told the other guys they'd felt they might not be coming back. They weren't apprehensive . . . they just had this feeling. Never once did I have the feeling that I'd be shot down or wouldn't come home. That's not me being clever; it just never entered my head that this might be a possibility.

Mr Hatcher
Air Engineer Mechanic First Class, 801 Harrier Squadron,
HMS Invincible
The ship broadcast information over the television, then every night there was a video piped through to all the mess decks with a good supply of films. We were issued three cans of beer a day, but as I'm not a beer drinker, I never drew mine. On board, you work and sleep, so running round the flight deck was a break.

Captain Jeremy Edmund Larken
HMS Fearless
I was one of the many who had to go to the map to see what shape the Falklands were; about the size of Wales, with one end of the east island as far from Stanley as Llandudno is from Cardiff.

Major Simon Ewen Southby-Tailyour
Royal Marines
I met Julian Thompson in Hamoaze House. We were great personal friends; he's the only person I've ever lent my yacht to. He told me to tell him all I knew about the Falkland Islands but I refused until he promised to take me with him, as there was no way I was going to hand over all my maps, photos, sketches and charts.

Captain Jeremy Edmund Larken
HMS Fearless
I had a conference on board HMS *Invincible* with Captain Jeremy Black, when we looked into some of the tactical problems we might encounter. For additional advice we engaged the services of the Maritime Tactical School, and during one of our tactics discussions I recall Captain Black remarking: 'Exocet versus Exocet. Hmmm, that's not nice, is it?'

Lieutenant Colonel David Robert Chaundler
Replacement Commanding Officer, 2 Para
I was working in the Defence Intelligence staff in the MoD. When the crisis blew up, our whole department was rearranged to cover Argentina. I was

moved into a team looking at arms trafficking, to see where the Argentines were getting their weapons, and what we could do to frustrate them. Our main priority was Exocet missiles. It's an area best glossed over.

Commander Robert Denton Green
Intelligence Staff Officer to Commander-in-Chief, Fleet HQ, Northwood
One of the biggest troubles was trying to keep in touch with the Exocet missile supply, and the Super Etendard aircraft, which was French. Enormous effort was put into trying to sort out what was going on in the French factories.

Rear Admiral Anthony John Whetstone
Deputy Chief of Naval Staff (Operations), MoD Whitehall
Events moved on with an inevitability that didn't surprise me; it was certainly an unnecessary yet inevitable war. The debate was in Parliament on Saturday morning and everybody said how marvellous it was that the ships were sailing on the Monday morning. Well, of course, the ships had been made ready the previous week from Gibraltar under Sandy Woodward. When it's absolutely necessary, the civil service are absolutely marvellous at sweeping away their own bureaucracy – probably because their top men start taking an interest.

4

Demonstrations of Serious Intent

We wanted to give everyone a leg-stretch ashore, to zero weapons and exercise. There were no ranges at Ascension but the Pan Am manager provided empty oil drums as targets. We fired thirty-seven years' ammunition allocation in one day, so the boys realised how serious this was.

Major General (John) Jeremy Moore
Commander, British Land Forces
We were ordered to sail a task force very quickly, to demonstrate serious intent to the Argentinians. They invaded on Friday, and by early on Monday morning two carriers had sailed from Portsmouth, then within five days the assault ships had also sailed. But we had no military aim, and were going to have to stop somewhere en route to reload.

Rear Admiral Anthony John Whetstone
Deputy Chief of Naval Staff (Operations), MoD Whitehall
We needed to avoid tackling the Argentines too soon, and not before softening them up a bit first. There were several serious limitations to consider. The troops wouldn't stay battle fit if cooped up in ships for too long. The Sea Harrier was a fantastic performer, but we had so few and they were the key to winning. Our new carrier *Illustrious* wasn't yet ready to take over from *Hermes*; and the Antarctic winter was coming, and so the end June or early July was the latest date we could possibly go ashore, after which we'd have to reconsider the whole business.

Captain (John) Jeremy Black
HMS Invincible

We slipped on Monday morning. My cabin didn't overlook the dockyard, so I missed the flavour of what was happening until I set off from my cabin on the five-minute walk to the bridge. I suddenly saw people on the dockside with banners, not just dockyard mateys. I've sailed from Portsmouth many times, without anything like this, and it made me feel immensely responsible. The mission was undefined, but clearly these people were expecting us to bring it off – whatever it was.

Michael Thomas Nicholson
ITN correspondent

I was recalled by my office from holiday with my family in Ullswater, and told to join the task force at Portsmouth, where I went on board HMS *Hermes*. We learned very rapidly that Mrs Thatcher had ordered the navy to include the press, and that Admiral Fieldhouse, who was a cussed old devil who loathed the press, did not want to take any of us, which is a typical naval senior officer reaction, so that only six or eight writing press were on board *Invincible*, with me and Brian Hanrahan sharing one cameraman and soundman between BBC and ITV. The send-off was tremendous. ITN filmed it from the shore and I did a radio piece from *Invincible*, but we felt like cheats, as we were sure we'd be back pretty soon, after a cruise round the Scillies. Unknown to us, Fieldhouse had signalled the captains of the carriers to starve the press of information.

Commander Ralph John Wykes-Sneyd
Officer Commanding 820 Sea King Squadron, Fleet Air Arm, HMS Invincible

I was in the sky within an hour of our sailing. The ship was then at flying stations continually for the next seventy-five days, which I think is the longest period ever that a western aircraft carrier has spent on operations at sea. The temptation was to go immediately to battle stations, but we had several weeks before we might expect to be engaged by the enemy, so we began developing skills to match the very different capabilities and weapon systems of the Argentines – as opposed to the current Soviet threat. The Exocet missile was something new. We also needed to consider how helicopters could deal with being attacked by fighter aircraft flying from land in coastal waters, as we were used to high seas operations beyond land fighter range. Fighter avoidance manoeuvrings needed a good deal of practice, particularly to avoid being too severe on the controls and slowing down.

As anti-submarine helicopters, we had to counter the Argentines' small but formidable 109 submarines, which, although not fast, were very quiet and difficult to detect, particularly in the South Atlantic, which has a lot of marine life in it. We were going to have to use active sonar, as our normal passive sonar detecting buoys were most unlikely to pick up such a small, quiet vessel.

Captain Jeremy Larken
HMS *Fearless*
We managed to sail by ten o'clock on Tuesday morning, the day after *Hermes* and *Invincible*. Our passage down Portsmouth harbour was one of those events one won't readily forget. There was tremendous enthusiasm from the dockyard. Their efforts were prodigious, and the support and enthusiasm was very impressive, although jingoistic, which has never come happily to me. We weren't a very jingoistic ship and never looked at events that way.

Petty Officer Brandon Christopher Smith
HMS *Fearless*
We had one young lad who'd jumped ship from the *Hermes*, under the impression that as he'd missed his ship he wouldn't have to go. He was put under my wing until we got to Ascension, where he could rejoin *Hermes*. He kept asking, 'Do you think we'll be hit?' This went on and on, and began to affect our morale. I was still thinking the Argies would back down. We were relieved when we got rid of him back to *Hermes*. He was a frightened boy.

Staff Sergeant Richard James Elliott
REME, 3 *Commando Brigade Air Squadron*
We were in *Sir Tristram*, one of the RFAs, which was going to be at sea without any port stops for very much longer than they'd ever done before. They had long-standing problems that hadn't been repaired, like air conditioning and water purification plants that didn't work. There were six engineers on board, so we put our heads together and did all the repairs.

Major Simon Ewen Southby-Tailyour
Royal Marines
On April 6, I flew with Julian out to HMS *Fearless* in the English Channel – and we were off, which was tremendously exciting. It might not be popular to say of a war, but I thoroughly enjoyed it. I was going off to a place with which I was having a love affair – the place, not the people.

Captain (John) Jeremy Black
HMS Invincible

Three hours after sailing, my engineer officer came and told me he could hear a knocking in the gearbox, which is the size of a house. We'd had this trouble since being launched, spending three weeks in Portsmouth while replacing a section of the gearbox. My heart sank. I closed Culdrose in Cornwall and had a piece of gearbox weighing three tons brought down from Rolls-Royce, to be flown on board by an RAF Chinook. But the Chinook had no radar, so in thick fog we had also to fly a Sea King, using its radar to find us, with the Chinook flying extremely close behind. The Chinook crew had never landed on a ship before, and then the gearbox piece had to be got down to the engine room – all challenging stuff. While we continued sailing and flying using the one propeller shaft, the engineers replaced the gearbox in just ten days, a remarkable piece of engineering ingenuity.

Michael Thomas Nicholson
ITN correspondent

What wasn't publicised was that *Invincible* kept breaking down and eventually had to have a new gearbox, delaying the armada. We heard Captain Black promised the engineers a crate of champagne if they fixed it quickly. Our problem, on this uneventful journey south, was that the British public was gasping for information and the story was leading the news every day, but we had nothing to give them for six weeks.

Captain (John) Jeremy Black
HMS Invincible

We had several additional pilots on board, plus five press men, who'd joined at the last minute on the orders of the Prime Minister no less, thinking it would be a quick trip around the Isle of Wight. They were completely unprepared, with no kit or clothing suited to what we were doing, so we had to sort them out with everything – and find them somewhere to sleep.

Michael Thomas Nicholson
ITN correspondent

I'd managed to leave the UK without a tape recorder, so I bought one from a naval rating. It was the oldest thing imaginable, but it worked and I've still got it. To begin with, we were talking about 'our troops, our ships, our soldiers', but I was reprimanded by my editor, and told to be more objective, saying 'the British troops, British ships'. But these were *our* troops, and we felt

ITN correspondent Michael Nicholson on the flight deck of one of the carriers.

this was *our* war, and in fighting alongside our own people, we did become less objective.

Captain (John) Jeremy Black
HMS Invincible

These five press men took up as much of my time as the Argentinians and my thousand sailors, from reading the despatches they were churning out daily, to complaints. Five men reporting daily produce quite a lot of copy, which it's very difficult to read to decide if there's serious intelligence in there or not. You could easily gloss over something that was very important. MoD instructed us not to deal with taste or tone.

I didn't interfere with their copy very much, but once, when two Harriers vanished in an inexplicable accident losing ten per cent of our total force, I told them they couldn't report it. Then later that afternoon, the loss was broadcast on the World Service news, having been reported to the House of Commons by the Secretary of State. These press men woke me to complain that they were risking their lives reporting, and I was preventing them from doing their jobs.

(James) Robert Fox
BBC correspondent

Some editors feel that reporters should not be accredited to the armed forces, as they become biased and therefore propagandising. But the actions of men and women fighting for their country can only be reported by media people with the military units. There is no choice.

Captain (John) Jeremy Black
HMS Invincible

I sent a signal to the chief of staff, a great friend of mine. I needed to know how the country was reacting to this press. I wasn't used to this sort of thing, and was growing nervous.

> Signal to Chief of Staff: 'Having five press men on board may be likened to having five houseguests reporting daily on your most intimate family affairs. I am living with this emotional strain in the hope that it is doing some good more often than it is an embarrassment . . . Problems lie not between individuals, but between our very different aims and terms of reference. As each day passes post Ascension, the pressures will rise on both sides, and both are aware of this. I've made clear that I will become more secretive, and my decisions on their copy more arbitrary . . . the presence of the press

could become a threat to the morale of my ship's company or their families if we are committed to action. I would be grateful if the MoD or DPR takes final responsibility for the final release of copy, and secondly any tips or nuances, which could help me crawl through the minefield.'

Brigadier Julian Howard Thompson
Commander, 3 Commando Brigade

My staff was planning where we would land. We had charts from 1830, which had been reissued every fifty years but not altered, with few accurate inshore soundings. Major Ewen Southby-Tailyour came with me and was able to give me the details we needed, thanks to his having surveyed most of the Falklands coast a few years earlier.

The place the Argentines expected us to land was Foul Bay, north of San Carlos. The maps did not show that it actually had extensive rock reefs running out to sea. We were able to dispense with very time-consuming, detailed surveys of the beaches, which can compromise security.

Major Simon Ewen Southby-Tailyour
Royal Marines

On *Fearless*, I spent all my time briefing, and realised I had to be very careful, as I was very subjective. For example, I wasn't recommending landings in my two favourite places: Volunteer Bay because there is a penguin colony, and Carcass Island which could have been used as a stone aircraft carrier but had marvellous wildlife. I falsified some of my answers – as with Volunteer Bay, because I wanted to protect the wildlife. I told them it was the most God-awful place for a landing. That's not the way to go to war!

Captain Jeremy Larken
HMS Fearless

We were also trying to get to grips with the plans and the direction coming from Northwood. Our whole command structure was in a state of flux, as was the overall objective of the operation. Admiral Fieldhouse was the four-star commander, and with Admiral Woodward being the senior officer afloat, it was assumed that he would be generally in charge. But this was never really sorted out. Misunderstandings were perpetuated through this period, and never ironed out.

Brigadier Julian Howard Thompson
Commander, 3 Commando Brigade
There was no joint force commander in the theatre of operations down south, which was an error. Admiral Fieldhouse had three task group commanders under him: Admiral Woodward with two carriers plus escorts; Commodore Michael Clapp commanding all the amphibious ships; and, third, myself commanding the landing force, of my brigade reinforced by other units. We needed a three-star vice admiral sitting over the three of us in theatre. Instead, we all three reported back up to Northwood, who had to draw together the threads of a battle taking place eight thousand miles away.

Air Marshal John Bagot Curtiss
Air Commander, Northwood
No decisions were made about what the task force was actually going to do until it arrived at Ascension.

Captain Jeremy Larken
HMS Fearless
There were various aims developing regarding what we were actually going to do: for example, landing on the Falklands Islands *with a view to* repossessing the islands, landing *to* repossess the islands – and so on. A very small change in the wording can lead to very large changes in what you've actually got to do, and the diplomatic situation was unfolding, changing every day. We were already planning on repossessing South Georgia, and Admiral Woodward was in the process of establishing area control with his task force.

Air Marshal John Bagot Curtiss
Air Commander, Northwood
The Americans held the lease on Ascension from us, but gave us sole use of it, with fuel and water from American tankers sitting offshore. Then later on, the Americans also let us have some special anti-radar missiles, which we needed to take out a radar that was locating the position of our fleet at sea. These missiles were used a few weeks later, on a number of the Vulcan raids.

Captain Michael Ernest Barrow
HMS Glamorgan
As the advance group, we sailed south to Ascension Island while diplomats attempted to convince the Argentines we would fight for the Falklands. We arrived at Ascension on April 11, as the RAF and RN contingents were flying

in, activating Wideawake airfield as the vital stepping stone for stores from the UK and tankers. There were a number of scares – an Argentine and then a Russian submarine were lurking, so we remained underway for most of our time there.

Lieutenant Commander Graham John Edmonds
Operations Officer and Squadron Warfare Officer, HMS Broadsword

At Ascension we painted everything grey, including removing all the numbers from the sides, which not everybody agreed with. We were a very experienced ship, and very comfortable with each other. Nobody was frightened – not even the Chinese laundrymen. We worked the same routines as we'd always done. We kept good food coming, and stood people down as much as possible so they could sleep.

Commander Ralph John Wykes-Sneyd
Officer Commanding 820 Sea King Squadron, Fleet Air Arm,
HMS Invincible

We became part of an enormous logistics operation, three days of solid helicopter delivery from the airfield to the ships, with twenty aircraft in the sky at any one time. We then sailed in rather a hurry, after a tanker reported seeing a periscope, which somebody's sonar appeared to confirm. My feeling was that this could have been a bigger nation having a look, as it was too far north for the Argentines.

Captain Jeremy Larken
HMS Fearless

I already knew Admiral Woodward, as a mentor and personal friend, and realised it was going to be very difficult building a relationship between him and Brigadier Thompson, who'd never met. Their meeting was going to be crucial. Admiral Woodward would be provocative, firing out ideas, some not very near the mark, to get responses, to stimulate debate and define the parameters. I did my utmost to prepare and brief my two bosses in *Fearless* as to what to expect. They met on *Fearless* just before we arrived at Ascension. Admiral Woodward insists this meeting was a success. But Brigadier Thompson found many of the Admiral's ideas outlandish, which set a pattern that was to continue to create difficulties throughout the campaign, and was very sad.

The next day *Fearless* arrived at Ascension. I went to *Hermes* for a meeting with Admiral Fieldhouse, who'd flown out from UK. There was a certain amount of resolving differences, debate over the aims of the operation, and the shelving of some of the outlandish ideas of the previous day's meeting. Then Admiral Fieldhouse returned to UK by VC10 and Admiral Woodhouse sailed south with his battle group, while the rest of us were undergoing a submarine scare.

Brigadier Julian Howard Thompson
Commander, 3 Commando Brigade

With the landing plans now determined, we should have taken everything off the ships and re-stowed it all in a more sensible order, but there was nowhere at Ascension to do this. The only bay on Ascension (English Bay) could take just one landing craft, and the only place helicopters could land was on the airfield tarmac, thanks to the volcanic dust which would get sucked into the engines and destroy them. Instead we played a huge Chinese puzzle game using one hundred and fifty-foot long MEXE floats to park things like trucks on, while we moved other stuff around. It was very complicated keeping a tally on where everything was, amid a continued Atlantic swell of six to ten feet.

The second task was amphibious training for people like 3 Para who'd never seen landing craft or assault ships. To further complicate this, we had ships like the *Canberra* which we'd never operated before. We were well used to *Fearless* or *Intrepid*; nine helicopters flying at once from the deck while running landing craft from the docks. But we had to be able to get battalions off these other ships as fast as possible with all their kit. We also wanted to give everyone a leg-stretch ashore, to zero weapons and exercise. There were no ranges at Ascension but the Pan Am manager provided empty oil drums as targets. We fired thirty-seven years' ammunition allocation in one day, so the boys realised how serious this was.

At Ascension, we were pretty sure the Argentines were too far away to try air strikes on the fleet. Submarines were a worry, but after an Argentine merchant ship made a huge dog-leg to investigate what we were doing, the navy thought demolition divers had already landed on Ascension Island, to swim out and put limpet mines on to the ships, backed by an intelligence report suggesting that Argentine Special Forces might have flown to France as civilians, then boarded a merchant ship. I had to deploy a company on to Green Mountain to investigate whether such a force was lurking up there, glimpsing at us through binoculars. The navy put to sea every night, to prevent frogmen from catching up, meaning we couldn't load at night, or do night-time troop rehearsals.

Captain Jeremy Larken
HMS Fearless
We had a rousing concert on one of our large vehicle decks but the Royal Marines' bandmaster could barely get my sailors to sing. It wasn't that they were downhearted or there was any depression; I realised afterwards that they were simply very thoughtful. They were far from jingoistic, which pleased me.

Brigadier Julian Howard Thompson
Commander, 3 Commando Brigade
We had very little intelligence, and what we had was often wrong. For example, the Argentine commander Menendez was labelled a hard-hitting, tough guy, but actually was a conciliatory sort of chap, probably selected to be a governor, who in my view was not a good choice to fight a battle. The intelligence picture did improve, mainly from radio intelligence monitoring. Although we built up an accurate picture of which units were where on the islands, we didn't know what equipment they had.

Commander Robert Denton Green
Intelligence Staff Officer to Commander-in-Chief, Fleet HQ, Northwood
We were heavily dependent on the USA for intelligence, with virtually no intelligence sources on the ground in Argentina – as they'd been our friends. We were severely embarrassed. What we needed was a guy at the end of the mole at Puerto Belgrano, using a fishing rod as an HF antenna. All this business about satellites providing wonderful instant coverage round the clock is absolute rubbish especially if you've got bad weather and it's dark. We were given occasional snapshots, which were quite useless as they were too old. It's no good knowing that the *25 de Mayo* aircraft carrier was in harbour twenty-four hours ago. Electronic intelligence from the American radar intercept satellites was very confusing; merchant ships appeared similar to naval ships, and there were also a lot of fishing vessels. Because civilian shipping had not been cleared out of the area, we had to spend huge amounts of time classifying ships; and because we had always to assume the worst case, there were lots of scares.

Brigadier Julian Howard Thompson
Commander, 3 Commando Brigade
We were soon able to add to the intelligence from London by landing SAS and SBS from the carriers, into areas defined by Commodore Clapp and myself. We'd radio ahead to the carrier group to say what we wanted them to

look at, leaving the detail of where they would land and so on to those who had to do it. Our special forces provided good information on the enemy's state of training, morale, equipment and so forth.

Commander Robert Denton Green
Intelligence Staff Officer to Commander-in-Chief, Fleet HQ, Northwood
But amid all this difficulty, GCHQ managed to break the Argentine codes. They were not terribly sophisticated, but we got a lot of very high-quality political and battle-planning intelligence. It took between twelve and twenty-four hours to decipher and translate the messages, so we were always trying to extrapolate forward to see what they meant for us now. But it was good intelligence, although often ambiguous. On balance, I think we had a reasonable picture of what was going on inside the minds of the main Argentine commanders, although the political side was a little bit confusing.

Federico Mirré (Argentine Ambassador, 2006)
Foreign Office, Buenos Aires
The political plan was to withdraw most of the Argentine military forces from the islands, then remain as a civilian government. The eventual garrison would have been the size of something similar in Patagonia, a few planes with around fifteen hundred men, plus naval ships for fishing patrols.

Maria Fernada Canas (Head of Political Section, Argentine Embassy, 2006)
Argentine school teacher
Everybody in Argentina has a political point of view and a solution to everything. Some people said that having made the point, we should now leave. In the cafés and bars of Buenos Aires, some people thought this was totally crazy, others that this was the only way to solve the Malvinas problem; and others that nothing good could come from this government. But even though many people did not approve of the use of military force and the methods being used, nobody ever said that the islands were not ours.

Captain Jeremy Larken
HMS Fearless
The Chinese laundry in *Fearless* had developed an anxiety about going to war, but the Number One Boy, as we rather arrogantly call the splendid man who runs it, had been very firm about continuing. He and the more stalwart members were saying, 'All same as Korea sir. We stay with ship.' This developed into a curious mutiny within Chinese circles, and a forlorn

gathering of Chinamen landed in one of the bays at the extremity of Ascension Island, waiting for a bus to the international airport. In the end we were able to fly the ones who wanted to leave back to Hong Kong.

Major Simon Ewen Southby-Tailyour
Royal Marines

I was going round all the ships and units, endlessly briefing, but I had great trouble with many officers, and staff officers back in England who didn't understand that although the Falkland Islands are the same latitude as Great Britain, it isn't like northwest Europe. There were no real settlements, and what looked like a village on the map would be just one man, maybe with a wife and dog, possibly with a couple of farmhands. There were no roads and no communications. People had to realise that once we landed, every mouthful of food would have to be brought in by us. And with the total exclusion zone operating, the Argentines would be suffering similar difficulties and would have to be supplied by air, which we could stop. I don't think Admiral Woodward took this seriously.

Air Marshal John Bagot Curtiss
Air Commander, Northwood

Port Stanley airfield was a great concern to us, even though it was too small for modern frontline fighters. But we were determined that the Argentines should never be able to operate their Skyhawks or Super Etendard aircraft from it.

Brigadier Julian Howard Thompson
Commander, 3 Commando Brigade

Commodore Clapp and I believed that there would be operations to take out the Argentine airfields near to the Falklands. We had twice been promised we would have air superiority, which is the normal precondition for amphibious operations, learned through bitter experience in places like Norway and Crete. But as it became clear that political permission for bombing Argentina would not be given, the unpleasant reality dawned that we were going to have to land without this basic air superiority prerequisite.

Admiral Woodward signalled Northwood his concern that the air battle wasn't being won. The Argentine air force was holding back until they could see where the landings would take place. He finished this signal by saying: 'Because of this, a ticket on the train going back to Ascension is going to be very expensive.' I obviously didn't show this signal around, but wrote a letter to Northwood, which I gave to a staff officer to hand-deliver for me, saying that without air superiority, casualties would be high before we even landed. I received a very silly reply that said: 'Don't worry.' It would have been much better if they'd been honest and just told us to get on with it.

Captain Michael Ernest Barrow
HMS *Glamorgan*

We wanted to conceal from the Argentinians the precise area in which the amphibious landings were to be carried out in three weeks' time. The first stage was a programme of naval gunfire bombardment designed to confuse while keeping the Argentine force awake, to soften up targets that might oppose our troops, and make life generally difficult for them. It also kept us awake too. The moon and state of tides suited making the landings on May 20, but they were delayed a day as some of the key elements were not ready.

Petty Officer Brandon Christopher Smith
HMS *Fearless*

When we were anchored at Ascension, the Royal Marines group on *Fearless* accidentally released the date for the landings, May 20, in their daily routine orders. These orders were very quickly withdrawn, and censorship imposed. Letters had to be left unsealed in the post box for the chaplains to read. Bits were literally scissored out.

5

Vida En Las
Islas Malvinas

A little Argentine soldier standing at the crossroads with poncho and rifle asked me for a cigarette. I said pompously: 'No, and if you're going to invade people, you should bring your own cigarettes.' He said: 'We did, but we've run out, and do you know, they don't accept Argentine money here?'

John Fowler
Superintendent of Education, Stanley
I looked out of the window to see a group of very weary-looking Argentine Buzo Tactico blokes coming by. They looked hostile. Then a group of Falkland Island Defence Force were marched past by these Argentine special forces guys, carrying their helmets and other kit wrapped up in a large Union Jack flag, wearing a motley collection of Second World War uniforms and things. It was very *Dad's Army*, and yet they looked so defiant and proud, surrounded by these others in black with all their weapons.

Stephen Luxton
Falkland Islander
Us kids hid beneath the front window most of the morning. They hammered in the door of the house next door, which belonged to Don Bonner, the guy in charge of public works, booted the door down and went in. We were next. They herded us into the garden while they searched the house looking for Royal Marines. They searched the freezer, but ignored the loft where half the garrison could have hidden. They imposed a total curfew for twenty-four hours, so all we knew was what Patrick was broadcasting over the radio.

61

John Fowler
Superintendent of Education, Stanley

We had a three-year-old daughter. My wife was heavily pregnant with my son Daniel, who was born ten days later in the King Edward Memorial Hospital. Another family of four were staying with us, plus their mother-in-law and another couple with twins – all camped out in the bedroom corridor.

The radio was broadcasting some rather strange things, in both English and Spanish. We were informed that we'd been 'liberated' by the forces of Argentina, and assured that in a few days, everything would be back to normal and we would be afforded all the rights and privileges of Argentine citizens, but that owing to the situation pertaining in Argentina, we were likely to be given *more* rights! We were to remain in our houses, and if we needed anything we were to hang white towels out of our windows and someone would come and see to our needs. This system, like many other messages, was never passed on to their soldiers, as people waved white flags furiously and nobody took any notice.

The kids in the school boarding house were having a great time; I was alarmed to learn the girls had been up all night soldier-spotting from the windows. On the Sunday, we took the children to the radio telephone hut to talk with their parents. In the middle, HMS *Endurance* called up. The Cable and Wireless operator Eileen Videl Davis took over, and kept saying, 'You'll get me shot . . . but here's another thing . . .' Eileen was very much a part of the glue of our rural society in those days. Every settlement had one radio, usually kept in the manager's house, used for ordering goods, talking to the doctor every morning; everyone listened in and knew who had what complaint, and so on. The Doctor's Round, as it was called, was continued by the Argentines.

On the way back, Governor Rex Hunt passed us in his red London taxi, in full diplomatic uniform, being driven by his chauffeur Don Bonnet to the airport to be flown out by the Argentines.

The children said goodbye to him, and he was clearly emotionally affected by it. Davis Street had columns of little barrel-chested guys from the north of Argentina like porters, carrying huge loads in a continual file as far as you could see, either side of the road.

John Pole Evans
Falkland Islander

On April 4, we drove in a convoy of Land Rovers all day to Fitzroy where some of the farmers met us, taking in children while their parents returned to Stanley. We changed our vehicle and carried on to Goose Green where we stayed the night with relations.

Concern at Number Ten. After being flown by Argentine C-130 aircraft from Port Stanley airport, Governor Rex Hunt and Royal Marine Majors Gary Noot and Mike Norman (far left and second left) returned to the UK via Uraguay along with other members of Naval Party 8901.

Stephen Luxton
Falkland Islander
Being only nine, I didn't know too much about what was happening, except that it was very shocking and upsetting. When we heard the task force was coming, we went from total despair to elation. The Colony Club had a riotous drunken session, which went on well into the afternoon. My mother remembered she'd put a chicken in the oven so at about four p.m. there was a weaving drive back to the house to get it out. I remember an altercation with an armoured personnel carrier on the way back, as my father decided he wasn't going to drive on the right-hand side of the road. I don't know which gave way.

Pat Whitney
Green Patch, East Falkland
An Argentine police vehicle came down the same side of the road as me. I stopped and beckoned him past, but he drove out around me and continued on my side of the road. I met him again and he stopped and beckoned me to drive around him this time, with a big smirk on his face. They were trying to get us to drive on the right-hand side of the road, but I wasn't going to do that. The day after, they painted big arrows on the road and we had to drive on their side of the road.

Colonel Manuel Dorrego
Head of Public Works Department, Islas Malvinas
I didn't share the idea of making people drive on our side of the road, but the majority of the vehicles came from our side, and the few vehicles that were there already had been taken over by our people. It seemed logical that they should adopt our system of driving, including for security reasons. There were no crashes fortunately . . .

General Mario Benjamin Menendez
Military Governor, Islas Malvinas
There were problems we could have avoided, and changing driving from the left-hand side of the road is a good example. But General Garcia made this change immediately after the occupation because we knew the problem they have in England with driving on the left-hand side. General Garcia thought that it would be better for the few islanders who came out on the road with their vehicles to drive on the right, rather than make the change for the drivers of military vehicles, trucks and armoured combat vehicles, etc., who

Argentine Marines from the *Batallón de Infanteria de Marina* 2 pose outside Government House in Port Stanley.

Falkland Islanders in Port Stanley, and *Amtracs* of the *Batallón de Vehiculos Anfibios*.

could cause very serious accidents. General Garcia was very worried for the physical well-being of the people.

Private Jose Omar Ojeda
Compania Comando Servicios, 3rd Brigade

On about midday April 2, they tell us: 'You will prepare the trucks because there is a mission to accomplish.' We left at six or seven the next morning, then as we leave they tell us: 'Well, men, we are going to the Malvinas.' We learnt that they had taken the islands on April 2. They explained that everything was all right, that we should be relaxed, that we should maintain calm, and that we had to defend our country. At that time we were not frightened. We were twenty, and for us it was like a joke, we felt no fear of anything. From the moment we left Argentina until the moment we arrived in the Malvinas it was all a laugh.

General Mario Benjamin Menendez
Military Governor, Islas Malvinas

The troops were prohibited to enter the town. We knew that the supplies of Puerto Argentino were limited. Had we allowed the soldiers to go to buy at the shop, the town would have run out of goods needed for normal life. At times one had to explain this to the military commanders. This was enforced because firstly, I was governor, secondly I was commander, so I was the one who gave the orders.

John Smith
Falkland Islander

Their soldiers would often break into people's houses and steal clothes so they could pretend to be civilians and buy food. They were quite obvious; tracksuit bottoms, tweed jacket, Argentine boots and a swarthy look.

Maria Fernada Canas (Head of Political Section, Argentine Embassy, 2006)
Argentine school teacher

In 1982, a right-wing junta ruled Argentina, which was using secret police, arresting people and using various techniques and procedures against the people. I didn't think that those procedures would be applied in the Malvinas. I was more afraid that the military presence would cause overreactions that might lead to other things.

Tony Smith
Falkland Islander
We didn't bother listening to the local radio because the Argentines were broadcasting propaganda and horrible stuff, which depressed us more. I never listened to it again until the war ended. Instead, we listened to the World Service on shortwave, which was very crackly, but our only contact with the outside world.

Air Vice Commodore Carlos Bloomer-Reeve
Secretary General, Islas Malvinas
Arriving on the islands, my mood was confused. I called my wife in Bonn and she was shocked. She and our children had so many friends from when we lived here previously. We were thinking that the islanders should take over the administration of everything that could be taken from the British: Chief of Police, Public Works and so on . . . But we didn't discuss this with any islanders. We brought an air force lawyer-brigadier to be the Secretary of Justice, to compensate the islanders in money for anything they lost or broke.

We had a genuine belief that we could make the quality of life in the islands better, while improving the friendship of the islanders to us and to the continent. We brought in three doctors, and we were about to bring in two dentists as well. Colonel Doreyo brought some civilian engineers, machinery and volunteers to make roads and other work. They arrived, but didn't have time to start.

John Fowler
Superintendent of Education, Stanley
The Colonial Secretary Dick Baker convened a heads of departments meeting on the Monday, in what is now called the Liberation Room in the secretariat. We stood before a heap of Argentine military brass sitting round the table with Dick in the middle. He made a little speech about how we were a peaceful democracy and they had no right to be here, and then we were allocated our new bosses. Mine was a naval captain of British origin called Barry Melbourne Hussey – a man who under different circumstances I could have taken home for tea. He offered the services of an Argentine obstetrician to ensure that my wife's birth went all right. She wasn't very keen on this idea.

After that, Dick summoned us to clandestine meetings in the nurses' room at the hospital. We were told to approach from different directions, so at the appointed time you'd see us sidling up to the hospital. We decided our primary

The Argentine commanders in Port Stanley after the town's capture. Left to right: An unknown air force officer; General Osvaldo Garcia, the joint army/air force Malvinas Task Force commander; Rear Admiral Carlos Büsser, commander of the Marine assault force; Rear Admiral Gualater Allara, commander of Task Force 40, the naval units supporting the landings.

duty was to keep the community going, even though that might mean collaborating with the Argentine administration.

Air Vice Commodore Carlos Bloomer-Reeve
Secretary General, Islas Malvinas
When I arrived the British governor had gone, but Dick Baker, the chief secretary, was still there. He gave me all the plans necessary to keep the community running then I asked him to leave. We were very friendly, but we thought it was better for the British to leave. We moved into his house. People came to see me, trying to keep the friendship going, but I would say thirty per cent of the people were afraid to come near us because of what other Falklanders would say.

It was to be a military-civilian government to operate for at least forty days. After that civilians would take over and most of us were supposed to return to the continent, leaving a very small military base: about a thousand men with air force planes. But we didn't get that far.

John Fowler
Superintendent of Education, Stanley
About thirty teachers were on contract from the UK. I released them from their contracts, but they had to decide what to do. The Argentines were extremely keen to get the schools going again. As far as I and the headmaster of the junior school were concerned, we should continue to keep the schools going as best we could, but everybody else said the Argentines would only use this for their propaganda purposes.

Federico Mirré (Argentine Ambassador, 2006)
Foreign Office, Buenos Aires
The instructions given to the military forces on the islands were that they were to be extremely careful with the feelings and property of the British settlers there; very severe instructions to minimise interference with the day-to-day life of the settlers. Buenos Aires authorities knew that there were no subversion activists in the islands – no guerrillas or terrorists in the farms. It would have been very unintelligent to provoke any such reactions.

John Fowler
Superintendent of Education, Stanley
On the Monday, I took the teacher with young babies back to see how his house was. He was bemoaning his freezer being full of shrapnel, how his bed

had been shredded and many other things. A little Argentine soldier standing at the crossroads with poncho and rifle asked me for a cigarette. I said pompously: 'No, and if you're going to invade people, you should bring your own cigarettes.' He said: 'We did, but we've run out, and do you know, they don't accept Argentine money here?'

I don't think he had the faintest idea where he was. Most of the ordinary soldiers assumed they were in Chile, which Argentina had been very close to invading not long before. They'd been conscripted, stuck on aeroplanes or boats, and didn't much care where they were, except they were out of fags.

We had to tell the Argentines the schools would remain closed, first returning home to change as we knew Argentines didn't respect people who weren't wearing suits. The town hall was still surrounded by hard-looking guys with blackened faces toting guns. We pottered along in my Deux Chevaux, and were shown up to an office where a very pleasant colonel speaking very good English said he was sad we wouldn't open the schools. I then became aware of another person behind me, and turned to see Major Patricio Dowling staring very menacingly at my right ear. I knew he had a bad reputation, which didn't cheer me up at all. The great thing was, we didn't get shot . . . We knew of the Argentine propensity for dropping people out of helicopters and generally getting their own way with dissidents, so it was pretty alarming to be refusing to do what they wanted on Day One.

Tony Smith
Falkland Islander
On the third day, a helicopter landed at West Falkland and some Argentine soldiers jumped out. An officer jumped out and shouted at them. They pointed weapons at us. One guy spoke some Spanish and asked the pilot: 'What's going to happen when the British get here?' The pilot was very arrogant. He laughed: 'Oh, the British won't be coming. In a few weeks it will all be back to normal, except we'll be in charge.'

Captain Barry Melbourne Hussey
Administrator of Health, Social Services and Education, Islas Malvinas
The day after General Menendez and I arrived in the islands, we made a flight by helicopter around the islands to Fox Bay, where Menendez spoke to the people.

General Mario Benjamin Menendez
Military Governor, Islas Malvinas
The first subject of conversation was the rights of Argentines or the British

over the Islas Malvinas. Hussey was there to help with the English, but they wanted to listen to me. We talked of the fear the islanders have of Argentine tourists. The Argentine tourist is a rogue, he shouts, writes on walls and takes things. I said to the islanders: 'We shall limit numbers so that they will be manageable, so that you will not feel invaded.'

We talked about the roads, communications, and the younger ones complained about the lack of work. So I said: 'Well, let's see what can be done, for example, industrialising the fishing business.' It was important to make it clear that priority for jobs would not be given to people from towns in Argentina. I had received many letters from Argentines who were rejoicing in what had been done and said that they were willing to go to the Malvinas, as long as they were given a house, a good job and a good salary, and I said: 'This is no use to me, I prefer an islander.'

Captain Barry Melbourne Hussey
Administrator of Health, Social Services and Education, Islas Malvinas
All islanders who worked for us were paid in Argentine money, and they would go straight to the secretariat and change it back into pounds.

John Fowler
Superintendent of Education, Stanley
I showed Barry Hussey on the map where all the schools were and who owned them – some by the government, some by the farms and others jointly owned. He scratched his head and said it was far more complicated than he had expected and that he would rather be chasing submarines. I was determined to avoid our new-born son Daniel becoming Argentinian. I waited outside the town hall until our two new Argentine registrars had left for lunch, then nipped in to persuade the clerk, Fran Biggs, to stand in as acting registrar and sign a proper Falkland Islands birth certificate.

My daughter Rachel, at the age of three, asked all sorts of very difficult questions. We'd be watching groups of morose soldiers being led up into the hills and she'd ask: 'Are they bad men, Daddy?'

I'd say: 'No, of course they're not bad men, and some of them are probably very good men, but what they're *doing* isn't very nice.'

'So why doesn't anybody like them, then?'

Air Vice Commodore Carlos Bloomer-Reeve
Secretary General, Islas Malvinas
The islanders were Argentine citizens who had been born on the other side of

the ocean. We had promised them dual nationality as one of the guarantees the Argentine ministry of foreign affairs had given in talks in New York with a delegation of kelpers. But we found out from our foreign affairs people that this had not been passed on to the islanders.

John Fowler
Superintendent of Education, Stanley

One of the weird things for us was living in close proximity to the 'enemy', who were being soldierly but also scratching around for food, begging a cup of coffee, being shouted at by NCOs, bullied by officers and generally having a miserable time. My office had been next door to the Argentine military police office, run by a corporal who didn't have much English, but was always tapping on my window asking for a cup of coffee. He would say things like, 'How are things now, under the new administration. Everything OK now?' I'd say: 'No, no, it's very bad. You shouldn't be here, it's a transgression of our rights.' He took this very well. One day I was driving along Ross Road by the post office, and this military police corporal drew himself up to attention and saluted me! I thought: 'For fuck's sake! I really don't want this sort of attention from the enemy.'

We learned that Stanley had been renamed Puerto Rivero, and the military police corporal asked how I felt about that. In 1833, Rivero led a group of gauchos who murdered the manager, storekeeper and various other people at Port Louis by dragging them apart with horses and in other unpleasant ways. I said Rivero had been a murderer, an assassin, a criminal and one of the worst gauchos that ever lived. He said: 'Oh . . . we think of Rivero as a hero of the liberation of the Falklands,' and went off to tell his comrades what I'd said. A few days later we were renamed Puerto Argentina.

Air Vice Commodore Carlos Bloomer-Reeve
Secretary General, Islas Malvinas

Somebody in Buenos Aires had decided Port Stanley was now called Puerto Rivero. I called and told them it's not acceptable: 'You can't call this place Puerto Rivero; he was almost an Indian without any culture; he killed everybody that went near him,' and they told me, 'All right, give us six hours.' Later they called again: 'It's called Puerto Argentina.' I told him it would be nice to call it Puerto Mestifea, who was in charge of the Malvinas when it was taken over by the British. I thought the name did need changing, but Mestifea was French. I had tested if Buenos Aires was paying attention to my observations and they did. It was a victory.

Stephen Luxton
Falkland Islander

Convoys were leaving Stanley as most people thought it was safer out of town. My father had a small Cessna 172 light aircraft, but decided it would be too risky as somebody might use it for target practice, so very early one morning we joined a convoy of twenty vehicles heading out to Darwin. We arrived at Darwin very late that night after numerous boggings in our very old Land Rover and stayed with Brook and Eileen Hardcastle, then drove to North Arm and stayed with Lyn and Tony Blake. A local boat took us across Falkland Sound to Fox Bay West, where the people from Chartres settlement picked us up – so we were home.

John Pole Evans
Falkland Islander

My dad drove us out of town, to a bay near Goose Green. A radio message said to expect the Argies by ship in a few hours. They came ashore, and took names of everybody who was there. Some people sabotaged vehicles and equipment, so the Argentines couldn't use them.

Neil Watson
Long Island, East Falkland

On the morning of Day Four six guys in camouflage walked towards our house at Long Island – Royal Marines who'd escaped from Stanley, one with hypothermia. We made them very welcome, and warmed them up. Three were very young guys. Some wanted to hide out in the hills. We said we'd supply them with food. Then we heard on the BBC World Service of a British task force being sent down, which would take at least a month to get here. Common sense prevailed, so they asked me if I could get in touch with Stanley. I spoke to Bloomer-Reeve on the phone. He asked how they were, then asked me if we could keep them overnight. So we sat back, opened a bottle of whisky and relaxed, then the phone rang, telling us they were coming to get them. The Marines had all their weapons with them and a lot of ammunition, grenades, 66mm anti-tank missiles and so on, so we hurriedly buried all this in the sand.

Air Vice Commodore Carlos Bloomer-Reeve
Secretary General, Islas Malvinas

Our intelligence service was trying to find out where British soldiers were moving around in the Camp. We found two soldiers at Long Island from

Naval Party 8901, and we had to rescue them. But our intelligence was not against the local people.

Neil Watson
Long Island, East Falkland
It was quite dramatic actually. They arrived in two big helicopters plus two twin-engined Pucara aircraft giving air support. All this lot came flying in over the top of our house, just to collect six Royal Marines who'd decided to surrender!

After they'd gone, the kitchen door was kicked in and two Argentine officers entered, one with a .45 pistol, the other with a 7.62mm FN rifle. They were very, very agitated – sweating. We found later that this first officer was Argentine but of Irish ancestry, Major Patrick Dowling. He ordered us to stand up against the stove, and I thought: 'This is it . . .'

Glenda Watson
Long Island, East Falkland
There were the two of us, plus Paul and our other son Ben. Our daughter Lisa was eleven, and was a right little madam then – as she is now. She was sitting by the wall sucking her thumb. Major Dowling told her to stand up against the stove as well, but she said she wasn't going to do it. We said, 'Please stand up against the stove or he'll shoot you,' but she wouldn't. It was frightening, but we realised that we had to calm these guys down, so I asked them if they wanted a cup of coffee. I really didn't want to give them anything, but they were so agitated, we had to do something.

Neil Watson
Long Island, East Falkland
Before the invasion, the place had been alive with Argentinians. They created dossiers on all of us, and knew that I'd been politically active against the Argentines being in the islands in the Seventies, and that I was great friends with the Royal Marines, so they seemed to think that we'd be a problem. They knew everything about us islanders, particularly who could be the local troublemakers, and I was one of them.

Major Dowling was in the Argentine military police, but he didn't behave like a policeman as we would understand it. He saw we had an Irish tea towel on the wall, and asked if I had Irish ancestry, and I said, 'No.' He said he was Irish, so I asked him, 'Northern or Southern?' His face dropped, and he said, 'Southern, of course.'

He then asked how long our family had been in the Falklands. Well, my family the Watsons were among the original settlers, and Glenda's came here in 1840. He was cooling down by this stage, and said, 'Oh, that makes you more of an Argentine than I am.'

I said: 'Not fucking likely.'

He said: 'It's only joke.'

I was looking him right in the eye, and I realised then that in a way, we had gained the upper hand, and were out-psyching him. It happened a lot during the conflict ... that these people realised they'd made a mistake. But every day for about a week a Huey helicopter landed with troops to search our house. They went through every room, but never disturbed anything. I reckon they thought there was one more Royal Marine who we were hiding somewhere. They'd made a mistake, and this was their way of dealing with it.

John Pole Evans
Falkland Islander

We'd been brought up to know they'd always claimed us, and we didn't really like them. We weren't nasty to them, we just got on with them. But now they were here in control, whatever they told us, we had to do. It was pointless trying to argue with them. You just had to get on with it.

Air Vice Commodore Carlos Bloomer-Reeve
Secretary General, Islas Malvinas

I'm a doctor in sociology. I did the degree because the air force sent me – and paid for it. But I started using it in the Malvinas. I thought we should use our own structure, then take over the other systems, but I needed help from the islanders. Islanders came to my office seeking guarantees or to ask for special treatment; for example to leave the town, or some privileges. That made it easier for us.

John Pole Evans
Falkland Islander

The Argies didn't bother the civilians, but took over farm machinery and moved into what used to be a boarding school up between Darwin and Goose Green settlement. They brought in aircraft and more troops to the airstrip, and confiscated civilian vehicles including our Land Rover, which put an end to our chances of returning to Stanley. For the rest of April we carried on separately to them. They had blackouts so we had to be in before dark with light-restricting shutters on all the windows, plus a couple of armed guards in each of the houses to make sure we didn't go anywhere. In one house, a guy opened the outside door to tip out hot ashes from the peat fire, and the jumpy Argie guard fired at him, missed and made a hole through the doorpost. You knew where you stood; you couldn't mess them about.

Colonel Manuel Dorrego
Head of Public Works Department, Islas Malvinas
We endeavoured by all means to understand the islanders and to win their confidence, not to confront them. But we had to make them understand the situation from our point of view, that we were occupying a territory we considered to be ours, which was nothing against them . . .

Gerald Cheek
Director of Civil Aviation, Falkland Islands
They told me to get the government air service going, but I refused, which they were unhappy about. Even if I had agreed, the pilots wouldn't have flown, and in any case there were so many military aircraft flying, it would have been impossible to co-ordinate and their troops would probably have shot us down anyway.

General Mario Benjamin Menendez
Military Governor, Islas Malvinas
The islanders' chief of police was not willing to work for the military government, as he considered it to be an act of treason to his country. He made his conditions. The engineer who managed the water plant said: 'I feel responsible that the town has water and therefore I will stay.' But the director of the hospital – I believe he was a doctor and had been an officer in the English Army – said: 'I will not.' He did not have an obligation to stay and we could not force him to do so.

John Fowler
Superintendent of Education, Stanley
The director of public works was away in the UK, so Harry Bonner had to show the Argentines all the drains, water supply, electricity sub-stations and so on. He'd been staying with us, but had gone back to his house, where his wife Doreen would visit him every day.

Within a couple of days of our being invaded, the town was empty and their troops were either camped on Stanley Common or up in the hills where the poor guys stayed. They had scoured Argentina to find officers who spoke English, who often told us how they had been called up from civilian life to come over to the Falklands simply because they spoke English. Captain Hussey commented at how quiet it was and how things were now back to normal. When a couple of Argentine Mirage jets flew over, he said even that would stop fairly soon.

The Argentines genuinely thought they were liberating us from British rule, and so we would welcome them. I think most of their soldiers had little idea of where they actually were. Their Amtrak tanks would drive around the streets of the town flying pennants, the crews smiling and waving at everybody, and were clearly puzzled that nobody was waving and smiling back.

They seemed to comprise two completely different sorts of people; some apparently reasonable and decent, and others clearly not. The Argentine army and navy were doing some pretty dodgy internal security operations back in Argentina. I didn't know what Barry Hussey had already been involved with, even though he seemed a decent person. Major Patricio Dowling, on the other hand, was clearly used to imprisoning and frightening people, using torture and all the rest of it.

Federico Mirré (Argentine Ambassador, 2006)
Foreign Office, Buenos Aires

During the years of the military dictatorship, a great many of my friends in Argentina were subjected to this kind of activity. Several of my friends in the Foreign Service were persecuted and had to live outside Argentina. My own brother had to flee Argentina in the 1960s. My first wife's cousin was tortured almost to death with his wife. She gave birth in prison and the child was tortured. They both escaped and lived abroad. These are just cases that I knew. But I know the methods used in continental Argentina were not used on the Malvinas.

General Mario Benjamin Menendez
Military Governor, Islas Malvinas

In the first few days of the occupation, very severe orders had been approved by my commander, General Garcia. Major Dowling was an Argentine Army intelligence specialist who had been made the chief of police. When I arrived at Puerto Argentino on April 4, I noticed Major Dowling was very angry but I did not have time to investigate why. I think he considered General Garcia's orders had been violated; Mr Luxton was one example, and Major Dowling took measures. I was not there, but it escalated a great deal and it produced a bad image. For Major Dowling, everyone was the same, part of a population he considered hostile.

Stephen Luxton
Falkland Islander
Our home was Chartres, in the middle of the West Falkland, which eventually we reached on April 13, and seemed peaceful. But then a helicopter arrived full of Argentine Special Forces bristling with weapons, grenades and so on, headed by Major Patricio Dowling. They took our ham radio and weapons – shotguns and .22 rifles used for slaughtering, and locked them in the farm office in our house. They then sprawled around our sitting room, weapons everywhere, and told Dad that my family were being arrested and taken into Stanley for questioning.

Air Vice Commodore Carlos Bloomer-Reeve
Secretary General, Islas Malvinas
I had to get Luxton out of the country for his own security. He had some trouble with the Argentine chief of police, Major Patricio Dowling. I couldn't get rid of the chief of police – although I tried.

Stephen Luxton
Falkland Islander
My father was a government councillor and very anti-Argentine. Major Dowling told him he was 'a threat to the security of the Argentine government of the Malvinas', which Dad took as a compliment. Major Dowling said they'd got dossiers on five hundred islanders and had worked out the ones they needed to pin down first. Dad was accused of having tried to set fire to the office of the Argentine national airline, LADE. He'd been in hospital with a broken back at the time, so this accusation didn't hold much water, but they wanted him out of the way. They interrogated him in our house, when I guess they put the wind up him, before flying us all back to Stanley with them.

Air Vice Commodore Carlos Bloomer-Reeve
Secretary General, Islas Malvinas
This chief of police Dowling was worrying for all of us. The governor had orders to make things comfortable for the islanders and this man had not been indoctrinated. Some called him the 'IRA man', as he was the son of an Irishman, but that was a joke. He considered every islander an enemy. Many NCOs and some young officers thought the same, only they didn't have the power – but Dowling did.

Stephen Luxton
Falkland Islander
We were locked in the Upland Goose Hotel for the night, then flown to
Argentina. My mother was very upset, but I was too young to appreciate the
gravity of the situation. As we flew out of the airfield, she shed tears of rage,
anger, fear, sadness, regret at being thrown out of her own country. Thankfully
I didn't appreciate what might happen to us. My parents feared we were about
to join the ranks of the twenty or thirty thousand Argentines who had
disappeared. They were well aware that the Argentines had no compunction
about knocking off their own people, so a couple of troublesome kelpers
wouldn't be much of an increase of the head count.

General Mario Benjamin Menendez
Military Governor, Islas Malvinas
We decided to change the chief of police, and Major Dowling returned to
General Garcia's command on the continent and continued his career. I was
relieved. We put in a new chief of police, and that was that.

Air Vice Commodore Carlos Bloomer-Reeve
Secretary General, Islas Malvinas
One of the generals ordered the arrest of a lot of people, over my authority.
They were trying to find an illegal radio station, and some people were arrested
for three or four days. Also, there were several islanders from Puerto Argentino
who didn't understand the situation and were bothering the soldiers and the
officers. There was a bar, The Rose, where a lady Velma was in charge. She
started being aggressive so we calmed her down; I think I sent somebody to talk
to her. But she had a very strong personality and it was not easy.

I asked Menendez to evacuate aggressive people to Fox Bay. Many of the
persons asked us to be taken to Fox Bay because they thought it was dangerous
for them to stay in town. I know it caused a lot of resentment, but they
were taken to friends. They were talking too much, fussing, trying to show
off, trying to be like the French resistance. It was useless, and complicated my
job.

General Mario Benjamin Menendez
Military Governor, Islas Malvinas
As in all nations there are falcons and doves, and the falcons would meet
together after curfew. We had our contacts. Puerto Argentino, or Stanley, is
too small to maintain secrets. There were Argentines who were living in

Stanley, and other connections. But I am not going to say how one carries out intelligence work in order to know who is who.

John Smith
Falkland Islander

We'd run a guesthouse, and before the invasion, one of the Argentine captains now in charge had stayed with us, so we knew they'd been preparing for some time. Another Argentine had taken photographs of places and people while being pushed around in a wheelchair.

Stephen Luxton
Falkland Islander

We were flown to Buenos Aires, then to Montevideo, and on to the UK. At Heathrow there were lots of Special Forces, MoD and other intelligence people waiting to talk to us. It was great for me; I was sat down with this huge Jane's books of weapons of war and aircraft, and I told them exactly what I'd seen. For some reason, the Argentines had taken us on a guided tour of military installations on the islands and in Buenos Aires, so this session was very helpful. I don't know why the Argentines hadn't blindfolded us – it was like so many of the things they hadn't thought through properly. After about a six hours' debriefing session, we emerged to see a group of press waiting for us. They asked us how we were going to get back to the Falklands, and my mother made headlines by saying, 'We'll bloody well swim if we have to.'

Gerald Cheek
Director of Civil Aviation, Falkland Islands

On April 27, I was told I had to leave Stanley. I was taken from my house at pistol point to the airport, with no idea of what they were going to do with me. The doctor and his doctor wife were there too. We were put into a search-and-rescue helicopter and flown to Fox Bay East, landing as it got dark. The Argentines there told us to go away. We flew half a mile across the bay to the other settlement at Fox Bay West, where they also knew nothing about us, and didn't want us either. The pilot said it was too dark to carry on and shut the helicopter down, so we stayed with the farm manager. Next morning the Argentine major in charge of Fox Bay East told us he didn't know why we'd been sent and didn't want us there, but provided we stayed within the settlement and acted sensibly, we'd be OK.

General Mario Benjamin Menendez
Military Governor, Islas Malvinas
We had information of English special troops infiltrating, making attacks or searching for information. I knew there was at least one who arrived and was in Puerto Argentino. We had information, but we were unable to locate him. Because of this we had to limit entry and departure from the town. In general we did not take any special measures, like if the special forces agent was not produced we would kill ten others. I would have cut off the ears of any Argentine soldier who touched a local woman. This was like the honourable war I had studied, the North Africa war between the British and Rommel.

Major General (John) Jeremy Moore
Commander British Land Forces
Remembering Montgomery and the portrait of Rommel he kept in his caravan, I sent for an intelligence report on the Argentine commander, Menendez. It said he was a parachute soldier and commander of elite forces, so I expected him to be very offensively minded. I was continually worrying about when he was going to counter-attack. In fact there were five Menendezes in the Argentine Army, and I'd been given an intelligence report on the wrong one.

General Mario Benjamin Menendez
Military Governor, Islas Malvinas
I could not use the people as hostages, nor could I make the people suffer privations in order to pressure the English commander or the English government. For me, the people were not the enemy, but we made a curfew from the start. If they were found moving around they were going to be shot. We put them inside the houses, and made our patrols in the safe knowledge that if we saw anything we could shoot; and that we would not later find it was Mr Smith or Mr Jones, or a lady who needed sugar and crossed the road to a neighbour's house.

John Smith
Falkland Islander
The curfew was serious and no one ventured out at night as it was clear that you would get shot. We had a guard outside our house as they thought we were up to something, probably because our two boys quite often had friends around for a few beers.

Air Vice Commodore Carlos Bloomer-Reeve
Secretary General, Islas Malvinas
The intelligence people tried to make ID cards for everybody. I told them it wouldn't work, but they wanted to do it. It was out of control, completely stupid. But somebody thought it was a good idea. We didn't bother about it because it kept the intelligence people busy.

Gerald Cheek
Director of Civil Aviation, Falkland Islands
We dismantled a radio and hid the bits around the house, plus we kept a small transistor radio hidden from the searches so we could listen to the World Service. Without that daily information it would have been horrendous, especially as the Argentine officers told us stories of *Invincible* being sunk, of a Harrier bombing a house at Goose Green and killing a lot of people, and how the British were getting everything wrong. We kept the radios secret from the children as well, so they wouldn't let anything slip.

General Mario Benjamin Menendez
Military Governor, Islas Malvinas
There were some shots with low-calibre weapons, no real danger. A family in San Carlos had one son, Miller, who blew off his hand, apparently making a home-made bomb – for what? We thought he was punished enough by what happened to him. Our people were saying that islanders were violating our orders, and should be punished severely. But I was the military governor. Even today there are military people here in the Argentine who say I was too soft with the people. Even the Red Cross said this. When the Red Cross visited Puerto Argentino, they said: 'General, why don't we put all the people on board the hospital ship and take them away?' I said: 'Why do you want to do this – for humanitarian reasons?' If I had done as they asked, the Red Cross were going to say the Argentines were eating ten people a day and for this they had to remove the people. But I am dealing with *looking after* the people, and the people do not want to leave their houses because everybody is attached to their houses and the things that we all have in our houses.

Air Vice Commodore Carlos Bloomer-Reeve
Secretary General, Islas Malvinas
We knew that the SAS could have been in Stanley but we never saw them. The great danger was at night. I remember there might have been somebody

moving through the bay and grenades were thrown into the water to prevent frogmen moving around, but we never found anybody. Menendez was always moving around a lot, and even he went walking. He changed his meeting places: sometimes in Government House, sometimes in my office, sometimes in Stanley House and other places.

The search for the illegal radio transmitter continued. One time, people from the communication service found the working radio in the medical corps office. They cut all the wires. Next day somebody from town came and told me that there could be no more medical broadcasts because the radio was damaged. The medical corps broadcasts to the islanders were very important for us, and so six hours later the radio was fixed. The locals were sabotaging phones. We found it, but didn't do much about it. The man knew what he was doing, but he never bothered us because we had our own radios.

General Mario Benjamin Menendez
Military Governor, Islas Malvinas

We had people from Buenos Aires at the exchange listening to all the telephone and radio conversations, on the wavebands we knew the islanders would use if they still had equipment. But the telephone exchange was very old, and the existing operator knew where to place each plug, so we had our people who spoke good English with earphones on, controlling the connection and checking who was speaking. We intercepted all communications by radio from the British troops.

Trudi McPhee
Brookfields, North Camp

We were ordered to take down all our two-metre CB radio antennae, and the Argentines cut the telephone line to Stanley. We decided to see if the line could be connected for a couple of hours every day so we could contact a doctor if necessary. They had no telephone at Johnson's Harbour, so we also thought we'd ask if they could keep their radio to speak with Stanley. We motorcycled in to see Bloomer-Reeve. The scary thing was that even though he said everything was OK and that nothing was any problem, somebody else could easily come along and shoot you. They just didn't know what they were all doing, so we asked to have it all in writing. We didn't want the guys at Johnson's to put up their aerial and then have a problem.

General Mario Benjamin Menendez
Military Governor, Islas Malvinas

There was a register of all the owners of radios, radio hams, etc. A radio in a house is a temptation to try to communicate with the outside – and what is on the outside? The British fleet. If we had found someone transmitting and he was considered a spy there would then have to have been a court martial, which could end up in an execution. It was certain that islander Peter Luga communicated with the British fleet on the first day. Because we did not go from establishment to establishment checking, Luga had continued using his antennas and communicated with Sandy Woodward. Brigadier Miara from the judicial section said: 'Mr Peter Luga, we had told you to dismantle your antennas and not make communications. You did not comply. Why?' Peter Luga said that he had done it for humanitarian purposes. We said: 'But you did not comply with orders, what shall we do with you?' Yet we still did not execute him. We dismantled everything and put him in Puerto Argentino in a house. He wasn't even in prison. He was very annoyed, but I told him: 'Sir, if one had strictly complied with the laws of war . . .?'

Ailsa Heathman
Estancia Farm, North Camp

We kept our two-metre radio, even though we didn't have permission from the Argentine authority to use it. The aerial was on a broom handle that we used to stick up outside the house after dark to talk with our neighbours across the bay at a prearranged time.

Air Vice Commodore Carlos Bloomer-Reeve
Secretary General, Islas Malvinas

People were transmitting information to the British using radios, and our communication officers were trying to find them. What bothered us was not information concerning the movement of troops, but the location of our radars, which would be bombing targets. The best thing would have been to concentrate all the population on another island, but we didn't have the capacity to move the people, and houses were not available.

Trudi McPhee
Brookfields, North Camp

A Chinook landed and these soldiers jumped out, training machine guns on the house. Two very fat Argentine officers demanded to speak to whoever was in charge. When I said that was me, they didn't want to speak with a woman.

They lined us all up and said that if we helped the British our families would suffer, and asked if they could search the house. I said yes, but no guns as my eighty-one-year-old auntie was staying. They didn't like that, but eventually agreed, and then told us: 'You can put your antennas back up and speak with your amigos.' No one else was allowed to do this. We had a girl here who spoke Spanish, so we listened to all the Argentine military broadcasts from around the mountain tops. They were cold and wet, and certainly didn't want to be here. The Argentines used to jam the BBC World Service really bad, but we still used to listen. We had an FRG-7 transceiver radio, a very good radio which could also pick up British naval transmissions. They'd change frequency every four hours but we'd follow them. We knew this was the task force, on their way to save us.

Air Vice Commodore Carlos Bloomer-Reeve
Secretary General, Islas Malvinas
Many local people wanted to do business with us, particularly selling sheep. It was good business for them, and we needed the animals. We rented a cooling room, and workshops to repair vehicles. Argentinians cannot live unless they eat bread. The bakery had been closed for several years so I said: 'You can rent it to us, or we can take it!' This was a great improvement: an Argentinian who eats bread is still on the continent.

John Fowler
Superintendent of Education, Stanley
We got four supply ships per year from the UK, so we must have had a recent delivery. The teachers had all departed saying: 'Don't let the Argies raid our freezer,' so we had an abundance of food, and even a daily milk delivery from Michael Ashworth and his daughters. The supply difficulties didn't start until we were liberated.

John Smith
Falkland Islander
When it became clear there was going to be fighting, we built a bunker under the conservatory of our house, and eleven of us slept there. It was obvious that the fighting was going to end up in Stanley, so we would need the protection. I was always worrying about how it would end – in carnage, or would the Argentines give up before that?

Air Vice Commodore Carlos Bloomer-Reeve
Secretary General, Islas Malvinas

I was working for the Argentine government, and for the armed forces. But I did everything I could for the islander population until the government ordered me to do something against the islanders. I would have done it, because that's the way I was educated. I followed orders, but I don't think anybody was really trying to hurt the islanders.

John Fowler
Superintendent of Education, Stanley

My main memory is of how scared witless one could become, and how long that state of affairs could continue, from long before things started going bang in the night. We lived in constant lurking dread of the potential for evil that existed within this situation, should the façade of being nice to us slip, and the Argentines reverted to their ordinary reflexes and the way they treated their own population back at home. They were acting out of character, even though various individuals like Bloomer-Reeve and Barry Hussey were doing their jobs in a civilised and friendly manner.

6

Sun Tans and Rifle Oil

*We did circuit training on the helicopter decks, and ran all around the
ship up and down the ladders, but after complaints about the noise,
we changed from boots to trainers.*

Captain Dennis John Scott-Masson
SS Canberra
On April 2, *Canberra* arrived at Naples where we heard on the World Service
that the Argentines had invaded the Falklands. We didn't think this
would have any effect on us, but between Naples and Southampton, I was told
to slow down off Gibraltar and pick up some naval personnel, but not
under any circumstances to let the passengers know what was going on.
Seeing a dozen bullet-headed, short-haired gentlemen climbing the pilot
ladder at ten o'clock at night was hard to explain. Rumours were wild, but as
the requisitioning of *Canberra* required Parliamentary approval, nothing
could be said. By the time we arrived in Southampton, we'd been requisitioned by the MoD to take troops down to the Falklands. It was to be 'in
the vicinity of the islands', after which the troops were to be transferred
into naval ships of some sort. My reaction was one of shock and some
apprehension.

Commodore Michael Verney Bradford
SS Canberra
Originally we were contracted as a troop carrier and hospital ship, but under
the Rules of War you can't do both, so although we could have worked five or

six operating tables with all the necessary staff, these roles passed to the *Uganda* and other hospital ships.

Captain Dennis John Scott-Masson
SS *Canberra*

I 'Cleared Lower Decks' after dinner, and told the crew we'd been requisitioned. I gave them until the following morning to decide if they were prepared to go to near the Falkland Islands as a troopship. The Asians were excluded for political reasons, and were unhappy: they were losing their jobs with no guarantee of the ship returning. Gratifyingly, only one of my ship's company didn't want to go, one of the officers who was an official conscientious objector.

We couldn't take casino operators, ladies' hairdressers and various other fringe members of the ship's company. The question of whether we should take our women went all the way up to Whitehall level. Finally we were told women could go as they had many important jobs, my secretary for example. We ended up taking fifteen ladies.

We sailed on Good Friday, only sixty-odd hours after disembarking the passengers, having added two helicopter pads and other structural changes. There'd been no contingency plan to convert the ship, which was done over the weekend. The rest of the ship remained untouched, with the troops using our normal passenger accommodation.

Captain Adrian Robert Freer
3 *Para*

We sailed out of Southampton Water with three battalions of soldiers on board, 3 Para and two Commandos. 3 Para were mainly on D deck, and I had a cabin with a porthole. It was very comfortable.

Private Jose Omar Ojeda
Compania Comando Servicios, 3rd Brigade

We travelled in a truck to Santa Fe through the river tunnel, then in flatbed goods carriages on a train, on which we serviced the trucks. We travelled through Bahia Blanca until Rio Gallego on the train, without sleep, without rest, unfed, cold. We suffered like wretches. For this sort of work we needed rest; the routes were dangerous, curve after curve, coming downhill and climbing. We needed some kind of rest to be able to travel calmly, but nothing, not one break. We arrived at San Antonio Oeste about one in the morning. In all this, we rested two or three hours. At five in the morning we

Members of 3 Commando Brigade embarking into SS *Canberra* at Southampton on April 9, 1982, each man carrying the stipulated suitcase, bergan and personal weapon.

had breakfast and didn't stop until we reached the point of departure. But we were not able to embark, so we returned to Puerto Deseado, where we had two days loading a great number of trucks and helicopters with floating mines, all kinds of armaments; a hundred trucks in total, into an the immense ship. We were two days loading everything, then we got on to the ship the last of all.

Captain Dennis John Scott-Masson
SS Canberra
We were sailing with a small cargo ferry Elk, loaded with highly volatile ammunition and vehicles, totally out of touch with everybody. There was no direction from London, so we sailed vaguely south across the Bay of Biscay, then after much discussion, went to Freetown to bunker. The flight deck workmen had now finished, so they were flown off and we sailed full of oil for Ascension Island.

Private Jose Omar Ojeda
Compania Comando Servicios, 3rd Brigade
But when the ship was ready to leave they said: 'No, men, you will now go to the other side by plane.' We had struggled to go on the same ship as our trucks but we were not allowed: 'You have to load up and return to Commodoro Rivadavia, and from there you take the plane and wait for the trucks at the other end.' So we drove seven hundred kilometres, arrived at dawn, rested for two hours and then went to the airport to get on a plane.

Captain Adrian Robert Freer
3 Para
Once we'd sailed, we established a strict regime for training. Rooms were cleared, and Julian Thompson laid down the skills and subjects he wanted us to concentrate on. A central agency allocated training areas and space within the ship, day by day. People were running for at least an hour each day on the promenade deck, which was two hundred and fifty yards long.

Private Jose Omar Ojeda
Compania Comando Servicios, 3rd Brigade
When we were nearly on board the plane, an urgent order came to say that the trucks would not go into the ship, so we had to go back again to Puerto Deseado. It wasn't that one just got in the truck, loaded it on and it was done; no, we had to load the munitions by hand. We laboured like wretches, and

then we went again to the airport, where we loaded trucks and munitions on to the plane, plus a field kitchen.

Commodore Michael Verney Bradford
SS Canberra

The troops created fewer problems than you'd get on a passenger liner under normal steaming conditions. Just before we arrived at Ascension it was decided food supplies were going down a little too fast, so people could have either fish or meat for main course – not both, which went down OK. But then I discovered this message hadn't got to the P&O restaurant, so we had the crew eating better than the troops, which I found rather amusing. There were the two pools for relaxation in the warmer weather, and some of the cabins were still fully equipped. But when they ran around the promenade deck in step carrying their equipment, you could feel a vibration that ran through the whole ship, so that you could actually see parts moving.

Private Jose Omar Ojeda
Compania Comando Servicios, 3rd Brigade

We finally arrived at Puerto Argentino on April 10, with only ten or eleven of us from my unit. There were a lot of people, and we went into the town, keeping out of the way because our company was all scattered. We should have been one hundred and sixty-five, but the company was not together. From the moment we arrived on April 10, our forces were already in full combat readiness.

Major Philip Neame
D Company Commander, 2 Para

My family were on holiday, climbing; at least I was climbing, everybody else was swanning around in the valleys, when we read about the Argentine invasion in the newspaper. I phoned Aldershot, to find the battalion had been recalled. H Jones had already flown back from skiing in France, and was busy berating UKLF to get 2 Para to be the battalion to be sent, which was very much par for the course where H was concerned.

Private Graham Carter
2 Para

I'd literally just finished my recruit training at Aldershot, my recruit platoon had been split up, and I didn't know anybody in 2 Para. I'd been hoping to go to 3 Para.

My section corporal, Paul Sullivan, took me under his wing; he was very experienced and looked after me. There was a lot of training and people were too busy to bother with 'the new Joe' as they called me.

David Cooper
Chaplain, 2 Para
H Jones was a very charismatic leader who saw things in black and white. The soldiers thought the world of him. We'd been very lucky as a battalion, as the previous CO, Colin Thompson, had established the battalion's administration and internal workings in a most effective manner. He'd handed over to H, then sadly died of cancer.

Major Philip Neame
D Company Commander, 2 Para
I was very much the new boy among the other company commanders, and still getting to know the soldiers. 3 Para was earmarked to go, so in fact there wasn't a role for us. But H wasn't having any of that, and eventually got us stood by as reinforcements for the Commando Brigade. A Royal Marine captain, David Constance, was attached to us as deputy operations officer; he was a superb individual. There was a week of indecision, then things began to happen fairly quickly. We had mixed feelings; that we'd sail to the equator, top up our sun tans then come home; but on the other hand, we were Parachute Regiment; it would be nice to put the training to the test at some stage before we finished our military careers. We really wanted a little war, with all the apprehension that goes with that. People who'd left were phoning the battalion wanting to come. There was also a 'Servants of Maggie' dimension. We served the Queen, but the sort of leadership Margaret Thatcher provided from the very first days grabbed everyone's consciousness, from H downwards, in a quite dramatic and personal way. When he didn't agree with what people were saying, H came out with extravagant expressions like: 'I'll get onto the phone to Maggie, who'll sort it out.'

Major John Harry Crosland
B Company Commander, 2 Para
Once I'd found out where the Falklands were, it was clear that a light force was going to have to spearhead whatever action there might be. The army considered it a very dodgy operation. However, the navy seemed keen, perhaps out to prove they could control a situation by sheer naval power.

Private Graham Carter
2 Para
You don't particularly join the army these days to actually go to war, but for a career. Most people don't particularly want to go to war, even though you're trained to do that. So I wasn't really looking forward to the prospect of going down to the Falklands in that respect.

Company Sergeant Major Peter John Richens
B Company, 2 Para
Having said farewell to our families in the morning, we'd be back home again in the evening. In fact, after a week of this, when we did actually go, it seemed like yet another false alarm – only we ended up on the coach and arriving in Portsmouth.

Captain Donald Arthur Ellerby
MV Norland
I didn't feel apprehensive, because I didn't actually believe we'd ever get beyond Ascension, and that the Argentines would bow out under the pressure. Even though *Norland* was a well-built ship, I wondered what would happen when we hit the Atlantic storms. The lorry spaces were taken up by refrigerated containers filled with food for the troops, as our normal stores were only large enough for a few days. We also carried very large fresh water bags, for up to four months.

David Cooper
Chaplain, 2 Para
Our soldiers were very gung-ho, seeing it as a large live-firing exercise in which the casualties would be the enemy and not us. Company commander Dare Farrar-Hockley had described it as 'an adventure' on the part of our government, which in view of the uncertainties, I agreed with. We stood at the rail of *Norland* and waved as we sailed, which was a very emotional moment. Parachute soldiers normally go to war in the early hours of the morning from an airfield with no send-off at all.

(James) Robert Fox
BBC correspondent
The BBC radio news department had already tried to get people to the Falklands via Ascension and Miami, so I clearly wasn't their first choice. Apart from the usual Northern Ireland reporting, I had no specific military

experience. I was convinced the whole thing was going to be diplomatic – even until the Peruvian initiative at the very last moment. On the weekend before the departure of the carrier group I was sent on a two-day trip to Portsmouth to see the ships leave. I was told to wait there, and then that I was to go with the troops. I managed to sneak back to London to see my family and organise my kit, and sailed on Good Friday, April 9. I was reluctant to go, as a retired general had advised me the navy was just going to sail round Ascension until it was resolved diplomatically, and that it would be a complete waste of time for me.

Captain Donald Arthur Ellerby
MV *Norland*

For most of the time, the troops were training: shooting off the stern, doing bayonet practice, fitness training – everything. There were very few discipline problems. They had very little space and sometimes left gear in the companionways, which got in the way of the ship's running. We did fire drills, boat drills and so on. We all got on very well, but the military life is very different to the merchant service.

Company Sergeant Major Peter John Ritchens
B Company, 2 Para

We upset the Royal Navy party very, very badly by shooting an albatross. The guys were fed up shooting at floating gash bags, and it was a tempting target . . . We did circuit training on the helicopter decks, and ran all around the ship up and down the ladders, but after complaints about the noise, we changed from boots to trainers. We also did a lot of medical training; our Medical Officer thought this through in great detail, and explained how in the Arab-Israeli war the Israelis had each carried their own saline drip kit, so this became 2 Para's standard operating procedure. By the time we reached Ascension, every man could put a drip either into his arm, or into his rectum, which works almost as well.

Major John Harry Crosland
B Company Commander, 2 Para

I was by far the most experienced in our battalion, so I insisted that we be realistic. I was as honest as I could be, and talked with the men about what would happen when people were injured and killed. The wounded would have to be left behind, and so must be able to look after themselves. In parachute operations, the preponderance of officer and NCO casualties is very high. In the Falklands, seventy to seventy-five per cent of our killed and wounded were officers and NCOs, and that's the nature of our game.

Company Sergeant Major Peter John Richens
B Company, 2 Para

I was doing room inspections, sorting out discipline problems, determining how much ammunition we should carry, and thinking hard about our firepower. We'd asked for more machine guns and were very encouraged when we got them. The Education Officer produced a newspaper to keep everybody informed. We ate very well, had a good drink in the evenings with a good social life.

2 Para was looking for a fight, with a country that had dared to try to knock Great Britain off its pedestal, rather than to save the Falkland Islanders.

David Cooper
Chaplain, 2 Para

There's no training pamphlet to tell army chaplains what to do as troops approach battle. I was asked to take charge of casualty clearance. I wanted people to discuss and accept the fear of injury or death without destroying their commitment. The general reaction was that they feared injury and permanent incapacitation more than they feared death. I spent a lot of time talking about this, and also about private matters. People would talk to me on the ship's rail and in the canteen.

Major Philip Neame
D Company Commander, 2 Para

The women crew members of *Norland* were put ashore at Freetown, but one of the remaining crewmen preferred to dress and behave as a woman, and was christened 'Wendy' by the soldiers. Apart from his/her penchant for non-heterosexual relationships, Wendy's saving grace was that he/she was a very good piano player and had a sharp line of wit, and so this man was taken under the wing of the battalion who made him an honorary member, presented with a battalion tie.

David Cooper
Chaplain, 2 Para

My main role in the battalion was as a sounding board at all levels. Our commanding officer, H Jones, joined us at Ascension. He told me that whichever side won, the first battle would win the war, which underpinned his subsequent actions at Goose Green. Some of our soldiers had left home

Despite hockey being considered an officers' sport, the more robust 'deck hockey' variant proved very popular. Officers and men of 2 Para on *Norland* contest an inter-company match on the way south from the UK.

having had a row with their wives, or had unresolved matters they feared might not get sorted out because of what they were doing. Some were worried they might not see their wife again. Private soldiers were probably better catered for by talking with other soldiers and company officers, but sergeants, warrant officers and officers needed somebody else they could talk with, and everyone needed the alternative of talking with someone outside the military system. I was quite involved in this pastoral work.

Private Alejandro Ramon Cano
Grupo Artilleria Aerotransportada

Our unit, Grupo 62, including conscripts doing obligatory military service, started to do parachute training every day, making ready. We were confined to our quarters, so we knew our unit was going to the Malvinas, probably in one week. During this time so many things went through my head, like wanting to go back to Buenos Aires, wanting to go to see my family. I started to think what would happen if I became a deserter, to see my family, my girlfriend, but I also wanted to go as well . . . I could not abide the boredom of waiting. On April 15 our battery was gathered together and we were asked: 'Anyone who doesn't want to go to the Malvinas, raise your hand.' Only three boys raised a hand, and they stayed. The rest were crying to go, we wanted to go at any price. We struggled for our place to go.

Federico Mirré (Argentine Ambassador, 2006)
Foreign Office, Buenos Aires

Nobody in either the ministry or the educated population thought we could hold the islands against the superior military strength of the British. But our foreign ministry officials calculated that the USA might help us find a compromise solution with the UK, so that we would not lose the favour of our population through losing the islands, which seemed to be supported by General Haig and others in the US State Department.

(James) Robert Fox
BBC correspondent

Wideawake Airfield at Ascension was crammed with absolutely everything from missiles, aircraft and ammunition. By that stage I would have been prepared to look at it under the rules of war censorship of that time. But although we spent three and a half weeks at Ascension, we thirty or so journalists on board *Canberra* were not allowed ashore. Some television crews succeeded by using the most extraordinary subterfuges.

Commodore Michael Verney Bradford
SS *Canberra*

One of my most difficult jobs was controlling reporters on board. We had satellite communications, and the reporters would ferret their way into things that were not their business. I had to keep a close watch on some who were a nuisance, and the naval captain had great problems censoring their reports. We heard stories on the BBC about things we didn't know ourselves.

Captain Jeremy Larken
HMS *Fearless*

The press had been kept rather in the dark in *Hermes*, *Invincible* and *Canberra*, as their respective captains didn't have much time for them – which was unfortunate. We made them very welcome on *Fearless*, and told them what was happening. They arrived thoroughly disaffected, then appeared overjoyed at the welcome they received. We made some firm friends.

Captain Christopher Charles Brown
148 *Commando Forward Observation Unit, Royal Artillery*

There was animosity between the journalists and the Royal Navy, with whom they'd been cooped for the last three weeks. They hadn't been allowed access to the communications and freedom they were used to. They were sceptical – but not quite anti. The Royal Navy's attitude is that you have to earn your living; if you're not firing a gun, stoking the boilers or helping to point the ship in the right direction you don't get fed. The peacetime navy, not having been to war for such a long time, was not used to living with the media. We knew from Northern Ireland that every time you had a rock thrown at you, there was a media man watching, and if you threw it back, it was that picture they used in the newspaper. The army was more used to dealing with them.

Captain Donald Arthur Ellerby
MV *Norland*

We'd been told that the *Norland* wouldn't enter the danger zone – the one hundred and fifty-mile limit. The troops were to have been taken off by helicopter, which we'd practised at Ascension. Then somebody realised we had side doors that would fit the landing craft. I'd been to one meeting on board the flag ship, but nothing had been said about what each ship was to do, as this was all top secret. Then a few days later, the commodore flew on board to see me, and told me that we were to be used as an assault craft – thanks to these side doors, which were the perfect height for the landing craft.

I was pretty worried. I asked the commodore if the company knew about this, but he said that my ship had been given to him to use as he wished. I asked to make contact with my company, which didn't know anything about it. I told the commodore I needed to speak with my crew, as they were merchant seamen with their own rights, and I don't suppose they'd thought they'd be going in as an assault ship either. They hadn't signed any forms to say they would do that type of job and had every right to refuse. But not one of them did. They said that if I was happy about it, then they would be too.

Captain Dennis John Scott-Masson
SS *Canberra*
I was asked if I would be prepared to take *Canberra* into the Falklands landing place. I discussed this with my deputy, and we decided that as we were this far involved, we should continue and do what was required of us.

Major Philip Neame
D *Company Commander, 2 Para*
The *Norland* were the unsung heroes of the Falklands, a superb ship and we had a great rapport with the civilian crew. She was used as an amphibious assault ship, and spent most of the time in the thick of it. It was unfortunate that in the early days, the military didn't level with them. When we were well south of Ascension, it was announced that the merchant ships were to go under naval orders, then immediately the *Norland* was designated an assault ship. The captain and crew were pretty put out by this, feeling used and less than flattered, especially at being threatened with naval orders to force them do something that they would have agreed to anyway. There was understandable resentment, even though I suppose it was the safe way for the navy to have played this.

7

Racing South

Lefties like Tony Benn and Tam Dalyell back in the UK were saying
we would fail, which was deeply sapping to our morale. It was our lives
on the line and they should have supported us.

Captain Michael Ernest Barrow
HMS *Glamorgan*
The weather was very cold, very rough with high winds, superimposed on very
long swells. But there were also very high winds, which would drop off to
nothing, then high winds from different directions, unique to the South
Atlantic.

Federico Mirré (Argentine Ambassador, 2006)
Foreign Office, Buenos Aires
After a couple of weeks of working most of the night collating and dissemi-
nating intelligence in the Foreign Ministry in Buenos Aires, I asked for a
fifteen-second private exchange with the Under Secretary, when I expressed
my doubts about the Malvinas operation to him. I asked, with regret, to be
assigned to different functions in the service. He was profoundly unhappy
about this, and asked me to go home.

Then very early the next day I was asked to come in and see the minister,
who told me they had decided to give me a very delicate mission that would
take me out of the diplomatic 'war cabinet'. I was to be the diplomatic link
between the Red Cross and our government, as their assistant, with the power
to request facilities from the military, and deal with matters like exchange of
prisoners. That same evening, I was flown south. The flight was normal from
Buenos Aires to Bahia Blanca. But five minutes before landing, the window

curtains were closed so we couldn't see out. From there we flew very low and landed at Commodoro Rivadavia, and as soon as I stepped out of the plane I could see the difference with Buenos Aires. Commodoro Rivadavia is the seat of one of the army corps, and the air force and army's headquarters for the Malvinas campaign. There were soldiers everywhere, and the airport was completely surrounded by trenches, with anti-aircraft artillery and military vehicles. Hercules and other planes took off direct to the islands. Commodoro was the epicentre of intense military activity.

The Red Cross team knew what they were handling, but had no first-hand experience of an actual war. They were doctors, two with experience in Cambodia, and one in Palestine.

Commander Ian Inskip
HMS Glamorgan

Lefties like Tony Benn and Tam Dalyell back in the UK were saying we would fail, which was deeply sapping to our morale. It was our lives on the line and they should have supported us. But once we heard the missile range at Aberporth was working on a Sunday, we knew the rest of the country was behind us!

Federico Mirré (Argentine Ambassador, 2006)
Foreign Office, Buenos Aires

We had meetings with General Juan Garcia who was the commander of the Fourth Army and also of the joint army/air force task force in the Malvinas, and General Menendez's immediate commander. We heard of the measures taken to protect our civilian population in case of British landing or bombardment of the Patagonian coast or inland, and measures to protect the British settlers in Malvinas – how military operations there would not put their houses or installations in danger.

General Garcia confided to me privately that he hoped the United Nations solution would come through, and that he didn't see any positive outcome to the war because of the disparities of forces, hasty organisation and the logistics involved. He was one of the few at that time who expressed his views and doubts. I think it's important to make a record of this. We also met air force brigadier Crespo, who was commander of the air branch of the operation and went on to become the air force chief of staff. He had more of the 'Patton' attitude, with very few doubts.

Commander Ian Inskip
HMS Glamorgan

Heading south-west, we took things with increasing seriousness. We moved to wartime damage control conditions, rules of engagement were imposed from London, and we knew that nuclear submarines were patrolling ahead of us and where they were.

Federico Mirré (Argentine Ambassador, 2006)
Foreign Office, Buenos Aires

The Red Cross wanted to know what kind of hospital installations were available. Crespo took us to an incredibly new, modern, inflatable military hospital that you could carry inside two Hercules, which was ready to take casualties.

Lieutenant Commander Peter Walpole
Signal Communications Officer, HMS Sheffield

Admiral Woodward had been a previous captain of *Sheffield*. When he visited us, he sat on a chair the wrong way round, like John Wayne. I wasn't sure if he had intended this to be a 'Chin-up' chat or an 'It's going to be quite tough' chat, but it was all commendably informal and rather Nelsonian. He couldn't tell us very much.

Federico Mirré (Argentine Ambassador, 2006)
Foreign Office, Buenos Aires

Civilian and military authorities were ready for a British landing. We visited some enormous sheep-shearing sheds which had been converted into shelters for people in case of bombardments, and disembarkations of UK forces into Argentine mainland. The local population in Patagonia were far more impacted by the war, compared with the 'party goes on' attitude in Buenos Aires.

Radio Supervisor Stewart Anthony MacFarlane
HMS Coventry

Everything was rationed. The NAAFI was a joke; you could have one Mars bar per man per day, and when you went for breakfast it was one egg or one sausage as we didn't have enough food on board. You couldn't have chips as hot oil was dangerous, with stew all the time – 'Pot Mess', with everything in it. But every night Les Kellet, our petty officer chef, baked bread rolls.

Federico Mirré (Argentine Ambassador, 2006)
Foreign Office, Buenos Aires
The Red Cross team could not physically go around everywhere themselves, so I was asked to collect information for them. One night I was on a hilly coast road, totally deserted, pitch dark, about one hundred and fifty kilometres from Commodoro Rivadavia. It was bitterly cold – one to fifteen below zero. The car engine stopped, so I got out, and with another Argentine fellow we got a torch to have a look at the engine, shivering with cold. Then all of a sudden I felt something very cold in my neck – a sub-machine gun. A voice said, 'Put your hands on your head.' I explained I was a Foreign Ministry official, and my documents were in my pockets. The gun stayed in my neck, but a hand pulled out my documents. After some twenty seconds I was told to lower my hands and turn around; to see a lieutenant with some soldiers. He said we were risking our lives, as the military believed UK commandos might land here, so he was following orders . . . But he took us in his jeep and drove us back to Commodoro, where we had a beer together.

Lieutenant Commander Peter Walpole
Signal Communications Officer, HMS Sheffield
The Argentine Navy's Type 42 ship *Santissima Trinidad* had been in Portsmouth alongside us for six months during 1981. It had British equipment, its crew trained on British ranges by British navy staff. Most of the Argentine officers had their wives over, and we invited them into our wardroom for drinks. We helped them with problems, and had a *Santissima Trinidad* plaque on the wall outside our wardroom. They were not bandolier-equipped gauchos. Like us, they'd taken a Type 42 to sea, operated its systems, and conducted successful missile firings. I felt it would be most unfortunate if we were to encounter the *Santissima Trinidad* in action – people we'd had in the wardroom not a year previously, sharing jokes and drinking. It really brings it home to you, that the military are just pawns in the politician's game, to be moved around as the politicians see fit.

Federico Mirré (Argentine Ambassador, 2006)
Foreign Office, Buenos Aires
The Red Cross were particularly concerned about how the local population of Porto Argentino – or Stanley – were reacting to the presence of Argentine troops in their midst. They repeatedly asked to fly to the islands to check on the civilian population, so I was involved in a series of difficult interviews with the military, to get a plane to go across with the Red Cross. I never met

with General Garcia again. It was now getting more difficult for me to obtain any relevant information on how the war was going. I could see tension growing in the military.

Lieutenant Commander Raymond John Adams
HMS Coventry

From Ascension, we headed south-westerly, transmitting on radar and signal communications, ensuring that the enemy knew where we were, but so they thought there were more of us, as strategic deception. Two-thirds of the way down we paused to wait for everyone else to catch up, and *Plymouth* and *Antrim* were detached to South Georgia.

The vastness of the South Atlantic is not something you appreciate. South Georgia is just over eight hundred miles from the Falklands, with an Antarctic climate. The Falklands are like a very windy Shetlands or Orkneys. It's also about three to four thousand miles from the Falklands to Ascension Island, so the scale is horrendous. The task force sailing from Portsmouth could have been on another planet. Our world consisted of these eight or ten ships in the middle of the South Atlantic, exercising together all the way down, with a few maintenance days, working very hard, preparing for war as a group.

Air Marshal Joseph Alfred Gilbert
Assistant Chief of Defence Staff (Policy), MoD, Whitehall

I had been convinced there could be a diplomatic solution. There were even times when I felt relief as I thought we'd achieved that. But one of General Al Haig's telegrams from Buenos Aires during his diplomatic shuttling, in which he said, 'I do not know who is in charge here,' made me realise that with the out-of-control factions in Argentina, there was nobody who could actually sign up to an agreement. General Galtieri, if nothing else, was an alcoholic. Their air marshal did remarkable things, but in the event their admiral ran for cover. They had no coherence, unlike Whitehall, which in this crisis achieved a remarkable degree of interdepartmental cooperation.

Captain (John) Jeremy Black
HMS Invincible

I'd told my wife, before we sailed, that we would fight. Mrs Thatcher had nailed her colours to the mast to save the islands, and Galtieri had done the same thing by invading, and neither of them was going to give up. This was not a popular view among the sailors, who held out hopes of a diplomatic settlement.

After leaving Ascension, we were buzzed by the Argentinians' converted Boeing passenger liner reconnaissance aircraft, with its radar. We put up aircraft to get on to its tail, and as it became increasingly more intrusive, there was much discussion between the admiral and Whitehall about what we should do about it. It could have contained a group of nuns en route to some 'do' in South Africa. The Boeing was allowed to fly about for a while, then attitudes in London hardened and we were told to shoot it down if it came within fifty miles. Maybe the Argentines were warned, and the Boeing never returned. From London we received definite intelligence of submarine activity in the Falklands area.

I had thought at some length about how we were going to fight and the changes we should make to the ship and its routine. Unlike the Second World War, modern war is not a slogging match, but one in which a single hit decides the result. You have to get it right first time. My crew were going to be in two watches, so they wouldn't get much rest anyway, which might go on for some time, and they'd be under stress. People needed to be rested, and be as comfortable as possible when they did get a break, to give them the best chance of getting it right.

We sailed south with *Hermes*, whose captain I'd known throughout our time in the navy, doing similar courses and jobs. I would therefore have expected us to respond to this situation in a similar way – which, interestingly, didn't happen. We were weeks away from any sort of military event. To my way of thinking, a steady progression was required, from peacetime shipboard life, to being highly tuned for war. However, *Hermes* went straight to action stations on the day we sailed, and did things like evacuating people from mess decks below the water line, forcing them to find little holes all over the place in which to live. I decided to do it all by degrees; for example, at some point we might have to remove the mirrors from all the bathrooms, which would produce flying glass if we were hit.

Commander Ralph John Wykes-Sneyd
Officer Commanding 820 Sea King Squadron, Fleet Air Arm,
HMS Invincible
My crews and maintainers were able to get good rest, and were fit and alert. Life on *Hermes* was very different; they lived in cramped, very uncomfortable conditions, and were getting very tired. On the combat air patrol station changeovers with our pilots, the *Hermes* pilots sounded very tired.

A damage control team on HMS *Invincible*, wearing very thick fireproof suits and breathing apparatus.

Commander Nigel David 'Sharkey' Ward
Officer Commanding 801 Squadron, Fleet Air Arm, HMS Invincible
We had a very happy ship. It wasn't quite the same in the other carrier, HMS *Hermes*, where different personalities affected everything that went on. Also, the Harrier squadron in HMS *Hermes* were not at the same standard as we were, which had become clear before the Falklands crisis started. Because my squadron had spent the previous three years bringing the Sea Harrier through all its tests and into naval service, my squadron knew it inside out. We'd even managed to get the Harrier's radar to pick up aircraft at longer ranges than the designers, Ferranti – twenty-three miles, as opposed to their eighteen miles. 800 Squadron could only manage pick-ups of seven and ten miles' range, and didn't believe the results we were getting.

Commander Ralph John Wykes-Sneyd
Officer Commanding 820 Sea King Squadron, Fleet Air Arm,
HMS Invincible
A tremendous amount of work was done to study the Exocet missile, its parameters and how we best should deal with it. To protect *Invincible*, we strapped a dish radar reflector to the side of a Sea King, which would hover to one side of the ship whenever there was an air raid. We knew the height Exocet flew and exactly where it would hit in the ship. One of my observers came down into the operations room one night to debrief after a sortie, and by way of making an entrance, flung open the door and said: 'Well chaps, how are things in the Exocet Reception Area?' to several frosty looks. Exocet decoy duty was quite safe for us, as we flew just above the height at which the missile flew.

Commander Nigel David 'Sharkey' Ward
Officer Commanding 801 Squadron, Fleet Air Arm, HMS Invincible
When *Hermes* 800 Squadron was first formed, we'd offered them all the help we could. But . . . [they] said: 'We don't need your help, Sharkey.' So when we came to the South Atlantic, because 800 Squadron still didn't trust their radars or navigation kits, they couldn't use them properly. The result was that 800 Squadron couldn't do a lot of very basic things, which is astonishing and highly controversial. They couldn't carry out a decent combat air patrol, searching for an enemy aircraft with their radars, so most of their pilots didn't actually use the radars! *Hermes* was captained by a very good guy called Lyn Middleton, but he doesn't suffer fools gladly, and is a bomber pilot, not a fighter pilot.

Lieutenant Commander Graham John Edmonds
Operations Officer and Squadron Warfare Officer, HMS Broadsword

I was summoned to a meeting of the two air groups on *Invincible* as I was the expert on Sea Wolf. As far as everyone else was concerned, the missile was fully automatic and liable to shoot down anything that came within range, which concerned the aircrew. I had to tell them it wouldn't. Some of the captains were aviators, the others submariners with no experience of aviation.

The meeting commenced with Admiral Woodward asking how we were going to achieve air superiority. The two carrier captains were at loggerheads. Captain Middleton of *Hermes*, a Buccaneer pilot, was all for using the Harriers for low-level strike; to drop bombs, fire missiles, suppress their air defences by aggressive action and generally cause mayhem to Argentine troops on the ground. Captain Black and the *Invincible* air group were much more concerned with the air defence of the ships, and with the shortage of our aeroplanes compared to what the Argentines could put up.

The two air groups could not be reconciled, so Admiral Woodward said he'd have two separate air groups; one doing air defence, the other low-level air attacks. This proposal made the two factions realise that a split in roles would stretch them all to the limits, persuading the *Hermes* faction toward air defence, with the occasional combat air patrol into the islands to drop bombs along the way – plus some specific attack operations. The meeting broke up in some disarray and acrimony. The admiral favoured Captain Black, who was a fellow submariner, on *Invincible*, against Captain Middleton, who resented having a submariner admiral sitting in his aircraft carrier. It was even more interesting for us in *Broadsword* having Captain Middleton's son as a pilot, who received letters from his dad via the internal seamail, which indicated that the relationship between Captain Middleton and the admiral was not all it should have been.

Commander Ralph John Wykes-Sneyd
Officer Commanding 820 Sea King Squadron, Fleet Air Arm,
HMS Invincible

I'd just opened a letter containing some rather disappointing news. After about twelve hours, I observed that the mood of my squadron had changed; so thinking I might have something to do with it, I set off around the flight deck, crew room and so on with my smile rigidly fixed, and, surprise, surprise, all the tails came back up. I thought, 'Good Lord, is this the level of responsibility I have for these guys?' It did surprise me, but thinking about it, the confidence I felt in my captain was clearly a reflection of the same thing.

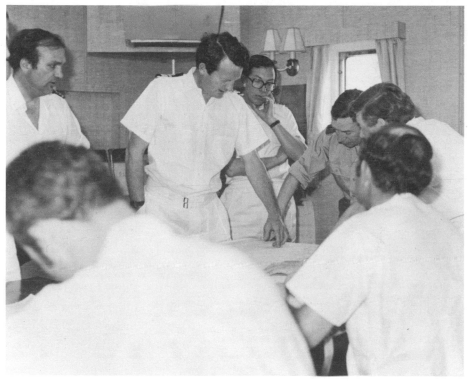

Rear Admiral Sandy Woodward and his staff on board *Hermes* at Ascension Island, discussing matters with a Royal Marine staff officer.

HMS *Hermes* making an RAS, with RFA *Regent* or *Resource* steaming close on her port side. The munitions on her flight deck include ARM.9 Sidewinder missiles for the Harriers, 40mm Bofors anti-aircraft gun ammunition, and M46 air-launched torpedoes.

Prince Andrew was a pilot in my squadron, and I had felt it crucial that he stayed with the ship when we sailed. I had some interesting conversations with him about how things could be made easier for him, and we discussed how we could get him out, if that's what needed to be done. He was as committed as any other pilot, but his role was never any more important than any other sub-lieutenant pilot. He was never given anything special to do, as he was not in my 'first eleven'.

Commander Nigel David 'Sharkey' Ward
Officer Commanding 801 Squadron, Fleet Air Arm, HMS Invincible

It was a winter climate down there, and you've got to wear woolly long johns and sweaters. Then you wear a green canvas goon suit with waterproof zip from the groin to the shoulder and rubber seals around the wrist and neck that keeps water out for a short time. Your G suit goes inside that, with an air umbilical to squeeze the body from the legs up to the abdomen, stopping the blood pooling down in your feet and bum so you don't blackout when pulling G. On top of that, you've got a Browning pistol in a shoulder holster and your life-preserver waistcoat, with goodies like a Sabre rescue beacon, and various other life-saving aids . . . You're attached to the seat cushion, which has a dinghy.

You're very restricted in walking, but in the cockpit, everything is within easy reach. You're strapped in very tightly and it's actually quite comfortable. You have a control column with quite a few buttons for trimming the aircraft, firing weapons, getting radar locks, then on the left there's a nozzle control lever, a throttle lever, and a radar hand controller with seven different switches. When you're working in the cockpit, you're very busy. You've got to control the radar, the navigation system, and engine power. Speed is critical to weapon delivery; plus the angle of dive and the height, and getting your missile release parameters right.

Sea Harrier pilots have to be aggressive and extrovert, with a high ego, competing all the time to get better, with a monkey-like ability to learn quickly. From the cockpit you can see all around you. Even though there's a lot of aluminium and engine behind you, you don't normally see it, so you feel very free – bombing around the sky in a high-speed machine like a space bubble. It's very exciting.

Commander 'Sharkey' Ward RN, in full Fleet Air Arm aviator's gear, ready to fly.

Part Two

THE
KILLING BEGINS

After making her unopposed landing and occupation of the Falkland Islands, Argentina reinforced her garrison there, ready to withstand possible British military action. General Osvaldo Garcia, commander of the Argentine Army's V Corps, and the Malvinas Theatre of Operations, appeared briefly on the islands soon after the successful invasion was complete, but commanded his forces from Comodoro Rivadavia in northern Patagonia. While the military governor Brigadier General Menendez, his Malvinas military government staff and the commanders of the fighting units lived on the Falklands, General Garcia and his staff remained in Argentina where they played little part in the military operations that were to follow.

Unlike the British, Argentina had no recent war experience. Argentine land commanders did not understand how the British would go about retaking the Falklands, and Argentine politicians seemed unable to gauge Britain's determination. Their plan was to achieve a huge superiority of numbers, weaponry and ammunition, then sit tight while advancing winter forced the British to return home. Thousands of Argentine soldiers were sent across by ship and Hercules transport aircraft, many being conscripted and trained specifically to go to the Malvinas. This sudden reinforcement was disorientating for individual Argentine soldiers, but took place in an environment of great rejoicing, as the unpopular and distrusted military junta tried desperately to hang on to power by satisfying one of Argentina's oldest and most strongly held nationalistic desires.

The US had strong ties with Britain, epitomised by the close personal relationship between President Ronald Reagan and Prime Minister Margaret Thatcher. But US internal politics did not allow Reagan to back Thatcher in what some were presenting as British aggression with forty million Hispanics in the USA, and some accusing Britain of colonialism. The Argentine government believed it enjoyed an important relationship with the US, based upon its staunch resistance to communism in South America – America's backyard. The junta believed this relationship would cause America to pressurise Britain into backing down without fighting. The United Nations played into Argentina's hands with ineffectual, dilatory measures of mild condemnation of Argentina's invasion, while also disapproving of Britain sailing its task force.

Behind the scenes, the US gave immediate covert military and intelligence assistance to Britain, on the basis of the 'special relationship' but also because the Falklanders' human rights had clearly been breached. In public, America began high-profile diplomatic efforts to solve the crisis without bloodshed. On April 8, 1982, the US Secretary of State, General Alexander Haig, flew to London to begin a series of intense mediation meetings in Buenos Aires and London. Two days later, the European Economic Community approved trade sanctions against Argentina, while General Haig flew to Buenos Aires for talks with the military junta.

On April 17, Haig again met with the Argentine junta, but two days later, after a breakdown in the mediation talks, he returned to Washington. On April 23, the British Foreign Office advised British nationals in Argentina to leave.

8

First Blood

Our boss decided to rescue the remainder of the SAS, so we stripped out all the dunking sonar equipment and ripped the guts out of the cabin to cut the weight right down. The Wessex 3 wasn't designed to carry troops. It was quite a big operation.

Captain Christopher Charles Brown
148 Commando Forward Observation Unit, Royal Artillery
I had a five-man team whose job was to conduct the forward observation of naval bombardments and control fighter-ground attack aircraft, plus field artillery. I'd been in bed on April 2, due to go on leave, but about six in the morning, one of my guys shook me and told me to get up to the office. I'd told him to fuck off as he was too late for the first of April. We'd packed everything away for Easter leave, but within a couple of hours were ready to go, though wondering how to get there. Parachuting seemed the most likely travel option, so we got all that together, then sat around waiting to see what would happen next. But we'd been in similar situations before, all ready but nothing actually happening.

We had five naval gunfire teams and a headquarters. One team disappeared south with the SBS, and then a further two sailed with *Canberra*. My team was left wondering whether we were going to be involved, only to be told to get ready for a pre-planned operation with the SAS to recapture South Georgia. The task force was getting further and further south, and the political negotiations were not going too well. Then a helicopter arrived to take us to HQ Commando Forces, where we were told we were retaking South Georgia with SAS and SBS, plus 42 Commando and a couple of Royal Navy ships.

Chief Petty Officer David John 'Fritz' Heritier
Fleet Air Arm, HMS Antrim

We'd sailed from Gibraltar to Ascension Island where we took on more food, plus a bunch of SBS and Special Forces troops – anonymous faces. *Antrim* went from our normal four hundred and fifty-strong crew, to eight hundred and fifty.

Captain Christopher Charles Brown
148 Commando Forward Observation Unit, Royal Artillery

My team sailed from Ascension in HMS *Antrim*, which I'd never worked with. We'd flown to Ascension, where people were still pretty relaxed. After check-zeroing our rifles, we flew out to *Antrim*, in an exercise rather than a war-type mood. Until you actually get fired upon, it's just like every other exercise. There's a transition; the navy don't just change into white pullovers and start passing round mugs of cocoa. Furthermore, as far as we were concerned, there was no guarantee of any action.

We sailed with HMS *Plymouth* – which I was rather worried about, because she had the oldest type of gun system in the navy, and was only accurate if the crew was well practised. I'd spent some time earlier in the year at the naval gunfire range in Scotland, where *Plymouth* had shelled everywhere but the target area. The navy had neglected the art of gunnery, considering anti-submarine warfare and air defence far more important. *Plymouth*'s lack of accuracy during previous practice was quite understandable, but on the way south it was vital for us to work up these ships. We put a liaison officer on board, and fired her as much as we could.

Chief Petty Officer David John 'Fritz' Heritier
Fleet Air Arm, HMS Antrim

I had twelve people working below me to keep our Wessex helicopter flying, which we called 'Humphrey'. The Wessex was twenty-one years old, and I'd had my doubts about its reliability.

Commander Ian Inskip
HMS Glamorgan

Almost immediately we sailed from Ascension, a periscope was sighted and a submarine racket heard on sonar. There was an emergency breakaway from replenishment, and the whole force turned away to the north. Once the panic died down, it was realised that this false alarm had been caused by the breakthrough of a ship's radar on dummy load into its electronic warfare detection equipment, and the periscope sighting was probably a fish.

Chief Petty Officer Terence Bullingham
Fleet Air Arm, HMS Antrim

HMS *Endurance* had escaped from the Argentine invasion of South Georgia by sailing south and hiding among the ice where other ships couldn't go. She came north to meet us, to take on stores: eggs, potatoes, and the all-important beer. I think she was pretty desperate for food. There was big cheering from her crew – all good stuff.

Chief Petty Officer David John 'Fritz' Heritier
Fleet Air Arm, HMS Antrim

We rendezvoused with HMS *Endurance*, then both headed for South Georgia, and it became freezing cold, a huge, strange, rugged island sticking out of the sea, and no sign of anything. That night it was too rough to put Humphrey into the hanger, then a chain lashing tore out of the deck.

Chief Petty Officer Terence Bullingham
Fleet Air Arm, HMS Antrim

Eleven of us went out, and even in full foul weather gear, anorak, trousers, overalls under that, plus full Number Eight action working dress and thermal underwear, it was as if you were naked – the wind just went straight through the lot. Anybody falling into the sea wasn't going to survive. We got ourselves round the helicopter by hanging on to each other's lifelines, and put on as many lashings as we could to make sure the helicopter stayed there. It was covered in salt. With a force eleven hurricane, and the temperature on the freezing point, it was the sort of weather you just don't see any other place than Iceland or the Faroes – a complete nightmare that only abated a bit at around four o'clock in the morning.

We had to insert the SAS into South Georgia covertly, so they could come in behind the Argentine marines, but the weather was a serious problem. We tried using Gemini dinghies, but one drifted off when the motor failed and was regained on its way to South Africa. Some SAS got ashore and up on to the Fortuna Glacier, but were stranded there by bad weather. Humphrey was tasked to recover them, with two Wessex 5 helicopters from RFA *Tidespring*, which was in company with us.

Chief Petty Officer David John 'Fritz' Heritier
Fleet Air Arm, HMS Antrim

That morning Humphrey became a hero all on his own. The special troops had suffered a very rough night with the high winds. They couldn't move

A crashed Wessex 5 assault helicopter from 845 Naval Air Squadron, on the Fortuna Glacier at South Georgia on April 22, 1982. SAS troopers are in the snow beside another 845 Squadron Wessex.

because of crevasses on the glacier and needed to be rescued. Humphrey and the two Wessex 5s disappeared up into the gloom, then we heard one had crashed. Humphrey clattered back out of the darkness on his own. I plugged in and asked the pilot where the other aircraft were: 'They've both crashed in a whiteout.'

Some of the special troops were in Humphrey, and when they got out we could see he'd been grossly overloaded, and there were several more loads of men to bring back. But the weather really closed in, we couldn't take off, so we got the aircraft ready to go again and waited. Having a single aircraft, you get to know their foibles, but Humphrey seemed to be able to cope with anything.

Chief Petty Officer Terence Bullingham
Fleet Air Arm, HMS Antrim
Our boss Ian Stanley decided to rescue the remainder of the SAS, so we stripped out all the dunking sonar equipment and ripped the guts out of the cabin to cut the weight right down. The Wessex 3 wasn't designed to carry troops. It was quite a big operation.

Chief Petty Officer David John 'Fritz' Heritier
Fleet Air Arm, HMS Antrim
There was a small break in the weather, so the boss decided to have another go up the glacier – his seventh time that day. We didn't know if they would come back, but after a very long time, we heard the noise of the rotors and Humphrey again emerged from the darkness, and with great gusto landed immediately – no hovering or anything. I was stunned; there were seventeen people in the aircraft; sitting in the door, lying on top each other, biggish people.

I was very concerned about the damage we'd done to the aircraft to carry all this. The boss assured me that the cold on the glacier made the air denser, so there'd been no problem, but that coming back, he'd had to land straight back on to avoid the added strain of going into the hover as he hadn't got the power. It was a very skilful, brave piece of flying.

Rear Admiral Anthony John Whetstone
Deputy Chief of Naval Staff (Operations), MoD Whitehall
Secretary of State John Nott was due to make a statement to the House about the progress of the operation. I'd broken the bad news and returned to my office when Admiral Halifax rang from Northwood to tell me a third

helicopter, loaded completely over capacity with both the SAS and the crews of the other two helicopters, had got them back safely. I ran and caught the Chief of the Defence Staff and John Nott just as they were leaving the Ministry of Defence.

Chief Petty Officer Terence Bullingham
Fleet Air Arm, HMS Antrim

We were very concerned about an Argentine Guppy class submarine called the *Santa Fe*, known to be in the area. Not knowing the location of this submarine was paralysing the whole operation. It wasn't a powerful or glamorous submarine – conventional and obsolescent, but it created a huge problem. But this is what Humphrey the anti-submarine helicopter was for, so we worked all night getting all the equipment back in and operating once more. It sounds easy now, but it involved a lot of red-eye from the maintenance crew.

Chief Petty Officer David John 'Fritz' Heritier
Fleet Air Arm, HMS Antrim

HMS *Brilliant* had joined us with two Lynx helicopters, and we moved back in to hunt the submarine which intelligence told us had sailed out of Grytviken at dawn. We loaded Humphrey with two depth charges.

Chief Petty Officer Terence Bullingham
Fleet Air Arm, HMS Antrim

Humphrey was flown away on the morning of Sunday April 25. The observer, Chris Parry, just managed to see a tiny blip on his radar, which turned out to be *Santa Fe*'s conning tower. They asked us to prepare a live torpedo.

Chief Petty Officer David John 'Fritz' Heritier
Fleet Air Arm, HMS Antrim

They found it on the surface, and made two passes, dropping the first depth charge right beside the submarine, with the second bouncing off the casing and rolling round the side – both exploding. This was the first time a helicopter had attacked a submarine, even though we'd been practising it for years.

Chief Petty Officer Terence Bullingham
Fleet Air Arm, HMS Antrim

Depth charges are like a beer keg filled with four hundred pounds of high explosive. A live torpedo costs hundreds of thousands of pounds, and contains three hundred and fifty-odd pounds of explosive. Handling these things is not for when you're tired, at ten o'clock on a Sunday morning. We loaded two depth charges and Humphrey went away again.

They found the *Santa Fe* again on the radar, but it saw Humphrey coming and tried to crash dive. Humphrey dropped another depth charge, which exploded along the starboard side of the submarine, crippling it. The boat was forced to run for South Georgia and get alongside the jetty.

Humphrey made it back carrying the remaining depth charge, which we had to swap for a torpedo – which is a pretty serious and tricky thing to do under pressure: winching the live depth charge carefully down, then fitting a live torpedo. HMS *Plymouth*'s Wasp and HMS *Broadsword*'s Lynx both had a go, before it was decided to leave the submarine, and instead *Antrim* and *Plymouth* were to do a naval bombardment of South Georgia – something the navy had never done for a long, long time.

Captain Christopher Charles Brown
148 *Commando Forward Observation Unit, Royal Artillery*
A hasty plan was cobbled together. I was to control the bombardment from *Endurance*'s Wasp, flown by Flight Commander Tony Allenbeck. He picked me up from *Antrim* and we flew in to Cumberland Bay, where we could see Grytviken with the *Santa Fe* alongside. It seemed no different to any peace-time exercise, but I knew that attacks never go to time. I asked Tony Allenbeck how much flying time we actually had. He had fuel for about half an hour, which wasn't long enough. I suggested we close down the engine to give us more time, but although the co-pilot and Tony Allenbeck were very worried about this, they agreed provided I cleared the area of Argentines. So I jumped out with my rifle, finding only penguins and seabirds. Tony shut down the helicopter, and we got out and sat on a rock, three people in a row, like on any naval gunfire exercise, waiting for the rounds to come down.

Chief Petty Officer Terence Bullingham
Fleet Air Arm, HMS *Antrim*
Moving at thirty-four to thirty-five knots, the ships were heeling over so much that you couldn't stand on deck; speeds never done in peacetime.

Captain Christopher Charles Brown
148 *Commando Forward Observation Unit, Royal Artillery*
The ships came into the area ready to fire, and in the meantime everybody on the ships was piling into helicopters for the assault. An Argentine flag was flying on a mast outside the survey base, but no Argentinians. So I set

about the normal business of conducting a fire plan with naval gunfire support.

I told a ship to lay guns on a bunker area, and in time she came back to say she was ready to fire with the time of flight for the shell. At that time it dawned on me that, in giving the order to fire, I was firing the first rounds of the war. There was a similar pause at the other end, during which presumably they also debated whether they should fire, then came their response – a report of 'Shot'. A puff of smoke and a big bang appeared at the other end. Although I was engaging targets all around Grytviken, I was not allowed to engage the buildings themselves. I requested permission to engage the old whaling station, but was told to engage the area immediately to the front of the enemy rather than the enemy themselves.

Our mini task force had no proper commando helicopters designed for troop carrying, so the assault force was a bit of a mishmash, taking several flights to get in. The other naval gunfire observer, Captain Willie McCracken, went in with them. As they started to walk off the landing zone, I saw a white flag flying alongside the Argentine flag on King Edward Point, with other white flags out of the upper floor windows. We got back into the helicopter and flew forward over the top of our advancing troops, landed, picked up the commander of the assault force, then flew into King Edward Point where the Argentinians surrendered, without firing a shot in return.

Chief Petty Officer David John 'Fritz' Heritier
Fleet Air Arm, HMS Antrim

Our shipwright was tasked to make a coffin. We buried an Argentine sailor killed on the submarine, in the churchyard at Grytviken, where Shackleton is buried. The prisoners were put into the empty hangar on *Tidespring* and taken to Ascension, where we thought the whole thing would end – but this was not to be.

Chief Petty Officer Terence Bullingham
Fleet Air Arm, HMS Antrim

The ships came into the old whaling station at Grytviken, and the Argentine marines were taken as prisoners into RFA *Tidespring*, with the notorious Captain Astiz taken into *Antrim* and locked up under special surveillance in the doctor's cabin. He'd been involved in torturing nuns before the campaign, and came through our flight deck guarded by our Royal Marine detachment. We'd been working all the previous day and night and were knackered, so we didn't take much notice of him.

A Royal Navy funeral party carry out the burial of Petty Officer Felix Artuso of the Argentine Navy, killed on board submarine *Santa Fe* on April 27, 1982.

Captain Christopher Charles Brown
148 Commando Forward Observation Unit, Royal Artillery

We'd had a marvellous day for the assault, in between gales, high winds and bad seas; and afterwards the weather again deteriorated. I spoke with one Argentine before they were taken away; he said: 'You were lucky to have such good weather.'

I said: 'Yes, each year we go to Norway and practise fighting in bad conditions.'

He said: 'Ah, but we have been here for thirty days, but at least in Norway there are womens.'

Chief Petty Officer Terence Bullingham
Fleet Air Arm, HMS Antrim

We came alongside, then escorted *Tidespring* with her prisoners of war back to Ascension, and thought that would be the end of it, with the Argentines having been given a bit of a lesson and a bloody nose. How wrong we were . . .

Captain Christopher Charles Brown
148 Commando Forward Observation Unit, Royal Artillery

One of the other whaling stations had a belligerent Argentine garrison, so we sent an SAS troop in HMS *Plymouth* and threatened them with naval gunfire and an assault. They surrendered after being told their colleagues at Grytviken had already done so. But it was interesting that when we moved into Grytviken, there were no obstacles to stop us from landing helicopters: stakes, barbed wire or anything at all. But the other whaling station had been booby trapped, and would have caused us casualties had we assaulted.

Chief Petty Officer Terence Bullingham
Fleet Air Arm, HMS Antrim

I remember a wounded sailor from the *Santa Fe* being brought on board *Antrim*. He'd lost his leg when our depth charge went off and knocked a torpedo from its mountings. I felt guilty that it had been our depth charge, and deliberately kept out of the way in order to avoid seeing him. I'd been one of the people loading the depth charge into the helicopter, and to my surprise I was thinking about how he might be a family man and how this would restrict him, and other disturbing thoughts. I deliberately didn't go and see him because I felt personally responsible. I was also thinking about how I might feel if I was a soldier and personally shot somebody. I couldn't work out how I would feel, and I didn't think I could do something like that.

HMS *Conqueror* with HMS *Antrim* (left) and HMS *Plymouth* (right) during the transfer of an SBS party from the submarine on April 26, 1982.

Chief Petty Officer Lionel Norman Kurn
Helicopter artificer, HMS Antrim

There was a suggestion that we were going home, as our role was complete. But after making a rendezvous with the task force, we turned south again, so we realised this wasn't going to happen. Having hoped that retaking South Georgia would solve the problem, the quickest way home was to get on with it. With all the ships together again, there was more shuffling stores around and a lot of activity.

9

Total Exclusion

We were shelling the airfield, and an Argentine Puma helicopter was ten miles away. We engaged with Sea Dart and knocked the Puma out of the sky in one. I was watching this from the bridge, and it made me think of the people in that aircraft, with wives and children. I think at some stage everyone has to realise that you are killing people.

Lieutenant Commander Graham John Edmonds
Operations Officer and Squadron Warfare Officer, HMS Broadsword
Once South Georgia had been captured, all the ships came together and we formed a vast task group heading south, entering the TEZ on May 1. A Sea King helicopter delivered mail to us, but after being handed on to the next ship, disappeared from our radar and crashed into the sea. The pilot escaped and was picked up having fired his flares, but sadly the crewman was drowned.

Chief Petty Officer Terence Bullingham
Fleet Air Arm, HMS Antrim
After reuniting with *Hermes*, we sailed back down to the Falklands, still not really thinking this would continue. We're the might of the British Navy . . . surely the Argentines are not going to pursue this thing to the end?

Captain Christopher Charles Brown
148 Commando Forward Observation Unit, Royal Artillery
We went on board *Hermes*, noticing a change in attitude between the crews of *Plymouth*, which had been in action, and the crews in *Invincible* and *Hermes*, who had the same exercise attitude we'd seen previously at Ascension two

weeks earlier. There was a clear split between we ground force people drinking and telling war stories up one end of the bar, and the rest.

Chief Petty Officer David John 'Fritz' Heritier
Fleet Air Arm, HMS Antrim

Around the roaring forties area, we rendezvoused with HMS *Antelope*, got rid of the more sensitive prisoners we had on board, then turned back to escort the *Sir Galahad* and support ships to the main battle group off the Falkland Islands. There'd been no political resolution and suddenly it was for real. Plans were being formed and there was lots of toing and froing, but that's not our concern. We just keep the aircraft flying.

Keeping Humphrey going required a lot of improvisation, but one day the engine blew all its oil out, just managing to land. Changing the engine on a Wessex 3 is a very long job, and a guided missile destroyer is very cramped. All helicopters were needed for cross-decking, so we had to get this done really fast. It normally takes four days – ashore at Portland. We worked forty-eight hours non-stop, while the other trades ran around doing the checks, getting supplies and feeding us with food and coffee. After thirty-six hours we got it on to the flight deck to test and adjust at full power with the aircraft screwed down in a special rig. We were very tired, doing stupid things like forcing in oil without realising the tank was already full.

Lieutenant Commander Peter Walpole
Signal Communications Officer, HMS Sheffield

There was consideration of whether we should shave off our beards, as beards break the seal on gas masks. The first lieutenant had a beard, and decided there wasn't going to be a chemical threat, unlike on the *Hermes* where they decided otherwise and had to shave them off.

Michael Thomas Nicholson
ITN correspondent

It only gelled for us once the diplomatic efforts failed. Winter in the roaring forties was a desperate prospect. The Argentines were delaying everything, hoping we'd be forced to pull out by the weather. Everyone was ordered to shave off their beards, which upset the naval types who'd had them all their lives. Brian Hanrahan shaved his beard off, making him unrecognisable from his official photo, which nearly led to him being refused going ashore because as the MoD minder said: 'His face was invalid.'

Captain Carlos B. Castro Madero
Weapons Officer, 5-Inch Anti-Aircraft Batteries, Warship Belgrano

The Argentine Navy was divided in three groups; one with *Belgrano* in the south, another in the north with our aircraft carrier and its screen, and a third group of corvettes. We were also updating our rules of engagement, as the negotiations were going on and we didn't know if the UK was going to send a fleet. But then we received information from our aircraft flying near Ascension Island, so we knew they were coming, and had to be ready for action.

Michael Thomas Nicholson
ITN correspondent

The navy were very, very restrictive and I have extremely unhappy memories of them. Our copy would first go to the captain, who was trying to fight a war so his first instinct was to cross out just about everything. It would go to his second-in-command, then to our minder, Commander Rupert Nicol, after which we were allowed to transmit; which meant waiting for a helicopter to take us across to one of the fleet auxiliary ships with a Marisat link, be winched down, then transmit our material, with Rupert there to cut us off if we said anything wrong. It could then take days for a helicopter to pick us up again, which I'm sure was deliberate, to keep us off *Hermes*. The guy in charge of helicopter operations told me: 'I loathe you guys. You are at the bottom of the list.' It was an astonishing attitude. But Rupert Nicol did become a helpful source of information because he could see that we were being treated unjustly.

I remember cameraman Bernard Hesketh, who'd been a Royal Artillery officer in the Second World War, hearing a senior naval officer on *Hermes* accusing us of being spies for the Argentinians. Bernard drew back his trouser leg and showed him a scar saying: 'I got that on the beaches of Normandy. Don't you ever call me a spy.'

Captain (John) Jeremy Black
HMS Invincible

My secretary told me that there was disquiet as the ship's company had concluded they were going to have to fight. The concern people have for their own lives became more apparent than I had expected. As the only person on board who'd been in battle, I decided to address them over the ship's closed-circuit television, and for half an hour went through how I thought we might fight the battle, my aim to give everyone an air of confidence.

Commander Ralph John Wykes-Sneyd
Officer Commanding 820 Sea King Squadron, Fleet Air Arm,
HMS Invincible

He ran through how he saw the opposition and our capabilities, and at the end, whether he'd thought about this or not I don't know, he said: 'Well that's about it then, but quite frankly I think we'll piss it. Good night.' This had a quite remarkable effect and dispelled a lot of tension, denoting our captain as being the man for the occasion. When you get into operational combat, the role of command takes on a very different aspect.

Captain (John) Jeremy Black
HMS Invincible

I left the television studio down in the depths of the ship, to climb the seven or eight decks back to my cabin. Several sailors stopped me en route, saying: 'You're right there, sir. We'll piss it.' Notices appeared above mess deck doors and on T-shirts saying: 'We'll piss it with JJ.' It just seemed to touch a chord, lifted them all up in a most extraordinary way, and is still referred to now.

John Keith 'Jake' Watson
Chaplain, HMS Broadsword

I had to decide what I was going to try to give people in this conflict. Because a ship is completely normal until the moment something comes through the side, I decided I would try to remain as normal as possible, rather than challenge people about being dead tomorrow and getting right with God. People hadn't thought things through; some thought turning to God in times of crisis was hypocritical, which may be an aspect of a ship at war being a normal sort of environment.

Captain (John) Jeremy Black
HMS Invincible

The day before we entered the two-hundred-mile exclusion zone, I asked the padre if he'd like to broadcast a prayer over the public broadcast as we actually entered. By declaring this zone, we were in effect determining when the war might start, so I wanted to give the padre the opportunity to lift everybody and give them confidence at that time. But, sadly, he just didn't grasp a moment that seemed to me to have been heaven sent.

Captain Carlos B. Castro Madero
Weapons Officer, 5-Inch Anti-Aircraft Batteries,
Warship Belgrano

The *Belgrano* was sent south with two other destroyers, for action if UK ships came from there. We sailed along the coast to our southern port of Ushuaia, then patrolled. Our commanding officer updated us on what was going on, but as a young officer I focused on the training of our people. I have to say the men responded very well. We knew we were on a very risky operation so we trained very hard so we could do well for our country.

Commander Robert Denton Green
Intelligence Staff Officer to Commander-in-Chief, Fleet HQ, Northwood

I was concerned about the anti-submarine nuclear weapons on board our ships; what the hell were they doing down in the South Atlantic? Some of the navy's nuclear weapons were taken off the ships before they sailed south, but others remained. This led me to speculate what might Thatcher's moves have been had we lost a capital ship?

Captain (John) Jeremy Black
HMS Invincible

I was shaving, the morning we entered the exclusion zone, musing about the Argentinians' rather good aircraft; that the Harrier was a totally untried aircraft, and we had so very few of them. I found myself wondering, very consciously, whether we'd have any of them left by nightfall.

The Argentines had very sensibly stopped transmitting weather reports from their weather station in Buenos Aires. In high latitudes the weather patterns race round the pole and come at you very rapidly, hitting the Andes and compressing, then jump over the coastal plain and move out to us at sea. It was either bad and windy, or foggy – both very difficult for flying aeroplanes. As the weather pattern cleared over the islands, the military people in Argentina could fly strikes at the Falklands. But being eighty miles to eastward where the weather hadn't yet cleared, we were still in bad weather and couldn't fly to defend the fleet. During these rather inconvenient windows, we bit our nails and hoped nothing would happen.

Commander Timothy John Gedge
Fleet Air Arm

The Argentines could launch into lovely hot weather and stable conditions from airfields in Argentina. We were launching a couple of hundred miles east in the Falklands, with fog and heavy sea states. The amount of deck pitch was very high, but this didn't limit the Harrier's launchability; you just had to judge the moment of take-off to when the ship was level, and hover on landing until a moment when the deck was stable. A conventional fixed-wing carrier would have suffered great problems in the heavy seas. We could operate at day and night and in zero visibility, sometimes by throwing flares into the wake and other extreme measures. We couldn't have recovered any other type of aircraft.

Captain (John) Jeremy Black
HMS Invincible

I had no inkling that the Harrier and its crews would prove to be so good: it was so manoeuvrable, and the Sidewinder missile was outstanding. With our well-trained pilots, we had an unbeatable set, but at seven o'clock that morning, I wasn't at all sure of it.

Commander Timothy John Gedge
Fleet Air Arm

The Argentines' Mirage 3 was a perfectly respectable fighter aircraft, with good missiles, weapon systems and track record, and we knew they were capable of putting up a very good fight against us. The Argentines had eleven times more aircraft in theatre then we did. They would have expected to have the advantage.

Lieutenant Commander Graham John Edmonds
Operations Officer and Squadron Warfare Officer, HMS Broadsword

The Argentines had two reasonably modern German Type 209 submarines, and some smaller, older American Guppy class submarines, including the one dealt with at South Georgia. One 209 was in port in Argentina and the other was at sea, operating off East Falkland. Brilliant, Yarmouth and some Sea King anti-submarine helicopters were sent close inshore, harassing it to the extent that it returned to Argentina. We found out afterwards, through naval intelligence, that the Argentines had been unable to perfect the firing of their torpedoes, and that the other 209 actually had torpedoes stuck in its tubes.

(James) Robert Fox
BBC correspondent

The navy likes to give all its orders in 'Zulu' – Greenwich Mean Time, by which they feel they can regulate orders to a fleet scattered all over the world.

But this is absolute hell if people are working through different times zones – as in the Falklands, Ascension, and South Georgia. This was a peculiarly naval irritation.

Lieutenant Commander Graham John Edmonds
Operations Officer and Squadron Warfare Officer, HMS Broadsword

We were working to Greenwich Mean Time, which in a ship without windows caused no problems, yet gave us a four-hour period at the beginning of each day to get ready for air raids. We could fight our air battles in our afternoon, after a proper breakfast and lunch. The Argentines would be fighting with the sleep in their eyes, and couldn't fly at night, so we could get a good night's sleep in between.

Lieutenant Commander Raymond John Adams
HMS Coventry

I remember May 1, as it was my sister's wedding, which I was supposed to have attended.

Private Alejandro Ramon Cano
Paratrooper, Grupo Artilleria Aerotransportada

The day before May 1, at five in the afternoon, we started to collect together all the munitions that remained around the bay, loading it into a ship then transporting it to the marine infantry. We never at any time expected to be attacked. We were exhausted. We couldn't do any more from transporting so much munitions. With my comrade we set up our tent well in order to rest. But after sleeping a little they got us up again to work. We loaded the semi-trucks up to the top, to be transported along the road in to Puerto Argentino, which we did all night until the first bombardment.

John Fowler
Superintendent of Education, Stanley

Everything was taking forever, with no signs of anything happening until May 1. In the early hours of that morning, I'd got up to poke the peat fire, so when everybody got up, it would be nice and cheery. Then it seemed the chimney exploded. I was lying on my back with my legs in the air still holding the poker, ears ringing from the enormous noise of explosions. Steve Whitley and I spent the next hours scouring the radio waves to find out what it was. An American station's news told us it was an RAF air raid. The BBC didn't tell us anything at all for some time.

Air Marshal John Bagot Curtiss
Air Commander, Northwood
We'd tried using Sea Harriers to lob bombs, an inaccurate and useless way of attacking an airfield, which is a long, slim target that is very hard to attack even with modern systems. Air force planners calculated that forty or fifty aircraft armed with ten to twenty thousand pounds of bombs would be needed to guarantee putting it out of action. The Argentinians were using the airfield for landing Hercules carrying spares and people, which weren't going to have much influence on the outcome of the war. But we very much wanted to send a message to friend Galtieri that we could attack targets at very long range. So with a great deal of effort we mounted six Vulcan bombing attacks on the Falklands Islands.

Private Alejandro Ramon Cano
Paratrooper, Grupo Artilleria Aerotransportada
The first bombing started at half past three or four in the morning. We saw it, and the first eight bombs that the . . . I don't know what it's called, the Vulcan aircraft? I thought it was a Harrier, but no, it wasn't.

Air Marshal John Bagot Curtiss
Air Commander, Northwood
The Vulcan force existed to drop nuclear bombs from high level on to the Soviets. A great deal of refurbishment had to be done so they could drop twenty-two one-thousand-pound iron bombs. Nuclear bombs don't need bombsights, so an aiming system was created for pilots by tracing a Heath Robinson drawing on to each windscreen. The crews practised dropping bombs on a small island off the coast of Scotland. Their in-flight refuelling systems had to be upgraded, and in fact we had to borrow one probe from a bomber in the Imperial War Museum's collection at Duxford, which I understand was returned after the war.

Private Alejandro Ramon Cano
Paratrooper, Grupo Artilleria Aerotransportada
Our chief sergeant, Pedro Arriba, told us to rest because we couldn't give any more. One sees the image before hearing the sound and I shout, 'Aerial attack!' and run when I saw the eight [bombs falling]. Our chief was dead; he had been working at our side, shoulder to shoulder, and at no time did he leave us. Suddenly I realise we are surrounded by all the munitions which might also explode . . .

Air Marshal John Bagot Curtiss
Air Commander, Northwood
It required seventeen tankers to get one Vulcan over the Falklands, plus good weather along the route for refuelling, and over the target to achieve accuracy. The run-in to the target was at low level. One Vulcan broke its probe on the way home and had to divert into Rio de Janeiro, where the aircraft and crew were interned but treated well by the Brazilians, who were very much on our side. When the Vulcan raids started, the dictatorship thought we might next attack targets within Argentina, so withdrew their Mirage 3 fighters to around Buenos Aires, where they stayed for the rest of the war, unable to escort their Skyhawk bombers on missions against our fleet, making life easier for our small number of Sea Harriers.

Commander Nigel David 'Sharkey' Ward
Officer Commanding 801 Squadron, Fleet Air Arm, HMS Invincible
I had wanted to do a Sea Harrier night attack on the airfield, all at once without any bombardment beforehand. We'd demonstrated this could be done, but Admiral Woodward's staff didn't want to do it. Instead a Vulcan was sent all the way down, with nobody allowed to shoot at anything while it was around.

Lieutenant Commander Peter Walpole
Signal Communications Officer, HMS Sheffield
We were faintly amused at the RAF's desperate attempt to get involved by dragging their ancient Vulcan bombers out of mothballs, flogging all the way down, to drop a few bombs somewhere or other. I've subsequently worked with the RAF and have a lot of respect for them in many ways, but I found the Vulcan raid rather amusing.

Lieutenant Commander Graham John Edmonds
Operations Officer and Squadron Warfare Officer, HMS Broadsword
Some of us stayed up all night to watch the 'Black Buck' bombing mission on our radars, but were surprised when none of the thousand-pound bombs appeared to have any effect on Argentine use of the airfield. It was an enormous and remarkable effort, and the RAF claimed to have hit the target, but there was no discernible effect on Argentine air operations, and seemed a worthless diversion of assets.

Lieutenant Commander Raymond John Adams
HMS Coventry
It was ironic. The navy had lost its conventional aircraft carriers because the RAF had promised to be able to provide air attack and air defence anywhere in the world. We had thought this was a farcical, unrealisable promise, which 1982 bore out.

Federico Mirré (Argentine Ambassador, 2006)
Foreign Office, Buenos Aires
In my efforts to get the Red Cross team over to the islands, we had another meeting with the air force's General Crespo. According to Crespo, the RAF had been bombing the Puerto Argentina/Stanley airstrip. He was talking at the top of his voice, telling us it was impossible to fly to the islands because the airstrip had two bomb impacts and that no plane could land there until they were repaired. He also said there was no helicopter available to do the crossing, which is true by the way. I then asked for a STOVL aircraft – a short take-off, vertical-landing aircraft. But the meeting ended at that point, the general having said what he wanted us to hear.

Michael Thomas Nicholson
ITN correspondent
On May 1, we weren't allowed to report how many Harriers took part in the first raid, so Brian Hanrahan got round the problem using a phrase . . . [from] a Second World War movie: 'I counted them out, and I counted them all back in again.' It was the classic phrase of the campaign and I kicked myself for not having thought of it.

Captain Michael Ernest Barrow
HMS Glamorgan
It was my admiral's wish that at 0800 on May 1, he would exercise his right to take action against the Argentinian invading forces within the total exclusion zone. It was also his fiftieth birthday. So with us and the two Type 21s, *Arrow* and *Alacrity*, a grouping that became known as the Three Musketeers, we were detached inshore to bombard Stanley airfield. The married men were more concerned that the worst might happen and that we might not return. The youngsters were still not entirely convinced.

Commander Ian Inskip
HMS Glamorgan

Intelligence interception of Argentine messages was telling us that the shores off Stanley were mined, which, as we were an inshore bombardment ship, concerned us. It did, however, appear from these radio intercepts that they'd left a small cheese of water free as an entrance, six miles from Pembroke Point light, which proved to be accurate, so we planned our bombardments accordingly.

We were without air cover. By eleven-thirty the Argentine air force had appeared, so we went to action stations. Unlike in war movies, people didn't grab their tin hats and rush to the guns, but went for a pee first. This continued throughout the war, with queues of twenty people waiting outside the wardroom heads during moments of excitement.

There was air activity all day, then in the early afternoon we sighted smoke from the Falklands where the Harriers had been attacking earlier, then the islands themselves. We closed from the south in a three-ship formation with the aim of opening fire together, to put fifty rounds apiece on to Stanley airfield, which we did at five o'clock.

Private Alejandro Ramon Cano
Paratrooper, Grupo Artilleria Aerotransportada

In the afternoon they transported us on to Mount Dos Hermanas because apparently the English were going to disembark there from ships below the mount, to take the mount from that side. As we were an artillery group of the Fourth Arsenal with our artillery, we had to support the infantry defending this area.

Captain Christopher Charles Brown
148 Commando Forward Observation Unit, Royal Artillery

On May 1, I was put on board the Type 21 frigate HMS Alacrity to coordinate the bombardment. We went in from the south, and I flew in a big detour round to the north in Alacrity's Lynx, to control it from the high ground. I think we got round without being spotted, and came in very low over the sea towards the coast, spotting an Argentine fast patrol boat and a Falkland Islands Company ship in a little cove.

To save weight and allow us more fuel, we'd taken off our anti-ship missiles, so all we had to engage these ships was a general-purpose machine gun manned by Alacrity's education officer, with me feeding in the bullets. On reflection it was completely foolhardy, but we decided to attack these two

Looking aft from the ski ramp launcher on the flight deck of HMS *Hermes*. One Sea King is landing with another waiting its turn, while a Harrier hovers before landing astern.

ships, which were flying Argentine flags. It was only when we got back to *Alacrity* and checked in *Jane's Fighting Ships*, that we realised a Z Class patrol boat has a twenty-millimetre cannon which could easily have knocked us out of the sky.

Commander Ian Inskip
HMS *Glamorgan*

Our master gunner, Brian Lister, was the only man on board who'd seen action before, at Suez, in the cruiser that saw off an Egyptian destroyer. He'd had his fiftieth birthday on the way down, and commented: 'What sort of a pension trap is this?' But as we were going into the gun line this first time, he rubbed his hands together and said: 'This is great, I haven't done this for a long time.' Knowing that Brian thought it was all right had a very calming effect on everybody else.

Captain Christopher Charles Brown
148 *Commando Forward Observation Unit, Royal Artillery*

We flew at them and poured down a lot of fire, which stopped them manning their cannon, and the patrol boat left for Port Stanley. We then decided to attack the other ship again, even though now we'd lost the element of surprise. We were engaged by their machine gun fire and hit. I could see a gaping hole in the spar, which runs up immediately to the right of the pilot's seat two inches from his right ear, and a shattered windscreen.

We broke off and went on to the hills, flying just above the ground, nosing over the edge. I could see Port Stanley clearly, with the ships coming in, and gave the orders for the ships to engage the airfield. I then thought what a good idea it would be to land, ostensibly to check the damage, and so become the first man to land back on the Falklands. The pilot was unwilling actually to land, hovered and I jumped out, to see fuel spewing from the tanks. Our flying time was very limited, and there could be other damage too. Told *Alacrity* we'd been hit and were returning, and that *Glamorgan's* Lynx with Captain Willie McCracken sitting in the back should get airborne to take over.

We headed back rapidly to *Alacrity*, landed-on safely, where we pointed out the bullet hole in the spar just two inches from the pilot's ear. His face went very white. We counted seven direct hits, with one through the tail rotor drive shaft. Losing the tail rotor makes the helicopter uncontrollable. Willie McCracken continued the bombardment from the other Lynx, damaging some of the airport buildings. Then as the ships pulled away, our ship came under attack from the Argentine air force, which was the first time for *Alacrity*.

Commander Ian Inskip
HMS *Glamorgan*

The three of us had gone into battle ensigns flying, very jingoistic, loosed off a hundred and fifty rounds, then retired to seaward intending to return singly to bombard selected targets. One Argentine Skyvan had flown between the hills, but I couldn't get a Sea Slug on to it. As we were retiring seawards, the heavens above Stanley opened up with fantastic amounts of flak, then an aircraft flew slowly across and was hit, flames coming out of its sides. Just before hitting the sea near the airport, it turned sideways revealing itself to be a Mirage and not a Harrier. I picked up the main broadcast and said: 'D'you hear there. The spics have just scored an own goal, shooting down a Mirage.' There was a lot of mirth and merriment at this, until our helicopter flight deck officer came on the broadcast sounding panicky, reporting a further three Mirage coming round Pembroke Point.

John Fowler
Superintendent of Education, Stanley

I was in the garden getting peat for my fire, when I saw the Argentines shoot down one of their own planes as it came in slowly and very low from the direction of Two Sisters. It was waggling its wings, and was clearly not in fighting mode. They opened up with everything they'd got, and eventually it was hit by a rocket and exploded. They all cheered. It seemed so very strange in a so-called civilised era to be witnessing one group of people trying so hard to kill another person. It was only after I'd checked, using a military aircraft book from the school text book store, that I realised it had been a Mirage, which the British did not have. It was so very strange, having been low enough and close enough to see the pilot – so personal and so strange, which you don't expect to see from your back garden.

Captain Michael Ernest Barrow
HMS *Glamorgan*

We'd completed the pre-planned bombardment using our helicopter and a spotter, aiming at the runway and some aircraft. Then as we were withdrawing to rejoin the battle group at sea, three Argentine aircraft jumped us from another airfield at the other side of the island.

Commander Ian Inskip
HMS *Glamorgan*

These three came at us with their after-burners open, below bridge height in a shallow dive, one heading for each of the ships in our group. Our Mirage attempted to strafe us, but the splashes he was whipping up stopped just before our stern – maybe because he took his finger off the tit as he was pulling up, or maybe because he had to stop to aim his bombs. Had he continued firing, he could have unzipped us with his shells. He released his bombs, and in the words of the midshipman on the gun deck: 'There was no way these were going to miss us, until parachutes came out of the rear and slowed them down,' and they fell either side of our quarterdeck.

As the raid was coming in, our PWO [principle warfare officer] had called the helm to 'Come hard left', applying thirty-five degrees of rudder. I went straight to the chart as this course change would take us into the minefield. Now we were safe, I countermanded the order. We also flashed up our gas turbines, which made a lot of smoke come from the funnel, giving the Argentines the impression they'd hit us. The bombs falling either side of the quarterdeck lifted our stern seventeen feet, putting a couple of shrapnel holes in the rudder as well as other damage. On day one we came as close as you could to having both propellers blown off in broad daylight under the guns of Stanley – which really shook us up. It was a good blooding.

Lieutenant Commander Raymond John Adams
HMS *Coventry*

We were shelling the airfield, and an Argentine Puma helicopter was ten miles away, not bothering to fly very low. We engaged with Sea Dart and knocked the Puma out of the sky in one. I was watching this from the bridge, and it made me think of the people in that aircraft, with wives and children. I think at some stage everyone has to realise that you are killing people. Once you get over that, it becomes easier to accept that what you are doing is what you *should* be doing. The war was very abstract, like an exercise.

John Fowler
Superintendent of Education, Stanley

From May 1 onwards, the Argentines did things they'd promised wouldn't happen; they built defensive positions, dug fortifications in Stanley and used our schools to house soldiers, the military imperatives thwarting their ambitions to administer a peaceful population. Then my office was commandeered, so I stayed at home.

Commodore Carlos Bloomer-Reeve
Secretary General, Islas Malvinas

Until May 1, things were working pretty smoothly. We had a curfew that started at eight o'clock at night. But then after May 1, everything got very . . . it was rather alarming.

Private Alejandro Ramon Cano
Paratrooper, Grupo Artilleria Aerotransportada

After these attacks, they said that there was an agreement to pull out the troops, and we were returning to the continent. That night there was great joy. We formed a ring, we came down the hill from Mount Dos Hermanas running, and we met up with other men from the front line and we hugged, tears were falling. It seemed that they all had the same information as ours. It was terrible to see so many bonfires on the hills, one behind the other, one every two metres; it was terrible, those lights all over those hills. Lit up on all sides, it looked like a Christmas tree.

But afterwards, the next day we were still there, again listening to the guns, and we stayed to the end. We knew we were going to lose the war when we saw the English pass over our heads. We saw that our boys couldn't reach us, but we were calm when we lined up every night and they informed us what had happened during the day.

The next day we were sent to Darwin. All our comrades saluted us, and the superiors who remained saluted us as if it would be the last time we would see each other. To explain, Darwin was under constant attack by air, Darwin was terrible. Every day we saluted as if we would never again salute.

John Pole Evans
Falkland Islander

When the Vulcans and Harriers bombed Stanley, the Argies in Goose Green thought they might also be bombed, so they moved helicopters and aircraft down from the airfield, around the settlement thinking the British wouldn't attack them knowing they were amongst the civilians. The Harriers attacked the airstrip, blowing up aircraft, fuel dumps and ammunition. I can remember standing by the window watching big plumes of flames. About twenty minutes later the Argies came down into the settlement, and rounded us all up. They were shouting, 'Out, out, out.' I was trying to put my boots on in the porch. A soldier came in and poked me with his gun, so I got out quite quickly.

General Mario Benjamin Menendez
Military Governor, Islas Malvinas

I was aware that civilians at Goose Green were imprisoned. What really happened was this. The military air base in Condor had an Argentine camp very near to the houses of Goose Green. After the attack of May 1 an un-exploded English bomb remained within one hundred and fifty metres from houses in Goose Green. What would happen if that bomb exploded in the houses or near to the houses? But more importantly, the air force had organised Condor into a campaign aerodrome.

John Pole Evans
Falkland Islander

We were rounded up on the green, then told we were going to the community centre for a meeting, where they shut us in. We had only the clothes we'd been wearing when they'd routed us out of the house; some were fully dressed, some weren't. The first night we had no bedding or anything, so we lay on the bare boards on the floor and it was quite scary.

For the first days nobody was allowed out. We had no food. Then on the second evening they let the storekeeper and a couple of others out to get food. Around the third night some people were allowed to go to the houses to get bedding – sleeping bags, mattresses, sheets and some of the single guys got sheepskins. Around the fourth or fifth day of being locked up in there, they let a couple of women go over to the galley to cook meals. We slept in family groups with about thirty-five children. During the day, us children played cards and games but there wasn't much to do.

A couple of the men fixed a broken radio. But because we weren't allowed it, they'd listen to one bulletin every night and pass on the news to the adults. The Argies would come in and walk around asking questions and checking on us. We were banned from listening to the news, as the adults couldn't trust us not to blurt anything out. We always had the feeling at the back of our minds that they might kill us.

In the middle of May they let a couple of people go back to their houses. One guy was caught listening to the local medical service on his radio receiver. They reckoned he'd been transmitting to the British, so they took him away, beat him up and tied him up out on a garage floor for a couple of days, torturing him into saying he'd been talking to the British, which he hadn't because they'd already confiscated the transmitters. Eventually they chucked him back into the hall, and we could see what they'd done to him – bruises, cuts to his arms, and the sores where he'd been tied up, so everybody knew what could happen if we didn't do as we were told.

General Mario Benjamin Menendez
Military Governor, Islas Malvinas
About May 20, I received a communication that Monsignor Espragon was worried, and so I called the commander of Lieutenant Colonel Piaggi, a general in Argentina, to investigate this immediately. The general sent his second-in-command, a colonel from Comodoro Rivadavia, who spent two days viewing the situation. He reported: 'In my opinion there is nothing detrimental. There is a safe situation there, papers are signed, the people are inside, the women go out to prepare the food, they are supervised by the doctor and I do not believe there is a better solution than this.'

Federico Mirré (Argentine Ambassador, 2006)
Foreign Office, Buenos Aires
The Swiss grew more and more worried that they couldn't check on the situation of the civilian population on the islands. Then, without any warning, I was summoned to the Comodoro Rivadavia military base at two in the morning without the Swiss, was put inside a plane with Red Cross markings, and we took off for the islands. We flew barely four feet above the sea, below the British radars, and the windscreen was soon obscured by salt. We flew over the western part of the islands, and dawn was beginning, probably around six in the morning. We then had a positive radar contact, so the pilot turned back to land at Comodoro, which was the limit of my thrilling experience over the islands.

John Pole Evans
Falkland Islander
After a few days they allowed us to stand outside in a small circle by the door for ten minutes or so. Our parents encouraged us to go out whether it was cold or wet or whatever, in the hope that maybe somebody from the SBS or an aircraft might see us, so that people would know we were in the hall – and not taken off to Argentina, so we wouldn't be blown up by accident.

There were one hundred and fourteen of us in the hall for over a month, with two toilets, but a lot of the time the water was off, so we kept buckets to flush them. Drinking water had to be boiled because of the way the Argies were living up around the reservoir. There wasn't enough food to go round, even on the days the women were allowed out to cook in the galley. We were all hungry, and some days my father would give my sister and I his meal, and he would go without.

John Fowler
Superintendent of Education, Stanley

From May 1 onwards, it seemed to take a long, long time for anything to develop, and by the time the British landed at Port San Carlos, everyone was in deep despair, which wasn't really alleviated by this news, as we knew San Carlos was the most difficult place from which to get to Stanley. Nobody would even consider driving to San Carlos in winter, and even in good weather we'd travel there with several vehicles, a person who really knew the area, and lots of ropes, spades, jacks, and so on. We weren't military and so couldn't appreciate why they'd chosen that place to land, and were despondent, as we couldn't see how they could get from there to Stanley.

It was interesting to have been on the wrong side of everything; for every piece of news it was 'Hooray!' then 'Oh fuck,' as we realised what each new British move towards Stanley could mean for us. People had a belief that somehow the bullets would miss us because they were intended for the Argentines. If you didn't have much to do, Stanley was a very worrying place to be.

Colonel Manuel Dorrego
Head of Public Works Department, Islas Malvinas

In the first stage of the operation we tried to understand how the islanders felt, and endeavoured that they should know how we felt. But when events were advancing, and they were telling us that the British were coming, from then on there were no possibilities of understanding. They worked against us by radio, they offered help to their people using any means, giving information, operating like patriot farmers in their country, defending their property. We were confronted, so the islanders lost the possibility of a normal life. After May 1, my work changed. I began to be more careful to whom I spoke, because of sabotage. They could have been poisoning the water, they could have made the generator houses explode, there could have been commando attacks.

Captain Barry Melbourne Hussey
Administrator of Health, Social Services and Education, Islas Malvinas

When the army started putting machine gun posts in the town, we had them taken out because the promise had been not to take the fight into the town.

10

Sinking the Belgrano

It was quite obvious to anybody who could read the general operations plot on our ops room wall that the Argentine navy was trying to execute a classic pincer movement. Even a curious stoker, coming into the ops room to find out what was happening, could see it.

Captain Carlos B. Castro Madero
Weapons Officer 5-Inch Anti-Aircraft Batteries,
Warship Belgrano
We thought the best chance was to hit one of the British aircraft carriers. Our carrier was patrolling in the north surrounded by a big screen, waiting for the opportunity to make a decisive strike. There were stories that our carrier wasn't serviceable, but really our carrier was fully operational. If we were able to put one of the UK carriers out of action, it would be very difficult for them to land anywhere in the Malvinas.

Lieutenant Commander Graham John Edmonds
Operations Officer and Squadron Warfare Officer, HMS Broadsword
We knew there were two Argentine navy task groups at sea, south being the *Belgrano* with much bigger guns than us and Exocet missiles, plus two destroyers – also with Exocet. Just north of the Falklands, they had a group of A69 frigates with Exocets and 4-inch guns, and further north there was the *25 de Mayo* carrier with its Type 42 escorts and two more destroyers. At one stage they were only eighty miles from us, which at a combined closing speed of sixty knots is only one hour's steaming, so we were growing anxious.

Our two nuclear submarines were in contact with *25 de Mayo* and the *Belgrano*, but did not appear to be permitted to attack, which, as these ships

147

were clearly trying to mount an attack on us, was a worrying puzzle. The last thing we wanted was a surface ship to surface ship engagement, exchanging missiles, with fifty-fifty odds.

Captain Carlos B. Castro Madero
Weapons Officer, 5-Inch Anti-Aircraft Batteries,
Warship Belgrano

Our carrier *25 de Mayo* had flown a Tracker S2E anti-submarine and radar surveillance plane which detected a UK main ship – supposed to be an aircraft carrier. Our authorities decided to make an attack. The UK battle group was on the north-east of the islands, so our carrier group started to move east from the north-west towards them. The *Belgrano* group was ordered to move from the south in a pincer movement, to be ready to attack, plus to complicate the picture for the British. The planes were to launch at dawn on May 2, as our A4 Skyhawks had to fly with no radars by visual flight rules, on a bearing to drop bombs; a very risky operation. The calculation was that fifty per cent of the aircraft would not return.

Lieutenant Commander Graham John Edmonds
Operations Officer and Squadron Warfare Officer, HMS Broadsword

It was quite obvious to anybody who could read the general operations plot on our ops room wall that the Argentine navy was trying to execute a classic pincer movement. Even a curious stoker, coming into the ops room to find out what was happening, could see it.

Rear Admiral Anthony John Whetstone
Deputy Chief of Naval Staff (Operations), MoD Whitehall

A lot of nonsense has been talked about the *Belgrano*. Our rules of engagement had been gradually extended for political reasons, to give our forces more freedom of action, and were a compromise between the sailors wanting full freedom to be able to do anything, and the political need to keep the Americans on side and for us always to be seen to be wearing the white hats. We gradually expanded the range of activity and geographical area in which our forces could behave aggressively.

Commander Ian Inskip
HMS Glamorgan

We left the task force for another night's inshore bombardment of the Stanley area. But when we were about halfway in, around nine p.m., we were ordered to return at speed, because the *25 de Mayo* was coming in from the north and the *Belgrano* was coming at us from the south. There was fourteen hours of darkness and *Belgrano* was within ten hours' steaming of the carriers. It wasn't out there for a sunshine cruise, and was a specific threat to us.

Captain Carlos B. Castro Madero
Weapons Officer, 5-Inch Anti-Aircraft Batteries,
Warship Belgrano
We sailed towards the British exclusion zone around the Malvinas. On the night of May 1/2 we were on hundred per cent watches as we knew there was going to be action by the morning. But to take off fully loaded with bombs, the aircraft needed a total of twenty-eight knots of wind. The carrier could steam at twenty-two knots, and so we needed at least an additional six knots of wind. We thought that God was Argentinian, but incredibly, unlike every other day in the Southern Ocean, there was no wind at all. So, at six that morning the operation was cancelled and we returned west to patrol close to the continent. The carrier group returned west as well. There's a big question mark over what might have happened if that operation had taken place . . .

Lieutenant Commander Graham John Edmonds
Operations Officer and Squadron Warfare Officer, HMS Broadsword
The admiral was negotiating to be allowed to attack the *25 de Mayo* and *Belgrano*. Our nuclear submarine to the north lost contact with *25 de Mayo* while taking measures to receive the permissive order to attack.

Captain Carlos B. Castro Madero
Weapons Officer, 5-Inch Anti-Aircraft Batteries,
Warship Belgrano
There's a lot of discussion about whether the *Conqueror* should have launched the torpedoes against us, as we were outside the exclusion zone. We were ready to launch our torpedoes or fire our weapons if we detected a ship or submarine. War is a risky business, and I was ready to hit and to receive. I received, but I was unable to hit back. But I was ready for that. The other side were doing their job . . .

Rear Admiral Anthony John Whetstone
Deputy Chief of Naval Staff (Operations), MoD Whitehall
We really wanted to sink the carrier, but the submarine in the north, tracking

her, lost contact. The carrier had some problems with her flight deck equipment, and turned around.

Captain Carlos B. Castro Madero
Weapons Officer, 5-Inch Anti-Aircraft Batteries,
Warship Belgrano
Navy against navy, we had certain advantage because of our aircraft carrier. It could send A4 aircraft with bombs to attack ships, whereas *Invincible* had only Sea Harriers, which were anti-aircraft with only limited capacity to attack ships. The key moment would be as the British landed, when they would need air superiority so as not to be hit by our air force.

Rear Admiral Anthony John Whetstone
Deputy Chief of Naval Staff (Operations), MoD Whitehall
The *Belgrano* was still manoeuvring around to the south, and Sandy Woodward was worried that the *Conqueror* would lose contact. As is usual, the *Belgrano* was steering irregular courses, but was close enough to present a serious threat. Her long-range guns and missiles would cause a lot of damage if properly fought.

Captain Carlos B. Castro Madero
Weapons Officer, 5-Inch Anti-Aircraft Batteries,
Warship Belgrano
We went back to normal routine; one-third on watch, one-third doing jobs around the ship and one-third sleeping. No one had slept all night. I did a watch until 1200 hours, had my lunch then went off to sleep. The ship was returning to the west.

Rear Admiral Anthony John Whetstone
Deputy Chief of Naval Staff (Operations), MoD Whitehall
Mrs Thatcher never said: 'Sink the Belgrano.' It was more prosaic than that. She said: 'You have freedom of action to engage enemy warships in the following areas of the South Atlantic . . .' I was the officer who personally approved these rules of engagement and sent them up to Terry Lewin. I cannot be any party to this idea that the sinking of the *Belgrano* was some sort of personal vendetta by Margaret Thatcher, of whom, politically, I am not a great admirer – for the record.

When this freedom of action signal was received and deciphered by the captain of the *Conqueror*, it just so happened that the *Belgrano* was in his sights and she was an enemy ship. It made no difference that she was steering towards Argentina at that time; she'd been steering all over the place all day, and could have turned around at any time. So he attacked her and sank her, then went away.

Captain Carlos B. Castro Madero
Weapons Officer, 5-Inch Anti-Aircraft Batteries, Warship Belgrano

Around 1600 there was an incredible explosion . . . Belgrano weighed ten thousand tons and was suddenly stopped. The first torpedo hit the bow, in a big space where the anchor is kept, so nobody was hurt or killed; but very close to the officers' mess decks, so I was woken by the explosion. A second torpedo hit in the centre. I went up to the main deck and helped injured people to get out. Even though a very dangerous moment, everybody acted well. Nobody panic, everybody followed how they'd been trained. In ten minutes the ship was listing sixty degrees to port, so we thought the ship would sink any moment. It was like an impossible dream. You have to walk with great caution or you slip into the water. It's very strange. I never thought this would happen. I've tried to remember what I thought, but couldn't believe this would happen to me or that our ship would ever be in this position.

Commander Robert Denton Green
Intelligence Staff Officer to Commander-in-Chief, Fleet HQ, Northwood

I was off watch at the time, at home when the Belgrano was torpedoed. I realised this attack was going to be very controversial and returned to the HQ. We had thought it a bit of a game, but with the sinking of the Belgrano, it became a complete living nightmare, a really nasty war that we could lose.

Lieutenant Commander Graham John Edmonds
Operations Officer and Squadron Warfare Officer, HMS Broadsword

Sinking the Belgrano spiked the Argentine attack, which was a huge relief, after which the Argentine navy literally vanished from the scene, and never left their twelve-mile coastal limit again, giving us much more room to manoeuvre.

Lieutenant Commander Peter Walpole
Signal Communications Officer, HMS Sheffield

When I read the signal telling us the Belgrano had been attacked and sunk, I remember feeling a certain doom as it meant the start of a major shooting war.

There had been some shooting already, but to all of us, the sinking of a major battleship or a cruiser meant that the shooting was really under way for the big ships – which meant us.

John Keith 'Jake' Watson
Chaplain, HMS Broadsword

When *Belgrano* was sunk, there was no elation on our ship, as we could be in the same situation ourselves. There was relief, however, that a threat had been removed.

Captain Carlos B. Castro Madero
Weapons Officer, 5-Inch Anti-Aircraft Batteries,
Warship Belgrano

I went down to the deep decks to get people out. People were still going down, even in the very last minutes, risking their lives and dying to rescue friends. When the torpedo hit, the damage control people did all they could, but we were hit so bad and the water came in so fast, they couldn't do anything about it.

Lieutenant Commander Raymond John Adams
HMS Coventry

Our only disappointment was that *Conqueror* hadn't also sunk both escorts at the same time, but maybe this would have been a bit unnecessary. We weren't aware of the controversy back at home about the sinking, and if we had we'd have greeted it with cynicism. It's the people who are doing the fighting who take the decisions. You can't have a half-hearted approach to operations, in which politicians keep trying to rein you back. Perhaps one draws the line at things like bombarding Buenos Aires, but if something is a threat in your area of operations, you should be allowed to remove it. I think *Belgrano* was removed reasonably well, with no loss of life to British servicemen – which was the important part of it.

Captain Carlos B. Castro Madero
Weapons Officer 5-Inch Anti-Aircraft Batteries,
Warship Belgrano

Twenty minutes later, our CO received the information from the damage control teams that the ship could not be saved, and he gave the order to abandon ship, the order that nobody wanted to hear. We threw our life rafts into the water.

It was easy for me; because of the sixty-degree listing we were only one foot from the water, so my team only had to jump a short distance into the life rafts. We had no immersion suits, only life jackets. I was totally tranquil, in control of myself with no problem at all. I don't remember much fear even though I was trying to save my life and help my people. There was no burning. There were twenty listed to be in my life raft team, and they were all there. I was second-in-command of my life raft. We were very close to the bow of the ship, which was all jagged steel holes, broken, sharp . . . The wind was blowing us on to this, and it punctured all our lifeboats, which sank, and we had to jump into the water and swim away.

I swam to another lifeboat about twenty metres from me, where there were only two people. The rest of the twenty were swimming behind me. When I reached the boat I couldn't pull myself inside because they used me like a ladder to get themselves inside. The water was very cold and I couldn't do anything, so I just hung on until they had all gone over the top of me. Then finally it was my turn and I could get in.

The lieutenant commander was missing. I looked out of the lifeboat and could see him floating in the sea surrounded by petroleum, and he seemed unconscious. I leaned out and pulled him in, and he was in very bad shape, totally unconscious, so I was in charge of the lifeboat.

The *Belgrano* was slowly turning over, and there were a lot of lifeboats all around, close to it. I was in despair, as when he sink, he will take all these lifeboats down with him. Then finally I see this terrible sight of the *Belgrano* turning round, the bow coming up, and then he started to sink very quickly. But as a noble warrior dying, instead of taking all these lifeboats down with him, he made a big wave, which pushed all these lifeboats away from him.

It was a terrible image that I still have in my mind, that will follow me for the rest of my life. In that ship there were a lot of people, comrades who didn't get out, who went down into the sea.

The ship sank at about twenty minutes to five – forty minutes after the torpedo hit us. The second torpedo hit in the area where the sailors have their cabins, where all the people are working on watch with the engines, and water came in very fast, so many people were drowned. My experience was much easier than for most people; they had to swim under water to get out of their cabins, fire came into the ship . . . Friends were stuck dead in the doors, and they had to get them out of the way to escape. There were two civilian brothers on the ship who sold sandwiches, candy, and Coke in a shop, who before leaving port were offered to disembark as we were going on a dangerous operation. But they said they were part of the ship's crew, and wanted to be part of the bad times as well as the good times. When the torpedo hit us, one got up to the deck, but went back down to find his brother – but never made it. They both died – terrible.

I was about fifty metres away when he sank. As he went down, we sang our naval hymn, then shouted, 'Viva la Patria.' I don't remember much noise, but after he disappear there were many explosions from the boilers which made it sound like another torpedo hitting. We made a prayer, and said that everything now depends upon us, that we had to put into practice all our navy training.

Our commanding officer was the last person to leave the ship – a warrant officer forced him, as he didn't want to do it. An officer took a photograph of the last moments of the *Belgrano*. In this picture you can see two men still on the ship.

Commander Robert Denton Green
Intelligence Staff Officer to Commander-in-Chief, Fleet HQ, Northwood
I always felt that Captain Bonzo, the captain of the *Belgrano*, was a very naive man, to think he could play cat and mouse in and out of an exclusion zone, with two British nuclear submarines itching to get at him if they could find him. It was an extremely volatile situation, and was the sort of risk the Argentines should have taken into account.

Captain Carlos B. Castro Madero
Weapons Officer, 5-Inch Anti-Aircraft Batteries,
Warship Belgrano
Then it began to get dark, with really bad weather, big waves which hit us and made us fear we were going to be turned over. The life rafts had a roof but the doors were open and water came in every time a wave hit us. We were wet and very cold, and had just lost our ship with many of our friends. I put everybody on the same side of the life raft as the waves, to stop them from turning us over. It was a very dramatic time, but nobody disobeyed my orders or behaved so I had to punish them.

Thankfully by ten o'clock in the morning the weather had calmed down. We were more than two hundred miles from the coast, so there was no chance of getting to land on our own. I knew we had very little chance of being rescued because I thought that if a ship came to rescue us, the submarine would sink them. I didn't want that. But I didn't tell my team what I was thinking. Then at five o'clock in the afternoon, we saw a destroyer on the horizon. It kept stopping then moving on, so I knew it was picking up people.

It was getting dark again, and I was very concerned about having to spend another night out. We had only some water, and a few emergency rations like cookies. The destroyer vanished, then a small ship approached. They were a long way off, but they were stopping to pick people up. It was getting dark, so we fired flares.

The ship was now coming to us, but it was dark, and the weather was very, very bad again. If he approach us too close he could go over the top of us. They throw ropes. In the waves, when the ship comes down to us and the lifeboat goes up to it, people jumped. Sometimes I had to separate from the ship, so it was difficult.

I was the last one in the lifeboat, and by that time the water was up to my knees. The operation had now lasted about thirty or forty minutes, and I had to do all the manoeuvre by myself. My legs were frozen and I was very cold. When I tried to jump my legs didn't work, so I just fell into the water, which was very, very cold. This time in the water, everything was like in slow motion. My mind was working, I was thinking, but my muscles wouldn't act like I wished. I started thinking I was going to die.

From the ship they threw me a life ring, which I put on to my right arm, but in the middle of being pulled up to the deck of the ship, I couldn't stand it so I went back into the water again. When they threw it back to me I tried with the left arm, but halfway up to the deck of the ship I was unable to hold on and fell into the water again. I thought about my father and my mother, how terrible it would be for them when they hear how close I was to being saved. I say I do it for my country and things like that – all pass through my head.

So they throw me the ring again, and in the last moments of consciousness, I say to myself that my legs are the strongest part of me, so I put my leg over the ring and hang on with my arms . . . and so finally they were able to pull me from the water. I was frozen, and I believed that my heart will stop in any second. But, I was twenty-four years old and in good shape. They assisted me to a cabin. I went to the engines to get some heat, and soon I was in normal shape again, and was able to help. I think my lifeboat was the last to be rescued. The ship normally carried forty crew, and we were now four hundred people. The next morning we were back at Ushuaia, where the war ended for me.

Commander Robert Denton Green
Intelligence Staff Officer to Commander-in-Chief, Fleet HQ, Northwood
The sinking of *Belgrano* was a great escalation. But after that the Argentine navy never appeared again, so the sinking was decisive. But I felt it was a

HMS *Conqueror*'s return to Faslane on July 3, 1982, with Commanding Officer Commander Christopher Wreford-Brown RN and his conning tower crew. The horizontal bar on the 'Jolly Roger' flag represents the sinking of the Argentine cruiser *General Belgrano* on May 2, 1982, and the dagger a special operation.

political decision to sink the *Belgrano*, not a military one. The *Conqueror* were doing their duty, obeying the politicians as they are supposed to. The decision caused difficulty for the British government, especially when they decided not to be straight about it, which was their real mistake. I always felt they must have had some conscience about it, and so got civil servant Clive Ponting to produce the two versions of events. That bothered me, but Admiral Fieldhouse told me: 'Let sleeping dogs lie.'

Captain Michael Ernest Barrow
HMS *Glamorgan*
If *Belgrano* hadn't been sunk, I think my fellow frigate captains and I would have been the next people to be sent to sink her with our Exocets. Although I was confident in my systems and had succeeded in various simulations, I had never actually fired an Exocet missile.

Michael Thomas Nicholson
ITN *correspondent*
The British public knew all about *Belgrano* before we did. I did report the sinking, using the line '. . . no sailor aboard our ship is celebrating. Sailors do not rejoice in the deaths of other seamen, no matter who they are'. It was true; the ship was silent; there was no cheering aboard *Hermes*, and I can't believe they were cheering on board *Invincible*. I'm sure that story was invented by the *Sun*.

11

The Argentines
Strike Back

*In the ops room there was dumb disbelief, with a gasping of breath.
This was the first Royal Navy ship to be sunk since the
Second World War. Seeing that ship burning from end to end
certainly made us look to our own laurels . . .*

Commander Nigel David 'Sharkey' Ward
Officer Commanding 801 Squadron, Fleet Air Arm, HMS Invincible
Invincible had been put in control of the air war by the admiral, and so had to
approve all air movements. But the admiral was launching aircraft from *Hermes*
without telling *Invincible*, making us very edgy. The radar emission from a Sea
Harrier looks very similar to an Exocet-carrying Super Etendard and some of the
other ships' radars too, so there were a lot of spurious Etendard attack warnings.

On May 4, the admiral's staff ordered exactly the same programme of events
as May 1, for a second attack on Stanley. The weather wasn't good enough to
carry out a dawn strike, so because the Harrier's range is much shorter carrying
bombs rather than fuel tanks, the ships moved in closer to Stanley. We were
flying as radar pickets, with *Coventry*, *Sheffield* and *Glasgow* as the second line
of air defence. There was a layer of low cloud down from around two thousand
feet, ideal for us to look down through with the radar. But then the admiral
started launching Harriers off *Hermes* to do visual searches and armed
reconnaissance missions over the islands. Then when the weather cleared
over the islands, the admiral's staff decided to attack the same targets as on
earlier days and Harrier pilot Nick Taylor got shot down. In all this confusion,
Sheffield was attacked.

Lieutenant Commander Peter Walpole
Signal Communications Officer, HMS Sheffield

By daylight we were awake, dressed, and had breakfast. I had the afternoon watch, which goes from after lunch to teatime at four o'clock. Before taking over, I went to the operations room for a brief from the on-watch warfare officer, Graham Tolley. One of the Argentine's small German submarines, the *San Luis*, was plotted on the chart in a position where she could easily have reached us by that afternoon. Although the sea was calm, it had the long remnant of a swell on it, with visibility quite reasonable at eight or nine miles. There were no indications of any air activity, and our assessment was that the biggest threat was this submarine. Up on the bridge, we listened to the World Service news, then my watch got under way. I delegated the conduct of courses, speed and manoeuvres to the second officer of the watch, who was young and under training, so I could take an overseeing role – a common arrangement. I was chatting to the air observer, Al Clark, who was in his overalls ready to fly.

Lieutenant Commander Graham John Edmonds
Operations Officer and Squadron Warfare Officer, HMS Broadsword

HMS *Glasgow* was the northern air defence picket and detected two aircraft coming in from the west-north-west, which she labelled as 'hostile interceptors' on the fleets' Link Ten data link. We went to action stations, and the two Etendards headed south and were picked up by *Coventry*, but disappeared again, presumably having detected the task group, and were now looking for an easy way in.

Radio Supervisor Stewart Anthony MacFarlane
HMS Coventry

Hermes hadn't detected the Etendard radar, and dismissed it as a spurious transmission, telling us we were not under attack and to continue with our previous orders. We and *Glasgow* then detected a second Agave radar burst, which we reported to *Hermes*, to the same response. Captain Hart-Dyke had realised this was a classic Super Etendard attack, with the aircraft flying very low below the radar cover, popping up for a quick sweep of their radars, locking the information of targets detected into the missile, before coming up twenty miles away to fire. So at twenty miles we again detected the Super Es' radar plus the Exocets' radar, so this was obviously an incoming attack. But yet again because it wasn't appearing on their radar screens, *Hermes* told us it was spurious.

Lieutenant Commander Graham John Edmonds
Operations Officer and Squadron Warfare Officer, HMS Broadsword
At this point the force anti-air war coordinator in *Hermes* declared *Glasgow*'s hostile interceptors detection as two returning Harriers, which we in *Broadsword* doubted, as it didn't tie in with the time we knew the Harriers would return. We had such little faith in the flagship's assessments of events that we remained at action stations.

Radio Supervisor Stewart Anthony MacFarlane
HMS Coventry
Because *Hermes* insisted there was no threat, *Sheffield* was transmitting on her satellite gear, which is banned in attack situations as it interferes with the electronic warfare sensors and is on the same frequencies as the Exocet radar and the Agave radar in the front of the Etendards. An MoD 'money-saving' measure meant that a set of filters was never installed so ships could do both at the same time.

Lieutenant Commander Peter Walpole
Signal Communications Officer, HMS Sheffield
Fighter Controller Lieutenant Colin Hayley in the operations room reported 'Bogeys' – the code name for unidentified aircraft. Then I heard the PWO calling for the AWO to come to the operations room, so we knew something was happening. Further reports from the fighter controller said there were two contacts off to the north-west.

Lieutenant Commander Graham John Edmonds
Operations Officer and Squadron Warfare Officer, HMS Broadsword
Sheffield was twenty miles from everybody else and closest in the air defence line to the incoming aircraft. The range of an Exocet launched from low level is not very great, so the main body of ships was not in any danger.

Lieutenant Commander Peter Walpole
Signal Communications Officer, HMS Sheffield
The first indication of the missile coming towards us was visual. I was seeing something rather strange, something I'd never seen before – a black dot that appeared to be smoking, so I did what most officers of the watch do instinctively and immediately took a bearing on it, and reported to the ops room, 'Something smoking bearing 297.'
I looked again through my binoculars and was having great difficulty

sorting out what it was. It wasn't moving at all – up, down or sideways, with what looked like smoke coming out of it, like one of those speeded-up films of a flower blossoming. The smoke billowing from behind made it grow in appearance without moving anywhere. Simultaneously with Al Clark and Allan Nation, we realised it was coming towards us, but that realisation came very late, at very close range.

Radio Supervisor Stewart Anthony MacFarlane
HMS Coventry

Our skipper and Glasgow's skipper decided to take the necessary action, and turned to head straight for the incoming missile at maximum speed, presenting the smallest radar profile to the missiles computer. The idea is then to turn hard to one side while chucking a massive cloud of chaff into the air, which the missile selects as the largest target. We proved that this does work, but in this incident, Sheffield was terribly unlucky.

Lieutenant Commander Peter Walpole
Signal Communications Officer, HMS Sheffield

The Sunday Times quoted me as saying, 'My God, it's a missile,' whereas I think what I actually said was, 'What the fuck is that?' I suppose I could excuse myself for not recognising it by saying that I'd never been trained to identify a missile coming straight towards me, but I don't see that as a shortcoming in my training. Nobody has subsequently given me a hard time for this . . .

We had only a matter of seconds before impact, but I remember distinctly that it was beginning to draw to the right. The perception of this sort of thing is something officers of the watch acquire in shipping situations, so just before impact I knew it wasn't coming straight for me but to the centre of the ship, so I had the possibility of surviving. But this was just a fleeting feeling.

I shouted twice down a handset to the ops room that they were to take cover. I wanted to go to the bosun's mate position to activate the main broadcast alarms. But I never got there, and at the moment of impact was lying on the deck. It really was the most frightful crash, and a very strange sensation, like your worst car accident but ten times worse – the noise, pressure wave, the sound of such a terrific explosion . . . There was also the sense of a perfect working ship, which, one second later, was irrevocably changed. Everything loose on the bridge was scattered in all directions, the air was thick with dust from inside the ventilation trunking and we were showered in paint fragments. Massive power cuts set off the alarms in the bridge, a tremendous noise. You cancel these by pushing the buttons and the noise stops, leaving just flashing red lights, but elsewhere in the ship alarm bells were still ringing.

Radio Supervisor Stewart Anthony MacFarlane
HMS *Coventry*

They took an Exocet in the starboard side, all because the people three hundred and seventy miles closer to South Africa thought they knew better. For the next few days we all felt pretty down; me specifically as I'd only just left the *Sheffield* to join *Coventry*.

Lieutenant Commander Raymond John Adams
HMS *Coventry*

We first heard she'd been hit on the air defence radio circuit, then we could see a great pall of black smoke about thirty miles away. It was quite a calm, sunny day – pleasant weather. The missiles weren't her main problem; but the raging inferno caused by fuel. If you start with an inferno, it's very difficult to put out.

Commander Nigel David 'Sharkey' Ward
Officer Commanding 801 Squadron, Fleet Air Arm, HMS Invincible

Two aircraft from my squadron had been sitting up-threat, ready in that area, transmitting and deterring, but had been ordered away one hundred and twenty nautical miles south-west by the admiral's staff, to make a visual search for surface targets. This created the gap in the air defences which was found by the Etendard that hit *Sheffield*.

Lieutenant Commander Graham John Edmonds
Operations Officer and Squadron Warfare Officer, HMS Broadsword

Sheffield caught fire very quickly. Because they'd relaxed, she was significantly less prepared than ships like us who were still at action stations.

Lieutenant Commander Peter Walpole
Signal Communications Officer, HMS Sheffield

After picking myself off the floor I checked the other members of the bridge crew, who were uninjured but very shocked. We were still under way. Smoke was seeping from the ventilation trunking, and we could see a major fire starting on the starboard side amidships. In a very short time, smoke made the bridge untenable and we had to evacuate. With hindsight, I wished I'd taken

HMS *Sheffield* on fire after being hit by an AM.39 Exocet missile on 4 May 1982. A Gemini assault boat with fire fighting team is approaching her starboard side.

more things with me; a chart perhaps, or one of the portable radios; but it seemed more important to get the people out and away from the suffocating smoke. I remember the quartermaster, Steven Yacavu, sitting at his post amid thick smoke with his gas mask on, briefing me that he was trying to take control of the steering, but was unable to do so.

A lot of the ops room staff had come out on the starboard upper deck. The missile gun director was incensed at having been attacked. He came out and, full of rage, leaped up on to the upper deck without his glasses on, got behind a 20mm cannon and started firing at the first aircraft he saw. This was a Sea King helicopter, which took a massive dive and scurried away at great speed. The captain shouted up from the fo'c'sle to ask me if I was in communications with the tiller flat, the space down aft where you could control the rudders locally as opposed to from the bridge. He said if we can steer the ship and are still running on some engines, head for South Georgia. He'd quickly appraised that the best thing to do was get the ship somewhere it could be repaired. I felt compassion toward him, a small, hunched figure, with a very heavy burden of responsibility.

Commander Ian Inskip
HMS *Glamorgan*

It was a nice sunny day; the sea was slight with a swell but not much wind. We heard *Sheffield* had been hit but not how, and we could see her and the smoke. We immediately turned towards her, but were told to get back into station, which made us feel very sad as she needed our help. The admiral was right; the carriers were the target and *Sheffield* was no longer a valuable unit. *Yarmouth* and one of the Type 21's went to assist.

Lieutenant Commander Peter Walpole
Signal Communications Officer, HMS Sheffield

The engines were ticking over using fuel from a small emergency fuel tank, and we were making six knots, in a small circle I think. I never did get control over the rudders. Communication was very difficult, by a telephone from the bridge wing, and we were getting horrendous crossed lines. The people down on the tiller flat couldn't actually get control of the rudders. Smoke was billowing so much from the bridge that we shut the doors, after which we never got back into the ship. We reassembled on the upper deck, and looked after some of the upper deck crew who'd been closer to the impact and had flash burns that made them unrecognisable.

Flames were leaping nearly one hundred feet into the air from the ruptured fuel tanks and paint on the side of the ship. This died down quickly into a smoking sort of fire, which was raging inside. It seemed important to establish some kind of command position at the bridge. I still had the binoculars round my neck. I climbed on to the bridge roof to see if there was a further attack coming, or if there were any other ships or helicopters. It was like being somebody's prey, trapped and unable to move, fearing a fresh attack. A Harrier flew over, which was a great relief.

Commander Ralph John Wykes-Sneyd
Officer Commanding 820 Sea King Squadron, Fleet Air Arm,
HMS Invincible
When *Sheffield* was hit, we all thought she'd been torpedoed. It took some time before we on *Invincible* realised an Exocet had hit her.

Radio Supervisor Stewart Anthony MacFarlane
HMS Coventry
Type 42 destroyers had torpedoes on board, and because *Sheffield* was burning so badly they were jettisoned. A helicopter from *Invincible* saw one of these torpedoes and decided a torpedo not an Exocet had hit *Sheffield*, so there must be an Argentine submarine in the area. Type 42s have extremely good sonar, so we told *Invincible* there was no submarine risk, that we could see *Sheffield*, and an Exocet had hit her. But nevertheless we were ordered to start fighting a non-existent submarine. So while *Sheffield* was burning and people needed to be got off, we were rushing round looking for a submarine.

Lieutenant Commander Peter Walpole
Signal Communications Officer, HMS Sheffield
HMS *Yarmouth* came very close along our starboard side, a very skilful piece of manoeuvring, using hoses from their fo'c'sle. One of our crew used our Gemini inflatable dinghy to get fire-fighting water into the hole. But then *Yarmouth* had a fleeting sonar submarine contact, so went off in a great hurry firing anti-submarine rockets.

Commander Ian Inskip
HMS Glamorgan
It took half an hour to determine how *Sheffield* had been hit. It was chaos and an absolute shambles. Torpedoes were being reported everywhere, usually due to the Gemini craft circling *Sheffield* or from ships' Unifoxer. Submarines were positively sighted, frigates attacking with mortars . . . It was obvious early on

that there weren't submarines, but it was a total shambles, caused by people going into action for the first time being extremely jumpy.

Lieutenant Commander Peter Walpole
Signal Communications Officer, HMS Sheffield
As we struggled to get fire-fighting water, the tremendous pall of thick acrid smoke pumping out of the side of the ship was being blown back on to us, and enveloped the bridge, so you couldn't see your hand in front of your face. It was suffocating, but thankfully the wind blew it away.

Air Observer Al Clark jumped down onto the fo'c'sle to take charge of firefighting down there, but we needed to speak with another ship, and our only working radio was in the helicopter. So they took off, to evacuate the casualties and also bring back more firefighting equipment for us. But when they landed to refuel on *Hermes*, they were stopped from taking off as it was decided after their traumas, they shouldn't fly again.

Michael Thomas Nicholson
ITN correspondent
We saw the smoke when *Sheffield* was hit. She was sacrificed to stop the Exocet missile from hitting us, as we were the real target. *Hermes*'s captain, Middleton, told us it would have taken four Exocets to sink one of the carriers, but that one missile would have affected our operational capability for some time.

Lieutenant Commander Peter Walpole
Signal Communications Officer, HMS Sheffield
With the fire being so intense, we couldn't get inside to the breathing apparatus and firefighting equipment. Helicopters came from other ships, hovering over the fo'c'sle, lowering breathing gear and fire pumps to us. Ships are full of very flammable materials, fuel, ammunition, cabling, and the metal of modern ships melts. The missile had entered the engine room and missile spaces, where there are lots of fuels that burned. In training, you fight an established fire, so you don't go through the stages of seeing a fire develop. In its first phase, our fire touched off all this fuel and paint, creating a startling flame which subsided quite quickly, but took hold inside with less physical evidence to be seen from the upper deck. I looked into the hole after the flames had died down, to see thick smoke billowing out. People were firefighting in a very matter-of-fact way. Nobody panicked.

The doctor set up a first-aid post with his Red Cross bag, and was tending people on the fo'c'sle. They could almost have been extras in a film. The *Arrow* came along our port side, and after using her own hoses, connected several cloth hoses together, which were passed over to us. The marine engineering officer used these hoses to try to get into the machinery spaces that had actually been hit. I don't think they managed it. Some of our people had been accidentally hosed by the other ships' firefighters, and, being unable to take shelter inside any part of our ship, were very cold. I shouted across to the *Arrow* that we needed food, and they threw over loads of Mars bars and nutty.

The deck in the bridge area was too hot underfoot to touch, but was even hotter closer to the Sea Dart magazine, so it was imperative that the ship's company be evacuated. We'd been firefighting five hours, which seemed to pass very quickly. I remember being surprised when the order came to leave, thinking we should stick it out a bit longer. But I didn't appreciate how much the fire had taken a good hold inside and was spreading. Also, Captain Salt knew we were stopping two other warships from looking after the aircraft carriers and the main body. I did feel regret that we couldn't carry on, but I think we'd have run out of steam pretty soon after.

When the order was given to abandon, we had to get aft, crossing the central area of the ship that was blazing with fire. I clambered down on to the port waist, then made a dash aft through the hot centre section to the flight deck, where people were jumping across the gap on to *Arrow*, which was very close. The gap widened and closed as the sea carried the decks apart and back again, and the two ships rolled into each other, *Arrow* sustaining quite a bit of damage as she rode alongside of us. I had this brief flash of all those days at school doing long jump, and thinking this was the time to make it work. I picked my spot, on a little companionway that runs along the port side of the hangar, near an HF aerial that looks like a birdbath.

Other guys already over there were shouting encouragement: 'Come on, you can make it . . .' I'd just watched the navigator make his jump, which he slightly mistimed, and after a scrabble in which his feet had slipped between the two ships, he'd been lifted out just before the two ships clashed together again. I thought: 'Right, I'm not going to miss this one,' made a jump for it and found myself on the *Arrow*. The buffer was over there already, a very stalwart character that you need to have at times like this. He was congratulating people at making the jump: 'Well done, sir, now off you go over there . . .' I'd still got the bridge binoculars round my neck, which I'd stuffed into my empty gas mask case. I'd used the gas mask itself as a scoop for water to cool the hot deck. Very soon after that, the *Arrow* was heading off at high speed to counter some new threat.

Radio Supervisor Stewart Anthony MacFarlane
HMS *Coventry*

We took a lot of uninjured survivors on board until we could transfer them into a merchant ship. The *Arrow* went alongside and took people off, while we stood off providing long-range air defence.

Commander Ralph John Wykes-Sneyd
Officer Commanding 820 Sea King Squadron, Fleet Air Arm,
HMS *Invincible*

As *Sheffield* lay dead in the water, her fires having been put out, intelligence indicated that the Argentines' small 109 submarines had been instructed to torpedo any ships coming to tow *Sheffield* away. I deployed two anti-submarine helicopters around her, and above this scene, there were two Harriers on CAP. My helicopter to the north-west detected a fleeting maritime patrol aircraft contact, which he called back to *Invincible*. The Harrier above him was told to investigate, but the other one came across too, and we think they collided. I flew out to see if there were any bits or traces, but there were not.

Lieutenant Commander Peter Walpole
Signal Communications Officer, HMS Sheffield

In *Arrow* we were split up, officers to the wardroom and junior rates to the junior rates' dining hall, which made me feel very uncomfortable, as I wanted to see that my division were all right. I went aft to the junior rates' dining hall, to find my yeoman and radio supervisor. We didn't yet know who'd been trapped below. I do remember knowing that one of our regulating staff hadn't made it.

Commander Ralph John Wykes-Sneyd
Officer Commanding 820 Sea King Squadron, Fleet Air Arm,
HMS *Invincible*

Later that evening, after I'd recovered from trying to find these two pilots, I was handed a signal from Admiral Woodward, which I read with some horror: 'This misreporting of one helicopter by another has led to the loss of two valuable air assets.' I went immediately to the Harrier squadron briefing room and showed the signal to my opposite number, fearing that if it were believed we'd have a serious problem between the two squadrons. My opposite number immediately said: 'That's a load of rubbish.' I later took the signal to the captain and discussed it with him, as it could have been totally disastrous to morale on board *Invincible*.

Captain Michael Ernest Barrow
HMS Glamorgan

The sinking of *Sheffield* had a very serious effect on morale of my men. In the ops room there was dumb disbelief, with a gasping of breath. This was the first Royal Navy ship to be sunk since the Second World War. Seeing that ship burning from end to end certainly made us look to our own laurels . . .

Michael Thomas Nicholson
ITN correspondent

Some of the survivors came aboard *Hermes*; one guy had been walking, but we heard he'd died a few hours later when they tried to take off his clothes and his skin came too. They were wearing polyester nylon clothing, which melts into the skin, after naval penny-pinching had done away with the cotton clothing they used to have.

Lieutenant Commander Peter Walpole
Signal Communications Officer, HMS Sheffield

The enormity of having suffered loss of life began to come through. I didn't think we'd lost anybody in the immediate impact, but some were overcome by smoke or just couldn't get out of where they were below, but we didn't know how many. I remember the dimly lit dining hall, the shudder of *Arrow* setting off at speed, and the relief at finding the rest of my division, as they were the people I was most concerned with. Splitting up officers and men at such a time was not the most sensible move. I desperately wanted a shower to get rid of the horrible smell of smoke. I then had this overwhelming desire to use a Q-tip to clean out my ears. The ship's medic told me not to poke Q-tips in my ears, but I did it anyway, and extracted a great amount of black gunge, for which I was most grateful and enabled me to hear better.

We were clearly a great burden to the *Arrow*, whose ship's company was swelled three times by our arrival. After losing the battle for our ship, the nervous energy and jocular spirits that had kept everybody going evaporated with a great deflation as soon as we stepped off *Sheffield*. It was a very demoralising time. Half of us were on the *Arrow*, half on the *Yarmouth*, and some had jumped into the sea to be picked up by a boat. I remember thinking that I wouldn't have done that.

But then *Arrow* went to action stations. If we were to be attacked again, I wanted to be high up in the ship rather than stuck down below, so I went to a secondary command position up at bridge level, thinking that somewhere higher up in the ship would be safer, where I could see out – a natural thing for an officer of the watch to do. It was frightening because we had nothing to do and were in the way of the other ship's company. When you are part of a crew, your mind is fully focused and occupied on something you've been trained to do. But just sitting around, you've got more time to think about it.

The admiral's staff were very keen to learn what had actually happened, so our captain was flown to *Hermes* with the warfare officers who'd been on watch. Al Clark and others who'd been on the bridge were able to confirm it was a missile they'd seen approaching the ship.

Michael Thomas Nicholson
ITN correspondent
When Captain Sam Salt and his men came on board *Hermes*, they were obviously shocked and were put into the tank deck – a sort of cargo hold where it was very cold and where they sat in semi-darkness for about half an hour. We were stopped from filming them; one isn't allowed to record tragedy. Then Captain Salt was taken away for several hours, after which we were allowed to talk to him. He was clean-shaven with new clothes on, debriefed, and had recovered his composure. When he'd been with his men earlier, he'd been in tears, devastated by the loss. We were not allowed to report the name of *Sheffield*, nor say the number of casualties, so that the families of every Type 42 – or indeed of every ship – were worried, which seemed to me to be very cruel. We were not even allowed to film *Sheffield* until four days after she was hit, when Sandy Woodward decided he wanted to see what the ship looked like but couldn't spare the time to fly over and see for himself.

Lieutenant Commander Graham John Edmonds
Operations Officer and Squadron Warfare Officer, HMS Broadsword
Before the Falklands crisis, the navy had gone four years without having flown fixed-wing aircraft at sea, or practised the air defence of ships by aircraft. Between losing the last of the fixed-wing carriers in 1978, and the very recent fitting of a Harrier launch ramp fitted to *Hermes*, we'd to re-learn how to run air defence aircraft at sea. By early May, we still hadn't sorted out our air traffic control procedures, which led to the loss of *Sheffield*.

Rear Admiral Anthony John Whetstone
Deputy Chief of Naval Staff (Operations), MoD Whitehall
The loss of the *Sheffield* was a real shock not just because it was the first, but because our intelligence people were assuring us that the Argentines hadn't yet got their Exocet missiles ready to use.

Commander Ralph John Wykes-Sneyd
Officer Commanding 820 Sea King Squadron, Fleet Air Arm, HMS Invincible

Sheffield was the price the fleet had to pay in order to get everybody into top gear and be really alert. A lot of people were still thinking it wasn't real and wouldn't affect them. People were also realising who were the pawns, and that the king and queen of this chessboard – the two aircraft carriers – were vital to the taking of the islands, and that a lot of pawns were going to be lost before the end of the game.

Radio Supervisor Stewart Anthony MacFarlane
HMS Coventry

A couple of days before *Sheffield* had been hit, the carriers told us aircraft were coming in, giving their height and speed, ordering us to engage with 4.5-inch guns. We told them there were no aircraft out there, but were ordered just to get on with it and fire, so we ended up killing a group of albatross, which if you were superstitious, you'd believe sealed the fate either of *Sheffield*, or of ourselves, *Coventry*, later on.

Robin Knowling Hopson-Hill
Family Services Officer, Portsmouth

After the *Sheffield* was sunk, and before we had received the list of casualties, every wife was imagining their husband had been killed. Because of the difficulty of ensuring the casualty list was accurate, it took some time to arrive. The casualty signal was just a list of names of people killed or seriously injured. Relatives would say: 'That's not good enough. How did he die? How was he injured?' but we didn't know. They were very demanding, more so than in the Second World War when I served in the navy. Families then received a brief telegram followed by a very blunt letter. Today the media provide blow-by-blow accounts of the war, and expect us to be able to provide detailed information immediately. We tried to find out what we could, but it took weeks. After the loss of *Sheffield*, we realised that a lot of the families had no idea that their next of kin were even involved in active service.

The media behaved in an unbelievable way. On the estate where the families of the *Sheffield* men lived, wives were being pounced on by journalists asking: 'Are you a *Sheffield* wife?' trying to get stories out of them, making the families' lives even worse.

Michael Thomas Nicholson
ITN correspondent

When the dead from *Sheffield* were buried at sea, we were told we couldn't film it, that 'it would not be decent'. We told them, time and time again, that it would be weeks before any of our pictures would ever be seen, by which time some of the scars would already be healing. It's a very pig-headed military attitude. I'm not there for my own glory or ITN's glory, but as a representative of the people. I'm there risking my neck so that people back home can be told what's going on, and recording events for posterity.

Commander Nigel David 'Sharkey' Ward
Officer Commanding 801 Squadron, Fleet Air Arm, HMS Invincible

We were astounded at what had happened on May 4; then a few days later, we received a signal from the admiral to *Invincible* saying: 'I didn't think much of your command and control on May 4.' I was there when the captain received this signal, and he showed it to me. I said the same thing as him: 'What a fucking cheek. What is the man thinking of?'

12

Softening Up

We'd been briefed on the Latin temperament; that they'd fight like tigers while everything was going well, but if we could hurt them often enough for long enough, they'd suddenly fold. Our bombardment schedule was designed to test this temperament.

Lieutenant Commander Graham John Edmonds
Operations Officer and Squadron Warfare Officer, HMS Broadsword
After losing *Sheffield*, we had to sort out every part of the carrier task force's operations. The misidentification of the two Etendards by *Hermes* made us more trigger happy, which the Harrier pilots returning to the task group were very aware of.

Commander Nigel David 'Sharkey' Ward
Officer Commanding 801 Squadron, Fleet Air Arm, HMS Invincible
Most of my pilots wouldn't argue with orders as I did. On one occasion *Hermes* ordered me to go east one hundred miles away from the threat to intercept two aircraft. I queried this and was told: 'Vector oh-nine-oh, now eighty-five miles, two bogeys, trade,' which means get on to that heading and intercept.

I said: 'Negative.'

They said: 'What?'

I said: 'Negative, they can't be enemy aircraft.'

There was a short pause, then: 'From the admiral. You are to vector oh-nine-oh. Trade now eighty-five miles. Get on with it!'

I said: 'Negative. Check who's just taken off from your own deck.' I knew who was taking off from our deck.

There was a pause, then they said: 'Ah roger. That's our red section. Carry on with your combat air patrol.'

It was so ridiculous, as those targets should have been engaged with Sea Dart anyway, and in any case the targets were coming out of *Hermes* and could only be friendlies. They didn't apologise, but the pomposity went out of their RT.

John Fowler
Superintendent of Education, Stanley

As things wore on and military imperatives took over, Hussey and Reeve became increasingly frustrated. I'm not so sure about the soldier member of this Falklands 'junta', Colonel Dorrego, as he was more concerned with public works.

Colonel Manuel Dorrego
Head of Public Works Department, Islas Malvinas

May 1 was the beginning of the second stage of the campaign, in which I took on the post of Commander of Engineers, studying the most possible routes to protect our troops from the English invasion. Engineers all over the world install minefields so afterwards they can take them up. Our mines were installed with great precision, using points of reference, with diagrams of the entire minefield with maps, in a pink-coloured file three centimetres thick, which after the surrender I delivered by hand to Major McDonald, when they asked me for it. But some of our mines were installed in an arbitrary and disorderly way. A little time after we started installing mines, one of the sub officers had his arm blown off.

Air Vice Commodore Carlos Bloomer-Reeve
Secretary General, Islas Malvinas

After May 1, we tried to make a civil defence system. I think Blinley and Bucket asked for it. I told them it would not be necessary, as we were not planning for anybody to bomb the town. But somebody told me: 'Look, Carlos, it's the British we're speaking about. Remember the Boer War.' So we asked for sandbags and started looking for places for shelter.

Commander Nigel David 'Sharkey' Ward
Officer Commanding 801 Squadron, Fleet Air Arm, HMS Invincible

Having lost aircraft on May 1, the Argentine air force decided to avoid us, ditching their weapons if we were around, to go home and try again next day.

They should have sent out wave after wave of fighters to take on Sea Harrier; we'd have lost aircraft, and if the numbers got critical, the whole operation would have folded and we'd have gone home. They respected us; but Admiral Woodward and his staff didn't. But they kept coming even when we thought they couldn't do any more. It must have been terrifying for them.

John Fowler
Superintendent of Education, Stanley

We had no idea of the magnitude of the task force operation, and had the naïve view that the Argentines would just piss off once they realised the Brits were coming. As the task force drew near, the Argentines started preparing for fighting in Stanley. One Argentine officer reassured me, saying: 'So long as you can see senior Argentine officers walking around you may feel quite safe. It's only when they all disappear that you should worry. We're not going to die in a ditch here.'

Federico Mirré (Argentine Ambassador, 2006)
Foreign Office, Buenos Aires

In Deseado, a town in the middle of Patagonia with less than ten thousand people, all buildings were blacked out, and car lights camouflaged. The sheep-shearing sheds were ready as emergency accommodation, with a code of ringing bells from the railway station, fire station, church and school to indicate attack, a wounded person, fire, for people to congregate in the church and so on. They were ready for war if it came to them. From Deseado we flew back to Comodoro Rivadavia, and were re-called to Buenos Aires where we gave a full report. The Red Cross remained adamant they wanted to visit the islands, to see for themselves how the islanders were being treated. But the military were increasingly disinterested in our requirements.

Commander Nigel David 'Sharkey' Ward
Officer Commanding 801 Squadron, Fleet Air Arm, HMS Invincible

We . . . [were told] not to use the Harrier's radar to look down for targets coming in low, and to keep it switched off until we'd been directed to within ten miles of a contact. I still don't understand this. On May 1 we'd achieved one good kill and damaged another enemy aircraft through looking down with our own radars. Maybe the admiral thought our very small Blue Fox radars would give away the task group's position, like the bloody great beacon of a ship's radar. In using our radars, we successfully turned back many air attacks simply by them knowing we were in their area. I told my captain 'No way' to this ban, and then wrote several papers for the admiral explaining how the radar worked and how it should be used, to which we received no acknowledgement. But later we . . . [were told] not to use Blue Fox radar *at all.*

Federico Mirré (Argentine Ambassador, 2006)
Foreign Office, Buenos Aires

I couldn't believe the contrast between Buenos Aires and Comodoro Rivadavia. Despite everybody understanding there wasn't going to be a good ending to the war episode, it was business as usual, with no outward signs of being a country at war. Whether this was a way of evading reality on a massive collective basis, or misinformation, I couldn't tell. People seemed convinced that in the end we would have the islands. I was replaced on the Red Cross team by a general, I think because the authorities were unhappy with my trying to be objective towards the Red Cross position. I was then isolated from the Foreign Ministry and any sort of policy decisions, execution or discussion.

Commander Ian Inskip
HMS Glamorgan

For the next three or four days after the sinking of *Sheffield* we didn't actually do anything, and our morale was definitely sagging. We'd taken a hit but were not apparently doing anything about it – sulking in the corner with a bloody nose. From my point of view, it would have been better if we'd got stuck in again.

Captain Michael Ernest Barrow
HMS Glamorgan

For the next twenty or so days, my job in *Glamorgan* was by day to escort the carriers and the other 'heavies' – the RFAs and merchant ships – and by night to go inshore at high speed and bombard Argentine positions on 'softening up operations', which later came to be known as 'diversionary operations'.

For the naval gunfire part of this plan, to reach the targets we had to get within a half mile of the shore, where there was kelp, an extremely coarse form of seaweed moored to the bottom of the sea and floating on the surface. Kelp showed up on radar if the weather wasn't too bad, but there was always the risk of getting generator inlets blocked up just when you were very close to the shore in a force nine gale. We got quite a lot in our inlets, but were never stopped. There were also coastal minefields to be avoided.

Lieutenant Commander Graham John Edmonds
Operations Officer and Squadron Warfare Officer, HMS Broadsword
On May 9 we went inshore with *Coventry*, to do a bombardment of the airfield from just off Stanley. We both had a pulse Doppler radar that would detect any moving targets over land. The idea was to stir up aircraft to come and attack us. *Coventry*'s gun jammed, but a Puma helicopter appeared. *Coventry* fired a Sea Dart and obliterated the Puma, which we watched on the weapon system video. This was our first direct action with somebody killed as a result, and those who saw it were affected. We consoled ourselves by saying the pilot would have been unaware of the missile coming straight down from above, through his rotor head. A second Argentine helicopter – a Chinook – arrived to investigate, but we were refused permission from *Hermes* to hit it, which was an extremely silly decision. Our job is to shoot down aircraft, and the less assets the Argentines had, the harder it would be for them to do their job. We then withdrew back to the task force.

Commander Nigel David 'Sharkey' Ward
Officer Commanding 801 Squadron, Fleet Air Arm, HMS Invincible
Around two-thirds of all the Argentine attacks around San Carlos were turned back by Sea Harrier. At sea, not one Etendard or other aircraft came through an area where Harriers were in the air and transmitting. But the admiral's staff misused the Sea Harrier assets in *Hermes* to do all sorts of stupid things, like sending four aircraft one hundred miles north-east, away from the threat, to eyeball search for surface threats.

It takes just one Harrier to sanitise an area immediately of all surface contacts, up to a hundred miles out. While we were working very hard to put up aircraft to defend the fleet, the admiral's staff were wasting four aircraft at a time on fan searches, flying fifteen degrees between aircraft on a heading, then ordering them to fly together back to the ship. I was actually in *Hermes* when they were being tasked like this. I'd gone across to see what was going on. I lost my cool and asked 800 Squadron's Senior Pilot Clissard: 'What the fuck's going on? What are you doing?'

He said: 'We've been told to do this by the staff.'

I said: 'Tell the staff to get knotted. If they want a task done, take the task and do it the operational, efficient way.'

He said: 'It's not like that over here.'

So I said I wanted to see somebody. Then Chris Honeyball, the staff aviation officer, came in. I said: 'What the hell's going on, sir? What is this nonsense?' Only using words stronger than that.

He said: 'It's none of your business, Sharkey. It's the admiral's staff's business. If you don't like it you can lump it.'

I said: 'Right, I'll leave it there.'

The admiral's staff were interfering on a daily basis, not only with Harrier business, but also misusing Sea King anti-submarine helicopter assets, again to do visual searches. Being a bloody good Buccaneer pilot who likes hitting surface ships, Captain Lyn Middleton probably wouldn't quarrel with the idea that we should sanitise the oceans for surface ships. But it seemed the admiral didn't believe ships could be protected from air attack by aircraft. So the twelve Sea Harriers on *Hermes*, sixty per cent of our force, were misused most of the time, before and during the war, because the admiral's staff didn't understand the weapon systems. Thankfully the admiral's staff didn't interfere in the way we on *Invincible* operated, and we ignored their orders about not using the radar.

Private Alejandro Ramon Cano
Paratrooper, Grupo Artilleria Aerotransportada

After Dos Hermanos, Darwin was very bad, with constant shelling from the British ships. This was where nobody wanted to be. Just before we were about to leave Puerto Argentina for Darwin they punished us, because one of our chaps was said to have pinched a kilo tin of food, when it was a corporal who'd done this robbery. We had to do physical training; I cried before leaving because we couldn't do any more. Then sub lieutenant Manzini comes over and says: 'Calm yourself, you are going to Darwin with the first lieutenant.' I didn't want to go, but he says: 'You have to go, because he wants you to go.'

Lieutenant Commander Raymond John Adams
HMS Coventry

On the fourth day of shelling the airfield – May 12 – we stopped after four Skyhawks attacked *Glasgow*. One bomb went into one side, through the after engine room, bouncing out of the other side without exploding. The other three aircraft were taken out by *Brilliant*'s Sea Wolf system. But *Glasgow* had to retire. From the original Spring Train contingent, we had now lost two out of the three ships of our type. This realisation didn't have much effect on our morale, as we hadn't actually seen *Sheffield* on fire, or *Glasgow* being hit. We also knew that other air defence ships were on their way to join us.

Radio Supervisor Stewart Anthony MacFarlane
HMS *Coventry*

I remember reading Admiral Woodward's signal to *Glasgow*'s captain after she was hit: 'Report your dead and injured immediately.' He replied: 'Slight damage to one generator. Thousand-pound bomb through starboard side forward auxiliary machinery room, exited port side. No dead, no injured. One chief stoker in dire need of a change of underwear.'

Michael Thomas Nicholson
ITN correspondent

I described one operation when we were on a ship that went in and bombarded an Argentine garrison, then scarpered – all great fun. At the end of the report I said: 'This has been so successful, we'll do it again – you can bank on it.' This got back to Admiral Sir John Fieldhouse as being: 'We'll go back tomorrow night.'

Fieldhouse lost his rag, complained to Woodward who summoned me to his office and told me that he was waiting for the transcript, and that if I had warned the enemy that we were going back, I was sacked and would be going home. He then broadcast this over the tannoy to the ship's company – that I'd given information away. People who'd previously been friendly were coming up to me and saying things like: 'The best place for you, mate, is a canvas bag over the side.' I felt so bad that I didn't want to go into the wardroom as I felt they would boo and throw things at me. But Bernard Hesketh told me I was going in, even if he had to carry me.

When the transcript came through from Northwood, it proved what I'd said, but nobody told me, and Woodward certainly never apologised or made any sort of correction over the tannoy. I never forgave him for that, but it was just part of the way they all were; quite happy to give you little interviews on deck because of their own egos, but when it came down to a proper relationship, it wasn't there.

Private Alejandro Ramon Cano
Paratrooper, Grupo Artilleria Aerotransportada

We left Puerto Argentina for Darwin thinking that we were going to lose, and so therefore we *are* going to lose. I wanted to destroy the English and I didn't mind how. But at that moment the majority with me didn't think this. We knew what was possible.

Everything in those days weighed heavily – what happened to us because of this land. We were angry, but we also wanted to get through this. I have forgotten everything else. I forgot that I was hungry, I forgot other things that I had seen in those days ... with the punishment they had given us for stealing the food, I forgot everything.

Commander Ian Inskip
HMS Glamorgan
We'd been briefed on the Latin temperament; that they'd fight like tigers while everything was going well, but if we could hurt them often enough for long enough, they'd suddenly fold. Our bombardment schedule was designed to test this temperament, and was the softening-up phase of the campaign, prior to the invasion.

Private Alejandro Ramon Cano
Paratrooper, Grupo Artilleria Aerotransportada
While we were over there, I received letters from people at home, above all from my family. I kept them all. We knew the Argentines were with us; but we knew that when letters did not arrive because of the blockade, nothing could arrive anywhere. But at no time did we question, or at least it never passed through my mind, why were we not sent food. The military had us by the balls, but that wasn't because we thought they might not feed us.

Commander Ian Inskip
HMS Glamorgan
The San Carlos landings were now scheduled for May 21, and the deception plan was called Operation Tornado. We sailed in to the east coast every night, making as much noise as we could to convince the opposition that the landings were to be on the other side of East Falkland, near Stanley. We fired at worthwhile targets, but the main point was as a distraction. We varied the times we fired, changing the direction of the circuits from which we fired, sometimes at the end giving an extra five shells to the first target, everything calculated to damage Argentine morale; keeping them out of their nice warm tents and up to their knees in the water of boggy trenches. But having been doing this every night for three weeks, we were getting very tired. Our usual naval gunfire support liaison officer was Lieutenant Colonel Eave. He wanted to fire hundreds of shells here, there and everywhere. We had to tell him there were only seven hundred shells in our magazine each night, and we preferred to fire ten or twenty at each target. He gave us targets to fire upon and we decided how to do it.

Captain Christopher Charles Brown
148 Commando Forward Observation Unit, Royal Artillery
Pebble Island is small, with an airfield, which the Argentine forces were using
to fly Pucara light attack aircraft – a light, propeller-powered monoplane,
carrying bombs, rockets and cannon; fairly slow, but a considerable threat to
helicopters and troops. D Squadron SAS were to raid the island and destroy
the aircraft.

The recce was done by SBS small boats, and they saw eleven aircraft, which
they thought were real. We would have put out mock-up aircraft in the hope
that somebody might attack them. The reconnaissance officer thought it was
all too good to be true, unprotected, and he rightly suspected a trap. Anyway
we decided to go in by Sea Kings using PNG, and were dropped four
kilometres from the airfield.

Commander Ian Inskip
HMS Glamorgan
We couldn't go direct to the gun line as the Argentine submarine was in
position along the route, so we had to go around it. The chart of Pebble Island
didn't go far enough north so I had to attach a piece of cartridge paper to it,
then draw the latitude and longitude grid and my bombardment lines on to it.
Our 1006 radar had lost its training rotor so we had to improvise on that too,
by fitting wind scoops to the dish so it would rotate: sometimes it was
wandering around in a breeze, other times it was spinning furiously like a
train. What the Argentine EW team gollies made of it I don't know.

Lieutenant Roger Edwards
Fleet Air Arm
I'd been here in 1973 with HMS *Endurance*, and with my wife being a
Falkland Islander, I'd travelled around extensively, particularly Pebble Island,
and other islands in the north near to where my wife's family farmed. I helped
the SAS with geographical information. The intelligence assessment was of
three hundred to four hundred Argie military on the island. The SAS were
quite happy to take on being outnumbered ten to one by the Argies.

Commander Ian Inskip
HMS Glamorgan
It was a moonlit night with three-eighths cloud, and we knew from intelligence gained from a frigate damaged by the Royal Marines at South Georgia
that they'd got an Exocet somewhere ashore, so we were feeling very exposed.

We arrived on the gun line at 0400 and spent the next three hours slowly steaming up and down the coast about five miles off, preparing our gun system.

Lieutenant Roger Edwards
Fleet Air Arm
There was a last-minute delay, when somebody realised *Hermes* was two hundred miles too far from Pebble Island to drop us off to do the raid then recover the helicopters. So we got out of the helicopters and waited for six hours while *Hermes* steamed closer to Pebble Island. Once we'd landed, the ship would be close enough so the helicopters could return to the ship, refuel then pick us up once we'd done the deed. But because of this delay, instead of having eight hours on the island we were left with just two hours.

Captain Christopher Charles Brown
148 Commando Forward Observation Unit, Royal Artillery
We were late getting ashore. I'd been allocated HMS *Glamorgan* in support of the attack, which wasn't going to hang around when daylight broke. It was obvious we were going to be very pushed. I radioed the ship and asked them to stay as late as possible to provide us with fire until the last moment. The captain agreed to stay till first light, but no longer as he knew he was likely to be hit by Argentine aircraft.

Commander Ian Inskip
HMS Glamorgan
We should have left the gun line, and were exposed to increasing danger the longer we remained. But Captain Barrow decided that we were there to support the SAS, so we remained.

Captain Christopher Charles Brown
148 Commando Forward Observation Unit, Royal Artillery
We made good speed towards the target, to just outside the airfield. The plan changed from attacking the aircraft then attacking Argentine forces in the village, because that would take too much time. Instead we set up an ambush to intercept any of the garrison that decided to come out. The rest of the squadron went on to the airfield and destroyed the aircraft, with me firing high explosive from HMS *Glamorgan* on to the planes, and also into suspected Argentine positions to neutralise them, interspersed with illuminating rounds to help us make sure we didn't miss anything.

Commander Ian Inskip
HMS Glamorgan
We were told the SAS were approaching their target. We received the order to fire twenty salvoes, the rounds catching the Argentines as they were running for their guns – one hundred and fifty yards from the SAS. Bearing in mind that two hundred yards is the standard error for the initial round, the SAS's naval gunfire forward observer was being rather optimistic in assuming the rounds wouldn't land on them. We were given a large spotting correction, bringing the bombardment to the end of the airstrip, then six or seven identical corrections as the spotter walked our bombardment down the airstrip. Seven Pucara were destroyed with several other aircraft, significantly improving the chances of the landings in San Carlos scheduled for later in the month.

Lieutenant Roger Edwards
Fleet Air Arm
It was already getting light, so the helicopters picked us up only three miles from the settlement rather than at the pick-up point, as it was obvious we weren't going to get there under the cover of darkness.

Commander Ian Inskip
HMS Glamorgan
We'd now overstayed our welcome and with a force nine blowing by the time we finished, we retired at twenty-nine knots on both steam and gas turbines flat out.

We had a huge quartering sea, so the helmsman couldn't steer the course. The only way we could get back was by facing aft, looking at the waves, then just before they got to us, apply the appropriate amount of rudder, then at the right moment take it off again. If you got it wrong, the ship would yaw fifty degrees at a time, heeling quite significantly. It was quite exciting, and when dawn broke we were still to the west of Stanley. So having stirred up a hornets' nest and done a lot of dirty work, we were feeling very exposed. The Argentines didn't react, and we were mightily relieved when we got back.

Captain Christopher Charles Brown
148 Commando Forward Observation Unit, Royal Artillery
We destroyed all the aircraft, pulling out with planes exploding and in flames. They made no attempt to counter-attack from the village or reinforce the airfield. If we'd had longer we would have attempted to weed them out, but there was the danger of inflicting damage on civilian property, or killing

villagers. But we really didn't have time, so we called a halt, having achieved what we'd set out to do. Destroying those aircraft removed a considerable threat to the future landings. We moved out to a safe place and were picked up by Sea King helicopters and whisked back to *Hermes* for breakfast.

Air Vice Commodore Carlos Bloomer-Reeve
Secretary General, Islas Malvinas

The British Harriers were able to fly at night and had good radar, but we could monitor planes flying over the water with our radar. We had three radars: the Westinghouse at the German camp on the top of the town was the only important one; and the other ones were for locating artillery gun sites. We broke it before we left. We destroyed everything we could, of course. That's the normal thing in war.

Captain (John) Jeremy Black
HMS Invincible

The key to the South Atlantic battle was the aircraft carriers; had the Argentines managed to knock them out, they'd have a very good chance of winning. We realised that the Argentines could survey all our aircraft movements using a radar located in the middle of Stanley. As our aircraft returned to the carriers, the Argentines could observe them drop down out of their radar lobe to land, and so deduce where our carriers were – then send in Exocet attacks. Fortunately we realised this, so I instructed all aircraft after take off to fly fifty miles very low then lift; and likewise when returning, drop down as if landing fifty miles west then fly low level to the carrier. The pilots really hated this as flying low level used up a lot of fuel, and there were long and heated arguments about it.

All the Argentine Exocet attacks were directed at the carriers. Initially they flew at us from the west through our ring of anti-aircraft ships, which didn't work. Next they tried an ingenious plan, which very nearly succeeded, using two Super Etendards carrying one Exocet, escorted by four A4 aircraft. They took off, climbing to altitude to meet a tanker and refuel, flew to the south of us, then came north-east until east of us, behind the aircraft carriers – on a sunny, clear afternoon. For this attack, my own Sea Dart missile launcher had broken, the only time it was unserviceable during the whole campaign.

These aircraft appeared on our radar, coming from the south-west at low level about twenty-five miles out. At that moment, there was nothing between the enemy and me. And unusually, I didn't have an air defence frigate with me, so things didn't look too bright. But thanks to our constant practice of deception when taking off and landing the aeroplanes, they thought we were fifty miles further west, so at the last moment they turned north-west. I had no means of retaliation, so it was only their misappreciation of where we were that saved us. Instead of finding us, they flew over a couple of frigates, which shot down three of the A4s. They launched their Exocet and some bombs were dropped, but there was no damage.

One of the CAP pilots observed a trawler, which he bombed and hit. We knew from intelligence this was a spy ship, so Admiral Woodward told me to go and capture it. I got together helicopters, commandos, marine engineers to get the trawlers' engines working, and medics to treat the injured, plus a Harrier to ensure the helicopters wouldn't be shot down. With planning and briefing, this took some time.

But after they'd taken off, London informed us that the Argentine spy vessel had surrendered, but the helicopters were flying low level and out of radio contact, so we couldn't tell them. The escorting Harrier was told to pass this on to the marine commander in the helicopter, but it took a long time.

Eventually they abseiled on to the deck of the spy ship, to find one man killed from the bomb, and the engines unable to run. Twenty-four Argentine fisherman were on board, commanded by an Argentine lieutenant commander, who'd commandeered the vessel at pistol point in Argentina. On searching the vessel, the commandos found all this officer's charts and intelligence reports, so no matter what the Argentines might say about this being an innocent vessel, we had the proof. But having no communication with the assault force, I knew nothing of this, and it seemed like an age, particularly as we knew the helicopters would be running out of fuel.

The Argentines refused to believe that the *Invincible* was still afloat, their authorities having announced its sinking several times. The fishermen were incarcerated in the ship's chapel; we fed them and buried the dead one, and a hospital ship took them and some wounded back to Argentina. But very interestingly, we subsequently intercepted a radio call from their intelligence lieutenant commander reporting back to headquarters on what he'd seen of our ship. I was very impressed with the detail of his observations: the number of aircraft and so on, gleaned from just one walk to and from our flight deck. This taught me a lot about the handling of prisoners, and what they should be allowed to see. An intelligence officer is, of course, a professional, trying to take it all in.

Captain Hugh Maxwell Balfour
HMS Exeter

The Argentines had aircraft stationed at airfields very large distances apart, and with the need to train and plan, it took time for them to generate more attacks. All the intelligence efforts back in UK to determine how many Exocets they had, and frustrate any plans to buy more, were taking effect. We thought they probably had just one left. Then on May 26, there was another, and very serious, Argentine air attack.

Captain Carlos B. Castro Madero
Weapons Officer, 5-Inch Anti-Aircraft Batteries, Warship Belgrano

We had bought only five AM Exocet missiles from the French in a package deal. When we had this problem with the British, the French technicians working on the system left us. Our engineers had to finish off. Two missiles were thrown in the operation that hit *Sheffield*. Two more were thrown in the *Atlantic Conveyor* operation, and so we had one left, an AM-39, for use against aircraft carriers.

Captain Hugh Maxwell Balfour
HMS Exeter

On the afternoon of May 30 we were on our south-west station, one hundred and fifty miles east of the Falklands, and were alerted to an incoming raid. The flag signalled us to stand down, then thirty seconds later we detected two sweeps of an Etendard radar. Our electronic warfare equipment was very close to me, and the operator had a whistle round his neck, which he blows and everybody shuts up. He blew his whistle.

A raid was due south, well away from the carriers, flying north towards us. A Type 42 has two 909 J band radars with a very narrow pencil beam, which you lock on to the target once you've located it, using the broader search radar. If you lock on very quickly, the attackers will hear a warning and break off. I'd worked with the Argentines, and from Portland training they knew that our system worked and that we made good use of it. There were two aircraft. I think they'd come up, had a look without seeing anything, got locked on and flew low level again for about twenty-eight miles. I think they came up again, had another look and released the missile. And because this was their last Exocet, they also sent in four Skyhawks to distract the defences, which was a most exciting, enterprising mission, requiring a lot of refuelling. A good, brave operation by anybody's standards.

My first personal problem was controlling myself, to allow my team to get on with the job. It was like dying. I seemed to have all the time in the world, but it seemed to take forever. I think I was cursing.

But there occurred a strange safety problem, with HMS *Avenger* off to do a night bombardment, and a Lynx helicopter, both smack on the same bearing as the incoming attack. The Lynx thought we'd locked on to her, so we shouted at her to freeze and climb; so I was happy we wouldn't hit them. But would we hit *Avenger*? Safety in war is just as important as in peace.

I decided to give the ship's company a description of what was going on: telling them the number of seconds to impact, to count and if they got to zero without a bang they would have survived – which caused a degree of mirth.

We fired the first Sea Dart missile, then a second, hitting one A4 fifteen miles out, and the second A4 at about seven miles. I decided I was just going to have to go for it, or somebody like *Avenger* or us was going to get sunk. I didn't know what the missile profile was, so I just prayed to God and fired.

We became aware of the additional A4s when *Avenger* reported being bombed. Modern operations rooms are always blind, not knowing if it's day or dark, relying on reports from the bridge – but at the crucial moment I hadn't asked for a feed of information from them. We turned downwind, accelerated to twenty knots and were still covered and unrecognisable in the efflux from the missiles, which I think the surviving Argentine pilot saw and led him to believe that they'd sunk *Invincible*.

Captain Carlos B. Castro Madero
Weapons Officer, 5-Inch Anti-Aircraft Batteries, Warship Belgrano

We had information about a main ship in a certain position, so we sent four A4s from the air force and a navy Super Etendard. They had to make two air-to-air refuellings, a very risky operation. But the A4s have no radar, so the Super Etendard used its radar and threw the missile, which is fire-and-forget. The missile detected the ship and the A4s followed it so they could bomb the ship as well. But the Exocet missile was shot down, along with two A4s; and the other two A4s said they bombed *Invincible* and returned to Argentina. But it was a great operation – with very brave pilots.

Lieutenant Commander Graham John Edmonds
Operations Officer and Squadron Warfare Officer, HMS Broadsword

If I have any criticism of Argentine pilots, it's that they're even worse at embellishing their stories than Royal Navy pilots. They even have a painting hanging in one of their navy messes of an Exocet hitting the *Invincible* and setting it on fire – which is a great mystery. By claiming to have hit *Invincible* during this mission, they had to assume that our air defences were in chaos, so further Argentine planning based on this presumption would lead to further disaster for them – which may be a reason so many of their aircraft were lost. Their pilots were arriving at what they'd been told was a defeated task group, only to find the opposite, making it even harder for them to cope with the stress of their attacks. They often chose the prudent way out, turning for home.

Captain Hugh Maxwell Balfour
HMS Exeter
I'd been down to ten Sea Dart missiles from twenty, and now was down to seven, and I didn't know when I could resupply, and also there were two Harriers chasing the remaining Argentine aircraft, so I decided not to risk shooting them down, and let the Argentines go. I sometimes think it would have been a really good day had we shot them down, but in the event it was a bit like missing the last two pheasants on a drive. It all took six minutes and was most interesting. We were very proud our ship had done so well. Then my steward Petty Officer Allen came in with a large glass of whisky, which I downed with a shaky hand, while wondering how he could have been so quick. I found out a few days later that he'd taken cover in my cabin, and having taken a glass of whisky to steady himself, thought it rather unfair and had brought me one, too.

We believed this was the last Exocet, but without being sure, Admiral Woodward couldn't bring us all inshore, which would have made quite a difference to the land battle.

Part Three

FIGHTING FOR THE FALKLANDS

In the outside world, General Haig's mediation effort was officially terminated on April 30. President Ronald Reagan openly declared US support for Britain, and imposed economic sanctions against Argentina.

On May 2, 1982 the president of Peru presented a peace plan, which Argentine President General Galtieri indicated he might sign after modification. Britain saw this as an opportunity for yet more Argentine prevarication, while in the South Atlantic the weather deteriorated, and, along with it, Britain's chances of making a landing on the islands. The Argentine fleet was at sea, evidently seeking to attack the British task force. The Peru peace initiative to all intents and purposes ended with the sinking of the Argentine cruiser *Belgrano* by the British submarine *Conqueror*.

Then on May 7, five weeks after the Argentine invasion of the Falklands, the United Nations started its own peace negotiations.

On May 9, after the initial British imposition of the total exclusion zone and the first attacks of May 1 on Argentine forces on the Falkland Islands, British forces again bombarded the islands, and two sea Harriers sank the Argentine trawler *Narwhal*. Then on May 11, the Argentine supply ship *Isla de los Estados* was sunk by British warship HMS *Alacrity*.

On May 14, six weeks after the Argentine invasion of the Falklands, Prime Minister Thatcher warned that a peaceful settlement might no longer be possible, on advice from her military commanders that the time frame within which successful operations could take place before the onset of winter was growing very short. Four days later, the United Nations Secretary-General, Perez de Cuellar, presented his peace proposal, which Mrs Thatcher rejected on the grounds that it was too little, too late.

13

Landing
in Bomb Alley

*Once we decided there was no submarine threat, we packed ships
very close together, under the shelter of a bluff of land about
eight hundred feet high, which was just high enough to
disturb the aircraft as they came in to attack.*

Major Simon Ewen Southby-Tailyour
Royal Marines
I'd chosen the beaches, and then I led the landing craft assault. That was right
and proper. I was the senior landing craft officer in the Royal Marines. I
wanted to do it because of my love affair with the islands, and it was a great
joy to me to lead the landings and lead the way down to San Carlos in the first
place, on to the beach. It was very straightforward, something I'd been doing
all my service career, for twenty-eight-odd years. I didn't give much thought
to what would happen after we landed.

Captain Jeremy Larken
HMS Fearless
The landing site at San Carlos had been chosen through taking the opinions
of various people, then decided ultimately by the War Cabinet back in the
UK. It was the ideal and obvious choice, which didn't seem to have occurred
to the Argentines, who seemed to be of the more myopic variety. I think they
believed that in order to take Stanley we would have to land near it.

Captain Christopher Charles Brown
148 Commando Forward Observation Unit, Royal Artillery
We mounted a diversionary raid in preparation for the landings, as part of the deception plan. This involved D Squadron SAS attacking the Argentine garrison at Darwin Goose Green, giving the impression that this was the main landing area, whilst the actual landings took place to the north around San Carlos Bay. We were to attack the outskirts of the settlement.

Chief Petty Officer Lionel Norman Kurn
Helicopter artificer, HMS Antrim
Our next operation was landing a team of special forces into the area of Fanning Head before the landings, to take out an Argentine unit that threatened the landings. Two Wessex 5s were to work from our deck, one fitted with special thermal-imaging equipment to locate the Argentine unit.

Captain Dennis John Scott-Masson
SS Canberra
Canberra was designed to advertise itself, with enormous windows and masses of light flooding out of them, so blacking out the whole ship was a mammoth task, using miles of black canvas to cover the hundreds of portholes and windows. There was always one light shining brightly over the ocean, until after a week or so, we finally became invisible.

(James) Robert Fox
BBC correspondent
As we got closer the weather got worse, making people much grimmer and more tense, but I vividly remember one sunny afternoon, and the marines going out on deck to sharpen their bayonets. It was an extraordinary sound, the endless scraping of a farm worker sharpening his sickle or pruning hook on a wet stone.

Captain Jeremy Larken
HMS Fearless
We arrived in the battle zone to the east of the Falklands on May 19. We had a two- or three-week 'window of opportunity' to get ashore and move forward towards our objectives. It was clear we were going to move very quickly. It was too risky to send *Canberra* forward containing three of our five infantry battalions, so we had to extract two and place them inside other ships. We also needed suitable bad weather within which to approach the islands, reducing our vulnerability to air attack.

Petty Officer Brandon Christopher Smith
HMS Fearless
There were rough seas and a lot of people were seasick in a very heavy swell, which was worse because the flat bottom of *Fearless* made it roll so much. One of my lads was very ill, and I left him in a bay to try and sleep through it.

Captain Jeremy Larken
HMS Fearless
Fate was really on our side, for when we arrived at the task group, the weather was calm enough to allow us to dock down *Fearless* and *Intrepid* in open ocean – an evolution only carried out in port or sheltered coastal waters. During the day we used the landing craft to extract the two battalions from *Canberra* into *Fearless* and *Intrepid* respectively. But we lost sixteen men from 22 SAS in a very tragic helicopter accident. The next day we had very bad visibility, yet not excessively unpleasant sea conditions, to cover our sea approach to the landing area. We made a zigzag track towards Port Stanley, then, late in the day, veered off to the north in very poor visibility, then in the night descended to our real landing area, entering Falkland Sound and San Carlos.

Brigadier Julian Howard Thompson
Commander, 3 Commando Brigade
I wanted to land just after last light, to give us time to be ready for the inevitable arrival of the Argentine air force next morning. But that would have meant the whole of the approach run to the islands taking place in daylight, which would be very dangerous. The naval preference was to land at first light, so we came to a compromise whereby only the last and most dangerous approach was done at night, with the landings at midnight GMT. London made the decision and signalled this to us, which I passed on to all the ships.

However, *Norland*, containing 2 Para, had faulty signals equipment (the literaliser) and couldn't decode this message. We were in total radio silence, zigzagging in close assault formation, communicating only by signal lamp, with *Norland* wondering what on earth was going on. She flashed us a signal saying: 'Do you know something we don't?' HMS *Broadsword* shot a paper copy of the signal to *Norland* using a Costan Gunline, a rifle which shoots a line over attached to a canister which you drag across – so they knew the landings were the next day. Luckily fog and drizzle concealed all of the daylight part of our approach, and as it got dark, the skies cleared and the stars came out.

A unit of Argentine troops with recoilless anti-tank guns were on Fanning Head, in a position to sink ships as they entered San Carlos Water. This task was allocated to a naval gunfire forward observation team and the SBS, on the night of D Day, May 20/21. So as we steamed south to the entrance to San Carlos Water, we could see the flashes of naval gunfire and tracer from the gun battle up there. We'd also sent an SAS squadron to duff up Darwin Goose Green, pretending that was where we were trying to land. Radio intelligence intercepts revealed the Argentines reporting they were fighting off a battalion attack.

Chief Petty Officer Terence Bullingham
Fleet Air Arm, HMS Antrim
The night before the landings, a naval gunfire forward observation team with SBS and some SAS were embarked, and totally black, we slipped quietly in towards the islands. There was a hill on the way in, where it was rumoured to be a company of over a hundred Argentine marines, which would interfere with the operation and so could not be allowed to continue existing. The SBS were to be inserted using the ubiquitous Wessex 5s – flying lorries. When the first Wessex 5 arrived, the SBS got in, and an inexperienced pilot took off, then immediately landed back on. He wasn't used to landing on small decks, and in the total darkness, didn't re-land in the right place, his tail wheel hanging almost in space, by good luck sitting on an overhanging lamp housing. We were praying that this lamp would continue to take the weight of the tail of the aircraft. His starboard wheel was way over, nearly on the edge of the deck, so if it slipped he'd be into the sea. This wasn't just a Wessex, but was filled with troops. Eventually the pilot got himself together, lifted the collective and got them all safely out of it – thank goodness! That would have been awful . . .

Company Sergeant Major Peter John Richens
B Company, 2 Para
We didn't know which day we'd be landing, so being woken by the *Ride of the Valkyries*, our regimental march, was a good hint, then a church service, which we enjoyed.

David Cooper
Chaplain, 2 Para
We were all bombed up and camouflaged, and the *Norland*'s forward lounge was totally packed. Everyone just piled in, with none of the usual officers sitting at the front.

Members of 2 Para waiting on board *Norland*, before the assault on May 21, 1982, in San Carlos Water.

I told them I didn't believe in a God of causes, but in a God who cares for every individual, who has the capacity for that care to extend beyond the grave. I said that whether or not you pray isn't going to divert the path of a bullet, and that you take your chances along with the next man, but that God would still care for you whatever happened.

(James) Robert Fox
BBC correspondent
British soldiers are only interesting to me when they are preparing to do something real. The social side I found tedious. It was only when the action started that one felt one ought to bond with these people – for one's own mental and physical survival.

David Cooper
Chaplain, 2 Para
We drew the remainder of our ammunition and hand grenades, prepared our weapons and got finally ready. I made myself a flask of coffee, and tried to get a bottle of whisky – my icebreaker. Soldiers knew me, and were always happy to share a nip from the hip flask, even if a visit from the vicar wasn't what they'd been expecting. But the barman wasn't allowed to sell bottles – only tots, to mitigate possible drunkenness. My problem was solved by Robert Fox who, not being a soldier, was allowed to buy bottles.

H Jones had insisted that I took ashore three or four wooden crosses, two feet or so high. I thought this totally unnecessary. I asked the pioneers to make them for me, which they thought macabre and pessimistic, and I hid them inside my pack.

Captain Jeremy Larken
HMS Fearless
We were a little late entering San Carlos Water due to a navigational error, which rather upset me. Time is of the essence in these things. Then it took more time to dock down and get the troops into the landing craft.

Chief Petty Officer Terence Bullingham
Fleet Air Arm, HMS Antrim
At about two in the morning the naval gunfire forward observer ordered us to fire two sighters from our forward twin 4.5-inch gun. Then he ordered 'Fire for Effect' – which is the sort of thing you only get to see in films, 4.5-inch shells streaking away from us towards this hill, Fanning Head,

which the forward observer ashore used to make the Argentines come running away from their own guns, towards where the SBS and SAS were waiting to get them in their ever-eager grips . . . I don't know exactly what happened, but suffice it to say that the Argentine marine company was no longer a threat.

Captain Donald Arthur Ellerby
MV Norland

We moved under darkness to San Carlos, navigating with charts, using short bursts of radar when we were close in. We were told where we had to go, the route to take and we got on with it. Later we were told we'd sailed under some heavy artillery positions. We heard and saw the naval gunfire, but I was so intent on what I was doing I didn't take much notice. It wasn't frightening, but it was different to what I was used to doing – and nerve-wracking.

David Cooper
Chaplain, 2 Para

We waited for ages sitting on our packs, until making our way down to the car deck in an interminable line. We were all carrying far too much, eighty-pound packs, but some, like the radio operators, were well over one hundred pounds. I carried as much saline fluid and medical supplies as I could lift, plus a large number of smoke grenades so helicopters could see us to pick up casualties. We didn't know how the Argentines would react or when we would be resupplied, so we took enough to deal with all eventualities.

Captain Christopher Charles Brown
148 Commando Forward Observation Unit, Royal Artillery

In the early hours of May 21, my naval gunfire team with sixty-odd men from D Squadron SAS, laden to the gunwales with all manner of weapons and ammunition, clambered into helicopters and were dropped north of Darwin, intending to create the impression that we were a much larger force. We attacked four separate targets with everything we had: mortars, rockets, machine guns, and naval gunfire from HMS Glamorgan. They did nothing, rather than react positively. At dawn we pulled out to the north. I damaged their Pucara aircraft on the ground at Darwin airfield with naval gunfire from HMS Ardent. One managed to take off and dropped its bombs in the area where we'd been five minutes earlier. We surprised the pilot by shooting him down with Stinger anti-aircraft missiles as he was flying away. He bailed out but his aircraft was destroyed. Signals intercept traffic afterwards revealed that the Argentinians believed they were under attack from the main force, which was our intention.

The most frightening part was nothing to do with the enemy, but later in the day, returning back through our own lines. 2 Para had landed and were securing the Sussex Mountains from San Carlos, so we had to move back through their lines. We suspected, with some justification, that they might be trigger-happy, so we waited until it got light.

Petty Officer Brandon Christopher Smith
HMS *Fearless*
The night we entered San Carlos there was a lot of firing, but I was still sure we weren't going to do any fighting. When I went up to the flight deck, I thought I was back in Scotland.

Staff Sergeant Richard James Elliott
REME, 3 *Commando Brigade Air Squadron*
We heard the machine guns firing on Fanning Head as the SBS cleared a company or more of Argentines out of there. We prepared the helicopters for flying, ready to take off at dawn to fly ashore. The next day, the remnants of this Argentine company managed to shoot down two of our helicopters.

Company Sergeant Major Peter John Richens
B *Company, 2 Para*
We'd allowed one hour to get the battalion off the ship, into the landing craft and away to do what we hoped would be an unopposed beach landing. But the sea was very rough, with the boats moving up and down a long way, so we had to judge when to jump with all our kit. This process took about five hours, and as B Company embarked early, we had a three-hour wait on the water in the landing craft, until the others were ready to leave.

Major Philip Neame
D *Company Commander, 2 Para*
Don Ellerby, a grizzled sea dog, had become our father figure, and when we finally went ashore in the Falklands, he came up on the ship's broadcast in a very simple, moving way, saying how much they'd enjoyed having us as passengers, to have a good time ashore and above all, to return safe and sound so they could take us back home again. He did this in his usual cruising style, thanking us for travelling with them and so on. While ashore, *Norland* was in our thoughts as the mother ship – the womb we all wanted to return to.

Company Sergeant Major Peter John Richens
B Company, 2 Para
There was one accident, when a soldier caught his sub-machine gun as he jumped, which cocked itself and shot him in the thigh. Then the CO's landing craft, which was to have been first ashore, had a mechanical problem which displeased him no end, so we were the first ashore. He did a lot of ranting, raving and shouting, but that's the way it went.

Major Simon Ewen Southby-Tailyour
Royal Marines
Once we'd got everybody embarked in the ships, the beautifully timed plan which I'd prepared with meticulous accuracy, because I am also a navigator, had to be abandoned. We were to have skirted the kelp which I thought would avoid mines, but by the time we crossed the start line, which we in the landing craft branch call the 'Line of Departure' or 'LOD', I threw the timings to the wind and ordered full speed straight down the middle, and sod it for the mines.

(James) Robert Fox
BBC correspondent
After two hours in the open boats going down the Sound, we landed peacefully as expected. I talked into my microphone, which became one of the most famous broadcasts; then there was this awful, brilliant, surrealist dawn with a very bright star which showed up everybody in silhouette.

David Cooper
Chaplain, 2 Para
We were ordered to make ready, and had been told that only rifles, not automatic weapons, were to be cocked. But when one of the Blowpipe detachment soldiers in front of me tried to cock his sub-machine gun, the cocking handle slipped out of his fingers and he fired a round into the deck. After the bang, I asked if everybody was all right, and there was no reply, and then a marine came down the side of the landing craft asking, 'Who stopped that one? Is anybody injured?' And again there was no reply. So the whole thing was ignored. We then grounded, and because we'd been told the landing craft could be lifted by the swell and come further inshore, we were hesitant at getting out.

Company Sergeant Major Peter John Richens
B Company, 2 Para
When the doors at the front of the landing craft went down, nobody

understood the marines shouting 'Out Troops', so at the critical moment everybody was staring at each other. In the Parachute Regiment the word of command for everything, stemming from jumping out of aeroplanes, is 'Go!' which I shouted and everybody understood. But the Royal Marines dropped us one hundred and fifty metres off the beach. When I stepped off the landing craft ramp, I went into the water up to my chest – and I'm six foot tall. My radio operator was six inches shorter, so I had to grab him by his bergan and keep him up as much as I could.

Major John Harry Crosland
B Company Commander, 2 Para

We got going up Sussex Mountain. I left my second in command, Captain John Young, to sort out the company, and walked off to liase with A Company. I saw two figures wearing white headbands – the sign of advance force units, so I let them get close to me before challenging. They were very surprised to see us, and were not expecting anybody to land for another three days.

Major Philip Neame
D Company Commander, 2 Para

There'd been a lot of small things go wrong which undermined our confidence a bit, and H was throwing tracks at the slowness of it all.

David Cooper
Chaplain, 2 Para

We set off towards Sussex Mountain and waded another stream, where a mortar man collapsed from heat exhaustion. As daylight came, we were nowhere near the top, and another soldier fell over and damaged his back. We carried him and all his kit in a groundsheet, which was impossible. I asked our adjutant to get him out, and he suggested waving down one of the helicopters that were flying overhead. All they did was wave back, so I told David Wood we had to make a proper request for casualty evacuation, and a helicopter arrived quite quickly.

Captain Donald Arthur Ellerby
MV Norland

When the sun came up we saw this plane coming towards us. The ships fired cannons and missiles that just missed us. I think it was the first time some of these ships had fired, but there was no damage done.

2 Para progressing from the beach up onto Sussex Mountain on May 21, 1982.

Captain Jeremy Larken
HMS Fearless

We knew when air attacks were coming, but the first one was a scene of great chaos. People hadn't settled down, guns going off in all directions, missiles whistling around . . . I watched a Sea Cat said to have come from *Intrepid* passing close down the side of my ship. We were extremely lucky not to have inflicted damage on ourselves – blue-on-blue as it's called.

Air Vice Commodore Carlos Bloomer-Reeve
Secretary General, Islas Malvinas

We had something they call Red de Observadores del Aire volunteers, who we mobilise into temporary military personnel. We placed these volunteer observers at places where there are small hills, with a radio. If an observer sees anything then we send a plane to investigate. These observers were able to bring in our air attacks very quickly. It worked very well, first for our air force, and then with information for the rest of our armed forces. But our radio equipment was not so good as some of the local radio equipment the islanders had, so we requested all the islanders who had equipment or radios to bring them to our communications centre. This was good for two reasons: first we prevented the islanders using the radios, and second we could use their radios for our benefit.

Captain Dennis John Scott-Masson
SS Canberra

As daylight came, an Argentine Pucara flew into San Carlos Water firing his cannon at us. This was our baptism of fire, and was quite frightening. We'd just anchored and I was on the bridge, but he turned away before getting to us and didn't score any hits. But he'd obviously reported that were we there, and it wasn't long until the first air attack arrived. We felt extraordinarily vulnerable, as we still hadn't been able to paint out our bright yellow funnels, which seemed to get brighter and cleaner every day. Our glistening white hull, although now rust-streaked, was still fairly obvious, and we were enormous, dwarfing every other ship and the land around us. *Canberra* is forty-five thousand gross tons, and the height-of-eye on the bridge is one hundred and ten feet, one of the highest in the world.

Air Vice Commodore Carlos Bloomer-Reeve
Secretary General, Islas Malvinas

When the British ships came into San Carlos, one of our two observers there, a military man Stefan, a hero, reported, so we sent two small navy planes to find out if it was true what he was saying. The two planes couldn't believe all the ships they saw. They fired all the ammunition they had on board, I think hitting nobody, and came back to town. Without Stefan and another air force-trained civilian on the other side of the water at San Carlos, it would have been a very easy job for the British to move in and finish without any opposition.

John Keith 'Jake' Watson
Chaplain, HMS Broadsword

At action stations when things were quiet, I moved around the ship talking to people, especially below the waterline in compartments that were unpleasant to be in: the steering compartment at the back, the engine room and so on. However, on the first morning in San Carlos I was on the bridge and saw a dot coming over the hills, which expanded into two dots, then our Sea Wolf system fired, taking out one of the dots, which by now was a plane, and the pilot parachuted out. The second plane fired at us with a cannon, and then was away over the hills. One minute later, I saw another plane, but nothing more as my head was on the floor.

People had been injured down the rear of the ship, so I went to the wardroom to help the doctor, who was extracting shrapnel and bandaging people up. One young man had his back peppered with small pieces. A senior rate had a piece of shrapnel the size of a chocolate egg which went through his boot and up his leg as far as the knee; another's head was covered in blood.

Lieutenant Commander Graham John Edmonds
Operations Officer and Squadron Warfare Officer, HMS Broadsword

We received an air attack quite early, a Mirage 5 Dagger coming across West Falkland towards us. Our Sea Wolf fired in automatic mode before I was aware there was an aircraft. The pilot ejected just as the missile went up his air intake, although ejecting into a cold sea during a battle indicated that he probably wasn't going to survive. Brilliant was quite badly damaged by cannon fire, affecting her operational capability, which she concealed from the admiral for some time.

Captain Jeremy Larken
HMS Fearless

I had a good view towards Fanning Head from within the anchorage, and saw three aircraft descend on the Argonaut, which was not far offshore. She was completely enveloped in an explosion and a huge cloud of smoke and spray. I was very relieved as it all cleared, to see that she wasn't all that different, although we later discovered she was quite badly damaged. She stabilised herself without power, and managed to anchor. I had her towed into the heart of the anchorage using landing craft, where she was able to use her weapon systems, and we helped patch her up, until she could make her own way out to the holding area and be patched up enough to get home.

Chief Petty Officer David John 'Fritz' Heritier
Fleet Air Arm, HMS Antrim
Humphrey had some electrical problems, and Terry Bullingham, our electrician, was working on the aircraft, up the side of the flight deck, just outside the hangar door.

Chief Petty Officer Lionel Norman Kurn
Helicopter artificer, HMS Antrim
I finally realised this was a real operation while watching Pucara aircraft attacking the ships. I was quite astounded that this could happen. We'd been told the Falkland Islands were too far away from the Argentine mainland for their air force to be a threat. But there they were – so it clearly wasn't true.

Chief Petty Officer Terence Bullingham
Fleet Air Arm, HMS Antrim
Two little propeller-driven Pucara aircraft bombed *Ardent*. First it was splashes in the water, and then it was hits with orange flashes. These aircraft dodged back behind the hills so we saw hardly anything of them. With a sickening realisation, we realised that our ships' weapon systems used radar, which couldn't lock on to any aircraft lurking behind the hills of San Carlos, so we were impotent.

Chief Petty Officer David John 'Fritz' Heritier
Fleet Air Arm, HMS Antrim
About mid morning, another Pucara came skipping across, rolling over the headland and disappearing very quickly. Then A4 Skyhawks were on us, coming straight down the Sound. The ship was turning at full power. They came astern, going for us. I was standing by the door and the flight commander suddenly shoved me down into the fuel space where we made a big bundle on the floor.

The two A4s hammered over the top of the ship with tremendous roaring, leaving the back of the ship enveloped in steam. Our pyrotechnic locker, where we kept flares, marker marines, phosphorus and other nasty things, was pouring smoke. We had fire hoses rigged anyway, as we were at flying stations. We didn't know a bomb had gone into the ship, and assumed this was a fire below decks, so we commenced boundary cooling to stop it spreading. We had no other information, but could hear damage reports over the ship's tannoy as search teams went round the ship. We couldn't find the key to the pyro locker, so I smashed it off with a hammer and hurt my hand, discovering there wasn't a fire, just steam from a calorifier. The unexploded bomb was discovered in the bathroom just below our feet. The damage control party wedged it so it wouldn't roll around.

Chief Petty Officer Terence Bullingham
Fleet Air Arm, HMS Antrim

While we were trying to stem the fire, two Mirage 5 Daggers came down the length of the ships in a coordinated attack firing their 40mm cannon.

Chief Petty Officer David John 'Fritz' Heritier
Fleet Air Arm, HMS Antrim

It was unreal. Calm blue sea, the ship was going flat out, turning hard to starboard to evade. The two aircraft closed on to us and followed us on the turn. I was trying to identify them and noticed the water between the aircraft and the ship becoming alive, in two parallel lines. I realised they were tracking us and firing guns. I was facing astern and they were banking to starboard to follow the ship round.

I was standing next to Terry Bullingham. I remembered thinking Daggers have guns mounted on their bottom, and as they are banking, those guns are pointing upwards, moving away from the port side of the ship – so I'm going on to the port side to hide behind the superstructure. Half the flight had come to the same conclusion and came with me.

Chief Petty Officer Terence Bullingham
Fleet Air Arm, HMS Antrim

They were going really low, just below the speed of sound. My eye was taken from the aircraft themselves to what they were producing. Below the aircraft I could see a straight line of splashes in the water every six feet – stitching the water.

Chief Petty Officer David John 'Fritz' Heritier
Fleet Air Arm, HMS Antrim

The flight commander was diving into the fuel locker again, but I'd already done that and didn't like being among all that fuel. One of the other petty officers managed to get all the way into the hangar, which I didn't think was possible.

Chief Petty Officer Lionel Norman Kurn
Helicopter artificer, HMS Antrim

I was pulled over to one side by another crew member, then fortunately decided to run down the starboard side of ship and avoided being hit, unlike other members of the flight deck crew.

Chief Petty Officer Terence Bullingham
Fleet Air Arm, HMS Antrim

Time stands still on these occasions, and realising the aircraft were pointing at me like the proverbial finger of fate, I got myself down and went into the foetal position, as everyone on the flight deck was spreading out . . . Then I felt a sickening impact like smashing your head in a car crash – much more than just being punched in the face or anything like that. I didn't lose consciousness, but the obvious expletive came from my lips, as it did from colleagues either side of me who'd also been hit. I went down like a sack of proverbial potatoes. That was the last I saw – ever.

Chief Petty Officer David John 'Fritz' Heritier
Fleet Air Arm, HMS Antrim

I don't know what happened with Terry to be honest, whether he froze, or was fascinated. I think he just stood and watched. There was an almighty roaring and these aircraft went straight over the top in reheat, afterburners going – a tremendous noise; they were actually climbing to get over the ship. I looked up the starboard waist of the ship and saw two white things in the sky, realising they were bombs with parachutes, and the ship was turning towards them. They just missed the bow and landed in the sea. But as I walked back to the flight deck I noticed the Sea Slug launcher was glowing with heat, and loaded with two war shots. Then it fired.

Chief Petty Officer Terence Bullingham
Fleet Air Arm, HMS Antrim

I remember seeing the two Mirage 5s as they came down alongside us, but after I went down, there was nothing – not even a red mist. I was just lying stunned. I remember doing a mental check, and felt pain in my legs and arms, nothing in the torso, but my mind was preoccupied with this sight thing. There were people on the flight deck who hadn't been hit, screaming on the intercom for a doctor.

Chief Petty Officer David John 'Fritz' Heritier
Fleet Air Arm, HMS Antrim

You're not normally on the flight deck when they fire these things because of the shock and blast. I thought: 'Blimey what are they going to do to us next?' Luckily for us on the flight deck, the missile was aimed off to starboard, so the jet efflux went over the ship's side. Had it been aimed astern, it would have blasted everyone off the flight deck. I watched the missile go down the Sound after the aircraft, but discovered afterwards they'd fired it blind as a last-ditch attempt to do something. I watched the aircraft go over the hill and disappear. I turned round the corner and walked on to the flight deck to see Terry lying on his back with his hands across his face and blood running down the flight deck from him. I went over to him. He said: 'I've been hit.' I said: 'I can tell that, you daft bugger. There's blood everywhere,' and pulled his hands away. His face was not a pretty sight at all.

Chief Petty Officer Terence Bullingham
Fleet Air Arm, HMS Antrim

When a colleague turned me over he said he thought my face had gone, but it was only blood from my eye sockets. A piece of shrapnel had gone into my left eye, but the concussion from the shell hitting the bulkhead two feet away from my head had also ruptured my right eye. But I didn't know this at the time. Goodness knows what would have happened to me if hadn't have been wearing double-skin, double-glazed goggles and an American-issue flight deck helmet, padded with fibreglass shells. Colleagues told me my helmet was literally full of shrapnel. If I hadn't been wearing it, I would have been dead.

Chief Petty Officer David John 'Fritz' Heritier
Fleet Air Arm, HMS Antrim

The flight observer came and took over with Terry, while I started looking at the damage. The flight deck was covered in debris and the aircraft was stitched full of holes. Other aircrew had also been hit by shrapnel, so we got on the phone and said: 'This is serious, get the medics here now,' and took Terry on a stretcher to the clearing station in the ward room.

Chief Petty Officer Terence Bullingham
Fleet Air Arm, HMS Antrim

Fosters, to my left, had been hit in the arm, and the petty officer air crewman to my right had been hit in the area of the prostate by shrapnel, which isn't a very nice area to be hit, which he was announcing loudly . . . A sergeant in the Royal Marines on the forward gun director position had picked up shrapnel in the lungs, liver and kidneys. There were also people below us hit as the 40mm cannon shells went through the decks. There was a lot of disruption, shouting, adrenalin, but not much panic, and a lot of people, *hors de combat*, injured – not seriously, but who would take no further part in proceedings.

Chief Petty Officer Lionel Norman Kurn
Helicopter artificer, HMS Antrim
It's surprising how a door or a fitting can insulate you from the action. I'd run down the starboard side, only a few metres away. Seeing some of the injuries inflicted on other members of our flight had quite an effect on me.

Chief Petty Officer David John 'Fritz' Heritier
Fleet Air Arm, HMS Antrim
We came under attack again. The aircraft had taken a lot of hits and fuel was leaking out and we were more worried about fire, so we covered the flight deck with foam. We debated pushing it over the side, but it weighed ten and a half tons and half a dozen of us couldn't do it. I de-fuelled the helicopter by throwing a long hose over the side to siphon the fuel out of its tank as we steamed along.

Chief Petty Officer Terence Bullingham
Fleet Air Arm, HMS Antrim
The ship's doctor saw me within two minutes, so I didn't suffer. Talking with paras who'd come from the shore, I know they suffered terribly. I was given morphia and the doc said he had to get me off the ship. The casualty station was the wardroom, and I remember lying in the floor wearing nothing but a pair of knicks. I used to drink with the petty officer medical officer, and I said to him: 'Steve I can't see.'

He said: 'You've just got a pair of black eyes, Terry.'

I thought to myself: 'Steve, you're a lying bastard . . .'

He was obviously wondering how to tell a guy his eyes were gone, and then there was obviously not the time to tell me.

Captain Jeremy Larken
HMS Fearless
I spent the first attack in the operations room not enjoying myself. I decided that trying to fight the ship open-ocean style from the operations room was not going to work. It was small and old, packed with the Commodore and his

staff, with radars that were not very good for looking through land features. By the second attack I was up on the gun direction platform, with two missile specialists, controlling our four ancient Sea Cat missiles. A lot of our people were very young – a number had their seventeenth birthdays when we were down south. They were very impressive; young men don't seem to be troubled by this sort of thing. Keeping an old Bofors gun firing successfully round after round requires coolness and good drill.

Commander Nigel David 'Sharkey' Ward
Officer Commanding 801 Squadron, Fleet Air Arm, HMS Invincible

The first guy I shot down was on May 21, the morning of the San Carlos landings. His name was Major Tombo. There were three of us on patrol rather than the usual two, as the reinforcement pilots from *Atlantic Conveyor* were making their first trips. It was the end of our patrol; we were climbing out at fifteen thousand feet, when the control ship HMS *Antrim* reported a slow moving contact overland fifteen miles to the south of us, and asked did we want to investigate. We were turning before the end of the message. Steven Thomas saw two Pucaras at low level over land, which you can't usually see until about two or three miles. On the first run I came from the back quite fast and hit it with my guns. I could see cannon shells chewing through the right aileron and the right engine was on fire, so I thought that's good news, what's he going to do now? I pulled off and jinked to get behind him again, while Steve and Alastair were coming in from the other side. They missed again.

He was sticking with it. We were between ten and fifty feet above the ground, and he was weaving gently to put my tracking off. I fired and hit his left engine this time, and some bits of fuselage came off, but still he didn't get out, so I came in for a third run, and all sorts of pieces dropped off, the canopy shattered and both engines were on fire.

It was like a World War Two film, with the aircraft disintegrating in front of the camera and going past you. I'd run out of 30mm ammunition when he ejected with his rocket seat, and the aircraft went into the deck. He was a really brave man sticking with it all that time. I hoped he would make it back. I heard later that he'd yomped back to Goose Green some thirty miles away, to be captured by the paras. Afterwards he sent me a Pucara sticker – which was nice.

Captain Dennis John Scott-Masson
SS Canberra

The air attacks continued throughout the day, while we continued discharging equipment by LCU and helicopter. Then finally at about ten o'clock in the morning, they decided our remaining commando battalion should be landed, to which they responded with great enthusiasm and alacrity. There's nothing a marine dislikes more than being on a ship under air attack, where he can't dig trenches and hide himself. We also had a public room converted into a field hospital, and received our first three wounded Argentines.

Michael Thomas Nicholson
ITN correspondent
I realised this was not a television war. Our film was going to take four weeks to get back to UK, so I had to do something else. I stuck close to the radio ships in the bay, and tried to do daily 'phonos' back to London and so managed to be on air every day. These 'phonos' were descriptive pieces of about eight minutes. I tried to paint the picture in words. In radio, you've got to bring the *smell* of it to the listener. People came up to me afterwards saying how they'd *seen* various reports I'd done, but in fact they'd only *heard* it, but had created their own mind pictures.

Company Sergeant Major Peter John Richens
B Company, 2 Para
We had a quite long approach march to the top of Sussex Mountain where we dug down as far as we could into the water-sodden peat, then built up the sides with rocks, making sangars. Being on the top of the hill we were relatively comfortable, but further down, B Company's trenches filled with water. It was cold and we were very wet.

Major Simon Ewen Southby-Tailyour
Royal Marines
The second half of the first wave landed, 40 Commando; then I collected the landing craft together, and went back to get 3 Para. Sand Bay was the one beach I hadn't actually landed on, so my planning had been guesswork – intelligent guesswork, of course. Without actual soundings, I couldn't guarantee we'd get a dry landing, which isn't the be-all and end-all, especially in temperate climates. But it didn't work out like that, and men got wet up to their waist, which is much worse than just up to their knees. There was a last-minute delay while we moved 3 Para into the smaller landing craft so they remained dry.

Captain Jeremy Larken
HMS Fearless
While we were waiting, I would talk at some length over the tannoy to

everybody on board. I believed it was very important to keep people informed, even though most of this information was classified 'secret'. I was rewarded by the confidence I felt the ship had in the management.

Petty Officer Brandon Christopher Smith
HMS Fearless

There were always rumours going round – 'buzzes' we called them. One of them was how every time there were disasters like *Sheffield* being sunk, around twenty casualties were always listed. We were convinced we weren't being told the truth, thinking we were being fed propaganda.

Captain Jeremy Larken
HMS Fearless

One of the most colourful characters to come on board was Lieutenant Colonel Mike Rose, who ran his SAS operation from two Portakabins on the upper deck, used more normally for midshipmen's navigation classes. They used to sit there with their curious communications equipment directly back to Whitehall, taking an objective view of the battle through their binoculars.

Major Philip Neame
D Company Commander, 2 Para

Our move through peat bogs and up the hill to the top of Sussex Mountain was harrowing. We'd kept fit, but were not tabbing fit. It was a relief when we realised the main Argentine effort was not going to be directed against us on the hills, but the ships below. After that, our monstrous bergans were left behind, and we carried fifty pounds or so in our webbing, surviving for a couple of days on whatever we could carry.

Brigadier Julian Howard Thompson
Commander, 3 Commando Brigade

The third wave, with the Rapier anti-aircraft systems, the artillery and its ammunition landed in broad daylight. We had to fly other things ashore before we could remove the deck hatches and get them out. This was very laborious, using cranes and helicopters, and took a long time. The Rapier battery commander had told me right at the start: 'You won't get much use out of the Rapiers for a couple of days.' The navy had imagined Rapier would be like one of their deck-mounted systems and immediately sprout into an air defence umbrella covering the whole landing area. In fact it did take two days to get them operating correctly, which we fully expected. I had told the navy, who'd ignored my warning.

Commander Nigel David 'Sharkey' Ward
Officer Commanding 801 Squadron, Fleet Air Arm, HMS Invincible
During the defence of San Carlos, *Hermes*'s Sea Harrier team were told by the admiral's staff to stay up at high level over San Carlos Water area, but not to attack the enemy aircraft until after they'd attacked their targets. Then, as the admiral later wrote in his book, they were to 'swoop down like hawks on the tails of the enemy and shoot them down', closing the door after the horses had bolted, in the worst possible way.

In battle we always fly side by side, turning in towards each other so we can cover each other's rear for enemy. We'd just come out of a turn and I saw these two delta wing shapes low under the hills below me. I was about three hundred feet, and these guys were about fifty feet, north-west-ish. My radio message came out in a garble but Steve saw them, then I flew right through the middle of them, thinking that at last we had a fight.

I was trying to accelerate from endurance speed to full power, horning it round while looking over my shoulder for them. Then I realised they hadn't turned for San Carlos as I'd expected, but home for Argentina. As I came out of the turn, Steve was firing his first missile, a Sidewinder 9L, which I watched with great wonder. It was lovely to see, climbing over the tail of this Mirage to break the back of the machine as it exploded. A big gout of flame obscured the whole aircraft. Just before the missile hit, the pilot's canopy left the aeroplane, then as it actually hit, the pilot ejected, and was swinging under his chute as Steve was attending to the second Mirage, which was accelerating away.

A Sidewinder flies under boost for four seconds to 1.8 times the speed of sound, faster than its launch aircraft. It has a lot of energy and keeps on tracking after motor burnout. The Mirage pulled up into some cloud, and the Sidewinder proximity fuse set it off just under the wing of the Mirage. This was a wonderful thing to see actually happening. But while I was thinking like that rather than being clever, a third Mirage was behind me. I was in the hard turn the whole time, and looked round to see this Mirage passing underneath me . . . It had beautiful camouflage colours.

I was only three hundred feet, and he was right on the deck. I got in behind him and fired my missile. It hit and the whole Mirage exploded. I could see what looked like the right wing, cart-wheeling along the deck. I thought, definitely that guy didn't get out. But he did. He must have seen the missile coming and ejected. That was very, very exciting. So I got two confirmed kills, much to the delight of the boys back in San Carlos. Then later it transpired the third aircraft hadn't got home either . . .

After shooting down the Mirages, I looked up to see what appeared to be seagulls orbiting between San Carlos and me; Argentine navy Skyhawks, orbiting about ten miles away. When they turned south, we realised they were going for the already crippled *Ardent*. We were flying at low level on the approach direction of the threat, disobeying Admiral Woodward's orders not to use our radars to search. When *Ardent* was first hit, she'd been a long way south in Falkland Sound. Her captain, Alan West, was bringing her back up under her own steam, trying to regain the safety of the other ships.

I assumed that *Hermes's* CAP aircraft, Red Section, were to the south at high altitude, so we headed off cross-country to try to intercept the Skyhawks before they got to *Ardent*. On the way I asked control ship *Minerva* to tell Red Section to come down fast and get involved. As I came out from the land over the water, I was too far behind the A4s to get them myself. Suddenly, just before they hit *Ardent*, I saw one Sea Harrier come in, fire a Sidewinder, knock out the trail man, then the middleman exploded, but the lead man got his bombs away into *Ardent*, before clipping the mast and later coming down round the corner near Stanley.

If *Hermes's* Sea Harriers had been at low level where they should have been, and where we always were, those Skyhawks would not have gone for *Ardent*, but would have gone home. The admiral's staff's orders to *Hermes's* 800 Squadron to come down on the enemy *after* they'd done their business was, in my view, incompetent.

His staff and the man himself were so self-assured of being intellectually superior beings – he says in his book that he's an admiral because of his intellectual superiority – that he didn't listen to his experts, who were us.

In trying to get to *Ardent* before the Argentine aircraft, I'd been haring along with no regard for my number two. In my squadron I was well known for this. I said: 'Steve where are you?' No reply. I thought: 'Shit, he's gone down somewhere,' and became really worried. I called the control ship and searched for as long as I could, and was feeling very miserable. I had two hundred and seventy miles to get home, and had to leave, so when I could see *Invincible* I told them I was very, very short of fuel, and they knew exactly what I meant. Immediately she turned into a speedboat coming towards me. I said: 'I've got bad news. I think my number two's been shot down.' But they said: 'Don't worry, he was hit by ground fire and his radio was damaged but he's fine and is just landing now.'

I was delighted. When I landed I tried to give him a bollocking for not staying with me. His answer was: 'I knew you could look after yourself boss, so I thought I'd better go back and get the aeroplane fixed.'

Captain Adrian Robert Freer
3 Para

A platoon-plus of Argentine soldiers had been in Port San Carlos before we arrived. As we landed on the beach, two Gazelle helicopters flew overhead, and were shot down by Argentines just beyond the settlement. Three of the crew were killed – one being shot up in the water by the Argentines, and one survived. Minutes later a Sea King helicopter over flew us with an underslung load, saw the two ditched helicopters, dropped the load and flew off rapidly. We were unable to get these Argentines, and it's interesting to wonder if we'd have taken them by surprise had we landed in darkness.

We then had to prepare the area for defence. We remained in the settlement, with B and C Companies moving to the high ground to the north, as part of a defensive bridgehead being laid out around San Carlos Water. We then settled into a routine, bringing supplies ashore, while also receiving conflicting orders that changed very quickly. I was very aware of pressure from the UK to get on with it.

Brigadier Julian Howard Thompson
Commander, 3 Commando Brigade

When the warships were under attack, they waved aircraft away and our helicopters took evasive action, hiding in folds in the hills all round the anchorage, which seriously delayed the unloading plan. By last light my brigade was ashore with artillery, but without the very large amounts of ammunition they needed.

Staff Sergeant Richard James Elliott
REME, 3 Commando Brigade Air Squadron

The landings were very like an exercise – even the air raids, which were like the Phantoms arriving at an exercise in Germany, leaving behind the smell of their after burners – except the Argentine aircraft left behind a little bit more ... And the noise was terrific; the small arms firing, missiles, people shouting and screaming, with several jets coming from different angles. The raids were very, very quick.

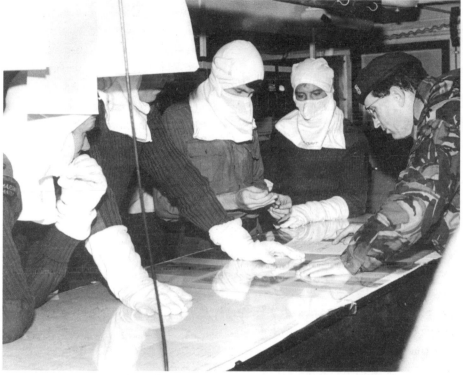

Brigadier Julian Thompson (right) monitoring progress of the landings on May 21, 1982, in HMS *Fearless*'s operations room. Surrounded by COMAW staff in anti-flash, he is wearing combat gear, ready to go ashore.

John Keith 'Jake' Watson
Chaplain, HMS Broadsword

I had nothing with which I could compare this whole experience, and noticed attitudes changing when people realised their lives could depend on how well the stewards had learned first aid. Also, unlike on an exercise when the first-aid teams went from their base in the wardroom or petty officers' mess to pick up casualties, it was up to people to get the casualties to us, as the ship was closed down at action stations. The doctor told us of an action in the Yangtze, when the ship's doctor had gone on deck and was shot.

Captain Jeremy Larken
HMS Fearless

As we could have operated small submarines in Falkland Sound, we thought the Argentines would know how to do it, too. They had probably received German naval training in the Baltic, which is similarly shallow. So on that first day, we spread the ships inside and outside San Carlos to counter the submarine threat, which was in turn directly responsible for some of the damage we sustained on the first day, to Antrim, and to Ardent, which was sunk. But once we decided there was no submarine threat, we packed ships very close together, under the shelter of a bluff of land about eight hundred feet high, which was just high enough to disturb the aircraft as they came in to attack.

John Keith 'Jake' Watson
Chaplain, HMS Broadsword

We were a mile away when Ardent was hit, spectacular to watch, horrifying to experience. The flight deck opened up like a tin can and she was ablaze. Several of the people killed had been on our ship a few days earlier, which affected people aboard. We took on two survivors from Ardent, including their doctor who'd gone to their flight deck to see a casualty but had been blown into the water. He'd managed to put on his once-only suit, but it took seven people hauling on a winch to get him out, as he was so full of water, which vindicated our doctor's position on not going to casualties.

Lieutenant Commander Graham John Edmonds
Operations Officer and Squadron Warfare Officer, HMS Broadsword

Earlier in the day, Ardent had remained supporting the SAS at Goose Green for too long and was abruptly called back at full speed by Fearless. She appeared not to be moving fast enough, so Fearless demanded she hurry up, but as we watched, Argentine aircraft attacked her from astern with bombs, stopping her just the other side of a reef. *Ardent*'s crew abandoned ship into *Yarmouth*. We picked up their doctor who'd been blown off the ship several hundred yards into the sea. Apart from being very cold, after a hot bath and clean clothes, he seemed in good spirits – maybe he lacked imagination – and was flown ashore to work in the field hospital.

Captain Dennis John Scott-Masson
SS *Canberra*

HMS *Plymouth* circled us all day as our air defence, as we only had machine guns. She went to get HMS *Ardent*'s survivors and bring them back to us, including her captain. They'd lost about twenty-two men, and were somewhat unhappy. We issued them with white boiler suits, and gave them what comfort we could.

Staff Sergeant Richard James Elliott
REME, 3 *Commando Brigade Air Squadron*

We spent about five days operating the helicopter from the ship, which we had believed would be a good idea. But everybody else had gone ashore and were now watching the ships being attacked, whereas we were still there being attacked ourselves – which was rather a mistake.

Captain Jeremy Larken
HMS *Fearless*

The Argentines knew we were all packed together, vulnerable to high-level bombing attacks from their Canberras, which could drop a stick of bombs along a line of ships and achieve damage if only by coincidence, so at night we spread out, reassembling the tight anchorage before dawn the next morning.

Company Sergeant Major Peter John Richens
B *Company, 2 Para*

We watched as HMS *Ardent* and HMS *Antelope* were bombed, and realised this could get very nasty. We had a lot of feeling for the navy personnel. On land there's places you can hide, but confined in a ship that gets hit, with ammunition exploding and fireballs going down corridors, must be horrific. We have a very sick sense of humour within the regiment, and use it to make fun of the problems and injuries we suffer; but we found watching ships going down, and knowing people on board, a very harrowing experience for everybody.

David Cooper
Chaplain, 2 Para
The soldiers treated the air raids like a fairground, firing enormous amounts of ammunition at Argentine aircraft. We realised the raids were serious but it seemed very unreal. We were more concerned with the effect of the weather on our capabilities, and that we were not contributing to the war. A war of attrition was something the Argentines could win.

Brigadier Julian Howard Thompson
Commander, 3 Commando Brigade
The intensity of the air attacks persuaded the navy to sail the vulnerable merchant ships from the anchorage. *Canberra* should have been my dressing station, taking the wounded out to hospital ship *Uganda*. She carried ninety thousand twenty-four hour rations and most of my medical people. Instead, we had to fly the dressing station ashore to set up in the old meatpacking factory at Ajax Bay. *Canberra*'s sailing left 3 Para, and 40 and 42 Commando, with only the equipment the men were actually carrying. The same happened to 2 Para, when *Norland* was also ordered to sail. So the three thousand men now ashore had to be supplied by the logistic regiment immediately, even though it was still off-loading. Unloading all the logistic supplies took a further five days. The helicopters and landing craft were fully employed doing this, leaving us no means of moving out of the beachhead.

Major Philip Neame
D Company Commander, 2 Para
When we got ashore and secured Sussex Mountain, there was a complete lack of medium-term objectives and no orders. We were in a limbo for four or five days because nobody knew what the Argentines would do next.

Company Sergeant Major Peter John Richens
B Company, 2 Para
For the first ten days ashore, we didn't dry out from getting wet making the landing. Feet were a big problem. My company strength was ninety-four; in the first week I lost fourteen men from immersion, or trench foot. We wore one pair of socks, and kept a second pair under our armpits drying off during the day, to wear at night. Our army issue boots let the water in very badly.

Private Alejandro Ramon Cano
Paratrooper, Grupo Artilleria Aerotransportad
When they informed us that the English had taken the beach at San Carlos, then we knew we had lost, and that's how it goes.

14

Sacrificing Pawns

A bomb had gone into the computer room and blown up eleven of my guys . . . then I saw Vic Sylvester sitting in the tactical bay with a Chinagraph pencil in his hand, which was on fire and he didn't realise it. I said, 'Put it out. Smoking isn't permitted in the ops room.'

Captain (John) Jeremy Black
HMS *Invincible*
The admiral decided *Coventry* and *Broadsword* should try and knock off some Argentine aircraft from the north of the San Carlos anchorage, one with Sea Dart, the other Sea Wolf, to test these two systems.

Lieutenant Commander Graham John Edmonds
Operations Officer and Squadron Warfare Officer, HMS Broadsword
The day before, May 24, we were out with *Coventry* twelve miles north of Pebble Island. *Coventry* shot down two aeroplanes using Sea Dart, and controlled a number of successful CAP intercepts. Although this is not in the official record, using a combination of fighter control and her own missiles, *Coventry* shot down more aircraft than any other ship. We were certain the Argentines would try something on May 25, their national day.

Radio Supervisor Stewart Anthony MacFarlane
HMS *Coventry*
We were in the wrong place, ten miles north of Pebble Island. The Argentines knew exactly where we were; as they flew up Bomb Alley we were sitting ducks. Our skipper asked to be moved further north between West Falkland and Argentina, to take out aircraft before they arrived at the Falklands and

give us a fighting chance. But the admiral refused. My friend was a Spanish radio intercept translator, and said they called us something like: 'The British bastard north of Pebble that isn't letting anyone get through,' a notoriety we could have done without. Our captain again asked to be moved north so our radar could shoot down aircraft coming at us from over the land. Admiral Woodward's signal said, 'You are to remain in your current operating position. You are a missile target.'

Lieutenant Commander Raymond John Adams
HMS *Coventry*
On May 25, during the early part of the afternoon ship's time, GMT – about four hours after sunrise – the first couple of Argentine aircraft had attacked the amphibious units and were on their way home. *Broadsword* picked them up moving over the land using her Doppler radar, and although we couldn't see them on our long-range radar, we transferred *Broadsword*'s data to our fire control radar using an inter-computer link and engaged with Sea Dart at long range, hitting both. That put us into a fairly buoyant mood.

Radio Supervisor Stewart Anthony MacFarlane
HMS *Coventry*
We shot down everything they sent at us, until dusk when we were congratulating ourselves at having survived another day. The skipper broadcast a message saying how well we'd done, that clearly we were one of the luckiest ships afloat.

Lieutenant Commander Raymond John Adams
HMS *Coventry*
We saw another couple of aircraft very fleetingly on radar, coming out of the Sound. We took out the front one with Sea Dart, and although we locked on to the second one, the pilot ejected before we had a chance to fire the missile. The captain was discussing whether we should change position. Four Mirages appeared about five miles away. Three were shot down by Harriers, but the fourth escaped. The consensus was that, 'Yes', we'd been spotted and were probably under threat, but that we couldn't move far enough to be safer, yet still do our job. So we stayed where we were. At 1745 we decided to go to action stations, so we would have the maximum damage control capability ready for immediate action.

Lieutenant Commander Graham John Edmonds
Operations Officer and Squadron Warfare Officer, HMS Broadsword

Around 1800 GMT, two pairs of Skyhawks attacked us. We knew their weapon load from intelligence, and had detected the raid one hundred and eighty miles out. I talked with *Coventry*'s air defence officer, and we agreed they would probably attack the amphibious ships. What we hadn't realised was that although Pebble Island had been attacked and neutralised, there were still Argentines there, who'd seen us and called in an air strike.

Radio Supervisor Stewart Anthony MacFarlane
HMS Coventry

Four Skyhawks came at us very low over West Falkland as the skipper had feared, and as expected our radars couldn't lock on because of thousands of 'land clutter' reflections.

Lieutenant Commander Graham John Edmonds
Operations Officer and Squadron Warfare Officer, HMS Broadsword

Coventry moved the CAP south towards San Carlos ready to meet them, but then the first two aircraft contacts appeared on my radar just south of us over Mount Rosalie, which I sent on the data link to *Coventry*, which she received then put on to another data link to other ships – so we knew she'd received the data. There was nothing more to do than wait for them to attack us.

Commander Nigel David 'Sharkey' Ward
Officer Commanding 801 Squadron, Fleet Air Arm, HMS Invincible

Neil Thomas's section from *Hermes* was called down by the control ship, saying: 'We've got a raid coming in towards Pebble Island – have a go.'

They did a good job to get down into a firing position, but were then called off by *Coventry*, who said they'd acquired the targets on their Sea Dart system. You don't follow into a missile engagement zone if the ship's happy to take it on.

Lieutenant Commander Raymond John Adams
HMS Coventry

Two Skyhawks came very quickly off the land, coming to us. We attempted to engage with Sea Dart.

Radio Supervisor Stewart Anthony MacFarlane
HMS Coventry

The ops officer announced, 'Birds away,' but instead of the usual 'Targets splashed' thirty seconds later, he said, 'Missed target.' We fired one more missile, and then heard small arms and the 4.5-inch gun firing, so below decks we knew we were in trouble.

Commander Nigel David 'Sharkey' Ward
Officer Commanding 801 Squadron, Fleet Air Arm, HMS Invincible

Broadsword tried to get radar acquisition, but then got visual acquisition with Sea Wolf, and locked up the targets. Sea Wolf is a brilliant little missile, and *Broadsword* was now just waiting for the targets to come within range.

Lieutenant Commander Graham John Edmonds
Operations Officer and Squadron Warfare Officer, HMS Broadsword

We elected Sea Wolf into fully automatic mode, turning it into a suicide mission for the Skyhawks. We had plenty of time, with nothing to do except monitor the attack. Sea Wolf had a software defect, which under certain circumstances required us to reset the system before we could fire. Imagine the horror when this defect occurred now, and we couldn't get the system on line before the aircraft came within bomb release range. . .

Lieutenant Commander Raymond John Adams
HMS Coventry

For some reason, *Broadsword*'s Sea Wolf didn't fire, so we engaged with our gun. I don't know whether the aircraft dropped any weapons, but nothing hit us.

Lieutenant Commander Graham John Edmonds
Operations Officer and Squadron Warfare Officer, HMS Broadsword

We engaged with our poor old Bofors 40/60s which were six years older than me, and an array of GPMGs and small arms on deck. Three bombs missed entirely, but one bounced on the water and went through us like a hot knife into butter. We didn't feel a thing at the front of the ship and with taking cover and no systems being affected, didn't realise we'd been hit.

Radio Supervisor Stewart Anthony MacFarlane
HMS Coventry

I ordered everyone in the radio office to lie down on the deck, hands over the head, in a 'hoping-everything's-going-to-be-all-right' position. I looked up and saw one of the young lads, Nobby Northeast, sat with his back against the remote panel. I told him to get down on the deck and he said: 'Oh, it's OK, sir, I'm doing fine here.' I shouted at him to bloody well do as he was told, and so he got down slowly with that look of obeying a direct order. This was when the whole world blew apart.

Lieutenant Commander Graham John Edmonds
Operations Officer and Squadron Warfare Officer, HMS Broadsword
Being only vaguely aware of the damage aft, and to avoid any further complications, I had selected manual mode for our Sea Wolf. I was locked on to the aircraft when they were twenty miles away, so it was literally only a matter of time before they came within range and Sea Wolf shot them down.

So it was with some horror that we watched *Coventry* turn to starboard and cross our bows, coming between the incoming aircraft and us. We still weren't worried, as she'd already said her Sea Dart system was locked on, which should mean the end of the aircraft. But when she fired her gun, we realised things weren't going so well with her either. She then crossed our line of sight to the aircraft, breaking the radar link with our Sea Wolf, which immediately reset itself.

Lieutenant Commander Raymond John Adams
HMS Coventry
As we finished the turn and steadied up, there was dull thud. We were already taking cover; I was lying on the starboard side of the bridge. We worked very closely together, and now eight of us were lying very closely together: the officer of the watch, the navigator, the quartermaster, a couple of signalmen, one of the warfare officers and the bosun's mate. Two bombs went off immediately, and the third after a short delay – in a sympathetic detonation. Within thirty seconds, the bridge was full of smoke, despite the bombs having hit four or five decks below us. We were reacting as we'd been trained to react, so it wasn't frightening.

Radio Supervisor Stewart Anthony MacFarlane
HMS Coventry
It was very quiet. All my transmitters had locked off. A huge piece of metal from one of the transmitters had imbedded itself where Nobby had just been sitting. The youngest lad I had on board, Tug Wilson, who'd opted to come south as he was only seventeen and didn't have to, was badly hit. The night before he'd asked me where he should lie if we did have to take cover. I'd

pointed out a place in between two strong bulkheads, and had assured him he'd be safe there. I hadn't counted on the metal door being shattered by a bomb, and the biggest bit of metal smacking Tug right in the back of the head.

John Keith 'Jake' Watson
Chaplain, HMS Broadsword

The gun started firing, there was a thump towards the stern and our ship keeled over to one side. I was very frightened. I feared I would be trapped, as all the access to the upper deck was on that side. I felt what I can only describe as ripples of dread, and was very close to breaking point. I also thought I might get away with not having paid for a Sony Walkman I'd signed for that morning from the NAAFI.

Lieutenant Commander Raymond John Adams
HMS Coventry

The captain came up to the bridge within seconds of being hit, and went out on to the port bridge wing. His orders were quite rational and calm, telling us to head east at best speed. We transferred to direct steering from the tiller flat, but were losing engine power as well. The ops rooms and crews from between decks evacuated very quickly because of the smoke. Within seconds most of the ops room were already out on the bridge and upper deck.

Radio Supervisor Stewart Anthony MacFarlane
HMS Coventry

I shouted through the hatch into the ops room: 'My computers have gone off. What the bloody hell's going on?' but received no reply. I looked in. There was nothing left. A bomb had gone into the computer room and blown up eleven of my guys, the blast coming through the hatch into the ops room. The ops room staff were just a pile of crap in the corner. Then I saw Vic Sylvester sitting in the tactical bay with a Chinagraph pencil in his hand, which was on fire and he didn't realise it. I said, 'Put it out. Smoking isn't permitted in the ops room.' He shook it.

Lieutenant Commander Raymond John Adams
HMS Coventry

Within minutes, it was fairly apparent we were going for a swim. The ship was heeling twenty degrees to port and we had very little power. The main broadcast was gone and there was no way of telling people to abandon ship. Nevertheless, the whole business seemed to happen anyway. A lot of people were pouring on to the upper decks; in the thick smoke there was no way you could survive between decks.

Radio Supervisor Stewart Anthony MacFarlane
HMS *Coventry*

I returned to the communications office, then one of the officers came in – we called him 'Tracker Ball' because he was bald, and said, 'Stand by to abandon ship.' I hadn't realised things were that bad, but then I found I was up to my knees in water.

The chief electrician and I agreed I would evacuate the main communications office and EW office, while he went to the port side to evacuate the transmitter room. As I was leaving the office I heard a voice saying, 'Sam is that you?' It was my best buddy, Chris Hill. I couldn't believe it. His action station was in the ops room at the EW desk. Every bit of clothing Chris was wearing had been blown off him in the blast – apart from the waistband and the right leg of his trousers, and we were wearing woolly pullover, eights and anti-flash, which had all gone as if it had never existed. His skin was hanging off him in bits. I got Chris up top, where my UHF room was being used as a first-aid centre.

Paddy, one of the steward first aiders, asked me to get some water as Chris was in a really bad way. Like a plonker I went back down below, not imagining that the taps wouldn't work or the toilets flush. I came back up and we decided the best we could do was get Chris into the sea as soon as we could. The only way to the UHF office was through a door on the port side, which was the way the ship was now listing, so it was pretty dodgy. The sea boat, ladders and everything else was strewn around on deck like rubbish. We clambered across, then said sorry to Chris . . . He said something like, 'I'll get you back, you bastard,' and we threw him in. He was swimming around, so the cold water had helped, but there was nothing else we could have done for him.

Lieutenant Commander Graham John Edmonds
Operations Officer and Squadron Warfare Officer, HMS *Broadsword*

When the *Coventry* emerged from the smoke, she looked quite normal. The main engines stopped, and she came to a halt on the water. People were standing on the upper deck looking puzzled about what had happened. But she was rapidly filling with water. The bombs had gone into the base of her fore mast, plunged down three decks into the diesel generator and engine room spaces, exploding deep down in the ship, blowing a twenty- to forty-foot hole in the bilge keel.

John Keith 'Jake' Watson
Chaplain, HMS Broadsword

My respirator was inside the wardroom, not round my waist where it should have been, so when the chemical attack warning went off I ran in to get it, only to find somebody else wearing it. This was about our tenth attack, so everybody was very calm, and the bridge recording shows there was no swearing or shouting. The officer of the watch says: '*Coventry*'s hit,' then '*Coventry*'s blown up.' At one point the captain asks calmly: 'Navigator, do we, or do we not, have a bomb on board?' Everyone had settled down to their jobs, with half working the ship while the other half were waiting in damage control teams. Then there was a pipe from the bridge explaining what had happened; a bomb had bounced around the stern of our ship without exploding, but had knocked open a torpedo inside our helicopter, which had led to the chemical hazard warning.

Lieutenant Commander Raymond John Adams
HMS Coventry

Time seemed to stand still. Within fifteen minutes the port gunwale was under water, with water up to the level of the deck on the port side, and we were heeling very heavily to port. People became abnormally calm. I've often tried to analyse my own actions. I was wondering what to do, and a little voice said, 'Go and see how your chaps are.' So I wandered round the gun direction platform to the signals deck. They were fine, no problems. People reverted to their training, and there was no reason for us to panic on the upper deck.

Radio Supervisor Stewart Anthony MacFarlane
HMS Coventry

It was strange. Everybody was so calm. Even trying to get out from down below, the ladders had been blown to pieces, so you had to climb over the bulkhead with your fingernails, with the ship going over, further and further. You'd help somebody, they'd say, 'Cheers mate,' and you'd help somebody else and so would they. Then somebody said we had to abandon ship, which I thought very strange, because that was not the sort of thing that happens to HMS *Coventry*.

I was trying to put on my once-only suit, which is orange and made of thin rubber, in one piece, with seals round the wrists and neck, and a hood. The idea is to stop you dying of hyperthermia so quickly that you don't make it into a life raft. I put some air into my life jacket, then I remembered them saying in training not to over-inflate your life jacket because when you hit the water it could break your neck, so I let some out. Then I thought, 'Hang on, is there enough air to keep me afloat?' so I blew some more in, which made me think again of breaking my neck so I let some out again, thinking, 'How the hell do you get a happy medium?'

The ship was going over so quickly to port that we couldn't use any of the life rafts on that side. The bloody things were so heavy and the ship was going over so fast that we couldn't get them into the water on the other side either. Eventually we got some into the water – but not many – although they were self-inflating.

Lieutenant Commander Raymond John Adams
HMS *Coventry*

On the starboard side we were launching life rafts from their canisters, and throwing down scramble nets. Having got the life rafts launched, it was obvious the ship was not going to survive, so after fifteen or twenty minutes we abandoned ship. We got into our once-only suits, in quite a hurry, but most of us put them on horribly wrongly and were very lucky to escape with our lives. Mine filled with water, so it was only my life jacket kept me afloat.

Captain Jeremy Larken
HMS *Fearless*

It was clear *Coventry* had been fatally hit. Commodore Clapp immediately sent every helicopter he could; it was a calm day, and we got to her very quickly, managing to get two hundred and ninety people off before she turned over twenty minutes later.

Radio Supervisor Stewart Anthony MacFarlane
HMS *Coventry*

There were two emergency radios on the upper deck to be taken in the life rafts, which you crank like a bicycle to transmit for help. On the top it says, 'This will float.' We lowered one into the water and it sank like a bloody stone.

Lieutenant Commander Raymond John Adams
HMS *Coventry*

A number of people were reticent about jumping over the side, which is usual with sailors. I was fit and healthy, so I decided to swim to the furthest life raft, which was about thirty yards away – my only little bit of leadership. The camber on the deck was very bad. Some people slipped down, others used the scrambling nets. I was able to jump straight into where there wasn't so much of a camber. There were quite a few people in the water already and I remember thinking it was a bit like 'Hands to Bathe'.

Radio Supervisor Stewart Anthony MacFarlane
HMS Coventry

I couldn't get my once-only suit on as I was trying to balance against a bulkhead that was leaning further and further over as the seconds ticked by. Like an idiot I rolled it up and threw it into the water intending to put it on in the water . . . But it sank like the radio, so I decided to jump anyway. But even that wasn't easy, as you had to jump a long way out to actually hit the water. Our First Lieutenant, Glen Robinson-Moltke, whose right arm was seriously injured from a 30mm cannon shell, tried to leap but couldn't get out far enough and smacked his head on the ship's side. Nobody saw him again.

Lieutenant Commander Raymond John Adams
HMS Coventry

Fully clothed, swimming wearing my once-only suit in the middle of the ocean, it seemed like miles. There was no thinking – it was all back to the immediate reactions of our basic training. I hadn't sat in a life raft since Dartmouth in 1976. We then tried to find the knife to cut the life rafts from the ship, and get sorted out. There were about thirty or forty people around our life raft. With people in rubber suits full of water, it was quite amusing – more like a game of sardines than a service drill.

Radio Supervisor Stewart Anthony MacFarlane
HMS Coventry

I was lucky and managed to throw myself out far enough. You never open your eyes in seawater, but this time I did and saw bubbles going up that seemed to go on forever. I thought: 'You're going too far down to come up son.' I panicked. Your life doesn't flash before your eyes when you're about to die; you just think: 'Oh bastard. So that's it then?' I was just about to say goodbye and release the air from my lungs, when I realised I was starting to come back up. Maybe I hadn't put enough air in my life jacket after all. Just as I reached the surface I had to release my air and breathe in – a bit too soon; so after swallowing a couple of gallons of seawater, I tried to find a life raft.

Lieutenant Commander Raymond John Adams
HMS Coventry

It was near sunset, which should have been worrying. We battened down the life raft and got organised. It was difficult remembering what to do. We bailed out the life raft with our plastic mugs, and paddled using our respirators like a large baseball mitt.

Radio Supervisor Stewart Anthony MacFarlane
HMS Coventry

My life raft had fifteen in it, and first we had to bail out the water seeping from our clothes. One of the lads was bailing using his steaming boot, which he handed to Paddy the steward to empty out of the door with the words, 'Here Paddy chuck this out for us.' Being Irish, Paddy chucked the boot out as well – which made everyone laugh. We then broke out the stores from the life raft – which included cigarettes. Like a lot of others, I'd given up smoking on the way down, but started again within minutes of *Sheffield* getting hit. I'd got a Zippo lighter, and when the NAAFI ran out of lighter fluid my buddy on the helicopter flight filled it with aviation fuel, so it lit first time. My watch wasn't waterproof but still works fine. Strange.

Lieutenant Commander Raymond John Adams
HMS Coventry

We paddled clear of the ship, and realised we had several very badly burned people in our life raft. *Broadsword* was still in attendance and several helicopters appeared quite quickly. *Broadsword* had a minor fire around her flight deck and cannon holes in her side. Her whaler was pottering around trying to shepherd the life rafts. We got a couple of our badly burned people off in the first helicopter. I was picked up on the second or third helicopter trip, by a Sea King Mark 4 commando helicopter, and winched up. We were in the life raft for an hour and a half, and by the time I left, the ship was floating upside down with just its keel above the water.

Radio Supervisor Stewart Anthony MacFarlane
HMS Coventry

One of the ops room guys was very seriously burned and in such agony that I injected him one of my ampoules of morphine, carried by all senior rates round their necks. They teach you how giving too much can kill, but the guy was so bad. Somebody said, 'Shit, he's on fire,' as there was steam coming off him. The morphine worked. They decided to tow us away from the ship using a Gemini assault craft with a powerful Johnson outboard. They threw us a rope but we were too heavy and the Gemini was pulled under and sank. One of my leading hands was in a life raft that had been sucked round the front of the ship and, despite their paddling, was being drawn close towards where she was going over. One Sea Dart remained on the launcher, and as the ship made another lurch, the bloody missile cone went straight through the life raft and they were sunk twice in the same day. Quite a few empty rafts were floating around, as when the water reaches life rafts, the clamps release automatically and they inflate in the water.

Lieutenant Commander Raymond John Adams
HMS Coventry

It was now the time of day when air attacks were normally finished, so we felt relatively safe. We flew to the Ajax Bay hospital to drop off a few injured people, then to another ship to refuel the helicopter, then a few minutes later were dropped off on Fort Austin.

Radio Supervisor Stewart Anthony MacFarlane
HMS Coventry

Somebody was clambering on the roof of our life raft. I shouted at him to stop buggering about and get into the life raft immediately. It was the aircrew man from a Sea King helicopter, who stuck his head in upside down and said, 'Who wants a fucking taxi then?'

I was a stubborn git and stayed until last. The crewman said, 'Out you come, don't worry about it. We'll get you into the helicopter. Get into this harness, and keep your arms tight around your waist so you don't fall out.' I was winched up into the Sea King where the crewman told me in sign language to go and sit down. He came across to me and took my anti-flash off, because I was soaking wet and freezing cold. He took my gloves off as I couldn't do it myself, then took my hood off and told me to clap my hands. I looked at him and he repeated: 'Clap your hands.'

So I shouted: 'I don't know why you want me to do this, but I will.'

I tried, but my hands kept missing and I couldn't do it. I couldn't understand why.

He then pointed at me and said, 'You. Get on the deck and go to the door.' I told him: 'You can bollocks, there's no way I'm going back into the life raft because I can't clap my hands. I'm not useless. Give me a chance and I'll show you.' He then grabbed me by the shoulder, pulled me on to the deck and shouted: 'Get over to the fucking door.'

I thought: 'You miserable bastard. Just because I can't clap my hands, you're going to put me back into the life raft.' I really didn't want to go back. I thought: 'Well, there's nothing more I can do. He's told me I've got to go.' He sat me down in the edge of the doorway and put me back in the noose harness, and said: 'Hold your hands down by your side. You'll swing out first, then you'll go down.' I called him all the names under the sun because I just couldn't understand what they'd done.

Then when I realised I was hovering over the *Broadsword* and they were about to put me down on to it, I tried to apologise to him, saying: 'Sorry mate, I didn't understand . . .' He just smiled and waved. And as I was swinging out I saw the pilot looking at me. He must have been about eighteen years old, and I thought: 'Bloody hell, he's a kid.' He smiled and gave me the thumbs up.

When I landed on the deck I couldn't walk. I thought: 'My brain's been done in. I couldn't clap and now I can't bloody walk.' Two blokes picked me up by the arms, carried me through a hatch and dropped me down a ladder, which hurt. At the bottom of the ladder, two other blokes cut all my clothes off with a Stanley knife. I remember thinking: 'This isn't a very nice way to treat somebody.' They broke my St Christopher chain, so I fought them off me and went scrabbling through the pile of clothes looking for the medal, which I found. They put a blanket round my shoulders and helped me take a tepid shower. I was gradually able to walk, and they gave me a boiler suit to wear, then I walked down the Burma Road, the main passageway in a Type 22. The *Broadsword* ship's company were patting us on the back. The radio supervisor came out from the communications office and said: 'You're really in bloody shit now, Sam. You didn't send the closing down signal for the broadcast list. Whitehall have got a right bastard on.'

I said: 'You're joking?'

'Course I am, but I have told Whitehall that you're off the broadcast list.'

And that's when it really hit me. The realisation that she'd gone, even though we'd sat in a life raft and watched her sink. We were saying: 'Oh that's a sad sight,' but not realising what it was. But it was being taken off the list of ships that were reading the signal broadcast that made me realise that was it for *Coventry*.

John Keith 'Jake' Watson
Chaplain, HMS Broadsword

The *Coventry* survivors came on board quickly; we had to cut the clothes off the ones who'd been in the water then warm them up in the captain's cabin shower, and dress the injured. I deliberately didn't go up to see *Coventry* because I didn't want to. People were burned and needed jigsaw puzzle-type dressings all over their backs. We had to rip up the ship's football strip when we ran out of dressings, which made people look twice at our club-swinger as he carried them from his store to the wardroom. One casualty was grinning like a Cheshire cat; he told me he'd signed a cheque for a hundred pounds that morning and had the cash in his pocket. The cheque was in the ship's office, which was sinking.

Radio Supervisor Stewart Anthony MacFarlane
HMS Coventry

I realised afterwards that in making me clap hands, the helicopter crewman was testing the extent of my hypothermia. Another crewman I talked to afterwards told me that how I had responded determined whether they took me to a hospital ship, or the nearest ship to get my clobber off me asap.

Me and the yeoman decided we should list the survivors, so we made a pipe for everyone to come to the communications office. We got seventy-four names. We looked at each other in total disbelief. We couldn't believe that only seventy-four out of two hundred and ninety had got off. A little bit of me died just then.

John Keith 'Jake' Watson
Chaplain, HMS Broadsword

We were busy with Coventry casualties until early morning, when we returned to San Carlos Water and transferred them by landing craft to Canberra. I led them through the darkened innards of Broadsword to the deck, where they climbed down a landing net into the LCVP, where they were covered in blankets, whereupon they all shouted, 'Three cheers for HMS Broadsword,' which was a bit like a John Wayne war movie.

Radio Supervisor Stewart Anthony MacFarlane
HMS Coventry

I needed to find out where my lads where. I saw Jack Daws in the sick bay having inhaled a lot of smoke, but in the end I couldn't account for two, Scouse Kelly and young Smudge. I badgered the radio officer until he discovered them both on the Uganda. Smudge was pretty serious, having been trapped underneath hydraulic pipework in the transmitter room which had split, forcing high-pressure hydraulic fluid into his face. He'd swallowed a lot of it and was in grave danger of dying. Scouse Kelly was found floating face down by a young sub lieutenant, who even though in grave danger of dying himself from hypothermia, gave Scouse mouth-to-mouth and brought him round. I'm extremely grateful to him.

Lieutenant Commander Graham John Edmonds
Operations Officer and Squadron Warfare Officer, HMS Broadsword
Coventry was riddled with small arms fire and we could smell aviation spirit all over the ship. But earlier that day she'd shot down five Argentine aircraft. More ships were coming down from the UK to make up the losses, but the Argentines were not getting any more aircraft, so even though she was gone, *Coventry* had done well – probably better than any other air defence ship. But we didn't know that later the same day, *Atlantic Conveyor* was sunk; and even when we did hear about it, we thought it was just another stores ship. May 25 could be considered the Argentines' one and only good day.

15

London Needs
Good News

*A little man came into the tent to tell me Atlantic Conveyor had been
sunk. She contained our four Chinook plus six more Wessex helicopters.
This catastrophe finally brought our whole effort to a grinding halt.
After a silence, one of my staff said: 'We'll bloody well have
to walk.'*

Rear Admiral Anthony John Whetstone
Deputy Chief of Naval Staff (Operations), MoD Whitehall
The troops landed earlier than we had expected, but Admiral Fieldhouse was
very concerned to push ahead, as troops are often so glad to be safely ashore
that they relax. We needed to exploit the landing as quickly as possible.

Brigadier Julian Howard Thompson
Commander, 3 Commando Brigade
General Moore had directed me to establish the beachhead, then push out as
far as practical to achieve moral domination of the area. But there were no
orders to advance, and it was only my assumption that Stanley was to be our
objective. The nearest enemy was twenty kilometres away at Darwin and
Goose Green, so I decided to mount a raid using 2 Para. They were to go in
and come out afterwards, causing as much mayhem and casualties as possible
– but not stay there. But as the days went past, it became clear to me that this
would be a diversion we couldn't afford.

Major John Harry Crosland
B Company Commander, 2 Para
I don't think anyone had thought through what we were going to do after we landed. We were getting frustrated and I'd lost four soldiers with immersion foot; it was like a bad day in Brecon. We were keen to get into action, so raiding Darwin and Goose Green was a much better prospect.

John Pole Evans
Falkland Islander, Goose Green Community Centre
The Argentines at Goose Green had increased their numbers to over a thousand and had taken over most of the houses, and were dug in all around in the hills, the airstrip and settlement. Navy warships shelled Argentine positions at night. We'd hear the Argentine air-raid warnings when British aircraft were around, and get together in families on the floor where we normally slept, so everybody could be accounted for. The adults had prepared shelters under the floor of the hall in preparation for fighting, but us kids didn't know the British were even ashore.

David Cooper
Chaplain, 2 Para
H wanted to test the Argies to find out what quality of men they were. He believed that one serious, effective fight with us winning would lead to an Argentine collapse, an aggressive and vigorous initial attack with no hesitation, and was adamant that we couldn't afford to lose men to the weather.

Brigadier Julian Howard Thompson
Commander, 3 Commando Brigade
We were putting final touches to our plan to move the brigade forward toward Stanley by helicopter, when a little man came into the tent I had behind my Land Rover, to tell me *Atlantic Conveyor* had been sunk. She contained our four Chinook plus six more Wessex helicopters. This catastrophe finally brought our whole effort to a grinding halt. After a silence, one of my staff said: 'We'll bloody well have to walk.'

John Pole Evans
Falkland Islander, Goose Green Community Centre
Helicopters landed on the green constantly, and their Pucara aircraft came in and out of the airstrip all the time. We knew what sort of damage they could do, because during April whilst we were still in our homes, they'd bombed the

The burnt-out hull of the *Atlantic Conveyor* after she was struck by an Exocet missile on May 25, 1982.

The burnt-out body of a Wessex 5 helicopter on board the *Atlantic Conveyor*.

tussock island in the harbour with napalm and it burned for a couple of days. This was like a warning of what they were capable of – that they could destroy the settlement if they wanted to. For them it was probably just some sort of target practice.

Air Vice Commodore Carlos Bloomer-Reeve
Secretary General, Islas Malvinas
The air force tried a napalm bomb on that island at Goose Green, but napalm is very nasty. Castellano had all the components but after he made sure he could use them, he deactivated them. I think we agreed not to use them.

Brigadier Julian Howard Thompson
Commander, 3 Commando Brigade
My initial reaction was that the sinking of *Atlantic Conveyor* put the kibosh on the whole thing until the reinforcements got here. Even if we did walk, without the *Atlantic Conveyor* helicopters, there was no way of moving artillery and ammunition forward fast enough to cope with Argentine reactions. When 5 Brigade arrived, it could then be done as a concerted move out with more helicopters.

But Northwood told me: 'No, you get on with it, plus remount the Goose Green operation, but not as a raid this time but to actually capture the place.' So I told Colonel Jones he was to seize Goose Green and Darwin based on his initial raid plan, which I'd cancelled earlier. I allocated all the helicopters in support of his operation, and told 3 Para and 45 Commando to start walking west; 40 Commando via Douglas Settlement and 3 Para direct to Teal Inlet.

Major Philip Neame
D Company Commander, 2 Para
We were told we'd be helicoptered down to Camilla Creek House at first light the next morning. We'd heard rumours of political imperatives. But with everybody lined up ready, we were told the helicopters were not available. H told me to secure Camilla Creek House as the assembly area. Having stashed all our GPMG SF kits and adjusted Camilla Creek House with artillery to give it a good pasting, plus as a navigation aid over very featureless terrain, we set off with an hour of so of daylight remaining. This was still to be a raid and not an attack.

Private Alejandro Ramon Cano
Grupo Artilleria Aerotransportada
We were three kilometres from Darwin. We went on with normal work, going forward. Every day at dusk we made a lot of gunfire to show our presence. I don't know who we were shooting at but every time we made a lot of gunfire, the English came with their silent helicopters. And every time the helicopters appeared we had to leave running because those blokes were up there firing with everything they had. We were not sure of what was going on. Everything for us was like wild party.

Major John Harry Crosland
B Company Commander, 2 Para
The Argentines' artillery fired on pre-selected points and the weather was bad. The Toms dived for cover at the first shells, so we stopped and I gave an introduction to the first signs and sounds of battle, pointing out some large holes in the ground that had no snow on them, explaining they weren't caused by moles and were obviously very recent. We moved very rapidly a hundred metres out of the area. They needed to become accustomed to the sounds and feel of battle, so they didn't immediately take cover, and lose the momentum.

Major Philip Neame
D Company Commander, 2 Para
I was unsure as to how far we were from Camilla Creek, so I called up a fire mission on it to see where the rounds would land. When they landed a thousand metres behind us, I couldn't believe it, so made the artillery check their calculations. On repeating the fire, the rounds still fell behind us, the result of a radical change in wind direction. Eventually we spotted one of the outbuildings. It was unoccupied so we posted sentries outside and got everybody into the main building – one hundred and twenty men.

Private Alejandro Ramon Cano
Grupo Artilleria Aerotransportada
A red alert came up during the night and they give information that an enemy ship was at sea. We aimed our guns towards Boca, where a ship was transporting troops to disembark. It was a bugger for us . . . we were dying of the cold, and didn't care if they disembarked. All we wanted to do was sleep. The only one who acted was a soldier, Gonzalez, and first corporal of the artillery, Fernandez. Gonzalez got ammunition, set the time on the fuse,

loaded it, fired a charge. He recalculated the timing, and then fired a shell, which exploded and lit up the whole of the ship. But it appeared that we had been fooled . . . I thought it was the *Canberra*.

David Cooper
Chaplain, 2 Para
We were shelled without effect; the bang of the air burst was more frightening than the ground burst, but as we hadn't known there was an artillery battery at Goose Green, it made me wonder if this might prove more difficult than we had thought.

Major Philip Neame
D Company Commander, 2 Para
When the battalion arrived three hours later, we were very comfortable, but the other five hundred men were intent on making themselves comfortable too, so it became rather crowded. One of my platoons fitted themselves into a downstairs loo, as everyone crammed in like sardines to escape from the elements and get some rest.

Company Sergeant Major Peter John Richens
B Company, 2 Para
With having only our belt order and no sleeping bags, we suffered the coldest night any of us had ever experienced, with the entire company in one garage and a Land Rover. I think we broke the world record for getting people into a Land Rover.

Major Philip Neame
D Company Commander, 2 Para
By now H was talking about this being an attack to recover Goose Green and Darwin rather than a raid. I didn't realise the significance of this until many months later.

Company Sergeant Major Peter John Ritchens
B Company, 2 Para
Towards the end of the day, one of our radio operators tuned through the channels to find the BBC World Service for a news update, and was horrified to hear the Defence Secretary John Nott telling Parliament that British paratroopers were five miles from Goose Green.

Major Philip Neame
D Company Commander, 2 Para
H threw a complete wobbly, getting Robert Fox in, berating him and demanding to know what the BBC thought they were up to. I didn't blame the BBC at all; they were reporting what was being said in Parliament . . . But this was the best possible warning for the Argentinians.

(James) Robert Fox
BBC correspondent
By the time Dave Norris and I arrived at Camilla Creek, all consideration of the aims of the Goose Green mission were out of the window, as, in Colonel Jones's mind, he'd lost all element of surprise, and the battle was now going to have to be an all-out slog. The Argentines had already shelled the paras, so it was clear that they knew they were being attacked from the north.

Major John Harry Crosland
B Company Commander, 2 Para
We were trying to hide five hundred men in a very open area, so we spread out and prepared to spend the day under the scrutiny of the Argentine air force. Some Argentine air reconnaissance flew over, and in the afternoon an army patrol motored up.

Major Philip Neame
D Company Commander, 2 Para
Knowing we were coming, it wouldn't be difficult for the Argentine commanders to work out the areas we were likely to be – either from the sea or from the north. The Argentines redeployed their troops, making it harder for us to fight our way in.

(James) Robert Fox
BBC correspondent
That afternoon H Jones was in one hell of a state. He wanted his wife to sue John Nott for divulging such vital information. I said: 'Why don't you sue the BBC for outright irresponsibility?' I was feeling rather sore myself, that the BBC might have reduced my chances of drawing a pension in due course. It was, however, quite jolly; Jones was in a state, and had to keep adjusting his orders for the battalion attack the following day. When recce platoon reported bumping an Argentine patrol, Jones shouted to his signaller that if they attempted to escape, they were to be shot in the back, to prevent any more

information about his presence or the impending attack getting back to Darwin.

David Cooper
Chaplain, 2 Para
Pete Ketley shot up an Argentine Land Rover and took the Argentines in it prisoner. Two were injured in the legs so we patched them up while the Royal Marine interpreter Rod Bell questioned the others. They couldn't tell us very much. We slept again until Colonel H gave orders, and then slept some more until it was time to move out.

Major John Harry Crosland
B Company Commander, 2 Para
This was the first time since Korea that a British commanding officer had led his battalion into an attack like this. Because of very little fire support, large numbers of enemy and the presence of civilians in two villages, it required a very complex plan.

The stress factor on H was high; he was an all-action type of man who liked things to go as smoothly and efficiently as possible, and he cared particularly for the welfare of the men under him. He realised the risks we were about to undertake. Most of the guys were young, with only Northern Ireland experience, and this was the first time they'd been in a full-combat arena. In some ways this was good; they had faith in the leadership, and so did what they were told. This, however, added to the stress and strain on the commanding officer, which H shouldered magnificently.

Major Philip Neame
D Company Commander, 2 Para
An SAS patrol told us there were only three or four hundred Argentines in the settlement, and all we had to do was 'knock hard on the front door' and the rest would collapse. People were taking it very relaxed, talking of hitting them hard then moving straight through. By the end of the day, recce platoon patrols had compiled some detail of what was north of Darwin.

(James) Robert Fox
BBC correspondent
Jones was very good, despite the BBC confusion, saying it was no reflection on me, and I was welcome to join him in the battle. He specifically invited Davids, Norris and I to witness his giving orders, which was a remarkable

experience. Jones described a very detailed six-phase plan with four of the phases to be completed at night. The intelligence was poor and the SAS patrol, contrary to what had been believed before, had not penetrated the settlement, so nobody knew where the settlers were. The SAS speculation was that settlers were not actually there, as only four or five had been observed walking around. The orders were disseminated down to company and platoon levels, and while the three artillery guns were flown in, we had scoff then went inside the house to have a sleep.

Major Philip Neame
D Company Commander, 2 Para

I remember discussing the narrow isthmus we'd have to cross with my sergeant major, saying either we'll take them by surprise, or it's going to be a long, bloody day. H called us in for formal orders that evening. After I'd marked all the enemy positions on my map, it was all red from one end of the isthmus to the other. I went back to my company sergeant major saying: 'I think it's going to be the bloody one.'

Company Sergeant Major Peter John Richens
B Company, 2 Para

It was emphasised that the whole thing had to be done and dusted by first light. On the start line, A Company was to be the left forward company, with us, B Company, being the right forward company.

(James) Robert Fox
BBC correspondent

I stood outside in the darkness with Chris Keeble after Jones had given his orders, listening to the distinctive sound of Huey helicopters, dropping Argentine reinforcement troops along the gorse line ridge running across the neck of the isthmus from Darwin settlement. Camilla Creek House stands out like a beacon – white with a bright red roof. One wonders why the Argentines didn't shell it, or bring in air attacks. We lay there in the house and chatted like boys in a public school dormitory with Jones as the prefect; jokes about whether the B Company commander was going to wear his woolly hat the following day, what colour beret the liaison officer Hector Gullin would be wearing – he was a paratrooper, but was also in the Marines, and in fact wore a green beret . . . But the following day we wore lids.

The last I saw of Jones was next day when he went off with the two lead companies into the swirling mist, squelching wet under foot. It was so dark with the fog that I grabbed the webbing of Sergeant Mann in front, just so I knew which way we were going.

David Cooper
Chaplain, 2 Para
On my way to the start line I found a senior rank who'd fallen down a bank, hurting his back. I put him into the captured Argentine Land Rover, then wondered how with a hurt back I'd managed to fold him to get him in. But he insisted he was hurt, so was evacuated.

Major Philip Neame
D Company Commander, 2 Para
I'd given my orders in the dark. It was a six-phase plan, and very complicated for people to get their heads round, particularly as we hadn't seen the ground. We left Camilla Creek at midnight, to be on the start line at 0200. B Company was at the back, as reserve for the first two phases, then moving forward on phase three. Battalion headquarters were in front of us for the march down. As we were crossing the last stream, they stopped, so we had to meander through this morass of bodies, radios and so on. As we came out the other side we missed the battalion guides and my lead platoon carried on in the wrong direction. We were five hundred metres or so off track and had obviously missed the route, so I ordered everyone to stop while I worked out where we were. I ended up in front of H's Tac. H believed in leading from the front, and was most upset to find his reserve company ahead of him, and proceeded to berate me loudly in his usual way. There was no harm done, except an affront to his pride.

David Cooper
Chaplain, 2 Para
When I got to the start line it was drizzling, and a herd of horses came galloping through us. We stopped behind battalion headquarters, and Phil Neame, OC D Company, was worried as he needed to get past us to his positions. There was some machine gun fire from the Argentine positions, red tracer going up into the air, which Chris Keeble declared was a good sign as it showed they were jumpy. I thought it was rather a bad sign, showing they were awake. We lay for some time on the start line in the rain, and I fell asleep.

Major John Harry Crosland
B Company Commander, 2 Para
Patrols company led us down to the start line. The ground was not easy, particularly leading A Company round to attack Burntside House, so the battalion was forty-five minutes late. It was very windy, cold, wet with some snow and a little moonlight. We had only one approach – straight down the middle, 'banging on the front door'.

Private Graham Carter
2 Para
Colonel H Jones was a little anti us, as we were late arriving on the start line. Feelings were quite apprehensive, as you can imagine. The Argentinians knew we there after the World Service BBC had told them. We had a bad start with being shelled – with real HE and phosphorus coming at us. I felt absolutely petrified knowing they're trying to kill me and my friends.

(James) Robert Fox
BBC correspondent
Then the guns started – the sound of ripping cardboard just above your head. Their fire was sparing; not a barrage, but a few rounds every two minutes. Then HMS *Arrow*'s gun started. But as the battle started, *Arrow* had to stop. Jones had brought down only two mortars, which was strange as in his youth he'd been a mortar platoon commander and should have brought all six. The mortar crews were shouting out the coordinates, firing, and by mid morning had run out of smoke rounds so Jones didn't have much cover.

Private Alejandro Ramon Cano
Grupo Artilleria Aerotransportada
The battle commenced at about twelve at night. We were sleeping and the mortars started to fall near to where we were resting. The colonel got us up and said to us: 'Be calm, you know what you have to do, go to your positions. Stay calm.' Each one of us knew what we had to do. He spoke to us with complete calm, and I think it gave us more confidence in ourselves, as it gave us a little more responsibility.

Then Colonel Vinasur told us to change position quietly, as the English were searching for us. We went outside and saw that the English were not so close, so we started to transport all the munitions to the positions where we had the artillery pieces.

Major John Harry Crosland
B Company Commander, 2 Para

We crossed the start line and very soon came into their first positions and were facing machine guns about one hundred and fifty metres range, in very open territory. The foul conditions gave us some cover, but then we heard that HMS *Arrow* had a very bad mechanical failure. Her fire could have made our approach much easier, but we were now going to have to do it all ourselves.

Company Sergeant Major Peter John Richens
B Company, 2 Para

In orders, we'd been assured we'd get Harriers, a couple of hundred rounds of HE from the ship, plus fire from the artillery to soften up the objectives. It was too rough at sea, so the air support didn't come. After a dozen or so rounds from the ship, they stopped. We had only a couple of mortars, the artillery didn't give us what we needed, so we were on our own.

John Pole Evans
Falkland Islander, Goose Green Community Centre

When the battle started, our family went under the floor of the bar and stayed there for the couple of days of the fighting, which took place outside the settlement. But the Argies rigged up a rocket launcher on the children's slide outside the hall, and brought their big guns inside the settlement to have less chance of being attacked by the British. The rocket launcher fired out over the top of the hall, and the artillery guns were firing all the time.

Company Sergeant Major Peter John Richens
B Company, 2 Para

We moved off, and a target appeared to our front, but after collecting a few rounds, it was revealed to be a scarecrow, relieving some jumpiness in the lead sections. We then came across trenches, and taking them out was very difficult and slow. Fighting at night has to be very deliberate. People have commented that we didn't take many prisoners. In pitch blackness, in the heat of the battle with a lot of firing going on and none of us speaking Spanish, unless somebody jumps up and throws their weapon away, it's very difficult to take prisoners.

Private Graham Carter
2 Para

All we were told was to clear the positions in front of us as we went. They

Argentine multi-barrel rocket launcher, which was fired from the top of the children's slide outside the Goose Green Community Centre in which some 112 islanders were imprisoned. Argentine artillery guns were also brought into the settlement, so they would be less vulnerable to British attack, where they fired throughout the battle.

were moving back, so in the early stages we didn't have to fight much. We were moving forward in extended line, seeing trenches in front whenever there was illumination fired. Occasionally the CO or company commander would come up on the radio and tell us which way to go. We'd come to trenches and throw in an L2 grenade, or if you couldn't find one of those, a phosphorus grenade, then climb in afterwards.

Major John Harry Crosland
B Company Commander, 2 Para
We started a series of individual platoon attacks, using 4 and 6 Platoons forward – Lieutenant Chiri Chapman on the left, Lieutenant Ernie Hocking in the right and Lieutenant Jeff Weyhill as my reserve platoon. It became a section commander's fight, at very close quarters – only a few yards. We'd come across a trench in the darkness; it was impossible to tell if the Argentinians were willing to fight, and I would suggest very strongly that we were not in the game of tapping on the door and asking them. You toss a grenade in and move on to the next trench.

(James) Robert Fox
BBC correspondent
A and B Companies seemed to go through tremendously quickly, with Jones's HQ behind them. Then we got going with HQ Company. We passed Burntside House, which A Company had thought occupied by Argentines, but actually contained a family of settlers who hid under the bed and mercifully were not killed. There was an enormous fire in the outhouse. It looked like the set of *Oklahoma* as we passed by, the barn burning, smoke pouring across the water of the ponds, confusion, and the dogs had run away.

Private Graham Carter
2 Para
If there was illumination up, you could see for a long way. With no trees or bushes you can see for miles. But sometimes you'd be falling into a trench, it was so dark. If we were under fire we'd leap into the trench, and if we heard any sound in that trench, we shot at it, so we were sharing the trench with dead bodies. When the fire stopped we were straight out and carry on.

Major John Harry Crosland
B Company Commander, 2 Para
I'd imbued my soldiers with the message that we must keep moving. If we

stopped and the enemy had a chance to radio back, we'd get enemy artillery landing amongst us; we were in the open and they were under cover in trenches. We left prisoners and casualties along the centre line, where the RSM could take charge of them.

Major Philip Neame
D Company Commander, 2 Para

A Company achieved their objectives, and B Company had a couple of platoons to attack, which from the radio they seemed to do without a great deal of opposition. Then H went stomping off down this little access track ahead of me while B Company were reorganising on the right. I thought they should just have pushed straight on, but the reason for their delay soon became apparent.

Private Graham Carter
2 Para

None of my platoon was wounded in the early stages, as we were going through clearing trenches. It was so dark, and we could only hear voices, shouting and screaming as people were hit. Screams of 'I'm hit' – in English so it was one of ours, or just screams and muffled shouts with no direction or location. When we heard the noise of incoming fire on to us, we'd move out of the way and take cover in trenches, which might have dead bodies, which we'd just tread on. I was too busy thinking about our people around me.

Major John Harry Crosland
B Company Commander, 2 Para

There were many actions, over featureless terrain under entertaining conditions. There was a problem maintaining direction, and after going through three positions I told my platoons to halt. We'd missed a position to the right, so I asked Jeff Weyhill's reserve platoon and company headquarters to attack, clearing it of twelve enemy anti-aircraft gunners who were either killed or wounded.

I carried a strobe light, and receiving no reply to flashes to the front, realised that my leading platoons were now behind me, facing the wrong way – which indicates how confusing a night attack can become. We were then heavily shelled, but thankfully not with variable time fuses, which explode the shells above the ground. The artillery fire was very close, rearranging the boulders and peat, and very unpleasant.

Private Alejandro Ramon Cano
Grupo Artilleria Aerotransportada

The chief of our battery Lieutenant Perez Fernandez gets hold of me and tells me: 'Calm yourself, you stay here,' in the command post, where we had a radio and a teleprinter. He said: 'You tell me the position to where we have to shoot.' A cadet from the military college told me: 'I received orders, that as long as the First Lieutenant Estevez is here, *he* is the one who gives the order to fire.' But he gave me the position and I passed it on to Lieutenant Perez Fernandez, and then the battery started to fire.

Major Philip Neame
D Company Commander, 2 Para

H was boiling over with impatience at the delay, as he'd set himself a very tight timetable of six hours to get outside the settlement by dawn, ready to do the fighting there in daylight – because of the risk to the civilians. It was very ambitious to fight through seven kilometres in six hours; we still had this sublime view that we'd knock hard and just steam through. B Company's delay reorganising was critical to this.

H came storming back, and having been shot at from another Argentine position, ordered me out of reserve to attack it. But in the murk and dark I couldn't see anything at all. I decided to advance to contact with one platoon up and hope for the best. I called in a fire mission with the ship's gun and illuminating ammunition, which I hoped might clarify things for us. The ship fired six rounds, including one illuminating before the gun jammed, leaving us in darkness and total confusion as we blundered towards this objective.

We attracted a lot of small arms fire from a small hillock, so knew we were heading for enemy positions. This was our first exposure to combat. But despite the enormous amount of tracer being fired at us, we managed to get on top of this hill and started to clear it, with 12 Platoon leading. Then from our right flank, between us and the hill B Company had just taken, some machine guns fired upon us. 10 Platoon took two casualties and were pinned down. I tried to fire at them but immediately John Crosland asked what the hell we were shooting at, as they were in the way.

Company Sergeant Major Peter John Richens
B Company, 2 Para

Colonel Jones was very annoyed that we weren't covering the ground as fast as he had planned. My company commander had gone forward to the lead platoon. Me, the company runner and the company radio operator went firm, and were opened up on. Rounds were dancing around our feet and it was very frightening. It might have been the enemy, but it could quite easily have been D Company, who was firing from behind us. If it was them, I don't blame them, as it's very difficult to hold control on night attacks. Rounds were thudding into the dirt feet from us.

Major John Harry Crosland
B Company Commander, 2 Para
Phil Neames's reserve D Company hit a position we'd all missed, took casualties then poured fire right across the tops of our heads. After brief congratulations to them on their shooting ability, they desisted – but this is all part of the chaos of a night fight.

Major Philip Neame
D Company Commander, 2 Para
I was caught off balance, but Chris Waddington and 11 Platoon saved us. Using his own initiative, he came round behind 10 Platoon and put in an attack on these machine guns, with no guidance at all from me. Chris was straight out of Sandhurst, and already showing a certain flair for this kind of thing. His platoon suffered one wounded and another killed as they went in to attack these positions. They'd gone to ground, but finding themselves literally feet away from the enemy, decided to keep on going.

Major John Harry Crosland
B Company Commander, 2 Para
We moved off again down the isthmus, moving as quickly as we could, continuing with individual actions. We'd underestimated the time it takes for such close-quarter battle fighting at night, and the level of natural chaos.

Major Philip Neame
D Company Commander, 2 Para
As we reorganised, I realised why B Company had taken so long. The terrain was so featureless that in the heat of contact, people had followed the line of resistance, losing their orientation in the process. I had to pull my company back together, which was complicated by 10 Platoon's two casualties being missing. We couldn't find them, and it took some time to decide to stop looking for them. We were very clear that in the attack we didn't stop for anything, but afterwards, how long do you spend looking?

In the end I put up a flare and told everyone to reorganise on it, which is not the approved method. We couldn't find the two missing people, so I decided to push on. They were eventually picked up by battalion head-quarters: Corporal Cork had been shot first, and his buddy, Fletcher, was found lying on top of him with a shell dressing in his hand, having been shot trying to give first aid. They were both dead, but that's the way it goes.

(James) Robert Fox
BBC correspondent

HQ Company, the regimental aid post, and Chris Keeble's HQ had set up on the track, which was probably a mistake. The lead companies had gone through so quickly they'd left behind pockets of Argentines, and we were now under artillery fire – phosphorus rounds, which somewhat alarmed the Regimental Sergeant Major. We were then told to get off the track and dig in, which is when daylight started to come up.

David Cooper
Chaplain, 2 Para

Roger Miller, the ops officer, called us forward to see some casualties, warning of snipers to the right. Small arms fire came banging past quite close as we were silhouetted against the flames of Burntside House. Steven Hughes patched up the injured while I gathered together the dead. We stayed there until daylight, when we realised we were in the middle of a large Argentine position that had run off.

Company Sergeant Major Peter John Richens
B Company, 2 Para

Finally Colonel Jones told us to get our arses in gear or he'd pass D Company through and they'd do a better job than us. A Company was firing to our left, but we just couldn't make the required pace, and when dawn broke we were in extended arrowhead formation in very open country with no cover at all. Two platoons were up front, with company headquarters in the middle and a reserve platoon behind.

Major John Harry Crosland
B Company Commander, 2 Para

Come first light, we found ourselves moving across very open country – like Salisbury Plain, and came under fire from Darwin Hill, and from the Bocca House stronghold in front of us. During the night, the boot had been on our foot; the Argentines had not liked close-quarter fighting, but in daylight they could stand off and fire at us from eight hundred to a thousand metres, with snipers, mortars, artillery and aircraft as well.

We were caught on the forward slope, so I took two platoons to the bottom of the hill with my company headquarters, leaving John Young and Jeff Weyhill to guard the exit route should we be forced to withdraw. We hid in this gully, grovelling in the gorse bushes, which were on fire. A Company was also under fire; with D Company in reserve.

Company Sergeant Major Peter John Richens
B Company, 2 Para

As we were going down a forward slope, we were opened up by an enemy in very well-prepared trenches, and had to double forward into the gully like rats down a hole, while the reserve platoon had to return and go firm over the top of the hill. There was nothing we could do about this, so my company was split in two. There was a lot of fire from the enemy on to us, so we had to stay in the gully. Their snipers stopped us from doing what we wanted to do, trapping us for about six hours.

Major Philip Neame
D Company Commander, 2 Para

Argentines were wandering southwards along the western shoreline, so we amused ourselves with long-range pot shots at them. Most were out of range so I stopped it, but something registered in my mind. Then incoming artillery adjusted on to us, so I moved us into the lee of Darwin Hill to avoid this fire mission, despite H's orders to remain on the knoll. Immediately we moved, a significant fire mission came right down on this feature. I had to explain to H why I wasn't obeying orders, which he accepted.

I was concerned that nothing much was happening, and wondered why, if the Argentines can move along the shoreline, couldn't we, and get into the Argentine positions without being seen. I thought we could turn this by making their Darwin Hill feature untenable. I put the idea to H who told me to mind my own business. We then came under more artillery fire, so moved to a hollow further west, closer to the shoreline, where I was joined by C Company who had similar problems.

Major John Harry Crosland
B Company Commander, 2 Para

The Argentines now had the advantage. We were short of ammunition, with no ability to mass firepower to neutralise or destroy what was hurting us. My company took our first casualties: Private Stephen Illingsworth, who was later decorated with the Distinguished Conduct Medal, was shot dead having rescued one man and gone back for ammunition; my 2ic John Young was very seriously wounded, and Private Street was also wounded.

This was now the time to think. We needed to sort out what was obviously a separate phase of the ongoing battle. There was consternation over at A Company where H was closely following up behind Dare.

Major Philip Neame
D Company Commander, 2 Para
I could see the shoreline, and was convinced my idea deserved some exploration. I again got onto the radio to H and said, 'From where I am now, I believe there's the possibility to infiltrate along the shoreline and possibly turn this.' H was clearly having a frantic time with A Company on Darwin Hill and bit my head off along the lines of, 'Don't you tell me how to fight my battle. Can't you see we're busy up here?' So there we were – it was his battle, so what could I do that was useful? I told the men to make a brew, which I think they found rather strange, but there was nothing else rational we could do, and they needed the energy to fight until evening. I'd literally just got my porridge on the boil when we received the news H had been shot.

16

Moral Domination

*Goose Green was won by the fighting quality of 2 Para without
any help from anybody else. The Harrier strike at the very end
just tipped the scales that final extra bit.*

Major John Harry Crosland
B Company Commander, 2 Para
We had now hit the main Argentine positions surrounding the settlements
and the airfield, so needed to devise some method of getting through the crust
of this defence, having lost our momentum. One option was to assault straight
at Boca House, but instinct told me there were mines in front, which proved
to be correct. H was agitated at the loss of momentum and the speed of the
attack. I asked him to give me an hour to turn the area of Boca House, then I
could assault the enemy facing A Company, rolling them up from above. But
about ten minutes later, H decided to carry out a personal attack, which led to
his gallant, but very sad, death.

(James) Robert Fox
BBC correspondent
Keeble was given the communication that H Jones was down. He knew very
quickly that he'd died, didn't tell the rest of us, and set off to take over the
battalion. I lost a good friend then, a good source, when he left.

Company Sergeant Major Peter John Richens
B Company, 2 Para
My company commander urged the battalion 2ic to bring up the Milan
missiles as bunker busters, and we also heard that the commanding officer had

been killed – although this tragic news was not passed on to the company at that time. Major Keeble took over, and gave command to Major Crosland, as Tac 2 was some distance away from the battle.

Major John Harry Crosland
B Company Commander, 2 Para

The Milan anti-tank guided missiles were the only direct-fire weapon I could think of that would hurt the enemy trenches in front of us, but were back in the battalion firebase some fifteen hundred metres west of us in a separate re-entrant, covering our western approaches. To get into position, they had to come all the way up the middle, under fire from the Argentines. Phil Neame was keen to make an attack on the right, but I said we should wait until we see the effect of the Milans.

Major Philip Neame
D Company Commander, 2 Para

The impact of H's death wasn't as bad as people might think. We were too far out of it for the significance to penetrate. I remember H transmitting on his own personal radio after he'd been shot, ordering that nobody else was to come up and help him, but as everybody says he went down and that was it, maybe I imagined it. But anyway, he was out of the equation and Chris Keeble took over command, but as he was some way back, he did the most sensible thing and gave command to the battery commander Tony Rice, who was H's right-hand man. But it very quickly became clear that having been embroiled in the skirmish that had killed H, Rice couldn't do anything either, so Keeble gave command to John Crosland, who could see what was going on, and told me to join and help him. This was very irritating to me as my porridge was ready and I was trying to eat it.

Bill Belcher
Helicopter Crewman, 3 Commando Brigade Air Squadron

We'd been flying four hours. I was dropped off at Camilla Creek House to reduce the weight, so Richard could take on more fuel. We heard that Col H Jones was down, and when Richard came back we offered our services. The paras said the ground was secured but we didn't believe them, so with another helicopter flown by Captain Jeff Niblet, RM, we went to 2 Paras' RAP, hoping to fly from there up to where Jones had been hit, to pick up casualties. We had no armament at all. As we flew towards Goose Green, there was a very low cloud base so there were no Harriers to help us. Then two Pucaras came towards us – the biggest threat to our existence. They could match our slow speed, and had lethal armament.

(James) Robert Fox
BBC correspondent

A Pucara attack came swirling in through the mist, and I curled up into a ball. It saw a juicier target just behind us, the helicopter of a man I travelled around with rather a lot, Richard Nunn.

Bill Belcher
Helicopter Crewman, 3 Commando Brigade Air Squadron

Captain Niblet briefed a break left and right; he broke left and we broke right, so low that Richard actually put a skid on the ground, which is the best way to make a rapid turn at low altitude. We immediately took off back towards Camilla Creek House where there were friendly ground forces. I wasn't strapped into the front seat as usual, but standing in the back ready to look after casualties, so I became Richard's ears and eyes as the Pucara were directly behind us.

They'd split to follow both helicopters, and one had latched on to us, in our six o'clock. I could see the flashes from his cannon, and told Richard he was firing. I was hit just below the right ankle with a cannon shell, and my right leg was gone. It was like somebody taking a felling axe to your leg. Richard suggested I get the first aid kit out. I'd been stood with one knee on the rear seat, and my right foot on the deck of the aircraft. I looked down and saw a soggy end with a few bits holding my foot onto the end. There wasn't much blood, so I picked up my foot and put it onto bench. I was in a lot of pain and needed to do something about it. I can only assume my body had shut off the blood supply. It was just oozing – not squirting everywhere.

I laid across the rear seat and started ripping open the first aid kit. But then the Pucara returned down our right-hand side, so I got back up to continue my running commentary. As he overtook, he banked on his left wing tip and came back at us head-on from one o'clock and let rip with his under-wing machine guns. He was flying as slowly as he could, probably on his limits. Now it gets a little bit hazy, but I now know Richard took a round through the face and I took a couple more through my other leg. Richard died at the controls. We bounced once, turned, then impacted.

The doors burst and I was thrown out – clear of the burning wreckage. It was the first time I'd ever flown without being strapped in, or on a harness. I came to among wreckage with everything on fire, and started applying first aid to myself. I was unsure of Richard's situation or position. I couldn't really move or crawl, so I got on with first aid for myself, injecting morphine into the leg that hurt the most, then took dressings out of the first aid kit, which for some reason was still clutched to my chest.

One of the Gazelles evacuating 2 Para casualties flew overhead, and saw the wreckage with me sitting beside it. I made the mistake of waving, which in aviation circles is a sign to go away because there's danger or a hazard. But fortunately they returned quickly and two crewmen got out and strapped up both my legs using a severed door pillar as a splint. Then Captain Niblet came back with a stretcher in his Scout and flew me to the field hospital at Ajax Bay.

(James) Robert Fox
BBC correspondent
The sad thing was that Nunn's brother-in-law was standing beside me as all this happened, 2 Para's ops liaison officer, Captain David Constance, Royal Marines.

Private Alejandro Ramon Cano
Grupo Artilleria Aerotransportada
All the night we had been firing mostly with charges 4, which makes the projectile fly through the air. The cannons were old and incapable of more powerful charges, but one time a soldier made a mistake and made up a shell with charge 7. This broke the gun, and it was a laugh because the cannon bent. The head of the battery then gets a skilled mechanic to come along and straighten it out with a giant mallet, in order to continue shooting. This is something that caused a great joke for the whole afternoon.

(James) Robert Fox
BBC correspondent
We were getting incredibly cross with the Royal Navy, an anger that doesn't leave me, even now. Since the end of the war, we've heard all their excuses and special pleadings, not least in the extreme self-justification of Admiral Woodward's autobiography. Things were going very badly wrong. Harrier fighter-ground attack would have made a huge difference, and air strikes were requested continually all day. There were several excuses: Admiral Woodward's ship told us that the Harrier crews were too exhausted and there was fog at sea.

Before the battle, for personal reasons, Admiral Woodward had not been the most popular officer with Colonel Jones. Inter-service rivalries have real point. There was much feeling that the navy at sea did not understand what was taking place on land, and were not prepared to admit it either. An earlier Harrier attack would have saved a great deal of fighting. I didn't think we were ever going down for a defeat, although that could have happened.

Major Philip Neame
D Company Commander, 2 Para
We crested the ridge before John Crosland's position and could see the enemy on the Boca Hill feature twelve hundred metres ahead, out of range. We thought we'd just push on gently and see what might happen, but came under small-arms fire and my signaller had his pocket shot off. Deciding I was being a bit bold, we pulled back off this ridge.

I got on to Chris explaining we couldn't get to John Crosland, but were uncommitted, and that I still believed by using the western shoreline on my right, we might infiltrate round the Boca feature. Keeble said OK, have a look, so I sent a section down, then took two platoons down myself, leaving a platoon on the hill to give us some support. I got within six hundred metres of the Boca Hill position, but we couldn't move any closer without exposing ourselves. But at least we could get GPMGs within range, so I brought all mine down in a firing line behind a small ridge, and opened up on the Boca Hill feature.

At the same time, John Crosland brought the support weapons up, which I felt should have been done a long time ago. Perhaps H had become too absorbed into what A Company was doing and had lost the full perspective.

(James) Robert Fox
BBC correspondent
A Company had a hit a formation at least equivalent to its own strength, probably larger, well dug-in on Darwin Hill. One of their rifle platoons was detached, taking the long way round over the causeway to take the settlement. John Crosland's B Company were having a heavy time on the forward slope going down towards Goose Green, fighting a physically courageous action of penetrating then withdrawing; the guns had stopped firing as the battery commander was worried about high winds and the closeness of friendly troops.

I was fascinated observing the unfolding pragmatism of a group of officers who were outgunned and seriously outnumbered, led by Major Keeble, with Hector Gullan the 3 Commando Brigade liaison officer, John Crosland of B Company and Dare Farrar-Hockley of A Company, but also the real unsung hero of the battle of Goose Green, Major Philip Neame, OC of D Company.

Major John Harry Crosland
B Company Commander, 2 Para
We combined our meagre fire support with the shock effect of the Milans to fire on Boca House, enabling D Company to get round to the right and have a fairly easy attack on the remnants of Boca House. We then regrouped the battalion, with Chris Keeble taking over command, having given command to me when H was killed.

Company Sergeant Major Peter John Richens
B Company, 2 Para
We were very short of ammunition, but for us the Milan firing was the turning point in the battle. D Company passed through us, down through to Boca House by the beach; then after sorting ourselves out, we moved to the side of the airfield. The Argentine triple As were firing at us in low elevation. We came to the bottom end of the Goose Green settlement, again very low on ammunition.

Major Philip Neame
D Company Commander, 2 Para
Shortly after we'd opened up with the GPMGs and John Crosland started firing with Milan missiles, white flags appeared on the Boca Hill feature. I wanted to take this as quickly as possible, but there were obvious problems of whether they were all surrendering.

John Crosland took a different view; to keep on blasting until nothing was moving, which would take a lot of ammunition. But I could see their position was finished, white flags all over, with no more serious opposition. I told Chris we should move up and take the surrender, but with everything laid on in case it went wrong. Communications from the coastline were difficult, so this had to be relayed through my 2ic who was up on the hill near John Crosland.

David Cooper
Chaplain, 2 Para
As I crossed the gorse line at the top of Darwin Hill, it was shot apart around me, the hedge disintegrating with the noise of an enormous amount of bullets going by, splinters, something pulling at my sleeves, twigs flying about until I eventually got through it and lay down beside another soldier. We could both smell whisky and I realised that my hip flask full of Bob Fox's whisky had diverted a bullet. I returned to the RAP very shaken as they were preparing to

move forward. I told them, 'I wouldn't bother if I were you. There's no fucking place to go.' They took one look at my face, realised I was serious and unpacked again.

Major Philip Neame
D Company Commander, 2 Para

But when we got the surrender arrangements squared away, Chris wanted to resupply the support weapons with ammunition before we moved, so there was more delay. Then I noticed the tide was coming in, and I didn't want to remain there in case the Argentines decided to continue fighting. So I told Chris the tide was coming in and I'd be cut off, a load of baloney, but it served to speed things up.

I was lying behind a rock with Corporal Harley, where we were discussing the merits of surrender with Jim Barry. I'd said: 'It's my decision, so it looks like I'll have to be the first one to expose himself and move forward – it's what officers get paid for.' I turned to my signaller to tell him to move, but Harley jumped up with his section and said, 'You're too valuable, sir, I'll do this one,' which I thought a fairly noble gesture on his part, which left me with rather a soft spot for the individual, who is actually a bit of a tearaway.

At first it all went smoothly. No fire was returned, so my two platoons started moving uphill towards the top. Then one of our Milan opened fire again, while we were out in the open. I screamed down the radio for them to stop – which worked and fire was not returned. I could see mines in the valley bottom, so I had to detour round by the coast. One of the soldiers tried to cut through, but snagged a trip wire, setting off a mine, which knocked him over but didn't seem to do him any damage. We got on to the position to find it empty.

Argentines were running for their lives towards the airfield. An officer was driving a tractor flat out towards Goose Green with soldiers running behind desperately trying to jump on. I thought: 'This is leadership from the front.' I wanted to keep them on the run, exploiting our success, so leaving some people to sort out the carnage on the position, I set off in pursuit with two platoons, ordering my third platoon to catch up.

Major John Harry Crosland
B Company Commander, 2 Para

We still hadn't achieved our objectives; A Company was eight hundred metres outside Darwin having taken severe casualties, the commanding officer and the adjutant killed. Anti-aircraft guns ringed the settlement, and we were unsure of the enemy strength. Chris Keeble arrived and we decided that D Company would take a direct line of assault towards the schoolhouse and into Goose Green, using the contours to encircle them with a big outflanking southern hook manoeuvre.

Major Philip Neame
D Company Commander, 2 Para

We were in some disarray, but I was convinced we should keep the pressure on them, but it did lead to confusion later on. Chris Keeble ordered us to continue, as he could see the Argentines running across the airfield. To my right, there was a command post with tents, so I detached 10 Platoon to investigate, while I kept going with the rest of 11, plus 12 Platoon. The high ground to our right was riddled with trips for mines, and we were being pushed leftwards into a valley, which led to Goose Green schoolhouse, and fetched up on the access road. We'd seen a lot of enemy heading towards the school-house, which had been highlighted in our orders as a potential defensive strong point.

Major John Harry Crosland
B Company Commander, 2 Para

The platoon commanders thought I'd gone slightly bonkers, walking over a very bare-arsed area in direct view to a battery of 30mm anti-aircraft guns. I told them the anti-aircraft guns couldn't fire low enough to hit us, so we'd walk underneath them. I don't think they had much faith in this, as these 30mm guns were splattering away and looked quite terrifying. But we did pass unmolested by them, then through three or four minefields where you could see the mines sticking up. I advised the Toms not to kick them. We were under fairly heavy fire – from artillery, anti-aircraft and aircraft, and knocked out a few of their anti-aircraft positions along the way. Some positions stood their ground; others fired a few rounds and left.

This southern hook outflanked the Argentinians and convinced them they were up against a much larger force. We continued into an open field some two hundred metres from the southernmost end of Goose Green village, among old Argentine positions. We'd been fighting all night and all day and were tired and low on ammunition. The Argentine 105mm artillery was firing at us over open sights, which was unnerving. Two of my Toms in a narrow dugout in front of me received a very close hit, so we called them back for a cup of tea, restoring their faith in the world and assuring them they were still alive.

Major Philip Neame
D Company Commander, 2 Para
There were mines either side of the schoolhouse track, then 12 Platoon got themselves into a minefield and were reluctant to move forward, so I told them to stay there and give us fire support. I brought 11 Platoon up and went across the track behind an old building, where we could see tents and some trenches about a hundred yards ahead, between the schoolhouse and us. We decided to blast these with 66mm light anti-tank rockets, even though it was a bit too far away. Several people had a go and missed, until one did hit, to no reaction, so we moved forward to an FUP, ready to attack the schoolhouse.

Major John Harry Crosland
B Company Commander, 2 Para
Pete Ritchens, my sergeant major, had just rounded up eighteen Argentine prisoners, and I had my eyes on a furry jacket I thought would be quite nice to keep *me* warm as opposed to the wearer. Then we realised a Pucara was coming in to attack. We blew it out of the sky using small arms fire, and were showered with the napalm it was carrying. The eighteen prisoners ran off like frightened rabbits, so I also lost my furry jacket.

Private Alejandro Ramon Cano
Grupo Artilleria Aerotransportada
One time in the afternoon we stopped firing and rested because three of our Pucara aircraft were attacking the English troops. I was then working as an ammunition supplier to the guns. The English were very near because their shouts could be heard. But because of the Pucaras shooting, they started to retreat, which was a relief for us because we couldn't go on. We were exhausted, we hadn't eaten all night . . . and it was terrible. We rested for a while, but it was terrible to come back to the same struggle.

In one of those resting moments, about half past three in the afternoon, in the middle of combat, a mortar bomb exploded ahead, in front of the howitzer. Three soldiers were saved, but one lost his head, and metal splinters wounded others. A mortar bomb usually destroys a gun; if it had not been for this being a lucky gun with a charm medallion, one of the wounded would have lost his leg. Another lost an arm but thank God nothing else happened to him.

Major Philip Neame
D Company Commander, 2 Para
Up on the hilltop, by a flagpole, 12 Platoon said they could see more white

flags. We were joined by C Company coming from Darwin Hill, and were being fired on by artillery and Argentine triple A in the ground role. C Company had suffered from this fire as they were coming down, losing their company commander, and were in some disarray, although still with bags of enthusiasm.

I called for fire support on the schoolhouse, but was told the artillery was unavailable as they were doing counter battery firing – a real waste of resources as we were under fire and about to make an attack, and the artillery battery commander, Tony Rice, was simply guessing where the Argentine batteries might be, which clearly he wasn't doing very well as we were still being shelled. One of my soldiers was hit and died in the fifteen minutes it took to get organised, which was very harrowing. We couldn't casevac him, as we were quite helpless. The first aid wasn't enough . . . Getting serious casualties off your hands quickly is absolutely vital. This poor bloke draining away in front of us was a telling moment; we were withering under the impact of it all.

Private Graham Carter
2 Para

We came up to the school house as our next objective, the last thing before we could go up on to the airfield. The Argentinians were standing up there, four hundred metres away with their weapons held in the air. Mr Barry decided this was a good opportunity to take a surrender, so we advanced towards them, covering him. Mr Barry kept shouting at them to put their weapons on the floor and put their hands up. But they just held their weapons in the air. We advanced, then we heard machine gun firing and we didn't know whether it had come from their side or from ours. We didn't know if anybody had been hit, we just heard fire from right next to us. And instantaneously the Argentinians dropped out of sight and started firing.

Major Philip Neame
D Company Commander, 2 Para

I blame myself for Jim Barry deciding to take a surrender from this flagpole position. He'd been listening to me talking about surrender, maybe without realising how carefully I was setting it all up – so everyone knew what was happening, with fire support on call. But he'd taken it on himself to go up there and start parleying with these Argentinians, without anyone else being aware. I'd ordered him to stop, but he didn't receive my message, which I then asked to be relayed to him via battalion headquarters. There just wasn't the scope to let everyone know what was happening.

Private Graham Carter
2 Para
In the first volley of shots, Mr Barry was hit quite badly and got tangled in the barbed wire fence. They then used him as target practice . . . In the same instance Paul Sullivan got hit directly behind me, in the knee, and then he got hit several more times in the head. I was really lucky, as with two others I was protected by a small scoop in the ground. The other gunner, Brummy, got hit directly after the first volley of shots, ricochets off the GPMG, which hit him in the shoulder and in the back, so he was in quite a bad way.

Smudge, our section 2ic, fired a 66mm into the trenches that were giving us trouble, but it must have been damaged in some way as the whole thing went off and damaged him badly in the face and chest. As he was only a few feet away I went across to administer first aid to him, but as I moved, I got a bullet in my helmet, which took a chunk of it away. There was no way I was going to try going across there again.

Major Philip Neame
D Company Commander, 2 Para
Our machine gun platoon, which tended to fire on anything that moved anyway, and without the best of communications, saw movement around the flagpole position, got into a position where they could engage it and opened up. The Argentines, thinking their surrender wasn't being honoured and as they had the parley party of Jim Barry and a section of his men a few yards away, just wasted them. There were other interpretations; the Argentines say they thought Jim Barry was trying to surrender to them! It was quite clearly a mishap – total confusion in the fog of war – but critical, with a platoon commander plus four killed, two wounded and only one unhurt.

Private Graham Carter
2 Para
I stayed where I was and looked after Brummy, who thought he saw exactly where the enemy were. Despite being badly wounded, he tried to lay down some rounds in their direction but all he could do was plough up the ground three feet in front of us, which was no good at all. They was still shooting at us. I then spotted a sniper who was doing the hits. I laid down fire in his direction, and finally took him out so he folded up over the banking. Meanwhile we were trying to get somebody to come up and give us a hand. There was dead ground to the right-hand side, so I got on to the radio and brought up the rest of the platoon to take out the position. Sergeant Meredith

came up to join us, then we pushed through to the enemy. But we hit an ammunition dump and had to withdraw.

Major Philip Neame
D Company Commander, 2 Para
So as the schoolhouse attack was going in, I decided Chris Waddington was competent, so I pulled back to rejoin 12 Platoon. I was relieved to see that the platoon sergeant, Sergeant Meredith, had quickly grasped the situation, and personally brought machine gun fire and anti-tank weapons down on to the Argentines who shot Barry, setting a bomb dump alight, making the whole area untenable, stabilising the situation. We were pinned down, under fire from other positions. The schoolhouse attack went in with lots of confusion between the two platoons, then the school caught fire and lots of Argentines – up to fifty – are said to have burned inside. In my opinion, it was impossible to tell.

Private Graham Carter
2 Para
I went back to look at Paul Sullivan, but there was no hope. He'd been hit twice in the head and had no pulse. I administered general first aid but there was no use really. Smudge had died by then too, which was cutting, because basically my section was demolished – there was nobody left. We regrouped just below the schoolhouse, which was now being taken out by 10 or 11 Platoon, who were running around the building like Indians, throwing in grenades and shooting. At the time, I thought this was quite funny.

Major Philip Neame
D Company Commander, 2 Para
11 Platoon and C Company were being fired at from Goose Green and from across the water, so they pulled back to join me. 10 Platoon were still dealing with the command post, and I didn't actually know where they were – apart from messages saying they were being shot up by our machine gun platoon. Corporal Owen, who'd been looking after prisoners on Boca Hill, had passed them on, but was trapped by fire on the forward slope of Darwin Hill, and my company sergeant major had only just joined me. We'd been sucked into all this and were in a state of some chaos, pushing the enemy hard, but a little unbalanced – because of circumstance and maybe my inexperience.

Private Alejandro Ramon Cano
Grupo Artilleria Aerotransportada

We observed that the English were quite close. The head of our battery, the First Sergeant Arribas, prepares the piece of artillery and makes a direct hit on a school near where they were. It exploded at the school. I will never ever forget that image.

And then it was my turn to fire. The Sub Lieutenant Chanela handed me a couple of rounds to fire in the artillery piece. Everyone was putting the munitions into the truck at the same time and working really hard.

Major Philip Neame
D Company Commander, 2 Para

We had about one hour of daylight remaining, but then Chris Keeble ordered me not to exploit any further forward – which I didn't immediately understand. He was hoping to start negotiating with the Argentines in the settlement, so we wouldn't have to attack it. I'd got everyone except 10 Platoon assembled by the track, and we were told to wait for an air strike. We heard the aircraft, but it wasn't Harriers but a Skyhawk, coming up the track with my company neatly laid out along it – the ideal aiming mark. I felt a complete prat. We were squashed into a trap between a minefield and small-arms fire from Goose Green. I had to lie there and pray, watching the cannon coming up towards us. It felt so close that I thought all I had to do was stick out my hand to be hit. But there were no casualties.

After that, I decided to take our chances with the minefield. Our own air strike came in and destroyed the triple As in Goose Green, with pilot Bob Iverson being shot down but recovered by us the next day. A Pucara came over, dropped a napalm bomb on my medical aid post and fired at us, but we shot it down with intense small-arms fire, everyone cheering like a goal being scored in a football match. We captured the pilot, who was rather twitched about what we might do to him.

(James) Robert Fox
BBC correspondent

Alex Ward, from the motor transport pool, who'd been looking after us, came up with supplies and to take away the prisoners. He helped us to cook an all-in stew using Marine arctic rations, with curry and Tabasco. I kept feeling bloody cold – really, really cold, and shivering. I wrapped myself up in my clothes, but foolishly hadn't brought my sleeping bag with me. I remember walking through the fires in the gorse line and still feeling cold. I realised I was suffering from battle shock.

Private Alejandro Ramon Cano
Grupo Artilleria Aerotransportada

I had a comrade who was called Cuevas, who was sitting on a box of English munitions. This worried us, that is to say that they were not for sitting on. He was saying he was tired, that he didn't want to know any more, that he would stay here, that we were going to die here. He wasn't afraid or anything, the bloke was just tired. He didn't want to do anything, and the English ammunition worried us. I treated him badly because I smacked him to get a reaction. They were going to trounce us and I told him, 'They are going to kill us, you mad man, you have to stop. Let's go from here, let's carry a box of munitions.' I had to hit him to get a reaction.

(James) Robert Fox
BBC correspondent

Just before sunset, the padre, David Cooper, asked me to go with him to help collect bodies, but Chris Keeble shouted at us not to go as there were mines. I think he probably saved both our lives.

Company Sergeant Major Peter John Richens
B Company, 2 Para

The battalion went firm around the settlement, while Major Keeble sent the Argentine garrison commander an ultimatum to surrender, which was accepted the next morning. The Harriers also came and dropped bombs into the sea as a firepower demonstration.

Major John Harry Crosland
B Company Commander, 2 Para

The Harriers did a bombing run, delivering the sucker punch to the Goose Green defences. We didn't know they were coming, and the two aircraft dropped six-hundred-pound bomblet canisters, which I think broke the Argentines' will to be aggressive. They frightened us, and did considerable psychological as well as material damage to the Argentinian defence.

Private Alejandro Ramon Cano
Grupo Artilleria Aerotransportada

I came from our gun to the storehouse, and found the battery was not fighting because we only had fourteen boxes of munitions remaining. We could not last much longer. When I came out of the storehouse I encountered a Harrier coming towards the storehouse. I find it so enormous, so big that to me it looks like a Hercules and I was frozen, then suddenly the Sub Lieutenant Chanela shouts at me and I react. I was thinking that they wouldn't shoot at me because it would be difficult for them to fire on us being in a house that is surrounded by their own troops. At this point I react, and I tell you that it was hard for me to recognise, but time helps you to analyse and tells me that yes, I was scared. The majority of my comrades didn't think, but were concerned with eating, resting, in carrying on, and at this moment they didn't think anything at all. I had always considered that I didn't have fear, and that if I had been frightened, I would not have survived. We left our position at nightfall, and were now without munitions, which we had left in a sort of base.

Major John Harry Crosland
B *Company Commander*, 2 *Para*
Just after last light, five Argentine helicopters landed south of our position, carrying one hundred and twenty or so reinforcements from Port Stanley, making me feel very isolated on our southern flank. With D Company still fighting on the northern part of Goose Green, and A Company wrapped up in the Darwin area having given platoons to D and C Companies, the battalion was too unbalanced to deal with any counter-attack.

Company Sergeant Major Peter John Richens
B *Company*, 2 *Para*
We heard helicopters coming in, which frightened us as we thought it might be a counter-attack force or mortar base plates, and we were very vulnerable. We saw their reinforcement troops arrive, but they went into the settlement, which was rather strange, and not what we'd have done.

Major John Harry Crosland
B *Company Commander*, 2 *Para*
I ordered my company to withdraw to a more defensive area on a slight rise where we could make a last stand if necessary, then fired a last-hope harassing shot at where these helicopters had landed, which was fairly accurate. We gathered up Argentine ammunition which is the same as our own, to be ready to attack the village of Goose Green if required. Chris Keeble told us: 'Hold firm as you are. Other ideas are being developed.'

Company Sergeant Major Peter John Richens
B Company, 2 Para

A lot of Argentinians were walking into the settlement, but all they wanted to do was surrender, which got a bit silly as I had only two sections with me. We separated the officers, NCOs and private soldiers, broke their weapons and took their ammunition, then told them to clear off into the settlement. We needed ammunition, not prisoners. We found thousands of rounds of Argentine 7.62mm ammunition and spare barrels for GPMGs, plus food in abundance all over the place. We struggled back up the hill and resupplied the company. It started to rain, only it tasted like aviation fuel. A Pucara had been shot down, dumping its fuel. There were also rumours of napalm being used, and later we found napalm canisters in the settlement.

Private Alejandro Ramon Cano
Grupo Artilleria Aerotransportada

We were told that they had made a ceasefire to clear the dead from the fields, and then they would see what would happen. The head of the battery came that night personally and gathered together all the battery: 'Men, do you want to go on? Do you want to go on? We are not going to surrender. Look for food and munitions where you can, but we are not going to surrender.'

We were tired, but the only thing in my head was to go on. I would stay, and if they made me surrender I would not give in. That was what was important . . . with enthusiasm, in a second you are involved. We broke all our artillery guns, we stole everything from them. We looked for 7.62 ammunition, munitions for our FAL rifles, and once we had loaded our pockets we left. But then night went by. It was my turn for the last guard. It was so cold . . . the moment, the feeling of defiance, passed. The chief of our battery tells me, crying: 'Well, sadly there is nothing we can do. The weapons must be handed over at half-past twelve.'

Brigadier Julian Howard Thompson
Commander, 3 Commando Brigade

That night 2 Para learnt of the civilians being held in the village hall. Through Captain Rod Bell in my headquarters, a letter was sent to the Argentine commander via two prisoners, saying that unless they surrendered, they'd be pounded; and if the civilians were hurt, he would be held responsible, so he'd better give up.

Argentine dead after the battle for Goose Green, May 1982.

Major Philip Neame
D Company Commander, 2 Para
We settled down on the reverse slope to the settlement. Nightfall came; we were down to two or three rounds of ammunition per man, no food, no water, with casualties and bodies we were trying to get back. Jim Barry's body had laid out there for three or four hours after dark before we could get him back. Chris Keeble was negotiating the surrender so we just waited to see what would happen. My gut feeling was that, psychologically, we'd won the day, but I didn't know there were eleven hundred Argentine troops in the settlement. It was freezing cold, but I managed to get some sleep. We were on our chin-straps and could easily have been taken out.

Major John Harry Crosland
B Company Commander, 2 Para
We were wet and exhausted, and had a very cold night. We'd suffered one killed – Illingsworth – and five wounded, the most serious being my 2ic, John Young. Despite atrocious weather the Army Air Corps flew in to take them to the field surgical teams at San Carlos Bay. This was the same flight who'd flown for us earlier in Kenya, and were intensely loyal to the battalion. John Greenhalgh and his pilots flew right into the front line, landing on torches at night to extricate our people. Our men had managed to survive for over fourteen hours after being wounded, which is a great credit to their courage, first-aid knowledge and fitness.

I told the men that even though our CO and others were dead and we were cold, wet and exhausted, we now had to pull our fingers out and produce the goods just as our forefathers had in the past. Although it sounded a bit Churchillian, they understood the message, and were perfectly willing to get up and go on again as they had been doing for the past thirty-six hours. But at daybreak, the surrender took place on the racecourse, out of sight to the world's press.

(James) Robert Fox
BBC correspondent
Chris had organised a parley with the Argentines, and I was one of the party of seven who went down to meet them. We nearly made a mistake though, with firepower demonstrations and the settlers being held as hostages. They could have held the hundred and twenty settlers inside the settlement and staged a siege. Had the thing broken down and any of the settlers been killed, then the whole campaign could have been stopped dead.

Major Philip Neame
D Company Commander, 2 Para
I supervised the surrender negotiation next morning, which Keeble did with Robert Fox. They were given an hour to come out, have a little macho parade, then ground their weapons and surrender. My company lined up and we watched with disbelief, as hordes of enemy soldiers poured out of the settlement. It could have been a very different story had the Argentines not accepted things quite so passively.

Company Sergeant Major Peter John Richens
B Company, 2 Para
We were most amused when the Argentinian army marched out of the settlement with a band, lined up in three ranks on the airfield, took off their helmets and laid down their arms. We thought: 'That's that then . . .' but the band struck up again, and out marched the air force and did the same thing, and finally the navy. The head count revealed there were eighteen hundred enemy, and we were about four hundred and fifty people, so it was quite a feat for us.

Private Alejandro Ramon Cano
Grupo Artilleria Aerotransportada
We handed over the weapons at half-past twelve, but one person was still armed. There was confusion because we had robbed many things, including alcoholic drinks. A couple of us got drunk and we didn't want to surrender. It was a big fuss, and I remember the row. We had fallen prisoner with no choice, but while we were still fighting . . . I think the English have to thank God and the Virgin that nothing bad happened there. Because had we acted in another way . . . Even though there was the row, we did not want to kill them. But then came a feeling of calm, although the row still existed.

Major John Harry Crosland
B Company Commander, 2 Para
I believe a lot of credit should go to Robert Fox, who speaks Spanish and understands the Spanish-American attitude. They wanted to sing their national anthem and have a parade, with which we had no problem provided they laid down their arms. Very few of us were privy to this plan, so suddenly seeing twelve hundred or so Argentine soldiers come marching out of the Goose Green garrison for this parade was a very sobering moment; there were far more than we'd thought. But we'd completed our mission, and taken the objectives we'd been set;

and with great respect to H and all the others who were killed and wounded, with relatively little cost. I think we had eighteen killed and thirty-five wounded.

Brigadier Julian Howard Thompson
Commander, 3 Commando Brigade

Goose Green was won by the fighting quality of 2 Para without any help from anybody else. The Harrier strike at the very end just tipped the scales that final extra bit. With hindsight, I made an error. I asked too much of 2 Para, and shouldn't have sent them there on their own. This is not a criticism of 2 Para. I should also have taken a commando, plus some of my eight Scimitar and Scorpion armoured cars, and gone down to command the battle myself, as a brigade operation. With the armoured car's firepower, we should have been through the Argentine positions in very short order. But because of my lack of personal experience in using light armour, I didn't believe they would make it across the rough ground, which was stupidity on my part. We could have done it with much fewer casualties had I done a two-battalion attack, and I kick myself to this day that I didn't do it.

David Cooper
Chaplain, 2 Para

Juliet Company from one of the commandos walked through our lines to support us, and it was nice to see them. One of our Volvo BVs came down with rations, so I went with it to see John Crosland at D Company, then drove down into Goose Green where the villagers had just been released from the village hall. We were alone in Goose Green with over a thousand Argentine prisoners, and one hundred and twenty villagers who couldn't return to their houses. Some houses had been wrecked and others booby-trapped as well. There were huge piles of ammunition and weapons, plus leaking napalm containers. It was a complete administrative nightmare. We set up a defensive position in case of an Argentine counter-attack.

John Pole Evans
Falkland Islander, Goose Green Community Centre

When the fighting finally stopped, the settlement manager came back to the hall and told us there was a ceasefire. We were so pleased to see the paras; we met them when they arrived, handing round drinks, and they put up a Union flag on the end of the galley. We were overwhelmed. We were free, which was all that mattered to us.

We remained in the hall the night we were liberated, as all our houses had first to be cleared of booby traps. The Argentines had used the floors as toilets, so after the British had cleared them for booby traps, we had to throw out all the carpets and gut a lot of the buildings. The following day my family moved into the house of another family member, after we'd cleaned it up.

Brigadier Julian Howard Thompson
Commander, 3 Commando Brigade

The commandant of Goose Green was my first contact with Argentine senior officers: an air commodore, as Goose Green was an airstrip and under air force command, with about six hundred army infantry and some twelve hundred air force. He was brought to my headquarters where I felt, out of courtesy, I should greet him. He spoke exceedingly good English and commented on how much he'd enjoyed a recent visit to London, so I said I hoped I might visit Argentina, to which he said: 'You are in Argentina now.' I just laughed.

Major John Harry Crosland
B Company Commander, 2 Para

D Company went into Goose Green first, while A Company remained in Darwin. B Company had to spend another twenty-four hours on the battlefield, then we got everybody into a couple of huts which Colour Sergeant Stevie Gerrard and his gang sorted out for us. We were made standby company, and after clearing an Argentine observation post on a hill overlooking Goose Green, had to help with cleaning up the battlefield – a very testing phase. The settlement was damaged from the fighting, and there were our dead, their dead, their wounded, our wounded, and the prisoners. Our chaplain and doctor had more experience of this phase of battle and so took charge, with us providing the help.

Company Sergeant Major Peter John Richens
B Company, 2 Para

We settled in an ironmonger's store, garage and barn in Goose Green, where we boiled water in forty-five-gallon drums to wash, shave and get cleaned up. The place had been left in a horrifically bad state by the Argentines, and there were a lot of prisoners. But we also had to go back and clean up the battlefield, which was very disturbing for the young soldiers. In our briefings for the attack, we'd been told to put our injured and dead on to the track that runs from the middle of the isthmus to the settlements. As the battalion rolled on, they were picked up or treated. We left the Argentinian dead where they fell, so had to send parties out to collect them. Nobody was buried on the battlefield.

David Cooper
Chaplain, 2 Para

I had the task of collecting and accounting for the dead. This wasn't helped by Dave Wood, the adjutant, being one of them. I suggested that the mortar platoon commander who was nominated as next adjutant, should take on the job immediately. Together with the RSM, we could start sorting out who our dead were, and trying to account for any who were still missing.

Company Sergeant Major Peter John Richens
B Company, 2 Para

During the mayhem of battle, with a lot of noise, screaming and crying, you just roll on and do your job. But when it all settles down and you go back and look for the bodies, it's different. It was very cold and they were frozen in *rigor mortis*; not lying on their backs with arms folded across their chests, but twisted as they fell, having been shot. They had to be picked up, and we commandeered tractors and trailers, and designated a field as the mortuary. This was quite harrowing.

Major John Harry Crosland
B Company Commander, 2 Para

The Argentine chain of command had collapsed and their officers had failed. Having tried to lead in a very macho, physical fashion, when faced with the professionalism and determination of our Toms, they'd cracked. The prisoners of war were shepherded into the sheep huts, while we attempted to find out who was alive, missing, wounded or killed, for the benefit of their wives, brothers, mothers and so on. The officers I saw were ignorant, arrogant and fearful for their own lives, through not having led their soldiers. They were now only worried about themselves, rather than their men's welfare.

David Cooper
Chaplain, 2 Para

We compiled a list of the names of the missing from the rifle companies and support company, plus information as to when they'd last been seen. So when I went out looking for bodies, I had a list of those I was pretty sure were dead, plus those reported missing by their companies. While I searched the battlefield and collected and identified all the bodies at Goose Green, our RSM, Malcolm Simpson, went back to Ajax Bay to search through all the dead there, to identify any bodies taken there without going through our battalion system.

Argentine prisoners of war living in the warm, dry clearing shed at Goose Green after the battle, before being moved to Ajax Bay. A soldier of 2 Para stands guard.

Major John Harry Crosland
B Company Commander, 2 Para
We were grieving for our losses, and that night I wrote letters to Sara Jones and Private Illingsworth's parents. But I was also very concerned about maintaining the momentum and deciding what we did next. Looking back in history, a successful attack is often followed by a failure or reverse. I was keen to build on our success, and having hit them hard, to keep on punching. This wasn't an easy attitude to put over, and was complicated by the arrival of General Moore and the new, reconstituted 5 Brigade. Clearly, with two brigades, there was going to be fewer resources to go round. The operation was entering a different phase and becoming more complicated.

We'd lost our commanding officer, and a new one, David Chaundler, was being flown in to take over from Chris Keeble. The land forces were being reorganised into two brigades. We hadn't got to Stanley, which was our objective, so we had to get our momentum back.

David Cooper
Chaplain, 2 Para
My next problem was actually collecting the dead, and I was able to use a Marine BV which had come down from San Carlos, and a small party of soldiers. I was still very concerned at where the Argentine mines were, and whether all the Argentines had surrendered, so it was with some anxiety that we set off visiting the various places the companies told us their dead had been placed. The area was criss-crossed by command wires from the Milan missiles, which I had to check in case they were mine trip wires. Once we got the bodies back to Goose Green, I was told they could not be flown out to San Carlos for at least twenty-four hours, giving me plenty of time to identify them.

Lieutenant Colonel David Robert Chaundler
Replacement CO, 2 Para
I knew that my old battalion 2 Para was fighting at Darwin and Goose Green, and on the Friday (May 28), we were told the objective had been taken, that casualties were light, and next of kin had been informed. My feelings were of relief, with envy that I was the wrong end of the world at the time. I was in defence intelligence, and our work was geared around the daily schedule at Number 10: the Prime Minister was briefed at 1000 hours, so we started work around five a.m.

After I'd put this particular morning's briefing together, I went down to the

MoD canteen with a friend of mine, Mike Jackson, who at that time was the only other spare Parachute Regiment lieutenant colonel. Colonel Peter Morton from the directorate of military operations was also having breakfast, and we said what good news it was about 2 Para, to which he replied carefully: 'Well, I suppose it is – if you call having the commanding officer and adjutant killed good news . . . you do realise that one of you two is going to have to go?' Mike Jackson and I got our bacon and eggs and looked at each other over the breakfast table. I'd already been pencilled in to take over 2 Para from H Jones, so we both knew it would be me.

David Cooper
Chaplain, 2 Para

There'd been pressure from brigade to provide a list of the dead, which we resisted until we were absolutely certain of its accuracy, which was of far greater concern to us than the speed of its release. There were difficulties back in UK, particularly with our families officer in Aldershot, as everybody there knew we'd been involved in a battle and people had been killed. It took between thirty-six and forty-eight hours to produce the list of the dead, which was a very long time for the families to wait.

Lieutenant Colonel David Robert Chaundler
Replacement CO, 2 Para

Back in the office on the Saturday, it was absolute chaos. The Argentines were trying to negotiate a particular arms deal in a European country, and the secure telephone on the other side of the room was answered by one of the civil servants who shouted that the embassy involved was on the line for me. At the same time my phone rang with Colonel Peter Morton, who said: 'It's you,' at which point I lost all interest in arms deals, picked up my briefcase and went home. My wife and I were having H Jones's wife Sara and her two boys round for supper that evening. It became very apparent that next of kin had not been informed of the deaths in 2 Para, which would not be done until all the 2 Para casualties were known. Sara Jones would be having supper with us without knowing both that her husband had been killed, and that I was to take over from him.

David Cooper
Chaplain, 2 Para

I put the bodies in the garden of the house we were using as our main headquarters. I remember telling the sentry that the bodies were part of his

2 Para bury their dead at Ajax Bay, San Carlos, May 28, 1982.

responsibility; to check regularly and ensure that they weren't interfered with by any of the dogs running loose around the settlement, which hadn't been fed. I told him to shoot the dogs if necessary, and he looked absolutely stunned. I was told afterwards it wasn't the shooting of the dogs, but guarding dead bodies that caused him some anxiety. I was able to get the bodies back to Ajax Bay the next day on a helicopter, where I believed they'd been buried. I was surprised to be summoned much later to attend the funeral – especially to be told at the last minute that I was taking it.

Michael Thomas Nicholson
ITN correspondent

We attended the burial of fifteen paras, including Colonel H Jones. It was a drizzly, dirty cold morning, perfect for funerals, and they'd dug a long pit. The paras stood around the pit, which was already filling with water, and they laid out the black body bags. A Royal Marine bomb disposal expert who wrote poems stood on the hill just behind the funeral playing a dirge on his fiddle, with the soft murmuring of prayer and the body bags being slowly covered by water. They allowed us to film it.

David Cooper
Chaplain, 2 Para

In the meantime, we also had large numbers of Argentine dead. The Argentine soldiers were prepared to help with this, so I went to speak with their senior officer. I told him we were collecting his dead soldiers and that I already knew some had no form of identification. I asked for NCOs, or officers from the units in the areas we were clearing, to identify the bodies – for humanitarian reasons, as I felt their families and next of kin would want to know what had happened. I was very taken aback when this officer said he knew who he'd lost, and didn't want to help us in any way.

John Pole Evans
Falkland Islander, Goose Green Community Centre

After the surrender at Goose Green, the farm workers helped dig out the new military positions. Equipment and vehicles that had been sabotaged were very quickly sorted out. Our Land Rover had been taken by the Argentines to Camilla Creek, where the British had captured it before the main battle. After removing the doors, it had become their only civilian vehicle, used for towing and carrying equipment forward.

David Cooper
Chaplain, 2 Para

We collected the Argentine dead and laid them out. Chris Keeble had planned to bury them in the local cemetery, but the Falklanders suggested we throw them into the sea. We said that if, as the ones who'd fought them, we were prepared to give them a decent burial, the least the islanders could do was to let us do it, and eventually the islanders recognised this. Only the senior of the three Argentine chaplains would help, and when we left Goose Green, the Gurkhas buried them, with his assistance and 5 Brigade's Roman Catholic chaplain.

An Argentine gun position, close to the sheep sheds where the prisoners were kept, was in a terrible condition with a pile of artillery and small arms ammunition mixed up with mines. This confusion did not equate to the obvious efficiency of the way they'd been firing at us, so Chris Keeble decided it was booby-trapped. But the ammunition technical officer who Chris brought in to examine it, said not. So when the Argentine prisoners wanted to move the ammunition as they feared an air attack might set it off, we agreed. We had nobody to do this for them, and made it quite clear they didn't have to do the work, but if they volunteered, we would pay them.

Company Sergeant Major Peter John Richens
B Company, 2 Para

We found a boat full of fresh food: ratatouille, tins of corned beef, which our quartermaster requisitioned, so for a few days we ate very well, which had a good effect on morale. The Falkland Islanders in the settlement were so pleased about what we'd done for them, something we'd never experienced before. We couldn't come to terms with people being so thankful to us. We had a church service of memorial, which after all the other services on the way down, seemed as if we'd become quite religious.

John Pole Evans
Falkland Islander, Goose Green Community Centre

We weren't allowed outside the settlement, because of minefields and booby traps. We'd go and look at the prisoners in the sheep sheds. There were a lot of dead Argentines, which the paras had collected and laid in the gorse near the garage. I can remember going up along there and looking at all those bodies. It's strange now to think of seeing them, and to say that we didn't feel sorry for them lying there on the grass. We hated them so much, after the way they'd come in and taken over, and the way they treated us while were locked up. We had no feelings at all for their dead. They were just lying there on the ground.

David Cooper
Chaplain, 2 Para
I was in the RAP building at the end of the settlement. There were constant explosions, but this one bang really rattled the building, followed by a soldier running in to report a fire at the gun position. We grabbed our bags and I helped a soldier carrying a stretcher. We came across an injured man, so I left the soldier with him and ran on towards the gun position. There was a very fierce fire in which the artillery charge bags were burning. Another soldier was trying to get a stretcher over a fence and making a ham job of it, so I grabbed it from him and threw it over. When I jumped over, for some reason he didn't follow, so I continued running towards the fire.

A medical corps sergeant had pulled one of the bodies out of the fire. Our RSM, Mal Simpson, shouted to keep clear as there was ammunition still in the flames. I decided it wouldn't make much difference to me, and pulled this Argentine casualty further from the flames. He'd lost both his legs, one at the knee and the other at the thigh, and one arm from the elbow, with a large wound from the base of his chest down to his abdomen. The flesh had been completely burned from these lost limbs, leaving the bones sticking out. He was still conscious, so we tried to put a drip into him.

Mal Simpson was still shouting about exploding ammunition, so we took this guy round the back of the buildings. He was in a bad way, and although we'd got a line into him, was now unconscious. We needed help to move him to the Land Rover shuttling casualties to the RAP. I looked up and saw a pair of Wellington boots standing there and shouted at this person to give us a hand, but nothing happened. I looked up to see it was the newly arrived 5 Brigade commander, Brigadier Tony Wilson, who was quite clearly too stunned to do anything. One of our platoon commanders, Pete Adams, arrived and helped us move this stretcher to the Land Rover.

I asked one of the Argentine chaplains, in French, to talk with the wounded and deal with the inevitable dead. Bob Fox spoke Spanish, but was in a real quandary as he'd got a helicopter coming and a Marisat slot booked to transmit the story back to the UK. I decided it was probably better that our families heard what we'd been doing, so Bob went off in his helicopter. We got the man I'd pulled from the fire evacuated, but he died later. One casualty was put into my sleeping bag, which I didn't mind at all, but thereafter whenever I got into it, all I could smell was burnt flesh.

Eventually we got the casualties out and restored some order. Two Argentines had been killed outright in the explosion. A third man was caught in the flames who nobody could reach, so one of our soldiers shot him – which

Ammunition technical officers from Commando Logistics Regiment RM sorting out abandoned Argentine ammunition at Goose Green after the battle.

I think was probably the best thing he could have done in the circumstances. It seemed to me some 105mm HE artillery rounds had gone off, suggesting that despite the ATO inspection, the dump was booby-trapped. It shook us a bit, making us even more aware that you couldn't lower your guard, and that there wasn't any such thing as a safe area.

Major Philip Neame
D Company Commander, 2 Para
More soldiers were going sick with problems like trench foot, and we didn't know when we'd get them back again. They needed a bit of reassurance, particularly the younger soldiers. It had been a pretty harrowing thirty-six hours, in an uncontrolled situation where we'd stuck our necks out quite a bit. There was the feeling that 'we'd done our bit, and the rest of the army could do their bit for a while'. They didn't want to have to repeat it again in a hurry. I ordered that nobody could go sick without first seeing the company sergeant major; he would give them reassurance they needed – either a pat on the back or a sharp pencil up the nose, and suddenly the numbers seeing the doctor dropped. We seemed to have solved the problem . . .

David Cooper
Chaplain, 2 Para
After one of our soldiers had escorted prisoners back to Ajax Bay, he complained to me that the prisoner-handling people there were treating them too harshly. He said: 'If I can treat them well, and it was me they were trying to kill, I don't see why they can't treat them properly at Ajax Bay.' We took this complaint seriously, and passed it to Brigade HQ.

Private Alejandro Ramon Cano
Grupo Artilleria Aerotransportada
In prison we had to deal with the English and they were very pleasant, very good treatment, at no time did they fail to respect in any way that we were soldiers. I showed them a little more consideration because they had treated us well. But unfortunately for them, at the end of the war, we continue feeling the same as before.

Company Sergeant Major Peter John Richens
B Company, 2 Para
We assumed Major Keeble would be made commanding officer automatically, but a few days later we learned that another CO had been appointed and was

on his way down. This made us all feel a bit sick, as we appreciated what Chris Keeble had done for the battalion. Our nose was put out of joint and at the time we all thought this was wrong.

Major Philip Neame
D Company Commander, 2 Para

Without a lot of luck and our total commitment, Goose Green could easily have gone wrong. As it was, we won it, stamping our psychological authority on to the whole campaign. After Goose Green, we were fighting an army that was staring defeat in the face, which is an enormous advantage. So although Goose Green was seen at the time to have been an irrelevance, strategically it was far, far more important. It was very fortunate that, despite all the shortcomings, we succeeded.

17

A Brand New Ship

During this flight, the Harriers were up looking for some alleged
Peruvian Sea Kings equipped with Exocets looking for our fleet.
I casually asked the pilot how the Harriers would know we were British
Sea Kings. He said he'd been wondering about that.

Captain Hugh Maxwell Balfour
HMS Exeter

HMS *Exeter* was a brand new ship, on exercise in the USA. We had shot
down real target aircraft, but our computer system kept crashing, so I had to
send a private signal to the chief of staff at Northwood, Admiral David
Hallifax, saying that although we were very willing to go to war, the ship was
not operational. We were giving a lunch party in Nevis, a lovely little island,
when we heard *Sheffield* had been sunk. We were first reserve and were
ordered to sail to Antigua, take on stores and pick up de-bugged software from
the afternoon BA flight, then make best speed to Ascension. Having been
hugged by a tearful Antiguan President, we slipped from a crowded jetty, with
the BA jumbo jet overhead waggling its wings. The locals were very
supportive of the UK's action.

We kept radio silence during the two-week voyage to Ascension. We were
only equipped for a tropical deployment, but the reply I received to my
detailed status report from Admiral Hallifax was unprintable. It dawned on
me that we'd been sent no operations order, and all the procedures had gone
out of the window, so I decided to shut up thereafter. The admin officer at
Ascension was an old friend, Captain Bob McQueen, so I flew ashore and he
told me what was going on. Bob was having a hard time with the RAF who
were still trying to do things by the book. We all wrote home for the last time,

with many like me sending a second, serious letter – to my brother, saying what to do if I was killed, with instructions to return the letter to me when we docked safely afterwards. An old friend, Sam Salt, on his way home after being sunk in *Sheffield*, came across to brief us on the pitfalls. This was invaluable. We had to refuel in seriously bad weather at forty degrees south, finding the tanker with so little left that we had no choice, which sharpened everybody up. We knew from the BBC World Service that the landings were taking place, then, once close enough to pick up the task force's air warning HF circuit, we got our first immediate information, listening as the above water warfare officers in *Brilliant* and other ships in San Carlos were attacked and bombed. Still with no orders, we headed for Falkland Sound, but three hundred miles or so out, were sent an OpGenAlpha, the list of who is in command of everyone else. We were to be air defence pickets for the battle group, one hundred and fifty miles east of the Falklands, out in front to take out low-level Exocet raids before they got within range of the carriers. *Coventry* was the only other air defence ship, and we were the new boys. We had to learn a lot very quickly.

Commander Timothy John Gedge
Fleet Air Arm

The navy had sent down every aircraft it could within the first few days of the crisis, so the problem was providing replacements and reinforcements. I was told to form a new Harrier squadron – 809 Squadron – to be ready for deployment as quickly as possible. I mustered all the Sea Harriers I could find from all over the place, some still being built.

I had three weeks to deploy my squadron. But both our carriers were already full of aircraft, so we had eight days to convert a merchant container ship, *Atlantic Conveyor*, into an aircraft carrier. On Saturday morning I walked around the ship and decided how this should be done, and immediately teams of marine engineers started work, cutting away huge sections of deck, with sheets of new steel being lifted into place.

One week later, she was swinging round a buoy in Plymouth Sound. I made six vertical test landings and take-offs from various directions, then climbed up to altitude and radioed back to Yeovilton that the conversion was satisfactory. After refuelling, I saw *Atlantic Conveyor* had already slipped her moorings and sailed for the South Atlantic. She would take ten days to sail to Ascension, where we would load her with our eight Harriers.

Many of the aircraft were brand new, so we had to complete their assembly, fit radars and repaint, plus work up the aircrew and ground crews. We flew to the Gambia, then Ascension, with thirteen air refuellings keeping the tanks topped up in case something unpredicted happened. This was the first time most of us had done air-to-air refuelling – as well as landing on a ship. The RAF Harriers also arrived, so once we were all safely landed on *Atlantic Conveyor*, we ran lectures and teach-ins about operating at sea.

Air Marshal John Bagot Curtiss
Air Commander, Northwood
The RAF's Number One Squadron were sent from Germany and turned overnight into a backup Sea Harrier squadron. The crews were retrained to operate as fighter pilots from a flight deck, the aircraft were sea-proofed to withstand the ravage of salt and the weather, and fitted with Sidewinder missiles. The squadron were flown to Ascension, flew on to *Atlantic Conveyor*, and were delivered to *Hermes* just before *Atlantic Conveyor* was sunk.

Commander Timothy John Gedge
Fleet Air Arm
The passage from Ascension took two weeks. I flew on to *Hermes* and refuelled, but the decision that I should continue to *Invincible* wasn't taken until after dark. When I got airborne, I realised there were several things I didn't know, for example should I use my bright flashing navigation lights in the war zone, was there any kind of threat around, and were there other ships around too? I decided to be cautious and used the bright lights for some two hundred miles to where I'd been told *Invincible* would be. When I got there, to my great relief they replied, and I was able to land. My lack of practice was not too apparent, but they didn't know I was coming and after some incredulity gave me a warm welcome. The rest of my aircraft flew across the next day. We had two days before the San Carlos landings to integrate ourselves into the programme.

Linda Kitson
Official war artist
The Imperial War Museum's Artistic Records Committee chairman, Freddie Gore, told me that the whole thing was mad, eight thousand miles away without air cover or air superiority. Field Marshal Dwin Bramall, the Chief of the Defence Staff and also on the committee, said it was impossible and the army wouldn't do it, but he was gunned down, and ended up putting his back into it. The military are not warmongers.

Major General (John) Jeremy Moore
Commander, British Land Forces

To fight a battle ashore, we needed reinforcements, but were given nothing like enough. Throughout the war, we were always outnumbered, so our planning had to be based on finding different ways of achieving superiority, moral rather than physical. With an extra brigade, we would also need a divisional headquarters, which it was agreed I should command, which meant me moving south. I needed to stay in UK until the landings were launched, to advise the chiefs of staff and the War Cabinet. I didn't want to arrive before the reinforcements, as I would be getting on the back of the bloke below me – Brigadier Julian Thompson, so I didn't go south until the actual landing took place.

Linda Kitson
Official war artist

My generation of artists had become ignorant of war. I am really ashamed to say that I had no knowledge of what war artists had done. There was a lot of fuss about having a woman war artist, and a horrible ten days when the press put my commission into jeopardy. The MoD said any photograph, statement or ripple of adverse comment and I was out of it. Two pressmen camped around my flat for twenty-four hours.

Captain Alan John Warsap
Regimental Medical Officer, 2nd Battalion Scots Guards

We were doing household duties and thought unlikely to be involved, but were recalled from leave. I had been too long a peacetime soldier, but our soldiers seemed to be one hundred per cent behind the enterprise.

Linda Kitson
Official war artist

I packed an enormous, cheap tin trunk with contents of an art shop, which the soldiers always cursed as it didn't have proper handles. I waterproofed it very carefully, and found an affinity with the sappers, who live as the result of the care with which they look after their equipment. I took oil pencils that would work in the wet, used a hardboard sheet as backboard – no question of an easel, and bristled with paper clips. My arrival at Southampton, and everywhere else thereafter, caused much hilarity – although not from the sappers; to them it was 'kit': my seven-foot fisherman's parasol particularly: 'Brought your umbrella then?' Folding stool, tin trunk, and a huge suitcase of

290

A 5 Infantry Brigade officers' cocktail party, complete with Gurkha pipe band, on board *QE2*.

Brigadier Tony Wilson (centre), Commander of 5 Infantry Brigade, with his brigade staff and Cunard stewards, aboard the *QE2* on their voyage down to the Falklands.

clothes suitable for the officers' mess on *QE2*. Particularly with the Guards, it's vital to be properly dressed – far more important than anything else.

I boarded *QE2* before anyone else, then watched the ship load a line of men that never ceased. They were building helicopter decks over swimming pools, removing mirrors, carpets, lights; it was like a floating town, people roaming everywhere with maps.

We cut the links with shore; the bands playing, the men realising they might not see their beloved ones again; and we left the quay. The military police gave up trying to stop people hanging over the edges of the lifeboats to wave goodbye. Then at the end, with everyone else gone, the only person left with me in the lifeboat was a huge soldier carrying a notice saying 'Mags' which he held up to a helicopter circling overhead. When he turned away, there were tears streaming down his face, which was immensely valuable to me as it made me realise they were emotional. He turned out to be the quartermaster of the sappers, an immensely brave man, and I'm still friends with him and his wife Mags. The send-off was terrible: festive on the surface, but they were all thinking, 'My God, what have we got into here?'

Guardsman Jim Mitchell
Scots Guards
We didn't know what was waiting for us in the Falklands. We thought we were going on a wee sail, just going out there, and then coming back.

Linda Kitson
Official war artist
The only women the officers saw were me and Jackie the barmaid. The four nurses and four female clerical officers were kept out of the way. Dining with the officers in the evening, I had to dress up, which I hated. I always wore trousers of velvet or silk, and jackets, with Royal Yacht Squadron buttons – as I reminded them. They're all awfully strait-laced and in a time warp, but very smart. The first sight of men ironing was a hoot, as ironing isn't a part of my life. Changing for dinner in the evening helped to reduce thinking about the increasingly alarming reality of what we were going to do.

I was horrified by military discipline, but I could see how it helped them. I only realised very late that I should have been learning things like survival in cold water, injecting morphine and so many other things – if only so the soldiers knew I could look after myself. Military people will always go back and help people weaker than themselves; it's the natural humanity in them, which moved me very greatly.

The medics were very angry with me for being a woman; one of the surgeons hadn't been allowed to take his anaesthetist, as she was a woman, because he said the Geneva Convention forbade women from going ashore. I told him I was on my own and understood his point of view, but not to take it out on me.

Captain Alan John Warsap
Regimental Medical Officer, 2nd Battalion Scots Guards
The troops were very motivated toward learning first aid, as it was going to save their lives. By the time I got to the Falklands, I felt that if I, or the rest of my regimental aid post, were to be killed it wouldn't matter.

Linda Kitson
Official war artist
I wasn't sure about asking what I was drawing, for example with a Rapier air defence missile detection machine. The next time I saw that machine, it was dug into the ground, doing its appalling job, targeting things in the air to bring them down, a dreadful weapon and part of war, and both sides have them so I was glad I'd drawn it. I was not judgemental, but was there to draw things so people could come to their own conclusions.

Captain Alan John Warsap
Regimental Medical Officer, 2nd Battalion Scots Guards
We sailed to Freetown, and cruised up and down the coast twenty miles or so away to reduce, as we were told, the threat from submarines. We were too fearful to ask why this was necessary. We called at Freetown, in the malaria zone, so everyone had to take a full course of Paludrin tablets. To complete the course and avoid malaria we had to continue taking them throughout the conflict.

Linda Kitson
Official war artist
At thirty-seven, I wasn't really fanciable to the average soldier. Although there were any number of approaches to me which were delightful, it was all overshadowed and easy to deal with because of the growing horror of what we were facing. I couldn't pass among the privates or appear at the sergeants' mess because I was of officer status; you wouldn't believe how hidebound and hierarchical it is.

Major General (John) Jeremy Moore
Commander, British Land Forces

The eight days I spent on *QE2* sailing south from Ascension Island were ghastly. There was nothing I could do, so I worried about my own performance, about people's lives; and also about my family and the stresses on them if anything happened to me, if one didn't come back or fouled it all up. My eleven-year-old son was at school, and every time there was anything on the television news, everybody looked at him. My goodness, he felt the stress.

Linda Kitson
Official war artist

The rivalry between all the units and regiments horrified me. I had to listen to so much malicious stuff. I know a certain amount of this is necessary, but it had the effect, throughout the campaign, of mucking up each other's operations, when units tried to maximise the glory to themselves, often knowing it would be at the expense of other units.

Major General (John) Jeremy Moore
Commander, British Land Forces

I wrote to the family but there wasn't much one could write about. The *QE2* library wasn't very military, and my taste isn't for whodunits, but more serious literature. There wasn't a lot of that. But, also, I couldn't sleep.

Captain Alan John Warsap
Regimental Medical Officer, 2nd Battalion Scots Guards

Immediately prior to getting to South Georgia it became misty. As people on the *Titanic* had said, I reckoned I could smell icebergs, which I found quite thrilling. When it got light and the mist cleared, we did see icebergs, and glaciers, coming down into the sea.

Linda Kitson
Official war artist

When General Moore moved across to HMS *Antrim*, I thought the warship looked alarming, very small but absolutely bristling with weapons and equipment. The *QE2* was very high, so we couldn't see the water between the two ships.

Captain Dennis John Scott-Masson
SS *Canberra*

Canberra got orders to proceed to Grytviken with *Norland*, to transfer 5 Brigade from the *QE2*. South Georgia is a most exciting, fascinating place, not on the normal cruising routes. We approached in poor visibility, among natural dangers like icebergs and growlers, so it was quite a challenge. HMS *Endurance* escorted us in. We anchored in absolutely flat calm, in rather eerie sort of weather, low cloud, poor visibility, and awaited the arrival of *QE2*, which had been delayed by icebergs.

Linda Kitson
Official war artist

Canberra looked like a little ship, and took two days to get into. I had terrible times of uncertainty, that they would leave me on the ship. We had to jump out of a hole in the Meridian dining room wall into landing craft. Large men were quaking with nervous anticipation, shit-scared, wanting to get on with it, wishing it was all over. Everyone seemed reconciled to the idea of never seeing their kit again, a thought that gave me hysterics. We got wet.

Captain Alan John Warsap
Regimental Medical Officer, 2nd Battalion Scots Guards

Next day, we all got off into Royal Marine landing craft, to San Carlos Settlement, and walked slowly and carefully along the mouldering jetty loaded with a ton of kit. It was really quite something to put one's foot on to Falklands soil after all that build-up, like being a man on the moon.

Lieutenant Colonel David Robert Chaundler
Replacement Commanding Officer, 2 Para

I had twenty-four hours to get ready to go to war. As I'd been working in the MoD, I hadn't worn combat kit for a year and couldn't find anything. I had discussions about 2 Para with the regimental colonel, Graham Farrell; but apart from H Jones and David Wood, the adjutant, being killed, we didn't know the extent of the remainder of the casualties, and I didn't find this out until I got to the Falklands. Even in war, peacetime arrangements grind on, so before I could be authorised to go down to the Falklands, the normal command board had to meet and appoint me officially to command 2 Para.

On Sunday morning a dilapidated Ford Escort Traveller arrived with a WRAC driver. I'd got my military kit together, except badges of rank. My ten-year-old daughter later reported my last words to a pressman as having been:

'Oh God, I've got a female driver'. Halfway to RAF Brize Norton this girl announced she felt ill, so I drove the rest of the way.

At Ascension Island nobody seemed to know who I was until eventually someone mentioned 'Captain McQueen at the mess'. When Captain McQueen appeared in his pyjamas it was quite clear that he wasn't some army transport captain, but a naval captain several ranks senior to me. I was concerned to ensure my onward progress from the Falklands, which I was certain would involve parachuting into the sea. I asked Captain McQueen if he had a parachute jump instructor.

'I've never heard of those. We'll have to see in the morning.'

'Have you got any parachutes here?'

'Not sure, we'll have to see about that in the morning too.'

'Did you know I was coming?'

'Oh yes, knew you were coming.'

I slept on Captain McQueen's divan for the rest of the night, and in the morning he said that they would sort everything out during his staff meeting at five p.m. He took me on his rounds; an incongruously glorious beach amid the black volcanic lava complete with white sand and a gorgeous young nurse; and a tunnel through to the inside of the volcano crater, where suddenly everything is green, with mist in the air, sheep grazing and a dew pond, in complete contrast to the rest of the island.

At the five p.m. staff meeting, an RAF group captain told Bob McQueen that the MoD had decided the RAF would take over Ascension Island from the navy and that Bob McQueen was to fly back to the UK. Bob was somewhat shaken by this. The RAF group captain turned to me and said: 'Oh, by the way, I can't fly you down tonight. All my tanking aircraft are being used on refuelling Nimrods and that sort of thing.'

Coming from MoD intelligence, I knew the Nimrods were achieving very little, so I phoned the MoD and said: 'Look, you bastards. You got me here at no notice at all, and now I've been told they're not going to fly me down tonight.' Half an hour later, the phone rang for me in the middle of the conference, saying I was first priority for tonight.

Flight Lieutenant Andy Valentine
RAF Hercules operations
The Victor tanker crews got up one hour before us. It took six of them to top each other up enough to get us down to the Falklands. They flew faster and higher than us, and after they'd checked their hoses were working, we took off in the middle of the stream.

Lieutenant Colonel David Robert Chaundler
Replacement Commanding Officer, 2 Para
I was in the hands of the army movers; a major promised he would wake me up and take me personally to the aircraft, and that all my kit would be packed so it remained dry. The next time I saw him was three weeks later on the flight back to UK, and all my clothes were totally wet. I woke myself up at 0200 and stood on the road five miles from the airfield wondering what to do. A truck came past, which turned out to be the Hercules crew. I hopped into the back. At the aircraft I was introduced to a PJI, my parachute and an orange immersion suit. There was also an army despatch team ready to push out kit, who slept for the whole journey.

Flight Lieutenant Andy Valentine
RAF Hercules operations
About a thousand miles south of Ascension, we would rendezvous and take our first fuel. We had no external tanks, and had to keep the main wing tanks as full as possible without dangerously tipping the aircraft. The second fuel was about eighteen hundred miles south of Ascension, from the fourth Victor. Being a jet, the Victor was faster, and as we took on fuel and got heavier, we had problems keeping up. We developed a technique called 'tobogganing'. Starting at twenty-two thousand feet, the Victor dives, enabling us to keep up while still taking on fuel, ending up around twelve thousand feet twenty minutes later. For each refuel, the Victor comes on the radio from behind us higher up, descends to our level on one side and trails his hose. We fly in behind him to the stable position in his slipstream, then when we know we've got enough power, fly up to him and get the probe into the basket. The captain is not supposed to look at the basket, but is talked into it by the navigator. A huge meaty spark of static electricity leaps across as you connect, then they switch their fuel pumps on.

Lieutenant Colonel David Robert Chaundler
Replacement Commanding Officer, 2 Para
The pilot had never done an air-to-air refuelling before, so that part was absolutely riveting, and took the pilot two goes to get the nozzle in. I didn't like to ask what would happen if he failed. We refuelled a second time just before I jumped.

Captain Michael Ernest Barrow
HMS Glamorgan
One of our tasks in the TraLa was to receive the huge and ever-increasing quantities of airdropped stores and equipment flown out from UK to Ascension, then dropped by the Royal Air Force from their C-130s. My junior rates were less busy than when we'd been firing on the gunline, boredom had set in and morale on board my ship was not as good as it could have been. The RAF's dropping techniques left a lot to be desired. Parachutes were not releasing as they hit the water, so one-ton loads were being dragged across the surface at up to thirty mph. With only a couple of sailors in a rubber dinghy, they took some stopping. Other times, the parachutes would release too early, so the enormous loads were dropping from quite a height.

Lieutenant Colonel David Robert Chaundler
Replacement Commanding Officer, 2 Para
Heavy headwinds were slowing us down, so the flight took eighteen hours. Looking down from the windows, the weather was bad and the waves had white horses. It was dusk and I was going to have to jump into a very unpleasant-looking sea. The PJI was saying: 'I don't think I can let you jump into that lot as you've not been water trained' – whatever that is. I said: 'You've just flown me eighteen hours down here, I'm not bloody well flying another eighteen hours back again, so you'd better let me drop.' So we agreed to differ.

An hour before the drop the crew came back and fitted *their* parachutes, so the only person not wearing one was me, which I thought a little off as I was the only person actually going to have to use one. We got to the drop point and although I could see a frigate down there, I couldn't see the horizon. On the first pass, the dispatchers threw a lot of heavy kit off the tailgate, and on the second pass my kit was dropped under a parachute and then I dropped – my first jump into the sea, which was interesting.

Captain Michael Ernest Barrow
HMS Glamorgan
One night I realised that among the boxes coming down was a human: Colonel David Chaundler, the replacement for Colonel H Jones, who'd been killed. I understand that the pilot of the aeroplane had decided the night wasn't suitable from dropping a person, and Chaundler had to virtually force his way out of the aircraft.

Lieutenant Colonel David Robert Chaundler
Replacement Commanding Officer, 2 Para

I landed in the water about a mile from a frigate, which I could only see when I was on the top of a wave. I began to think how stupid this was, as I had no form of beacon or even a torch. The frigate had no working helicopter so I had to float around until a small boat and three sailors arrived. My orange suit was leaking and I was extremely cold. They couldn't get me into the boat easily as I was waterlogged, and I suspected they were more interested in recovering my parachute for their own nefarious purposes.

I got on board the boat and we motored to the frigate, where I had to climb a rope ladder up the side. It was now blowing a force eight with large waves, and from the boat the ship appeared at one moment to be just above me, then the next, towering over me like the Empire State Building. The sailor just said: 'Up you go then, sir.' So I clung on to the rope and was dunked into the sea then hauled high into the air, then eventually hauled myself over the rope at the top and fell on to the deck, absolutely exhausted.

But the navy, with all its usual courtesy, had a man standing there blowing a whistle and the loudspeaker was saying: 'Colonel Chaundler aboard, sir!' All I could think was, 'Does one salute in a bright orange suit?' and decided one didn't, which I think was a mistake.

I was taken to the captain's cabin and told his steward that I didn't want to see the bright orange suit ever again. The captain came and offered me gin and a plate of Penguin biscuits, which I thought apt. The captain was called away and the movements of the ship got the better of me, so I tipped the gin down the loo.

My kit had also been recovered from the sea, then a Sea King took me to Admiral Woodward's carrier. After an hour of flying in the darkness, we landed, where they told me I was expected in the ops room. The carrier's heaving flight deck was without lights and I had to crouch low to look up to the sky so I didn't walk into things or fall over the side. I found the ops room where Sandy Woodward gave me a briefing on how he saw the war, and we had a chat about Exocet missiles.

Woodward explained his concerns about how losing another capital ship would change the complexion of the campaign overnight. He said this was why he was so far over to the east, and so only able to provide Harrier cover to halfway across East Falkland.

I had another two-and-a-half-hour Sea King trip to San Carlos Water and HMS *Fearless*. During this flight, the Harriers were up looking for some alleged Peruvian Sea Kings equipped with Exocets looking for our fleet.

I casually asked the pilot how the Harriers would know we were British Sea Kings. He said he'd been wondering about that.

We arrived at *Fearless* around 0200. Captain Jeremy Larken, who was charming, met me on deck. He said I'd better meet the General, who'd arrived a day or so before. Jeremy Moore made it clear that he hadn't asked for me, and didn't want me, gave me a whisky then told my escorting officer to take me to meet Brigadier Tony Wilson, who was commanding 5 Infantry Brigade. I knew Brigadier Wilson quite well from HQ Northern Ireland a few years before. He'd just gone to bed, and said: 'It's very nice to see you, but this is a most unfortunate time for you to arrive. 2 Para have just been through an amazing experience and are closely united behind the second in command . . .' I said: 'That is not your problem – it's my problem.' Then we argued until four a.m. when I finally said: 'Sorry, but I've had eighteen hours in a Hercules, three hours in a Sea King and have parachuted into the sea, and need to sleep.' He told me to come to his headquarters ashore in the morning and he'd take me to 2 Para, so I then tried to find a bed.

Next morning I found my way ashore to 5 Infantry Brigade headquarters, where I waited. By early afternoon I discovered the only person Wilson had told of my arrival was the 2 Para second in command, Chris Keeble, and that he hadn't the slightest intention of taking me to 2 Para as he'd already visited them several times that day. So with a few soldiers from the battalion, I hijacked a helicopter, which dropped us off at Goose Green. When I got out, I hadn't a clue where I was, nor did the others. We found a Gurkha who couldn't speak English but took us to see his leader who said we were at Darwin, not Goose Green.

When eventually I walked into Goose Green I met Chris Keeble and told him I was his new boss. He said: 'We'd better have a pretty serious talk.' We went into one of the settlement houses where Keeble told me that the honourable thing for me to do was to fly back to *Fearless* and stay there for the rest of the campaign. I said: 'You've got to be joking.' That was that, and I may say thereafter our relationship was extremely good, but I can well appreciate his disappointment that, having seen Goose Green to a successful conclusion, somebody else appeared to take over the battalion.

Linda Kitson
Official war artist
I was alone on *Canberra* and feared I'd been left behind. The intelligence officer asked me to draw the prisoners. Some were young hill farmers carrying their father's call-up cards, sent in his stead, with brutal officers who'd told

them the British would eat them alive as we were short of rations, having come so far. They were terrified, from a decadent country that needed to be smashed up, and were good to draw.

The Argentine injured were treated exactly the same as our soldiers, and, without sounding jingoistic, it's clear to me the British have a long tradition of doing the right thing in warfare. Some had become victims of their own minefields. I was horrified to learn that our young sappers had to crawl with metal prodders to find the small plastic mines, because despite all this technology there was no alternative. There were times when I wondered if I should stop drawing and help, but once the ship was transformed into a hospital, I could just draw. Afterwards, the people who bought those drawings were the amputees; when I asked why, they said they were determined never to forget what had happened. There were no photographers and they knew I was part of it, so my drawings were precious to them.

I was then told to land, so I discarded my evening clothes into a plastic bag and got my gear together. I was more worried about leaving my drawings with the steward than going ashore. My gear looked ridiculous: Samsonite suitcase, parasols, and tin trunk, with the label 'War Artist' impressing people, even though they didn't know that was me.

Captain Donald Arthur Ellerby
MV Norland

At San Carlos, we loaded up with the first Argentine prisoners – from the Goose Green battle – and took them to Montevideo in Uruguay. I was worried about this, as the war was still on and we were to sail there unescorted. However, the navy told us we were under 'free passage' and that nobody would bother us. I was worried the Argentinians might not honour their promise.

Flight Sergeant Ian Guttridge
RAF Chinook Air Load Master

I flew to Ascension on May 10, and sailed five days later to the Falklands, in company with the Atlantic Conveyor. In San Carlos Water, we watched Antelope fire an old Sea Dart missile at a Skyhawk, which went into reheat and was faster than the missile, so escaped. We'd been on to Antelope a few years earlier for a party, and it was quite sad watching it go down – like a friend disappearing. We then crossed to HMS Fearless, which we protested against, as it was clear the Argies were only targeting grey funnel line ships, not the merchants; but we were told, this is where you are going.

Three of our four Chinooks were lost, plus nine Wessex, when *Atlantic Conveyor* was sunk, plus tentage for four thousand people, and the complete Chinook spares and tool kit backup. Fortunately Brave November – X3718 – had flown off on an air test when the Exocet hit, but she had only her on-board equipment to keep her going for the rest of the time. The crew had a few tools in their pockets, and that was it.

We then sailed on *Europic Ferry* to collect the next batch of Chinooks from UK. One Chinook flew across from a container ship, and stayed with us that night before going on to the islands. The captain wanted us to check the safety lashings every fifteen minutes, but we refused, as there were no safety lines. We were very surprised to find it still there the following morning, even though three of the chains had broken. It was very wet inside, but started up, took off OK and flew ashore.

Air Marshal John Bagot Curtiss
Air Commander, Northwood

Two RAF Harriers were lost on ground-attack bombing missions, so we sent four more down to the fleet by flying them, with many air refuellings, from Ascension. The navy, bless their socks, thought I was mad trying this with a single-seat aircraft. There was nowhere for them to go in between although they had a tanker with them for some of the time, and at the end they had to land on a small speck of a flight deck bouncing around in the middle of the South Atlantic ocean. It was a very worrying period for me, waiting to hear that they'd met up with *Hermes* and landed safely.

18

Disaster at Fitzroy Roads

When we saw the Sir Galahad *sitting in the bay in broad daylight, everyone was immediately very concerned. The private soldiers were making bets as to how long it would take before the ship was bombed.*

Brigadier Julian Howard Thompson
Commander, 3 Commando Brigade
On landing at my headquarters, after blizzards and a series of curtailed flights, I discovered General Moore had arrived and was being briefed by my staff in a cowshed. I walked in and waited to say hello to him.

Major General (John) Jeremy Moore
Commander, British Land Forces
I had expected operations to have moved further towards Stanley.

Brigadier Julian Howard Thompson
Commander, 3 Commando Brigade
Eventually he said he was happy, and would land 5 Brigade, who were a day away in *Canberra*, sending them to be based at Goose Green. He told me they would keep 2 Para. I was to keep 40 Commando, and take 3 Commando Brigade on my current axis to consolidate on the high ground overlooking Stanley.

Major General (John) Jeremy Moore
Commander, British Land Forces
My orders to Brigadier Thompson had been to establish himself ashore, then to push forward while remaining balanced and secure in the landing area so we could reinforce through him. I think I actually wrote 'to seek to establish that dominance over the enemy which was going to enable us to build up, by breeding success on success'. The battle of Goose Green began establishing that, showing that we were going to win battles with anything like equal numbers. Things had developed along the right lines, but not as fast as I had hoped.

Brigadier Julian Howard Thompson
Commander, 3 Commando Brigade
As land force commander, General Moore had been out of communication for the critical ten days of the landings, the Goose Green attack and the breakout from the beachhead. I hadn't been able to discuss what I was being told to do, or even confirm that my orders and actions were what he wanted me to do. I didn't even know if he was getting my signals.

Major General (John) Jeremy Moore
Commander, British Land Forces
Having been working with the defence staff in London, I was known personally by the commander in chief, the chiefs of staff and, indeed, the War Cabinet. The commander in chief was a naval officer, not familiar with operations on shore, and had only briefly met Julian Thompson at Ascension Island; they didn't know each other personally. I had been needed in London as a buffer between Julian Thompson and the source of enquiries back at home. But once 5 Infantry Brigade arrived, I was needed on the islands, which argued for me travelling down quickly; I was a trained parachutist and could easily have parachuted.

Brigadier Julian Howard Thompson
Commander, 3 Commando Brigade
With hindsight, I think General Moore should have flown south from Ascension, rather than taking ten days sailing in *QE2*, and parachuted into the sea to join us much earlier, so he could monitor what we were doing from *Fearless*. This would have made things very much easier for us.

Major General (John) Jeremy Moore
Commander, British Land Forces

But one silly side issue did influence me: the press. They had overplayed various stories, done distasteful things like the 'Gotcha' headline when the Belgrano was sunk, even made breaches of security of one sort or another. I had a nasty feeling, which is silly now I look back on it, that parachuting would be an awful, overdramatic way for a major general to go to war. The press were creating great dramas, and my parachuting would be turned into one too. I think this was probably more of an influence on me than it should have been. I now believe I made the wrong decision in opting to sail from Ascension in QE2, when I should have been down there, interposed between Julian Thompson, who was getting on with fighting the enemy and the elements, and talking back to the commander in chief. After the whole thing was over, Willie Whitelaw said to me: 'It made a tremendous difference to us in our deliberations the day you arrived down south. The messages were coming from somebody with whom we had personally discussed things and we felt we had an understanding.'

Staff Sergeant Richard James Elliott
REME, 3 Commando Brigade Air Squadron

There was a bug went round in the Falklands, maybe from the water or the peat. You got diarrhoea and vomiting and felt really ill, so we isolated these guys into one tent, zipping them up into their sleeping bags until it went away. One of the pilots and an aircrew man got it, and an avionics specialist, but although we were fearful of being taken out by it, we survived. It cleared in a day or two, but made a real mess of people's sleeping bags. The guys on the front line were getting it too, and were being brought back in their sleeping bags, which needed to be cleaned up. A lot of the front-line guys just stayed out until it went away. It wasn't much fun and required a lot of morale to get through.

Commander Nigel David 'Sharkey' Ward
Officer Commanding 801 Squadron, Fleet Air Arm, HMS Invincible

On June 1, Steve Thomas and myself were on the climb-up back to Invincible. As we passed twelve thousand feet, HMS Minerva said she'd got an intermittent contact, three radar sweeps, forty miles north-west, do we want to investigate? This was the wrong direction for us, and she didn't want to order us to go as she knew our fuel was marginal. But we turned immediately to investigate. After all the stupid signals we'd had from the flag about Blue Fox radar, here was an opportunity to use it.

As soon as I turned on to the heading, I picked up a fat juicy contact at thirty-eight nautical miles, obviously airborne. I used the radar to check what height it was; four thousand feet below me. I called 'Judy' to take control of the intercept. Steve picked up the target at thirty-two miles on his radar. As we approached, the height difference remained the same, so the target was descending, but his range held at twenty-nine miles rather than decreasing rapidly, meaning he was turning away from us, so he knew we were coming. Although we had a good amount of fuel, it was not enough for a prolonged chase and to get back home. We followed him on radar through cloud. I told Steven to stay above the cloud in case he popped out, while I went down through it, and emerged about four miles astern of this guy. I told Steven to come on down.

It was a Hercules transport aircraft. My radar was holding beautiful contact on the guy the whole time, despite a fairly heavy sea state, so when I reckoned I was just within range I fired, but at one and a quarter miles I was too far away for a low-level attack. The missile just fell short, an error on my part. But I made no mistake with the second missile, closing to about a mile, aiming at the right-hand engine, setting the wing on fire. The aircraft carried on going west, so I called *Minerva* to get some ship's decks ready for us to land in San Carlos, as we'd be short of fuel.

I decided there was no time for messing around. I would have liked to have flown alongside him and indicated that he should climb and jump out by parachute. But *Invincible* was then two hundred and twenty miles away. So I got into firing range and kept my finger on the trigger, putting two hundred and forty rounds of 30mm into the tail area, the big slab door at the back, and his flying controls. The Hercules banked gently to starboard and very gracefully nose-dived into the sea. There was no chance of any survivors, and that was great. I felt really good. I didn't think about who was on board. That wasn't my problem.

We turned away into the climb, checked how much fuel Steve had, and I realised we could still get home. I estimated we'd make it with just two hundred pounds of fuel, which is nothing. But I trusted my system, so I told *Minerva* we wouldn't be landing at San Carlos as we'd got just enough to get home, and needed to rearm the aircraft. We landed very short of fuel.

Apparently they are very angry with me in Argentina for shooting down a Hercules – well, bloody hard luck mate! As long as it wasn't filled with Red Cross nuns or school children, I don't give a shit. But they seemed to think it was unsportsmanlike, even though they were carrying weapons, ammunition and whatever into Stanley every night. I watched this thing go plummeting into the sea with no feelings of guilt whatsoever. I'd love to pay a visit to Argentina and sort that one out. We didn't complain when they sank *Atlantic Conveyor* because that's the way war is. We're all trying to fight. There was no animosity from us in the air towards them.

Captain Christopher Charles Brown
148 Commando Forward Observation Unit, Royal Artillery
The landing force was preparing for the main attacks on Stanley. The artillery had two 105mm light gun regiments, and lacked any heavier fire. People had now realised that naval gunfire had taken the place of medium artillery. The accuracy of field artillery depends on meteorological data that could not be collected in the Falklands, but also changed radically, producing firing errors of hundreds of yards, whereas warships don't use meteorological data. Every time the artillery guns fired, they were pushed into the soft, wet peat five or six yards, and had to be dug out and pulled back into position before they could fire again, causing delays and inaccuracy, requiring huge amounts of hard physical labour from the gun crews. By contrast, the ships were floating easily, their systems largely automated, pretty much oblivious to conditions outside, firing a very powerful shell. At the beginning of the campaign, many people had imagined naval gunfire to be somewhat irrelevant, an anomaly from the Second World War. But by 1982, naval gunfire was often more accurate than field artillery. Naval guns fire with a regular, steady beat, which you can hear in the darkness; and as the Argentines didn't have any, you knew it was firing for you, putting down heavy shells on to the enemy positions, which was a great morale booster. Everybody realised this, clamouring for naval gunfire support. But we only had five naval gunfire forward observation teams which, because of the demand, were always in action, moving from unit to unit.

Captain Hugh Maxwell Balfour
HMS Exeter
On May 31, we'd been sent inshore, and immediately I saw how different it was, a buzzing world we knew nothing about. I'd also been briefed by Mike Clapp and Jeremy Larken. It was clear there were many misunderstandings between the shore and the offshore operations. I was determined to persuade Sandy Woodward to come and be briefed himself, but he wouldn't leave the carrier. He should have seen for himself what the Army were doing, what they required and what their problems were.

Commander Nigel David 'Sharkey' Ward
Officer Commanding 801 Squadron, Fleet Air Arm, HMS Invincible
Ian Mortimer from my squadron got shot down by a missile over Port Stanley on June 1. He obviously strayed too close and too low, and a missile blasted his tail off. He ejected from the aeroplane and went into the water. We didn't know where he was. We were a hundred and twenty miles further to the east from Stanley, and having heard a garbled radio message from water getting into his Sabre beacon, we knew he'd gone down in the water somewhere.

Commander Ralph John Wykes-Sneyd
Officer Commanding 820 Sea King Squadron, Fleet Air Arm,
HMS Invincible
While flying over East Falkland, I picked up a rescue beacon auto tone, but was too low on fuel to investigate. Returning to the ship, I discovered we'd lost an RAF Harrier pilot, so I organised a proper search and rescue operation.

Commander Nigel David 'Sharkey' Ward
Officer Commanding 801 Squadron, Fleet Air Arm, HMS Invincible
Our assistance squadron on board, 820 Squadron, were wonderful guys. Their boss, Ralph Wykes-Sneyd said: 'Don't worry, Sharkey, we'll find him.' They set off on a visual search of all the water between Grantham Sound, Choiseul Sound and Port Stanley. This was a very dangerous job, as at any time Pucaras could have attacked them from the ground. They searched four daylight hours, and five night hours.

Commander Ralph John Wykes-Sneyd
Officer Commanding 820 Sea King Squadron, Fleet Air Arm,
HMS Invincible
At two a.m. my captain told me he was quite keen for us to stop the operation, but I was very keen to continue, as at first light Argentine aircraft would be waiting for us.

Commander Nigel David 'Sharkey' Ward
Officer Commanding 801 Squadron, Fleet Air Arm, HMS Invincible
We then got a message from the admiral's staff saying: 'It's not worth searching any more. Knock it off and get on with business.' I said: 'Hey, that's not right,' and Ralph said: 'Don't worry. We'll ignore it. We'll search until we find him.'
Keith Dudley, the senior pilot of 820 Squadron, said: 'I'd bet Ian, if I had to come looking for him, it would be off the end of the Port Stanley runway.' So

Keith Dudley flew down there. Mortimer heard the helicopter coming. He was suffering from exposure, but decided he didn't want to die so it didn't matter if the helicopter was friend or foe, switched on his strobe light and they picked him up.

Linda Kitson
Official war artist
I finally landed on June 3. I wasn't the only person feeling dismay for having to pay such a price for this hostile, bleak, lifeless island, barely fit for human habitation. It wasn't inspiring, nor did it hold much magic. Stanley is a tiny, run-down place of final resort. Where there's a bit of movement in the landscape it can be quite beautiful and there's wonderful wildlife, but there were no roads. It didn't seem like a place one would choose to live, and there were very few people there. One seventeenth-century traveller with remarkable foresight described the Falklands as a 'blasted rock that will one day cost us dear'.

Captain Hugh Maxwell Balfour
HMS Exeter
Following my visit ashore, I did call on Sandy Woodward to explain how there were various things he could do to alleviate things ashore; for example, the land commanders' wish for him to bring the carriers in close enough for the Harriers to take part in the final land battle. But Woodward was adamant that he had to remain afloat and couldn't go ashore, even to see for himself. This revealed his long-standing difficulty, that he couldn't leave his flagship in the sure knowledge that his policies would continue to be carried out as he wanted them to be. He was never quite sure that his staff captains and his flag captain in *Hermes* were going to react as he would wish. I'm friends with Sandy Woodward, and have forgiven him for the outrageous things he wrote about me in his book.

Michael Thomas Nicholson
ITN correspondent
We met General Jeremy Moore when he arrived, and he said: 'I'm glad you guys are here as I want my son to know what I did in the war.' This made us think that the army might be different to the navy. But we were wrong.

Linda Kitson
Official war artist

Canberra had been a culture shock: it was very hot and we were often wearing life jackets because of alerts, with heavy seas, so we had to take seasickness medicine. *Fearless* was even more different. But these two changes were nothing compared to the landing, in this bay so full of ships accessible for destruction. It was a lovely day, and I had to go ashore in a little Rigid Raider, which seemed too small for all my kit, but then landed on the wrong beach, which had a very humble jetty that seemed too frail for the endless cargo coming off those ships.

The sky was noisy with helicopters unloading, the beaches filling up with heaps of containers and equipment, untrammelled bays becoming vast dumping grounds. Tiny hamlets suddenly received three thousand men, who disappeared into the hills. The helicopter pilots were taught to dig in by the marines, their elegance on ship transformed into unshaven constipation, living in the pits of life in waterlogged trenches, suffering stomach complaints from dirty water, slipping over on the muddy slopes. I was learning to live the mud life, courtesy of Commanding Officer Malcolm Hunt and 40 Commando, who were responsible for protecting us from attack. We had to learn passwords every day, which changed to numbers the Gurkhas could remember, and I got into trouble not remembering them myself. I wore black with a hat, was Gurkha-sized, and was saved by my red, white and blue leg warmers.

Major General (John) Jeremy Moore
Commander, British Land Forces

Things on the ground were different to what I'd expected. I knew it wasn't suitable for wheeled vehicles, but hadn't realised how well tracked vehicles would manage – especially over the huge rock runs, great rivers of tumbled, jumbled rocks, often the size of grand pianos and larger. Some parts are so boggy that vehicles sink, so with constantly pulling vehicles out, even for the locals, progress is limited to about five mph.

Linda Kitson
Official war artist

The first death of somebody I knew took place on my first morning: Mike Forge, who'd helped me with survival instruction, and I'd done a drawing of him on *Canberra*. He'd been flying to sort out a broken communication base. 3 Commando Brigade, who didn't know him, said he shouldn't have been flying so high. You hear so many derogatory statements like this. But it was his first morning, he was army so he didn't know, and he'd been shot down by one of our ships, as they didn't expect to see somebody there. They say the first person you know that dies is the worst, and I'm ashamed to say that thereafter it affects you less.

Major General (John) Jeremy Moore
Commander, British Land Forces

I admired my commander in chief's restraint. Despite having a secure voice link he never attempted to talk with me personally. Once he rang me to explain the likely political outcome of a proposal, and I phoned him with some bad news.

Linda Kitson
Official war artist

My first drawing ashore was of a command post dug out of the mud, a place where people knew what was going on, so I started there. I drew without moving for some eight hours. I had intended to introduce myself, but this proved unnecessary as I was 'under command to' the commanding officer. There was no great army of people to see as the camouflage was incredible, with the risk of being shot. The 40 Commando quartermaster had to be a man of integrity, as he was in charge of 'things', and any sort of black market in gloves and other stuff would be very lucrative. He was in a tin hut riddled with bullet holes, full of food and supplies, and my tin trunk, so I was forever stumbling in and out. The unloading plan seemed wacky; a huge pile of hand warmer sticks arrived, and as I was the only person using a hand warmer I was delighted, but everybody else was very angry. We took turns to guess what might be unloaded next, but it wasn't funny.

Major General (John) Jeremy Moore
Commander, British Land Forces

Northwood had calculated the carriers could sustain full air operations for one month, after which one carrier would have to be withdrawn. But the whole assumed schedule was wrecked when *Atlantic Conveyor* was sunk. On land, we were deliberately operating in the high mountains to come at the enemy from an unexpected direction. No matter how well trained your troops are in coping with arctic conditions – and these were very wet and much worse – men deteriorate if left out too long. But *Atlantic Conveyor* contained all our tentage – shelter for five thousand men.

Captain Jeremy Larken
HMS Fearless

I think the 5 Infantry Brigade units expected to be employed in garrison duties around San Carlos, leaving the battle-hardened units of 3 Commando Brigade to do the fighting. But it was decided that they should take part in forward operations leaving, to their great disappointment, 40 Commando to guard San Carlos. But when the Welsh and Scots Guards attempted to go forward on foot as everyone else had done, it became clear they weren't fit enough, posing very serious problems. 3 Commando Brigade was in the hills ready to attack, so it was decided to take the Scots and Welsh Guards forward by ship.

Captain Alan John Warsap
Regimental Medical Officer, 2nd Battalion Scots Guards

We had a quiet, safe landing at San Carlos settlement on June 2, despite good weather. As the early mist cleared, the navy ships appeared, alert, bristling with radar and weaponry, there to defend you . . . It's difficult to describe the safe, solid security of having a grey ship on your side. Then the weather deteriorated. Our main concern was that the men were overloaded with mortar bombs, ammunition, food and so on. On top of that, we'd heard so much about the Falklands weather, that most men were wearing far too much clothing; wearing it seemed sensible when there wasn't much room in backpacks. Paradoxically, my first casualty of the campaign was one of heat exhaustion.

We marched about two kilometres into the hills and dug in. After a few feet, peaty water ran into the trenches. The first night wasn't too bad, but the next two nights were progressively colder and wetter. The Welsh Guards moved off to try to walk from San Carlos to Goose Green, but had to turn back because of the wet ground and all the weight they were carrying. Certain reporters saw Welsh Guardsmen sitting down under their loads and wrote stories about how they were not able to yomp long distances like the Marines, which was given as the reason why the Guards didn't march all the way to Stanley.

Major General (John) Jeremy Moore
Commander, British Land Forces

I wanted to move everybody in one night, but as there wouldn't have been time to get the ships back to safety by dawn, we planned for a two-night move, using the ten-thousand-ton LPDs *Intrepid* and *Fearless* and their eight landing

2nd Battalion Scots Guards come ashore from HMS *Fearless*'s landing craft at San Carlos on June 1, 1982.

craft, which could each take a company from the ship to the shore. The danger was of losing one of these big ships whilst still loaded with troops, leading to enormous pressure on the government to halt things, leaving us unbalanced, very exposed with a fifty-mile LofC and no ability to maintain it adequately.

Captain Alan John Warsap
Regimental Medical Officer, 2nd Battalion Scots Guards
On my last night at San Carlos, I went to sleep in wet clothing and suffered cold exposure, with psychedelic dreams. The night was freezing, but I got up, changed into dry underwear and ran up and down until I felt warm again. I believe, as the result of this, that men must carry dry spare clothing, separately wrapped in plastic bags, and a dry sleeping bag. I was so impressed with the reliance and toughness of our men. I thought that was the worst night of my life and felt very miserable. But in fact the next night was even worse.

We marched back down to San Carlos settlement, embarked on landing craft and were taken to HMS *Intrepid*. It was absolutely super to get on to the ship, as it was warm and for a few precious hours we could dry out our kit. It gave our people a second chance, a respite for future operations, to repack and sort things out.

Lieutenant Colonel David Robert Chaundler
Replacement Commanding Officer, 2 Para
2 Para's B Company, commanded by Johnny Crosland, had earlier that day mounted a small raid on Swan Inlet House which they found empty of Argentines, but had a working telephone. Crosland had phoned Bluff Cove and Fitzroy and asked if the Argentines were there, to be told, 'No.'

General Mario Benjamin Menendez
Military Governor, Islas Malvinas
We knew there was collaboration. But we had to maintain the radio-telephone and the telephone lines for the civilian health service in the interior of the islands. But we knew it was being used because we monitored all the calls, for example, when Fitzroy communicated with Goose Green telling the British military officer: 'There are no Argentines here.' When in the early days Peter Luga called Admiral Woodward on the radio, we could find him; but when Fitzroy collaborated with the enemy we could not go and find them and say: 'You have passed on information to the enemy.'

Company Sergeant Major Peter John Richens
B Company, 2 Para
After a small helicopter assault on to Fitzroy settlement proved the place was empty, the Chinook helicopter arrived and our advance party took off. Thirty-five people with their kit is the RAF's limit, but we put eighty-five people in, each carrying four mortar bombs and bergans. It took off and landed, and we were very relieved.

Lieutenant Colonel David Robert Chaundler
Replacement Commanding Officer, 2 Para
5 Brigade failed to tell 3 Commando Brigade of our move in the Chinook – of which the Argentines had many and we just the one, and so the heavily laden helicopter was very nearly attacked by artillery fire. I decided not to take command of the battalion immediately, but wait until after this move, at first light. We piled into the second lift, twice its normal load. The Air Load Master had shouted: 'Everybody sit down,' but nobody could move.

General Mario Benjamin Menendez
Military Governor, Islas Malvinas
But after this last example of collaboration, we had some revenge. When the English started to disembark at Bluff Cove, first the Scots, then the Welsh, it was made possible to effect the most terrible air attack that the English suffered during the whole war . . . So which was better, collaboration or non-collaboration? But I hope that the residents of Fitzroy were very happy with what they did.

Lieutenant Colonel David Robert Chaundler
Replacement Commanding Officer, 2 Para
We landed on the hill above Bluff Cove, and while a patrol went down to check that it really was clear of Argentines, Chris and I had a very long talk about what had happened at Goose Green. The patrol returned and we went down the hill. I knocked on the door of settlement manager Ron Binnie, who invited us in for tea. I started to come out of shock, and had my first decent night's sleep on the floor of the Fitzroy community centre.

The first few days at Bluff Cove were a difficult time for us, as our bergans didn't get to us. But each morning another family, the Kilmartins, would ask me how many soldiers needed feeding that night, and Kevin would kill several Falkland Islands Company sheep – not his own – and feed the men, twelve at a time around his table.

David Cooper
Chaplain, 2 Para
We flew straight to Bluff Cove where we set up the RAP in a small shed close to the Kilmartins' house. It rained permanently for the next three days. The Kilmartins were incredibly helpful. We even used their dining-room table for operations: a soldier who'd been shot in the foot but hadn't been treated properly was the first. We slept in their shed.

Lieutenant Colonel David Robert Chaundler
Replacement Commanding Officer, 2 Para
I told 5 Brigade commander, Brigadier Tony Wilson, that as the Argentines were not going to debauch from the mountains to attack us, we should get the air defence and logistics elements flown in before bringing any more infantry forward. They fired at us using a 155mm artillery gun, but from my intelligence knowledge, I didn't think they had the will or capability to do anything more. This was my firm advice to him.

Well, he didn't do it that way. He sent the Scots Guards to Bluff Cove, intending they would go north of us into a defensive position. But we did get our bergans brought to us.

Captain Alan John Warsap
Regimental Medical Officer, 2nd Battalion Scots Guards
The plan was to sail down to the south coast in an adventurous right-hook movement. We were the spearhead of this move, and were to be dropped off at Lively Island, due to the threat to *Intrepid* from Exocet missiles. We were then to be landed at Bluff Cove, which was lightly held by the 2nd Battalion Parachute Regiment, who were waiting for us to arrive, as they couldn't hold this position for any length of time, due to their casualties and previous exertions at Goose Green.

Major Simon Ewen Southby-Tailyour
Royal Marines
The commodore had ordered HMS *Intrepid* to drop us some ninety minutes from Bluff Cove, but the captain of *Intrepid* said he didn't want to lose his ship to an Exocet, and refused. I said: 'Bugger that, you are launching us seven hours offshore and the loss of your ship isn't actually going to be that important compared to the loss of six hundred men in the Scot Guards.' I had a terrible row, with just the two of us together in his charthouse.

Captain Alan John Warsap
Regimental Medical Officer, 2nd Battalion Scots Guards
We were briefed by, shall we say, a very laconic amphibious operations officer from the Royal Marines. After hearing him, I gave myself very little hope of surviving the night, as I could see what was coming. We were to be put down in open boats well offshore, then have to negotiate round a lot of little small islands, rocks and headlands on our way to Bluff Cove. This was projected to take a minimum of four hours, but in the event took seven hours. The battalion was packed into four boats. There were even a few Land Rovers – which weren't much use – and with all our food and equipment, these boats were very low in the water.

Major Simon Ewen Southby-Tailyour
Royal Marines
I don't know where he launched us, and didn't know where we were until we closed with the coastline and I recognised it, which was disgraceful. The six hundred men of the Scots Guards deserved better treatment. But the captain of *Intrepid* wasn't prepared to risk his ship, so I had to launch the whole battalion in four unarmed, un-armoured, open landing craft in the open sea, with a seven-hour approach past enemy-held territory and the possibility of enemy fast-patrol vessels. Also, I didn't know there were British ships on the gun line that night, until we encountered them later on.

Captain Alan John Warsap
Regimental Medical Officer, 2nd Battalion Scots Guards
It was cold, the wind got up, we got lost and waves were breaking over the boat. Everyone got thoroughly soaked with seawater, and it went on and on. We were packed tightly, couldn't move, suffering muscle cramps. I thought the only ending would be a cold, quick death.

Major Simon Ewen Southby-Tailyour
Royal Marines
I headed north-east, hoping we were west of Lively Island. This gave me a hideous problem and I had no proper charts, just my memory, plus a huge chart of the whole islands. I had to circumnavigate the whole of Lively Island using this chart and a compass with a thirty-degree error, no radar, then find Bluff Cove. And then we were bombed by something that put high explosive into the water all around us – but there was nothing we could do but continue steaming at seven knots.

Captain Alan John Warsap
Regimental Medical Officer, 2nd Battalion Scots Guards

Then the skies were illuminated by star shell, and shells fell into the water around us. People said we were being fired upon from the shore by heavy mortars, but in fact it was our own ships. Fortunately the firing stopped, but we were critical of amphibious operations to say the least, for our own ships firing upon us when we turned up in the area of operations. We felt very poorly about this. Nobody was hurt, but it increased the apprehension factor.

Major Simon Ewen Southby-Tailyour
Royal Marines

We were approached by two ships, which because the captain of Intrepid had told me there would be no British ships in the area, I assumed to be the enemy's two patrol boats. We were then illuminated by six star shells. We were easily identified as British landing craft, heading for Bluff Cove. These ships told us to heave to, and although we tried to get away, at seven knots you can't get very far. It was now three o'clock in the morning and beginning to blow from the north.

The leading ship was within a mile and flashed. Through my binoculars I recognised she was a British frigate, but not which one. She flashed one little word of Morse, a pinprick of red in the darkness, saying: 'Friend.' I was so bloody angry I replied: 'To which side?' And yet instead of staying to look after us, the two frigates didn't answer my rude reply, but steamed off to the south-east at fast speed, leaving us militarily even more exposed, as the enemy would now have seen that we were British. That was sad, as Admiral Woodward had been told by Commodore Michael Clapp we would be in the area that night, and he'd replied saying he was putting no British frigates into the gun line that night.

Captain Alan John Warsap
Regimental Medical Officer, 2nd Battalion Scots Guards

There seemed to be no end to this journey and we got colder and wetter. Long after we should have landed, dawn light began to appear in the sky and we felt even more vulnerable to enemy attack, as we were in an area where the enemy was known to be.

But I believe it was due to the cool-headedness of one of our own company's commanders, Major John Kisley, who subsequently won the Military Cross on Mount Tumbledown, who is a small boats man. He went up to assist on the bridge, and managed to work out where we were; so instead of landing short of our objective as had been projected, we actually got to Bluff Cove beach safe and unharmed.

Major Simon Ewen Southby-Tailyour
Royal Marines

Well, come dawn we found Bluff Cove, thank God, and landed the Scots Guards, from boats that are designed only to operate within two or three miles of their parent ship, under radar control, in sheltered waters. It was quite interesting, and actually quite frightening, and I was quite miserable; not for myself, but I thought professionally the thing was a terrible cock-up.

Captain Alan John Warsap
Regimental Medical Officer, 2nd Battalion Scots Guards

I had three exposure cases verging on unconsciousness. My medics took them down into the heat of the engine room where there were three bunks. They were left to dry out for that day, until the landing craft sailed again that night. Most of us felt so vulnerable jammed in this wet, cold, steel box that this was the worst night of the whole campaign. All our four landing craft arrived at Bluff Cove beach, we landed, and although the weather was very bad, we marched up to the settlement where our battalion HQ were set up in the barns, and we dug in trenches in the surrounding hills. The walk up from the beach was one or two kilometres, into the teeth of a howling gale, blowing sheets of hail horizontally into our faces. The battalion was in a pretty tired state, and although they were willing to go on, we began to get a series of exposure casualties.

David Cooper
Chaplain, 2 Para

I walked back to Bluff Cove in the rain, where I found the Scots Guards had arrived. They were wet, miserable, unhappy, and looked like a defeated army. They were replacing us, as we were dropping back to Fitzroy to become the reserve battalion.

Lieutenant Colonel David Robert Chaundler
Replacement Commanding Officer, 2 Para

I was using the buildings in both settlements to rotate my soldiers off the hills. The Scots Guards second in command and ops officer arrived at my HQ, asking if I knew what they were supposed to do. Their CO wasn't with them. I told them everything they needed to know, but soon some horrendous exposure cases were brought in. I'd never seen anything like it; they were life-threatening and my medical staff were struggling to keep some of them alive. I found the whole of the Scots Guards battalion still outside, so I said to their second in command: 'What the hell do you think you're doing? If you don't get them out of here and into the countryside, digging in with shelters up, you're going to lose the entire battalion.' He said he couldn't do anything until the commanding officer arrived, about which I do not wish to pass comment. When Mike Scott, the Scots Guards CO, about arrived, I took my men out into the hills, then back to Fitzroy so they could take over the sheep sheds. My motives for this were not entirely altruistic; I needed to have my battalion together in one place, to get them geared up for the next stage.

Captain Alan John Warsap
Regimental Medical Officer, 2nd Battalion Scots Guards
Instead of pushing on towards Stanley, we stayed at Bluff Cove. We had a dozen serious exposure cases verging on the unconscious, plus others less seriously affected, who had to be revived in the barns.

Lieutenant Colonel David Robert Chaundler
Replacement Commanding Officer, 2 Para
The LCUs which had brought the Scots Guards round could take us to Fitzroy, but they had put back to sea and we didn't know which radio frequency they were on. I sent Chris Keeble off in a helicopter to turn them round. He found them just offshore and turned them back. We loaded our two companies into the landing craft and set off for Fitzroy. The weather was not good and, about an hour later, land appeared out of the rain looking suspiciously like Bluff Cove again. I got hold of the coxswain, who agreed that was correct. He blamed the weather and the kelp, admitting they were lost. We eventually arrived at Fitzroy jetty well after dark, and were met by our technical quartermaster with dry socks, tea and tureens of stew.

Captain Jeremy Larken
HMS Fearless
It was decided that Fearless rather than Intrepid should have a go at getting the Welsh Guards forward the next night. This was not an easy thing to do, and I decided afterwards it was not to be repeated.

Major Simon Ewen Southby-Tailyour
Royal Marines
I was determined I wasn't going to suffer the same problems, so I got a helicopter back to *Fearless* and told Mike Clapp what had happened. It wasn't his problem, of course, as he'd expected the captain of *Intrepid* to drop us in the right place. However, for the next night, because the landing craft were all at the far end, *Fearless* was to RV with us within two hours of the coastline. I obtained a list of the ships on the gun line, plus the night recognition signals which I hadn't been given the night before, got it all planned then flew back to Bluff Cove – only to find there were no landing craft.

Captain Jeremy Larken
HMS Fearless
It was very bad weather with a front coming through. I didn't have direct communications with Major Ewen Southby-Tailyour. We got very much farther forward than *Intrepid* had done, off Lively Island. From the intelligence, we knew there was an improvised Exocet missile system, probably on Cape Pembroke south of Port Stanley, so we had to keep out of its footprint. But we got fairly close to Bluff Cove, and although the front was going through, the weather for us was quite passable. However, for Ewen Southby-Tailyour it was still terrible, and after the experiences of the previous night he wasn't keen to set sail. But I couldn't talk to him directly, so he didn't set out.

I despatched two landing craft with half the Welsh Guards, and returned with the other half. I'd stayed too long, so we had a very exposed and uncomfortable daylight passage back up Falkland Sound, but thankfully there was no air attack and we got back to San Carlos unscathed.

Major Simon Ewen Southby-Tailyour
Royal Marines
Despite my having given orders for the landing craft to remain at Bluff Cove, they were gone, I assumed sheltering from bad weather. *Fearless* arrived at the RV carrying the Welsh Guards, but nobody met her. Although the weather was calm, I should have sailed to make this RV, but I decided not to admit that I didn't know where my landing craft were, so instead said I'd been prevented from making the RV by bad weather. I subsequently discovered that after I'd left by helicopter for *Fearless* the night before, Chris Keeble had ordered my blokes to take his battalion to Fitzroy. They quite rightly refused, saying they were waiting for their boss to return for the operation that night . . . [The Paras] then got extremely angry when they couldn't find

Fitzroy and ended up back in Bluff Cove. They had no charts, the weather was blowing a gale and was beyond their limits. They'd never been to Fitzroy, and were under orders to stay where they were. The landing craft ended up at Fitzroy; so bad weather prevented them from meeting me, missing the rendezvous with *Fearless* and the Welsh Guards. This is why only half the Welsh Guards got ashore. The other half returned to San Carlos aboard *Fearless*.

Captain Jeremy Larken
HMS Fearless
We still had half the Welsh Guards embarked. The next night we had to take charge of a very complicated operation to the north of the island, with another exposed return to San Carlos in broad daylight. So we decided to sail the Welsh Guards round to Bluff Cove in RFA *Sir Galahad*, in company with the *Sir Tristram*.

Major General (John) Jeremy Moore
Commander, British Land Forces
The senior Welsh Guards officer on board *Sir Galahad* had been informed that due to a bridge being blown, his companies faced a fourteen-mile march round the edge of the cove to their destination, so he decided to wait on board until landing craft arrived to sail them round. A marine's view would be different: 'If you see a shore line, you damn well get on it quick because you are very vulnerable in a ship.'

Captain Jeremy Larken
HMS Fearless
With Commodore Mike Clapp, I must take responsibility for the two RFAs being sent south, but the Welsh Guards should not have stayed on board as they did. In the north, two other unescorted RFAs were running a shuttle delivery service through Salvador Water. In a complex situation, you have to take chances. We needed to get the troops forward to keep the whole momentum of the battle going, and there was tremendous political pressure.

Captain Hugh Maxwell Balfour
HMS Exeter
Two minutes before we launched the San Carlos CAP, *Plymouth* was attacked. The raid had come in low from the south, split and gone north up the Sound

to attack the Harrier forward land operating base at Carlos Water. They'd found *Plymouth*, and the five aircraft dropped ten bombs on her instead. The Harriers took off before I ordered them and got two, and the Rapiers got one, so it wasn't a total disaster. But we didn't know until later that there was another raid coming in – to Bluff Cove.

David Cooper
Chaplain, 2 Para
We'd had an argument with the commanding officer of the field ambulance on the *Galahad*, who'd just landed and ordered us out of our building. But there was nowhere for us to go and as he hadn't cleared it with our battalion, we refused. He admitted that his medical facility wouldn't be ready for some four days, which, if we had to pack up then, would leave no medical cover at all.

There wasn't much to do at Fitzroy, so I'd persuaded some of the soldiers to go fishing, to get some fresh food. The islanders had given us some bread – the first since Sierra Leone, and life was quite comfortable. The RAP was looking after a few trench foot casualties.

Lieutenant Colonel David Robert Chaundler
Replacement Commanding Officer, 2 Para
The morning of June 8 was a lovely sunny day. I hadn't taken much notice of the two LSLs coming into the bay, as we were busy running a shooting range, and they were well out of our defensive umbrella. We'd had a quartermaster sergeant major and some men on board *Sir Tristram* bringing around some stores, but they'd got off as soon as the ships arrived.

Major Simon Ewen Southby-Tailyour
Royal Marines
When the Welsh Guards did finally agree to get off the *Galahad* . . . the commanding officer of the field ambulance, who was already ashore, thought that because he was a lieutenant colonel, he should get his men ashore first – which was wrong. The field ambulance was not needed as there was no war at that stage there; and the landing craft were not sent to collect him. They could have waited on board for another twenty-four hours. But the Welsh Guards *were* needed ashore.

David Cooper
Chaplain, 2 Para

When we saw the RFA *Sir Galahad* sitting in the bay in broad daylight, everyone was immediately very concerned. The private soldiers were making bets as to how long it would take before the ship was bombed.

Captain Alan John Warsap
Regimental Medical Officer, 2nd Battalion Scots Guards

The weather cleared and you could see a very long way. The padre and I were walking round the company positions, looking over to the west where we could see the upper parts of some grey ships. We then walked down to Bluff Cove beach, where we met the second in command of the Welsh Guards, who told us he was expecting the rest of his battalion to arrive by landing craft from the grey ships.

Lieutenant Colonel David Robert Chaundler
Commanding Officer, 2 Para

Four Skyhawks appeared, the first came in at mast level, the hatch was open on the deck, and this thousand-pound bomb went straight in. All these Welsh Guardsmen appeared on deck. We were absolutely appalled, as we had no idea there were any troops on board.

David Cooper
Chaplain, 2 Para

Within minutes we received an air raid warning red and the *Galahad* was bombed. The snipers I'd sent to go fishing put up the only fire against the aircraft. We were amazed to see troops aboard this ship – in daylight, which seemed to be criminal irresponsibility.

Lieutenant Commander Graham John Edmonds
Operations Officer and Squadron Warfare Officer, HMS Broadsword

We knew of the take-off of a large number of Argentine aircraft in Argentina. We knew the distance between the Argentine airfields and the targets, and we knew exactly when the aircraft should have been launched from *Invincible* and *Hermes* to intercept this incoming raid. We were therefore very concerned when no aircraft were launched.

Commander Robert Denton Green
Intelligence Staff Officer to Commander-in-Chief, Fleet HQ, Northwood
Special forces were put ashore on the mainland as well as the Falklands, to obtain intelligence on the ground. The idea was to get a guy on to the runway to tell us whenever aircraft took off. It worked, to a certain extent, but was very hit and miss.

Petty Officer Brandon Christopher Smith
HMS Fearless
I heard stories that we'd deployed a submarine, maybe the *Valiant*, sitting between ourselves and Argentina, acting as an early warning for air raids coming over. We certainly had very good warnings of the Argentine air raids.

Rear Admiral Anthony John Whetstone
Deputy Chief of Naval Staff (Operations), MoD Whitehall
Our conventional submarines did land special forces on a few occasions, which was very valuable. Our nuclear submarines were deployed to prevent the Argentine fleet getting into areas where they could engage us.

Lieutenant Commander Graham John Edmonds
Operations Officer and Squadron Warfare Officer, HMS Broadsword
We were aware of the disagreements between Admiral Woodward, Commodore Clapp who was in charge of the landings, and with Northwood, over the sea movement of troops around the Falklands. Even as bystanders, we were well aware of the dangers to the *Sir Tristram* and *Sir Galahad*, which it seemed our flagship was ignoring. There were plenty of pilots, who often were not flying, and plenty of aircraft.

My opposite number, Roy Birch, who'd been a fighter controller, phoned *Hermes* and told them that unless they launched CAP to protect *Galahad* and *Tristram* in the next ten minutes, it would be too late. He was told to mind his own business. But when finally CAP was launched, it was twenty minutes too late, and could only attack the second and third waves of aircraft after they'd attacked *Galahad* and *Tristram*. We were angry about that. We think there was an error of judgement in *Hermes*, which is a bit sad.

Michael Thomas Nicholson
ITN correspondent
Brian and I, with Bernard the cameraman, went to Fitzroy to film the Welsh Guards coming ashore. But they were still on board the ship, and even as

civilians we thought they should have been ashore. Major Ewen Southby-Tailyour was running around like a scalded cat shouting at them to get off. We were sitting down, having some tuck, when there was a huge explosion. We ran down to the water's edge to see the *Sir Galahad* on fire, about five hundred yards away.

Radio report by Michael Nicholson dated June 9, 1982

'The bombs hit *Sir Galahad* aft, through the engine room and the accommodation sections, and I watched from the shore less than four hundred yards away, as boxes of ammunition exploded, shaking the ground beneath us. And we crouched as bullets from the ship whistled and whirled past us. I saw hundreds of men rush forward along the decks pulling on their life jackets, pulling on their orange survival suits. Some, the ship's crewmen just off watch, were pulling on shirts and trousers. Many who were trapped on the wrong side of the ship jumped overboard as the flames spread. I saw men swim underwater away from the ship, to avoid the burning oil. And I watched other men, men who were safely away forward of the flames, risk their lives to jump into the water with life jackets, to save those men swimming below. Inflatable rubber life rafts, bright orange, were hurled over the side. Some immediately burst into flames as debris from the explosions hit them. Others landed, but were blown by the wind into the burning oil and exploded at the same time. Ropes were thrown over the side of the ship, men clambered down them, and, despite the wind, despite the heat of the metal on their feet, despite the movement of the ship, they got into their life rafts. The strong winds fanned the flames – enormous flames – and as the fuel tanks exploded, the ship was half enveloped in thick black smoke. But the Royal Navy Sea Kings and Wessex helicopter pilots and their crews ignored the flames, they ignored the explosions, they ignored the ammunition erupting around them, and they flew their machines into the smoke to lift off the queues of men below. The helicopters waited in turn in a queue, steady in the air, to move in over the bow to winch the men off.

'And I watched one pilot steer his machine slowly, and deliberately, into the black and hover. He was completely blinded, completely enveloped, and then I saw his crewman winching down on a line to pick men out of the sea. Three times I watched him go down. Three times he brought men up, out of the blackness that covered his helicopter. I saw

RFA *Sir Galahad* burning at Fitzroy Roads, after being attacked by the Argentine air force on June 8, 1982.

another helicopter almost touch the water, its rotor blades seemed to be spinning through the flames, to pick up a man in a bright orange survival suit who was clinging to the anchor chain.

'Lifeboats were launched from *Sir Tristram*, whose crew seemed to be containing their fire, and these boats, under power, began taking some of the rubber life rafts in tow. Other rafts began drifting, taken by the wind away from the inferno and as the breeze suddenly turned, towards pilots in the helicopters waiting at the bow, waiting to bring men aboard, they saw what was happening. They saw these life rafts drifting into the flames, and immediately took action. They came down low, and, using the down-draught of their rotor blades, began to push the rubber dinghies away – slowly, yard by yard, each helicopter taking care of one dinghy full of men and pushing them safely towards the beach.

'There was much heroism at Fitzroy, but this single tribute must be paid to the helicopter pilots and their winchmen, who saved so many. The casualties and survivors, many suffering from shock and burns, were picked up from the beach by soldiers who'd run from their trenches to help. Dozens of soldiers waded out into the freezing water, some up to their chest, to pull men to safety. I watched soldiers struggling in the waves, picking the injured out of the life rafts, and carrying them back on their shoulders to the shore, and then going back for more.

'Let me say this. It was a day of tragedy, but I vouch it was a day of extraordinary heroism and selflessness by every man who witnessed it. High above, maybe ten thousand feet up, were the thin vapour trails of the Harrier jets on their combat air patrols. Over the last few weeks we'd grown used to them, felt safe because of them, and were cheered whenever we saw their white trails cross like kisses. It meant all was well and that the sky was ours. As the smoke from the exploding inferno rose above *Sir Galahad* out in the bay, and men without arms and legs and open stomachs were carried past me, I looked up and saw those same kisses.'

Commander Nigel David 'Sharkey' Ward
Officer Commanding 801 Squadron, Fleet Air Arm, HMS Invincible
I was patrolling to the south of *Sir Galahad*. When she was hit the second time, the most devastating one, I saw the enemy aircraft that attacked her come off the land. *Hermes*'s CAP aircraft were overhead, but as usual quite high, and so were not a physical presence and were unable to eyeball the

attacking aircraft. If they'd been doing figure-of-eight over the ship, maybe she wouldn't have been attacked again.

There was big bombs and smoke everywhere, and the enemy set off, high-tailing it to the west. Dave Morgan and the other *Hermes* CAP guy came down, following Admiral Woodward's orders 'like hawks from above' and shot down three of the four with Sidewinders.

Captain Hugh Maxwell Balfour
HMS *Exeter*

We'd passed the message 'air raid warning red' to everybody including the two LSLs at Bluff Cove. I'd told Captain Green, in the *Sir Tristram* the previous day, that we'd warn him of air raids, but when we broadcast the warning to everyone on the HF radio, we didn't hear a reply from him, and I regret to this day not having sent a complementary warning message to him by teleprinter. But after the attack on *Plymouth*, we thought that was probably the end of Argentine attacks for that day – but we were quite wrong.

Michael Thomas Nicholson
ITN *correspondent*

A man was brought ashore on a stretcher, and was looking at the stumps of his legs, and we filmed him. I interviewed this man, years later, and he told me he didn't feel any pain, but was so angry that we were filming him. I had to point out to him that we were risking our lives in order to film what it was really like. It made me angry that there was so much enthusiasm for this war at home, and people had to be made aware of the consequences of sending young men to war. Young men lose their legs – and many lose their lives.

Commander Nigel David 'Sharkey' Ward
Officer Commanding 801 Squadron, Fleet Air Arm, HMS *Invincible*

I was haring north with Steve, and by the time the *Hermes* CAP were releasing missiles, we were three miles away. The fourth Argentine aircraft was eight or ten miles from us, but we'd got sight of it. We saw it go overland, ditch weapons or fuel that exploded on a little island, and we decided to get him. But then the controller from San Carlos told us to stop as there were six Mirage 3s coming in at high level towards us. We looked up and there were contrails in the sky over us.

We went for them instead. I got radar contact at fourteen miles, which was quite good for a Mirage contact, but when we got within twelve miles they turned away. They were obviously under control, diverting our attention from the A4s down below. They turned away to the north, and as they were higher than us with superior speed, we never saw them again.

Captain Hugh Maxwell Balfour
HMS Exeter

The six Mirages came in high as a distraction for the raid on Bluff Cove. We sent *Invincible*'s CAP to attack them, but then we played a very interesting professional game with them, withdrawing the CAP as they flew away, then when the Argentines turned back again, locking on with our 909s, holding the CAP off to within two or three degrees of bearing, shooting down two of the Mirage. It was a very interesting day for us, although very sad for the Welsh Guards. We were very upset that we hadn't provided the air defence co-ordination required, but we don't have a conscience – not really.

Captain Alan John Warsap
Regimental Medical Officer, 2nd Battalion Scots Guards

There were three air raid alerts, and we saw three aircraft flying over our positions about fifteen hundred metres away. People said they were Harriers, and only realised they were the enemy who'd bombed the ships at Fitzroy after they'd gone by.

David Cooper
Chaplain, 2 Para

Our medical officer, Steve Hughes, told our trench foot casualties to find somewhere else to shelter while he went down to the seashore with his equipment. I grabbed defence platoon of 9 Squadron Royal Engineers, and we organised a chain of stretchers from where the helicopters landed with casualties from the ships, to the village hall, where our medics carried out triage and treatment. After stabilising treatment, I put the selected casualties on to helicopters to take them to Ajax Bay.

I saw a Chinaman, soaking wet, wrapped in a blanket, having swum ashore, which really shocked me, as I'd not thought that somebody from the other side of the world would get involved in this. 5 Brigade headquarters, who were also at Bluff Cove alongside us, seemed to have closed down completely, and were making no decisions about anything. So I took survivors to shelter under a hedge and told them I'd fly them north once the injured had been moved out.

Captain Alan John Warsap
Regimental Medical Officer, 2nd Battalion Scots Guards
We saw the smoke and heard the explosions about five kilometres away. Then aircraft from those raids flew back towards Stanley keeping very low, foolishly right over the Scots Guards' positions who opened up with everything. There was a reverse cascade of tracer going up at them; their formation split up, some of them making smoke and throwing out foil to throw off heat-seeking missiles. Some were damaged and others crashed.

David Cooper
Chaplain, 2 Para
Welsh Guards soldiers were appearing, seeming stunned and inactive. Platoon commanders and senior NCOs were too dazed to do anything, so I sat them down under the hedge as well. A Welsh Guards company commander introduced himself to me, so I told him where his survivors were and that I thought he'd lost the best part of his mortars platoon. He immediately disagreed and told me casualties had been very light and they would soon re-equip. I asked him: 'How do you think you're going to be re-equipped?'
 'We've got a lot of stuff on the ship.'
 'Have you seen the ship?'
 He too hadn't grasped the situation, so I told him to go and determine who the survivors were, because I was going to fly them all out as they were a drain on our resources. Nobody else was making any decisions, so these people, including uninjured members of the Welsh Guards' support company, went back to Ajax Bay entirely on my decision. 5 Brigade headquarters stayed inside their shed, as if nothing was going on in the world, completely disinterested in the disaster right outside their door.

Lieutenant Colonel David Robert Chaundler
Commanding Officer, 2 Para
There were horrendous casualties. My soldiers had to do all the first aid, as Headquarters 5 Brigade hadn't got any medics in position. When things had died down a bit, my RSM, Malcolm Simpson, and I decided to have a look round. We found a hundred or so Welsh Guardsmen at the top end, with officers and senior NCOs, but very little of the equipment one might have expected them to have. A few were lightly injured, and by this time the Harriers were overhead. But every time a Harrier went over at about four thousand feet, they all ran off into the countryside and hid behind tussocks of grass. They were completely shot away – in shock, for which I'm not being in

any way critical of them. How lasting those effects are, I don't know. I was extremely relieved to learn the next day that we were to go under command of 3 Commando Brigade, to our north.

Captain Alan John Warsap
Regimental Medical Officer, 2nd Battalion Scots Guards
A sort of medieval, football-ground cheer of exultation went up from the crowd, from people who at last felt themselves to be combat troops who had taken part in an action. This was then tempered by the news of the casualties at Fitzroy, which was a great blow to the brigade. Up until this time, it had seemed to us that we were invisible to the enemy – but clearly we weren't.

David Cooper
Chaplain, 2 Para
For 2 Para the *Galahad* disaster was a turning point. Until then, we felt we'd done our bit, and it would now be nice if somebody else won a few of the medals. Now our soldiers were saying: 'We can't afford to leave it to the others and then suffer more things like this. Let's just get on with it and get it finished, even it does mean we have to take a few more casualties.'

Major Simon Ewen Southby-Tailyour
Royal Marines
I'd gone ashore to try to persuade 5 Brigade HQ to exercise some influence over the Welsh Guards officers who were refusing to leave the *Sir Galahad*. Their mistake was not getting off the ships. At the time I was extremely angry that they wouldn't take my word for it and obey my orders. There should have been air cover over Fitzroy that day, but HMS *Hermes* had steamed another hundred miles east to clean her boilers – against her captain's orders. You would have thought this was a bloody stupid time to decide to clean your boilers, but Admiral Woodward had ordered this, which meant that the CAP aircraft could only stay overhead for ten to fifteen minutes. Added to this, the CAP from *Hermes* were always stationed at high level, whereas *Invincible*'s CAP were always stationed at low level. Nobody has ever explained the reason for that, and it meant several Skyhawks got in under their defences while *Herme*'s CAP was chasing other aircraft.

Company Sergeant Major Peter John Richens
B Company, 2 Para
When it calmed down, I was asked by one of my platoon sergeants if I was

aware that the Welsh Guards were saying that they'd now done their bit and would be going home, and were giving their ammunition away. This annoyed me a lot, so I got hold of one of their company sergeant majors and told him to get things under control.

Captain Jeremy Larken
HMS *Fearless*

An enormous number of burns cases were brought from the *Galahad*, the most serious to the field hospital ashore at Ajax Bay, and we dealt with those with severe superficial burns – a brave but pathetic little group. *Plymouth* was sorting herself out. Two aircraft attacked from the east – a most unexpected direction from over the hills, causing a lot of damage, including to the Ajax Bay field hospital.

Then two naval Skyhawks came from the south and took a pass at *Fearless*. The first was breaking up, the pilot ejecting as he passed over us, his bombs dropping slightly ahead of the ship, the canopy landing on the bridge. He was bobbing about in the water two cables away so we fished him out. He had a seriously dislocated knee, having caught it as he ejected, and was in some pain, so I went down to see the poor chap. With a great spasm of agony we got his knee back into place again.

Major General (John) Jeremy Moore
Commander, British Land Forces

I was concerned about the morale of the two companies of Welsh Guards who'd been in the *Galahad*. I went to see the survivors, who were cold, wet and shocked, and had lost most of their kit. I too felt shocked, not just my own morale, but also because of the delay to our operations and the effect this might have back home on the government's determination to complete the operation. I told the Commander in Chief I thought it would delay the final attacks by four days, which ended up being two days. This was the second time we'd spoken on the secure radio link, and I rang him this time. I felt it was my responsibility to report the bad news personally.

19

Getting On With It

We watched the paras walking over the Marlow Hills,
coming like a line of ants from Teal Inlet. That evening we stood
on the Green watching a fire fight between Argentine special forces and
the SAS, in the rocks behind the house.

Captain Adrian Robert Freer
3 Para
After landing, 3 Para had dug in around the hills north of Port San Carlos, patrolling towards the northern coastline. On one occasion patrols were out from both A Company and C Company, but on different radio nets. The location of the patrol from A Company was somehow sent by battalion HQ on a different radio net to C Company as an enemy grid reference. The C Company patrol commander plotted this enemy position on his map and realised he could see soldiers there – some fifteen hundred metres away, too far to recognise who they were. Using great skill, he was able to bring down artillery and machine gun fire on to the A Company patrol, chasing them down into a re-entrant, wounding most of them, two with serious head wounds. It really doesn't reflect well on us, as it was the result of poor procedures. We didn't know what had happened. Helicopters were scrambled to get the casualties, and everybody was excited. A Company moved out to investigate. A Sea King came in too fast to get the casualties, and as it flared back to land, broke its tail rotor.

Captain Christopher Charles Brown
148 Commando Forward Observation Unit, Royal Artillery
We'd flown forward fifty miles to secure Mount Kent, prior to 42 Commando moving up with an artillery battery, as the start of a leapfrog movement across

the island. We didn't know if Mount Kent was occupied, but it was better that we should occupy this feature than the enemy. The weather was very bad and helicopters couldn't get through, so it took several nights to get us up there.

Brigadier Julian Howard Thompson
Commander, 3 Commando Brigade
We needed our helicopters to get reconnaissance people forward on to Mount Kent to ensure we weren't flying units into enemy-held areas. Even lightly held landing zones could turn a forward move by helicopter into a bloodbath. The weather was bad for five nights in a row, and helicopters had to turn back, before finally we established an SAS position on Mount Kent. By this time, I'd been ordered to move to Stanley, but I hadn't been able to confirm this with General Moore as he was still incommunicado, in the *QE2* travelling from Ascension Island.

Captain Christopher Charles Brown
148 Commando Forward Observation Unit, Royal Artillery
We sat tight on Mount Kent for a week, and were very conscious of being too far ahead for anybody to help us. By day I was able to call in aircraft to help us out, and by night a frigate would give us naval gunfire support. But we felt vulnerable to an Argentine attack, as there was only sixty of us, and at any time they could have put in a much greater force against us.

I'd called in an air strike on troops moving with what looked like vehicles, but the second Harrier had been a bit too far behind. The first aircraft made his attack, but the Argentines managed to hit the second as he climbed out, luckily only with small arms, puncturing his fuel tanks. I told him he'd been hit, so he called up the rescue helicopter from his ship *Hermes*, which was in position to rescue him when eventually he ran out of fuel and crashed into the sea. On another occasion we needed aircraft, and one of the Sea Harriers on CAP heard my cries and came up, offering to attack anything we could see. He was armed with air-to-air missiles and cannon, when I needed bombs or rockets, so I told him that although I was grateful, I felt he was better employed at his current task.

Commander Nigel David 'Sharkey' Ward
Officer Commanding 801 Squadron, Fleet Air Arm, HMS Invincible
Hermes ordered us to attack four helicopters on Mount Kent at dawn, with thousand-pound lay-down bombs, going in and out at low level along specified routes, and at the end of this order they told us to watch out for three

radar-controlled, low-level air defence guns in the area. We didn't receive this signal on *Invincible* until after we were supposed to have done the mission. I had a huge row with my commander air, who told me to get on with it. I said: 'No. I want to know the position of those air defence guns, which they know, and I will not be told how to enter or leave the target area. And we shouldn't be using thousand-pound retard bombs, which produce shrapnel all over the place when attacking the side of a mountain. We should use two-inch rocket and guns, which are designed for this type of target.' The captain agreed, and asked me to get the intelligence, but Wings wouldn't agree about the low-level bombing. So I fudged it by getting the Met man to say that cloud and fog prevented us from going low level, so we could do a high-level delivery with bombs, which would be very accurate, and is what we did, but I doubt the helicopters were still there . . .

Captain Christopher Charles Brown
148 Commando Forward Observation Unit, Royal Artillery
A helicopter dropped a group of Argentinians into the valley below us, and they moved up on to the mountain below our position. We had time to ambush them, and pinned them from two sides. It was getting towards last light, and was difficult to see if we'd killed them all. It was a rocky area, so some might have crawled away. The next morning we found bodies and a lot of kit abandoned, including various non-standard weapons with sophisticated sights that looked to be from a special forces reconnaissance patrol.

Commander Nigel David 'Sharkey' Ward
Officer Commanding 801 Squadron, Fleet Air Arm, HMS Invincible
The admiral's staff was telling us how to do things and getting it wrong. They never once gave us any scrap of enemy intelligence, despite getting lots of good stuff from the SAS boys ashore – about radar and missile sites, or anything at all.

Ailsa Heathman
Estancia Farm, North Camp
After playing Monopoly until late, we went to bed. I'd been complaining about the slow progress of the military. A machine gun started firing outside. I reached out of bed and turned the generator off, plunging everything into darkness. We got dressed, gathered up the children and hid downstairs under the kitchen table. I phoned Teal Inlet, telling them we were about to die. On the open line it was two rings for the manager's house, and as I was waiting, I tried to sit down but the telephone chair had been moved for the Monopoly

so I flopped to the floor in the darkness with a baby under each arm. Then there was a bang on the door and a shout, 'British Army.' The SAS had been watching Estancia for a week and as an Argentine helicopter had visited twice that afternoon, they thought there were Argentines in our cow shed, so they'd machine-gunned it.

Pat Whitney
Green Patch, East Falkland

Terry Peck was the ex-chief of police and a councillor, who wanted to get out of Stanley. He was the sort of guy who had to get into things and I suppose they knew about it. He wanted to take some ammunition and a pistol out with him, which I put inside the tyre of a spare wheel and pumped it up. Terry had a motorbike, but not much kit.

I'd got myself out of Stanley soon after, when they told me to report to the police station. I then travelled round the farms redistributing surplus stores. Most people were staying put. I painted my Rover blue with white squares, so nobody would think I was trying to sneak anywhere. I also carried a small tin of red paint and a brush, in case when the British forces arrived, they might want me to carry wounded under a Red Cross.

Trudi McPhee
Brookfields, North Camp

With sixteen of us living on the farm, we spent the time working, cleaning, cooking, eating, and the children would often drive themselves over to Green Patch for a break. There was just the two of us here when I saw Terry Peck walking past the window. He told us he'd left Stanley as he didn't feel safe there, and that when he met up with the British, he'd call us on radio frequency 7000 on the CB.

Neil Watson
Long Island, East Falkland

When Terry Peck arrived at Long Island on his motorbike, it was a dark night so, despite the Argentine mortar company, we decided to dig up the Royal Marines' weapons. We went into the dunes, dug up the weapons and put them into rucksacks, then walked back down the beach, staying in the water so as not to make footprints, and hid the weapons under the floorboards in the chicken house. We felt more comfortable knowing we had some arms. Terry Peck set off towards San Carlos with one of the SLRs, on his way to meet the British troops, and we kept the rest under the chicken house.

Captain Adrian Robert Freer
3 Para

We were probably heavier than we should have been, each with a hundred rounds of GPMG and five 7.62mm magazines, plus grenades. Even only with belt order, the weight was substantial. Our DMS boots and puttees were useless for walking across boggy, broken country in two or three inches of water, which, with the cold and blisters, destroyed people's feet. There's nothing you could do about this, you just had to crack on. Our clothing was bad too; they'd flown out some arctic kit to us from another unit back in UK, but it was in dreadful condition and needed sewing up, new buttons and so on.

The Argentines at Teal were gone by the time we arrived. The next morning it was snowing. One of our soldiers had an accidental discharge with a sub-machine gun, which wounded several people when the bullets ricocheted off the walls of the only brick building for miles around. We'd been marching for three days. Several people had bad feet, and our machine gun platoon, who were drums platoon back in barracks, the youngest and smallest, were finding it particularly hard work. I told them once we left Teal, they were on their own. I left some people behind as they weren't managing. We reallocated their kit, and they were left to work with the quartermaster in B Echelon.

Neil Watson
Long Island, East Falkland

At about eight o'clock one evening, there was a knock on the door and a guy was standing there in camouflage kit. He didn't look Argie, so I said: 'Who the fuck are you?' to which he replied, 'Who the fuck are you?' He had a 9mm pistol pointing at my navel. I said, 'You're Brits aren't you?' It was a team of SBS guys who'd been watching the farm for the past four days, seeing Argies coming in and out. They set up an observation post in the old house for a couple of days, and after I established that the Argies had gone from our area, we left early to drive them to Salvador Water, to be picked up by a Rigid Raider that night.

Ailsa Heathman
Estancia Farm, North Camp

We heard the paras were at Teal Inlet, and were listening to messages on the two metre from places like Port San Carlos, talking in riddles so we were never totally sure what was happening. We watched the paras walking over the Marlow Hills, coming like a line of ants from Teal Inlet. That evening we stood on the Green watching a fire fight between Argentine special forces and the SAS, in the rocks behind the house just to the west of Mount Kent. We could see the tracer floating backwards and forwards, and it was such a quiet still night, we could hear the GPMGs, and also the drone of the Scorpions and Scimitar light tanks coming from the other side.

Trudi McPhee
Brookfields, North Camp

We listened in to channel 7000 for Terry, until one night he came on and said: 'Could you get as many vehicles and people together as possible and meet me at the Estancia?' So we got everything ready to go, then went to bed. We were very jumpy, then in the darkness I heard a vehicle, and going out discovered it was Pat Witney. He said: 'I've brought you some British soldiers for coffee.' I was a bit rude to him, as we were getting up at four a.m., and asked him where they were. 'They're a bit nervous.' Four SAS guys had been on Green Island in the bay beside our house. Every night I'd heard this outboard motor, but had no idea it was them. They said because there was nothing on their map here, they'd assumed we were Argentine, and my effort of blackening out the windows was terrible. At two a.m., they decided they'd better get back to their boat, so I drove them back down the shore, but stopped when they said the other two SAS guys might shoot me, not knowing I was friendly.

Neil Watson
Long Island, East Falkland

We left Long Island in the dark with the Land Rover lights off, got to Green Patch and dropped the SBS guys off. I'd got an SLR plus the spare magazines and bandoliers of ammunition the Royal Marines had given us, and put it into the Land Rover beside my knee. The Argies were gone from Long Island, Goose Green had been liberated, the paras and marines were marching to Mount Kent through Estancia, and we felt that we were almost behind friendly lines. I wasn't prepared to be pushed around any more.

Captain Christopher Charles Brown
148 Commando Forward Observation Unit, Royal Artillery

We were relieved on Mount Kent by 42 Commando. As they were flying forward, some Argentine troops bumped into us, so we engaged them with mortar fire and machine guns. 42 Commando arrived in the middle of all this, having expected to be flying into a secure landing site. It was in fact secure, but we were just getting through a little local difficulty. Newspaper reporter

Max Hastings, who'd been allowed forward, came bursting out of a helicopter, and was immediately thrust under a rock so he would come to no harm.

Brigadier Julian Howard Thompson
Commander, 3 Commando Brigade
Over the next few nights, 42 Commando got on to Mount Kent, 3 Para walked up on to the neighbouring Mount Estancia area, and 45 Commando, which I'd held back at Teal until my brigade headquarters arrived and could defend it, marched forward to the base of Mount Kent. I now had three units with gun batteries forward, but with very little ammunition, so we were in a very delicate situation. I was therefore not best pleased to hear on the BBC World Service our defence minister John Nott announcing that my brigade was on Mount Kent and my brigade headquarters at Teal. We had intended to bring in supplies by sea to Teal using LSLs, saving innumerable one hundred-mile round trips by helicopter. But now the Argentine air force knew what we were doing, it was too dangerous to try.

Ailsa Heathman
Estancia Farm, North Camp
On the evening of June 1, there was a knock on the kitchen window and Terry Peck brought eight members of 3 Para in to see us – their recce patrol. They had sore feet, but were upbeat and looked in good shape. They said the rest would arrive the following evening.

D Company tried to set up in our shed until they were ordered out by the hierarchy. We took up the carpets so they wouldn't be ruined, and started making huge pots of soup and bread. But working on GMT, they arrived four hours early. This didn't matter, as we couldn't have provided for them all. D Company took over our living room, and then a troop of engineers arrived, so we went to bed and they took over the kitchen and passageway. I turned off the generator as usual, so when D Company guys went out on patrol they tripped over all the engineers.

Brigadier Julian Howard Thompson
Commander, 3 Commando Brigade
I kept asking General Moore for the return of my other unit, 40 Commando, which still remained guarding the beachhead. I'd already ordered them to move out, but this had been rescinded. I was not best pleased about this, but had to put up with it.

I now needed to know about the enemy we faced on the mountains

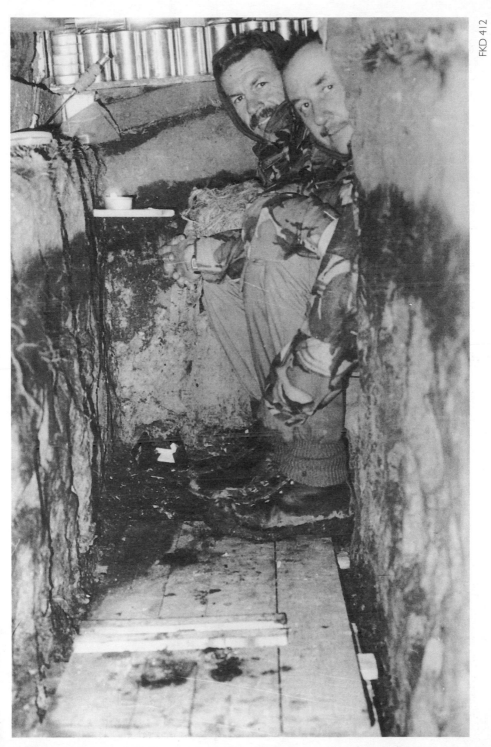

Two Royal Marines of 40 Commando installed in their trench near San Carlos.

surrounding Stanley, so my units began an intensive programme of patrolling, which also developed our moral domination of the enemy. It was exhausting, over very rough ground and very long nights, the men returning to sodden holes in the ground covered by ponchos.

Linda Kitson
Official war artist
One night 40 Commando said they were taking me 'out on the town'. We all lined up in the darkness, thousands of them it seemed to me. I hadn't brought a mess tin or eating utensils, but they gave me what I needed while they made do with cartridge cases and tins. I never forgot my eating utensils again. I made a lot of friends as I couldn't eat as fast as they could, so they could get seconds and eat mine as well. They dreamed nostalgically of 'joined-up meat' because all they ever got was out of tins. One was so hungry that it didn't matter what order you ate it in.

Private Jose Omar Ojeda
Compania Comando Servicios, 3rd Brigade
After many difficulties we'd finally arrived at Puerto Argentino over two months earlier, on April 10. We went into the town, keeping out of the way because our company was all scattered, one group here, another group there, another one of those '*kilombos*' mess ups. We should have been one hundred and sixty-five. Then twenty of us got together; we were with a signals communications group, drivers from an anti-aircraft gun unit. I'd lived and moved around like that for two and a half months, until of course the moment of combat arrived. We hardly ever slept, we didn't bathe, we didn't know what a passable meal was. When we could sleep, we slept half-standing up, or on top of the truck where we ate any bread we could get. We stole wood for the kitchens, which we kept in the truck. There was an anti-aircraft gun mounted in the truck. When one person came down, the other person stayed above with the anti-aircraft weapon. I was managing the radio and did the communications. I didn't go very far; to the village where the others were, or to another unit. I transported supplies or munitions, or I did the post; and as I had the radio, I carried and took messages. When I could get myself to the truck, I stayed there.

Brigadier Julian Howard Thompson
Commander, 3 Commando Brigade
After some discussion with General Moore's divisional headquarters, it was decided there would be three phases to the final battle: my brigade seizing

Mount Longdon, Harriet and Two Sisters; followed by 5th Infantry Brigade seizing Tumbledown and Mount William while I took Wireless Ridge; with finally my brigade pushing though to the airfield isthmus, hoping by that stage the Argentine army would have had enough. I was given 2 Para and the Welsh Guards, which I kept in reserve for the first phase.

Private Jose Omar Ojeda
Compania Comando Servicios, 3rd Brigade
I talked to boys from the 63rd Regiment, who didn't have much training. We were well prepared; more than a year of being ready – weapons training, shooting and everything, but it appears this boy had not. We were not allowed to converse with other units because military authorities are like that; and if we did, we were reprimanded.

Linda Kitson
Official war artist
I had far too many hats, and gloves: I used five different types of glove in doing one drawing. They were so distinctive that when I lost them, they were always handed back to me. The soldiers were envious of some of my kit; their Northern Ireland leather gloves were hopeless. I also had gumboots, yachting kit and fisherman's jumpers. Thank God the Gurkhas were with us, as they were my height. The commandos wore seamless tights, which made me laugh, but they gave me a set; 'City Queen', they were called – and so warm.

Private Jose Omar Ojeda
Compania Comando Servicios, 3rd Brigade
If I go to war, and can't eat well, and in two and a half months don't see water to bathe, how can the military authorities force me to shave? It happened to a comrade, and they put him in the glasshouse because he went around unshaven. We could not leave a comrade staked out because he was unshaven. Twenty of us joined together and rebelled, saying that if they did not release him we would start shooting. We were played out, what did we have to lose? But from then on, no comrade was pressured. I will never forgive how they treated us in this war, as though we were slaves. But we could not quit. Where could we go?

Major General (John) Jeremy Moore
Commander, British Land Forces
Throughout the campaign, the Argentines had been managing to fly at least one Hercules transport aircraft each night, in and out of Stanley. I was very

keen to break this air link back to Argentina, and was looking to fly a battery of artillery with an infantry company within range of Stanley airfield. I found a suitable area on the next peninsula clear of enemy – to the north of Stanley. But in the end, Brigadier Thompson, to whom I left the decision, decided he couldn't do it. The logistic effort of moving the troops, guns and their ammunition, then sustaining them, would have detracted too much from his main battle. I accepted that. But it was a nice idea.

Air Vice Commodore Carlos Bloomer-Reeve
Secretary General, Islas Malvinas
Our C-130 Hercules transport aircraft continued coming in right to the very end. They'd land then take off quickly without stopping their engines, in about two minutes. They needed more time to put wounded men in. The plane had to be at the end of the runway when the lights went on for one minute, and they took off without the lights. The British thought we were landing outside the runway. But every night engineers pushed fake craters on to the runway, always in the same position, so the RAF took photographs and the crater was always there – the idea of Brigadier Castellano. But it was risky. Comodoro de la Colina was killed when a Lear jet hit another plane. They were transmitting messages as they crashed . . . it was very disturbing.

Private Jose Omar Ojeda
Compania Comando Servicios, 3rd Brigade
The enemy looks to blow up your supplies and water, and in this way they start defeating you. I expected them to blow me up at any time. I decide the first thing I am going to blow up is the radio with the truck. There were times when it was useful or imperative to be sleeping in the truck and I was there, but when it wasn't necessary, I always ran off.

Captain Adrian Robert Freer
3 Para
We left Teal to walk around this very long bay to Estancia, a very small, one-family settlement, farmed by the Heathmans. We were only at Estancia for a very short time, then marched up a very steep re-entrant where we were ordered to stop. We didn't know why until later.

Ailsa Heathman
Estancia Farm, North Camp
It was the end of the year and we'd just cut the peat for the winter, stacking it

away out of the rain. Most of the sheep work was done and everything was slowing down for the winter. My parents lived in Stanley, running the Rose Hotel, and our first daughter was eleven months old. I'd heard that my parents had been arrested and taken to Fox Bay, which worried me quite a bit.

You can survive at the Estancia with nothing if you want to; we've a good vegetable garden and you go out and kill your mutton. I always kept a good well-stocked storeroom as, without roads, we didn't get into Stanley very often. Three other families from Stanley were staying with us. We'd had quite a few Argentine soldiers come asking for shelter and food over the previous weeks. Once my husband Tony knew British troops had landed, he'd been desperate to join them, to give them as much information as he could. But once we realised Terry Peck had already gone, he stayed put. We'd heard of the landings on the BBC, and had sat here wondering why they weren't advancing faster. We didn't understand the logistics of military operations.

Roger Patton, the 3 Para second in command, set up the battalion HQ in our shed with his radio operators. Their CO, Huw Pike, lived in the gorse hedge at the bottom of the garden. We had a well, but the troops had been told we had liver fluke, so would only drink water from the tap on the Green, even though it came from a spring. Helicopters were continually flying in to fill up jerry cans, and it was running constantly so we couldn't even get water for the baby. We had to send somebody down there for a couple of hours to keep the tap turned off so we could get what we needed.

Every morning we'd put cardboard down on to the floor from the compo boxes, and change it every day. We only had one loo, and on the first morning there was a queue out through the kitchen down the steps into the yard, three deep. By the end of the day there was so much mess we put a pair of welly boots outside the door as there wasn't any point tripping in there wearing your slippers. At five p.m. we said: 'That's enough,' and scrubbed it out to get the kids bathed. The troops were then banned from using our loo, and latrines were dug outside with a couple of posts across a slit trench. I'm glad I didn't have to sit on them. On a frosty morning, you could have lost half your backside. Every morning we'd go to one of the units and collect socks which we'd wash and dry, attempting to keep their feet OK. We had 3 Para complete, 9 Para Squadron Royal Engineers and the Blues and Royals armoured cars. The doctors were in the kitchen, dealing mostly with bad feet. I had four press living in the loft, including, according to a photo in a history book, Robert Fox.

Neil Watson
Long Island, East Falkland
After Terry Peck's radio message saying the paras were at the Estancia, all the farmers in our area, the North Camp, went over to there with tractors and Land Rovers with logistical and whatever other support we could give to 3 Para.

Trudi McPhee
Brookfields, North Camp
We left at four a.m. in very thick fog with Roddy McKay, meeting with everyone else about three miles from here. It was such a quiet day you could hear all the noise of the trailers and vehicles miles away. We reached Estancia, where there were hundreds of people. Trenches were dug everywhere. The queues for the loo and water went about six hundred yards, the troops waiting patiently.

Neil Watson
Long Island, East Falkland
When I came round Estancia Mountain I couldn't believe it; it was such a beautiful sight to see all the paras there, and these British helicopters converging on the Estancia. A supply ship was sitting in Salvador Waters, landing supplies into Estancia, which was a long way from where the paras were. So we helped the helicopters move all this stuff. I thought, 'We're free,' but I'm afraid Stanley wasn't free for quite some weeks yet.

Part Four

DOING
THE BUSINESS

British land forces were now making their way towards positions ready for their final assault on the very large numbers of Argentine forces defending Port Stanley. They had only limited amounts of ammunition and other combat supplies for these attacks, in particular for their 105mm artillery light guns. The bad weather had already begun in what was to be a particularly severe winter.

The lack of Chinook heavy-lift helicopters (strictly speaking they are designated 'medium lift') had forced several of the land units to walk across the island, and had caused a four-day halt to further advances whilst ammunition stocks were built up using limited numbers of light transport helicopters in very poor weather. The British were assuming that the Argentine garrison remained unaware that the main attacks were to come from the mountainous interior and not from the sea, but in fact by this stage the superior bad weather training of British ground troops gave them a distinct advantage over this very arduous terrain.

But British ground forces were becoming weakened by both the weather and the enormous physical effort of surviving and moving in the mountains, with their treacherous weather and constantly waterlogged ground. The rapid onset of winter left only days in which to complete the operation and retake Port Stanley. The launching of main attacks against the Argentine units defending the town began with only minimal ammunition stocks, because time was so short. It was a gamble which ran the risk of attacks having to be curtailed, and further days of stalemate, probably in exposed positions, while waiting for more ammunition to be brought forward from San Carlos, with British troops enduring both appalling weather and Argentine shellfire, from the many 105mm and heavy 5-inch artillery positions inside and forward of the town.

The prospect of hand-to-hand fighting into Stanley itself was not an edifying one either, a particularly dangerous phase of war known as FIBUA – fighting in built-up areas – which sucks in large numbers of troops, with many casualties and the total destruction of the town. With this in mind, the British were continuing to use radio links to encourage an Argentine surrender. At the same time, the Argentine junta in Buenos Aires were using international diplomacy in their attempts to obtain a ceasefire, an ideal outcome for them, which would have left British troops marooned freezing in the mountains, whilst the Argentines evacuated their equipment, weapon systems and troops, ready to fight another day. With a ceasefire in place, the Argentines could slow things right down, and seek whatever advantages presented themselves, courtesy of the declining weather and the degeneration of Britain's already grossly overstretched ground forces.

On June 1, Britain repeated its ceasefire terms, which required the total withdrawal of all Argentine forces and a reversion to the political and diplomatic status quo of before the Argentine invasion. Three days later, an alternative, pro-Argentina ceasefire resolution was presented to the UN Security Council by Panama and Spain, which Britain rejected. On June 6, the Versailles summit supported the British position on the Falkland Islands. It seemed that only an Argentine surrender could prevent the destruction and bloodshed of a large-scale attack on Port Stanley; but it was becoming equally clear that the military junta in Buenos Aires was incapable of backing down, regardless of the consequences.

20

Footsore and Ruthless

*The helicopter had been stripped out, so I had to sit on the floor.
Its canopy was held together with black masking tape because,
the sergeant pilot told me, they'd been at very low level and had
flown into a barbed wire fence.*

Lieutenant Colonel David Robert Chaundler
Replacement Commanding Officer, 2 Para
It was time to make myself known, so the men would know what I stood for. I visited each platoon, taking the RSM and doctor with me. The men were suffering badly from the effects of the weather; bleak, windy, hovering around freezing. We had no sleeping bags or food, as our bergans were still at Goose Green. Men were suffering from the weather and more minor wounds from Goose Green. If they got worse so they had to be evacuated, we had no idea when they might be returned to us. I wanted our doctor take these marginal cases to the warmth and comfort of the Fitzroy community centre. We brought twenty soldiers off the mountains, eighteen of whom returned after treatment. As the men came out of their trenches, I tried to identify somebody I already knew, so I could make a personal contact. Sergeant Barratt, a platoon sergeant in A Company who was to be awarded a Military Medal, told me later that his soldiers had thought they'd be OK as the new boss was chums with their sergeant.

Company Sergeant Major Peter John Richens
B Company, 2 Para
I knew Colonel Chaundler from our time in Berlin. He said: 'Hello, sergeant major,' so I said: 'Who are you?' He was actually well known to us, and a good choice as new CO.

Lieutenant Colonel David Robert Chaundler
Replacement Commanding Officer, 2 Para
I tried to tell the men how their achievements were regarded at home, reading messages from the Chief of the Defence Staff downwards, congratulating them on capturing Goose Green. When you're eight thousand miles from home, you feel lonely and detached. Then I said my aim was to get us back to England without further casualties, and would ensure we had the correct amount of fire support in future battles. Our soldiers felt they were more than a match for the Argentine infantry, but didn't like the Argentine artillery. I discussed Goose Green with the company commanders, and got the intelligence section to build a model of the hills around Stanley, which we used to think through possibilities. Our predictions were wrong, as we ended up attacking from the opposite direction.

Major Philip Neame
D Company Commander, 2 Para
We'd done our bit, it was somebody else's turn, and we thought we should stay in reserve for the last phase. We were pleased about being shifted back to 3 Commando Brigade.

Lieutenant Colonel David Robert Chaundler
Replacement Commanding Officer, 2 Para
It was a joy to go to 3 Commando Brigade Headquarters as, without putting too fine a point on it, 5 Brigade Headquarters was a complete shambles. By contrast, a 3 Commando Brigade Air Squadron helicopter picked me up, the landing zone was recognisable, somebody was waiting for me, then brought me to the tent where Julian Thompson gave the orders.

2 Para were to be in reserve on the northern flank behind 3 Para and 45 Commando, with orders to exploit forward depending on where we achieved a break. Julian Thompson didn't seem to know that 2 Para were still in the south with 5 Brigade. In the time he'd allocated, we couldn't get to where I wanted us to be. I was the new boy, so I didn't raise this problem during 'any questions' at the end of orders. So I got hold of him afterwards; he'd understood we were at Bluff Cove and not Fitzroy, which would have been closer. He asked, 'Where do you want to be?' I indicated the reverse slope of Mount Kent. 'You're going to need helicopters aren't you?'

'Yes, if we're to get there on time.'

'Right,' said Julian, turning to his brigade major, John Chester: 'Fix.'

David Cooper
Chaplain, 2 Para
We flew to rejoin the commando brigade at the back of Mount Kent. I was glad to leave Fitzroy, as everything there had been the consequence of ineptitude and military mismanagement, and I didn't want to be associated with that kind of incompetence.

Captain Adrian Robert Freer
3 Para
We knew about Goose Green and the deaths of H Jones, David Wood the adjutant who I knew very well from 1 Para, and the eighteen others. We were under no illusions about what was in store.

Ailsa Heathman
Estancia Farm, North Camp
Huw Pike was all set to move out on June 5, but the bigwigs flew in and clipped his wings for him. The southern flank units weren't ready so there was no point in 3 Para pushing ahead in the north. The *Galahad* bombing at Fitzroy had also slowed everything down. It was foggy for the first couple of days, so supplies were brought in by landing craft to the creek. When the fog lifted, helicopters were flying stuff in all the time. We were now living on compo ourselves, but we did kill a beef and hang it up, but the troops stripped it bare overnight. Tony killed a couple of sheep, and told them to leave it overnight until the meat was cold and set when he'd cut it up for them, but everybody was desperate for fresh meat so they also went pretty well immediately.

Captain Adrian Robert Freer
3 Para
Before we could make any sort of assault on Stanley, the guns had to be brought forward within range plus at least three hundred rounds per gun. So from June 5 to 11 we sat in the middle of nowhere, nine kilometres west of Mount Longdon, fifteen kilometres west of Stanley. We were in a very forward position, within range of the Argentine 155mm guns on the racecourse, which would fire at us – often quite close. The ground was soft and wet and absorbed a lot of the effect of these explosions, although we had some injuries from shrapnel. A Pucara turbo-prop aircraft with 30mm cannon and missiles also attacked us.

Ailsa Heathman
Estancia Farm, North Camp
The nearest Argies were on Mount Kent, and the day after D Company arrived we were told to go somewhere safe for the day as there was going to be a battle. Of course, we didn't want to miss it so I went upstairs with binoculars for a good view – but the Argies ran away, so it didn't happen. There was a blue-on-blue on Mount Kent and the four Royal Marines killed were brought here by helicopter and buried. They stayed in the one grave for three months and then were shifted, three to the cemetery at San Carlos and one back home. I think this was the first war the families were allowed to take their loved ones home. We always visit them, on May 21, for the landing day memorial.

Captain Adrian Robert Freer
3 Para
A Company became the battalion's patrol base, and our patrols platoon went out a lot, looking at Mount Longdon. I took out a patrol as part of a big recce operation, to get as close to the Longdon positions as we could, to establish where their positions were, find some covered approaches and determine where our start line should be. As we were going to be doing a night attack, we practised all the drills in the darkness, and generally got ourselves used to working the terrain at night.

Neil Watson
Long Island, East Falkland
In late afternoon, the para's night recce patrols would move out for the long walk on to Mount Longdon. We'd drive them, with their heavy gear, to the top of the Estancia mountain, then sit up there until they returned and take them home. This was a tricky job, as we couldn't use headlights. While we waited, incoming shells often got pretty close. The drill was to get off stony ground and under a peat bank. The beauty of the deep peat is that it absorbs everything, so there was very little shrapnel flying about. You could set your watch by it; at around eleven o'clock at night our batteries around Mount Kent would open up, and the Argies would reply, so I know what both incoming and outgoing artillery sounds like.

Ailsa Heathman
Estancia Farm, North Camp
It was a hive of activity here around the clock. Guys were driving all night, delivering and collecting stores and troops. People were sleeping everywhere

including the lofts. You got out of your bed, and somebody else would get into it.

Private Domingo Morel
Argentine Infantry Regiment (deployed on Mount Longdon since April 17)

On the first night that we went into combat, I was scared that I might not come back or that something would happen to me. When we were told by the under officer that we had to get ready to reinforce B Company, then I really had to face up to the fact that it was going to be the enemy or me, then yes I was afraid. Being there, listening to the boys shooting, seeing them being shot at, it would be him in front or me, so then I had to concentrate on fighting. You had to leave fear to one side, as this boy who died said to me. Before we went to the front line I was afraid. I was also scared when everything was over.

Trudi McPhee
Brookfields, North Camp

In the first twelve hours we took six hundred paras up the Estancia mountain, brought six hundred down to get a rest, and then went to Teal Inlet to collect para medics from the ship. We were working Zulu time, like the military, and started the day taking rations to the different locations, then moved ammunition up the mountain. Six of us used to take the guys going out patrolling to the top of the mountain, then drop them off to make their way forwards as far as they'd dare to check out the Argentine positions. We'd wait there and sleep until they came back – at about two in the morning Zulu (just before dawn), then we'd start ferrying rations again. We drove without lights using the moonlight, and it was very rocky and boggy, with six or eight of us in a convoy. It was cold, wet and miserable, and the paras were wet all the time, using whatever they could to keep the weather off them in their trenches. They had very little food, making a twenty-four hours ration pack last thirty-six hours. I lost about a stone in weight. At the Estancia, Ailsa kept an enormous pot filled with raw meat, which the paras helped themselves to. They needed it and deserved it.

Pat Whitney
Green Patch, East Falkland

Until the war, we'd never even seen a helicopter in the Falklands, so they were a real novelty. We heard there was two Argie ones shot up in front of Mount Kent, so I asked the 2ic if we could go over and have a look.

I found this Argie motorbike, which the 2ic told me his men had been

Standing up to relax and eat, in a reverse slope position in the mountains overlooking Port Stanley. The 7.62mm SLR on the left is fitted with an early generation image intensifying sight, probably used for sniping.

trying to start the previous day, so it wasn't booby trapped. I lost interest in the wrecked helicopter and started trying to kick this bike into action. Just as I got a splutter out of it, a shell landed about eighty metres away. I dropped the bike and took cover, but then as we could hear more shells on the way, I picked up the bike, gave it another kick, it burst into life and I was gone, back to the Estancia.

Commander Timothy John Gedge
RN *Fleet Air Arm*

As the ground forces closed on Stanley, we were dropping ordnance of various sorts, while also trying to defend the landing area around San Carlos. The navy hadn't even practised attacking ground targets, because modern surface-to-air missile defence systems were considered too lethal. Being one hundred and forty miles north-east of the Falklands, we were transiting for forty-five minutes, before patrolling for another forty minutes, then returning. Fuel management was a vital new skill, to be learned very quickly.

Commander Nigel David 'Sharkey' Ward
Officer Commanding 801 Squadron, Fleet Air Arm, HMS Invincible

I told my pilots their job was to remain on station for as long as possible protecting the landings, and not to land on with excess fuel or I'd kick their backsides; and fly on 'endurance' – a disadvantage to a fighter aircraft, which needs combat energy before getting into a fight. I told them the main thing was to stay there for as long as possible, and that even if we were too slow to start with, we'd still beat these guys. But as the carrier group moved further east in response to Etendard Exocet threat, and we were operating two hundred and thirty miles from San Carlos, there was no way we could spend more than twenty minutes on CAP. *Invincible's* air direction guys used to joke that I was ruining the ship, because they always had to steam flat out towards us, to prevent us dropping out of the sky.

But all this time, the *Hermes* team were spending only half that time on task – at high level, probably because they'd been told always to land with reasonable fuel to ensure they didn't lose the aeroplane. I was amazed and furious when I found out. It was like they weren't taking the bloody operation seriously. The guys on the ground and the amphibious ships were losing lives and having a hard time, so we should do everything possible to deter or intercept enemy aircraft, but Admiral Woodward's quotes in his book about how he was getting nowhere with aviation, and having to fight his war without it, were stupid.

Commander Timothy John Gedge
RN Fleet Air Arm
The process of transmitting the army's requirements for Harrier air attacks to the crews in their cockpits was so long, the targets were not getting hit, or aircraft were arriving too late, being shot at by enemy weapons, or were attacking the wrong targets. I was sent ashore to sort it out.

After a briefing in *Hermes* and a two-hour helicopter flight in terrible weather, I was winched down on to an LSL in total darkness. We sailed into San Carlos in thick fog as dawn was breaking. I went to *Fearless* in a small boat, and the fog cleared to reveal a scene of beautiful hills, warships all around and fearsome activity everywhere. I flew up to 3 Commando Brigade HQ on the back of Mount Kent, then down to Bluff Cove to see the remnants of the two bombed LSLs. The helicopter had been stripped out, so I had to sit on the floor. Its canopy was held together with black masking tape because, the sergeant pilot told me, they'd been at very low level and had flown into a barbed wire fence. We had tracer fired at us, which I'd never experienced before.

Linda Kitson
Official war artist
I became addicted to 'Biscuits AB', nutrient-packed cement bricks. There's also 'Fly Cemetery' which are 'Biscuits AB' with dried fruit. Chocolate is also very important to the military diet, as it's instant energy, and as it got colder one needs more food. At times there wasn't enough food, and people were always hungry. I was offered brews made on hexamine stoves, which were really filthy, made from powdered stuff. Later we were eating abandoned Argentine rations, which were quite good. The climate is perfect for the petrifaction of limbs and dead people. There was an arm at Goose Green ... and dead bodies that people seemed to have forgotten.

Commander Timothy John Gedge
RN Fleet Air Arm
Fitzroy was very cold with brilliant sunshine, and as I was going to the brigade HQ, I saw a Falkland Islander wearing a blue boiler suit, rodding his drains. I had to go over and speak with him as I'd never met an islander, which obviously perplexed him, as he couldn't see why I wanted to speak with him. But I had breakfast with him, a cup of tea and huge wad of thick bread and marmalade, which was light relief for me on a very horrific day.

Private Jose Omar Ojeda
Compania Comando Servicios, 3rd Brigade

We didn't have orders or anything, so we managed as we could, depending on the danger. They were attacking us here and we were shooting over there, and if they attacked us over there, we were shooting over the other side. We did not keep anything in order, we defended ourselves as if God was with us; we didn't depend on anyone, and we depended on ourselves.

Major General (John) Jeremy Moore
Commander, British Land Forces

My headquarters was on *Fearless*, alongside the Commodore Amphibious Warfare, whose operations and mine required close coordination. My headquarters remained on *Fearless*, because as we did not officially exist we were not equipped to operate in the field. But as things approached the final battles I did move a small tactical headquarters forward to Fitzroy, quite close behind where the final battles were going to be.

Linda Kitson
Official war artist

I'd been warned: 'No bright colours,' so I chose black. I'd say to the lads: 'What are you carrying then? Mortars, rockets, radios, plus you've got a hedge sticking out of your hat as well . . . to me, you're the ones who look weird. I'm a unit of one, so I'm carrying everything.' *Private Eye*, which we loved whenever we could get it, called me 'Kit bags'.

The men had problems with their feet, and other Crimean War afflictions. Lack of helicopters prevented evacuation of many of these cases. The wind was so strong, carrying my portfolio was a problem. I never anticipated the pain of it. You can get cold and continue, but it takes too long to thaw out – you lose half a day of working and it makes you ill.

Captain Michael Ernest Barrow
HMS Glamorgan

On June 10, the bombardment organisation was reinstigated, as the troops ashore were having some difficulty displacing Argentinian forces well dug into the mountains to the west of Stanley.

General Mario Benjamin Menendez
Military Governor, Islas Malvinas

We gave the order that because the English were shelling, during the night people had to gather together in places which offered safety: the west store building or the Anglican church. The people who did not want to go to those places of safety and asked for special permission to stay in their house were the ones who were killed. God willed the artillery fire from the English navy, for which General Moore had to apologise afterwards, reached that house.

John Smith
Falkland Islander
The nightly Royal Navy bombardments went from eleven p.m. until three in the morning. The noise became soporific and eventually we went to sleep while it was going on, even though salvos sometimes landed behind our houses. At daylight the Harriers turned up. We had a routine in our shelter, which worked well until someone needed to go to the loo. We were stunned, finding ourselves doing things like listening to announcements of ships being sunk, while under a bombardment ourselves.

John Fowler
Superintendent of Education, Stanley
The first few nights of serious naval bombardment of Stanley were sleepless, but then as it became part of our lives I found myself able to sleep through. We would take our two-year-old and the baby for a walk most afternoons, and sometimes a Harrier raid would come in. The unexpected things were the scariest. The naval gunfire got to be such a normal night-time activity that we'd carry on watching videos even though there were huge crumps coming down further along the street. We knew somebody was out there killing people on our behalf – an uncomfortable feeling of strangeness made worse by the warmth of the peat fire.

Captain Hugh McManners
148 Commando Forward Observation Unit, Royal Artillery
My five-man team were hiding on Beagle Ridge to the north of the town, with a Swift scope, binoculars, a night scope, and plans of the town's electrical and street layouts. We fired at night, using the grid of streetlights to locate targets, which were often inside the town, as we'd been told all civilians had been moved well to the east. Priorities were the Argentine 155mm medium artillery batteries, the Chinooks and other helicopters, and the radar sites. I took care not to damage the electricity substations, as the streetlights were so useful.

Once on target, naval guns are incredibly accurate and reliable. I would start firing on to the racecourse at the far west of the town, where stores of aviation fuel would often explode with a confirmatory flash of flame. I would then make very careful and gradual corrections, creeping on to the targets I wanted to hit from a safe direction, ensuring the shells were dropping on to ground that I knew, from intensive study during the day, I could see – not into valleys. This was very technical shooting, with the highest standards of accuracy.

Captain Barry Melbourne Hussey
Administrator of Health, Social Services and Education, Islas Malvinas
The worst night was the shelling of June 12. I used to put a blanket over my window, light a small light and read until it stopped. Sometimes it would last an hour or two, or just fifteen minutes, but it was a way of war; they knew what to bomb or what to shoot at because they were photographing us every day.

Captain Hugh McManners
148 Commando Forward Observation Unit, Royal Artillery
Every morning, the roofs of buildings around the previous night's targets acquired large fresh red crosses, and the Chinook helicopters were moved on to the green as close as possible to the actual hospital. We spent the days plotting eight-figure grid references of targets, and 'dead ground' that we couldn't see. It takes hours of painstaking telescope work to find camouflaged military positions, which only give themselves away when somebody takes a walk out in the open. But increasingly, Argentine military units were seeking refuge in the town, which meant we could see them more easily.

Colonel Manuel Dorrego
Head of Public Works Department, Islas Malvinas
When they started the bombardments over the city, we had put out fires with the fire engine. The civilians who drove the fire engine . . . [cooperated]. Bloomer was also helping to take out the furniture from some houses, but what a strange situation, very, very odd, helping people who were your enemy?

Captain Hugh McManners
148 Commando Forward Observation Unit, Royal Artillery
One night the firing was puzzlingly different; initially we hit some fuel at the racecourse, but the next shell vanished, with an audible bang but no flash. After making adjustments, which should have brought the shells out on to

higher ground to the west of the racecourse, I calculated an error in the firing, which I transmitted to the ship. She could find nothing wrong with her system, and was very put out when I terminated her firing and sent her away from the gunline.

John Fowler
Superintendent of Education, Stanley
Late in the evening, Steve Whitley the vet woke me up to say naval shells were falling one hundred and fifty yards away, in front of our house, and out in the harbour near the old wreck. There was considerable blast. We went outside into our porch, which wasn't very secure and I was worried about being injured by the glass. The firing stopped and we went to bed. Some time after midnight I was woken again by Steve who was sleeping in the other end of the house, who said a shell had landed on the concrete of the garden path. We went outside, which was a bit scary as it was curfew. The shell had ruined the porch, pockmarked the whole front of the house and broken all the windows. We had a cup of tea in the kitchen with some of the others who'd also been woken up.

Captain Barry Melbourne Hussey
Administrator of Health, Social Services and Education, Islas Malvinas
On the night of June 12, 1 Regiment was being shelled . . . real fireworks which we could see from the secretary's building. It was difficult to know if it was finished. Bloomer, Dorrego, somebody else and me were sitting in the living room. We heard one explosion very, very close so we decided to go into the garden where we sat in the shelter of the stone fence, and then the second shell came down. The telephone rang and we went indoors.

John Fowler
Superintendent of Education, Stanley
I knew the bombardments went on a lot longer and usually came from the west. I became spooked, and suggested we all should move into the middle of the house, then went to check on the children. Steve was in the hallway off the kitchen, my wife and this other lady were at the foot of Mary Goodwin's bed in the little central bedroom of this house. There was this unimaginable whistling sound which was clearly coming directly down on us, followed by something that wasn't a noise but a shock – a total assault on every one of our senses, followed I thought by rain, which was the punctured water tanks. Then there was the best sound of all, my wife shouting; then the sound of

Steve Whitley shouting at her to stop shouting, both of which were tremendously reassuring.

The house was full of cordite fumes, dust, smoke, smell and, particularly, water. My shelter was very snug and I felt great reluctance to leave it, but my wife said she thought the lady with whom she was lying on the floor, Doreen Bonner, was dead. I left the shelter to see her, and was struck by how her glasses were totally covered with dust. She was a very meticulous person, and this seemed very odd, as she would certainly have wanted to wipe them. The other thing that struck me was that you could see where the shrapnel had gone into her and cauterised the flesh underneath. I can see her now in tremendously clear detail, which I don't particularly want to go into. Doreen was dead, which was hugely sad, as she was a tremendously brave woman. Her husband had been staying with us. He'd gone to his own house on Davis Street, behind Argentine lines. Doreen had gone every day past the Argentine troops who frightened her, to make sure he was all right – a very brave, nice lady.

I then discovered poor Steve Whitley trying to get his wife into the living room to see if she was hurt, to discover she was also dead. I'd been having an argument with her after she'd said fifty people dying wouldn't be very much. I'd said it wouldn't seem like that if you were related to one of them.

I don't know how seriously Mary Goodwin, the eighty-three-year-old lady in the front room, was wounded. She hadn't been well to start with, and died three days later in hospital, maybe of shock. She was fantastic, a classic Falklands lady, and of all the people we were looking after, was the most useful: she cooked, made bread, looked after the baby and was a grand lady. It was such a shame that her life ended in that way.

Having survived this attack, I was convinced there would be more, so we got back into the shelter. Rachel was woken up by us lying on top of the children. It was soundproofed, with no light, so she didn't understand why we were waking her up. She said: 'What's happening Daddy? Is this a bad day?'

Captain Barry Melbourne Hussey
Administrator of Health, Social Services and Education, Islas Malvinas
The people from the house were calling me because they were trying to get to the hospital – Fowler, or maybe his wife. We were two houses away, so I ran across. I remember Fowler had told me: 'Two shots never fall in the same place' – well, they did. The house was destroyed, pieces of roof were falling around, hanging down, and this old lady was on the floor. Another was lying

in her bed and perspiring. I picked her up and put her on an armchair, and held her in my arms, and then an ambulance came and they started taking them out.

John Fowler
Superintendent of Education, Stanley
Laurie Goodwin, the one-legged man, didn't seem too bad, so we got him into the bunker, than phoned the hospital. Other people from the west end of town arrived at our house, so we packed out the shelter, and refused to leave as it seemed to represent the only safety there was. The Land Rover ambulance arrived and did a laborious turn outside, rather than drive round the block up a one-way street.

Air Vice Commodore Carlos Bloomer-Reeve
Secretary General, Islas Malvinas
Barry Hussey went to rescue them, and Comodoro Mendilash, an intelligence officer of the Argentine air force, went out into the curfew, picked up the people and took them to hospital. Hidalgo was there too. The British were aiming at our house, but something went wrong. It was a terrible night. We were expecting something like that. We were on the limit of the bombing zone of the ship, so we knew it had to come one day. The explosion of those shells was deafening.

Captain Barry Melbourne Hussey
Administrator of Health, Social Services and Education, Islas Malvinas
I smelt death there. I am a navy pilot so I have seen many accidents and people . . . but this was the first time that I had ever had somebody dying in my arms and I felt really sorry for what was happening there. I suppose that is what influenced my saying to Fowler: 'I'm very sorry about what is happening.' I don't remember the words, they come from inside and you don't write them down. I was really very sorry for all those things that happened.

John Fowler
Superintendent of Education, Stanley
As we left the house, Barry Hussey was standing by the gate and said: 'I'm really very sorry. We've come here and messed up your peaceful existence, and now we're causing some of you to be killed.' I said: 'Well, it would be really great if you have access to General Menendez, to go and tell him that. Your political objectives are not being achieved and you're going to lose the battle. It would be better to pack up and go.'

He said, 'I wish it was that simple.'

Later, Barry Hussey was quite instrumental in the radio-telephone conversations with the British, before the surrender – with our doctor, Alison Bleanie.

Captain Hugh McManners
148 Commando Forward Observation Unit, Royal Artillery
When we heard the sad news several nights later, it was not possible for me on Beagle Ridge to decide exactly on which night the tragedy had happened. The peculiarities of the shooting on June 11/12 seemed the most likely. The shells had not done what they should have done. When I had told the ship to check their system they had been unable to find anything wrong. I had 'lost' several shells in dead ground which should have landed well away from any houses. If it had not been that night, then I was extremely worried, as every other shoot had seemed to go well. I could not afford to have such doubts. Since it was I who controlled all the shelling around Port Stanley, the airfield and the hills to the west and north, it was one of 'my' shells, which I found deeply upsetting.

Once hostilities ended, 148 Battery gathered on HMS *Fearless*. Battery Sergeant Major Jock Malcolm, who had been liaison officer on board the gunship on that night, made a point of telling me what happened; that when the firing system had been checked, nothing was amiss and they assumed I was mistaken. I had then told them to 'check solution' a second time and an impasse was reached when still they could find nothing wrong, so I terminated the shoot. The next day, worried by my insistence, the gunnery crew made a complete check of their computers and firing system, discovering a small deviation on one of the tracking radars that would produce the error that I had calculated the night before. To be proved correct after the event was a small comfort, but I was very grateful to have been told.

John Fowler
Superintendent of Education, Stanley
My leg felt like I'd been jabbed by a needle. At the hospital I discovered a hole in my jeans, with a lump and a neatly cauterised puncture in my leg. The Argentine surgeon removed some shrapnel. By the time the British arrived this had turned a bit septic, and thanks to the famous naval doctor Rick Jolly hacking a great chunk out of my leg, my little hole ended up being an impressive scar. But I think our mental scars were bigger.

My daughter Rachel was very, very frightened by the whole thing. For the

Argentine 105mm artillery guns in fire positions inside Stanley. Buildings were used for concealment in the hope that British artillery would be reluctant to fire upon the town.

rest of that night and the next night, when we were in the maternity ward of the hospital, it was terrible as we no longer had any protection from the shelling. We slept on the floor under the beds, with another mattress balanced on top of us. There was a lot of firing and I was in a gibbering hysterical state. The Argentines kept moving artillery around the town, and had a group of guns firing just outside the hospital. I'd felt much safer in my little womb on Ross Road West than here, where people were shooting very close to us on purpose. If a thing has happened once, it enters the realm of things that can happen to you – so there's no comfort in people saying it won't happen again.

21

Night Killing

*The rifle platoons were in close-quarter battle – gutter fighting.
I was directing fire at muzzle flashes in the darkness, with the
occasional stab of light from exploding artillery, which revealed
the people we were firing at.*

Glenda Watson
Long Island, East Falkland
Back at Long Island, the females were keeping the farm going. There was
plenty of food as we've got a good garden, although flour and stuff like that
was running out. We also had plenty of beer. My fourteen-year-old son Paul
was the only male here. He'd been desperate to go with Neil and the other
men to Estancia, but Neil had insisted he stay, telling him: 'You'll get your war
some day.' Paul is a keen member of the Falkland Islands Defence Force,
working and training, and is still waiting. We had the children and grand-
mother to look after, and there wasn't much else we could do.

Neil Watson
Long Island, East Falkland
At the Estancia we were living in tents, using the military sleeping bags the
marines had left us at Long Island.

Trudi McPhee
Brookfields, North Camp
Because I was the only woman out of fourteen blokes amid all the paras, they
tended to get me to do things: 'Get that woman in here. We need Land
Rovers to do this and that . . .' At night time we'd stop around the diggings

and chat with the guys. They'd say: 'What the hell's a woman doing round here then?' and I'd say: 'Looking after you guys,' which seemed to go down quite well. They'd also talk about how wet they were and how they wanted to go home. They were fed up and wished Mrs Thatcher would give them the green light to go. They were really raring to get on with it.

Neil Watson
Long Island, East Falkland

When we weren't needed to ferry equipment, we used to come back home, and I'd get a good night's sleep. I'd just got back one morning and was in bed when an enormous explosion vibrated the entire house and woke me up. Some Argentines were flying these old Canberras, and had dropped their bombs, some in Berkeley Sound, and one of them hit this ridge of rock, miles from here near Brookfield Farm, but the tremor went right through, down to our house.

Pat Whitney
Green Patch, East Falkland

We could get about six people with their kit into a long wheelbase Land Rover, but with the trailer we could take more than ten guys with the bergans. They had a lot of kit, at least until the big push on the last night, when they went in for the final attacks with just their webbing, ammunition and a few bits of chocolate in their pockets.

(James) Robert Fox
BBC correspondent

The Marines got jealous that 2 Para were all over the BBC national and local radio, so I wasn't allowed to go with the paras round to Fitzroy, missed reporting the Bluff Cove disaster, and instead joined 45 Commando for half of their big yomp eastwards. Their extremely professional CO, Andrew Whitehead, never trusted me as H Jones had done, so sadly I never heard his orders for the Two Sisters action.

45 Commando and the paras were very different. The paras have very peculiar ways of doing things at times. It was exciting, but quite alarming to be with them. You feel their tremendous energy; they're assault troops in conventional and non-conventional warfare. By contrast, apart from their amphibious role, the Marines are heavy infantry. They do things more deliberately and at times it's better thought out, but with less spirit, I would say. I was very relieved not to have much to do with 5 Brigade, which seemed to be a class apart and badly organised.

Falkland Islanders help with ferrying 3 Para's equipment at Teal Inlet after the arrival of the British on May 28, 1982.

Captain Michael Ernest Barrow
HMS Glamorgan

On the night of June 11 we went inshore in support of 45 Commando who were having some difficulty taking the Two Sisters mountain. We arrived close inshore at ten-thirty and went to action stations, spending the next five hours on the gun line, responding to calls for help from 45. The Scots Guards were on the adjacent mountain, and another ship was supporting them.

Commander Ian Inskip
HMS Glamorgan

It seemed to us that the gun line was becoming more dangerous, especially with the shore-based Exocet that the Argentines had set up. On the way in, I'd spent a lot of time discussing the odds with Lieutenant David Tinker, and we mutually agreed things looked a bit dodgy. But as the admiral had said, escorts are expendable, they were running out of Mark 8 ammunition, so we Mark 6 ships had to go in and do the business. The land forces were now on the outskirts of Stanley, and our job was to support 45 Commando dealing with the Two Sisters Ridge, with Longdon and Tumbledown going on the same night.

(James) Robert Fox
BBC correspondent

Because the CO wouldn't tell me what was going on, Whitehead's ops officer and 2ic had to fill me in on the details, and I followed the battle from transmissions over the main headquarters radios. I had a grandstand view of the attacks on the Two Sisters, Mount Longdon and Tumbledown. From the forward slope of Two Sisters, it was an incredible display of pyrotechnics.

Captain Michael Ernest Barrow
HMS Glamorgan

These NGSFOs were extremely effective; army commando officers specially trained in firing naval guns, and also for fighter-ground attack. They sometimes worked from helicopters, but on this occasion he was on foot with his assistants and backpacks full of radios, going along with the forward troops.

Captain Christopher Charles Brown
148 Commando Forward Observation Unit, Royal Artillery

My naval gunfire team was given to 45 Commando for their attack on the Two Sisters. Because ammunition was short and we thought we could achieve surprise, it was decided to attack without prior artillery fire. This isn't easy, as you normally adjust the rounds on to the targets before you start, which slows things down if you have to do it during an attack. But that was the decision, and we got to within a couple of hundred yards before the Argentines opened up with heavy machine guns, which I'm glad to say were firing over our heads, as they didn't have night sights. With support from HMS *Glamorgan* and the guns of the artillery batteries, we took the mountain pretty quickly.

(James) Robert Fox
BBC correspondent
The battle was very tough and hard-fought because the defensive positions were so well laid by the 5th Argentine marines who were a hard, professional outfit. I curse the ITN television crew to this day, who, halfway through, wanted to go to bed! One had to learn as one was going on, what you were looking at, and there were great *longeurs* when nothing happened.

Captain Michael Ernest Barrow
HMS Glamorgan
It was very worrying to be listening to the spotter officer on the other end of the radio net. You could actually hear him panting as they went up the hill, whilst giving us instructions of where he wanted the rounds to fall, and where the last lot had gone. One almost felt you were fighting the action with him, although fortunately I was in my nice warm operations room, and I would rather be there than flogging up the mountain with him.

We responded to calls throughout the night, detailed gunnery, relying very heavily on our navigation, firing rounds at ranges of six to seven miles, hoping not to hit our own troops. I'm glad to say we didn't, but I have to say that we were firing as little as two hundred metres from our own troops. There was a lot of kelp around, and a 155mm howitzer fired at us, rather ineffectively. As a result of the help we were able to give them, 45 Commando did take that mountain, but we had to stay rather longer than we should.

Captain Christopher Charles Brown
148 Commando Forward Observation Unit, Royal Artillery
As we took the top of the Two Sisters mountain, I gave the all clear for HMS *Glamorgan* to leave the gun line so she could return, but she cut across into the arc of fire of the Argentine Exocet missile in Stanley.

Commander Ian Inskip
HMS Glamorgan

We had to get pretty close in, within Exocet danger range, and while we awaited the call for fire, we tucked ourselves in very close to East Island. Our orders were to be back with the carriers by dawn, but fifteen minutes before we were due to leave, we received the PIN from the carriers indicating they'd moved fifty miles further east, another two hours' steaming time for us, so we couldn't make it by dawn.

Captain Michael Ernest Barrow
HMS Glamorgan

We knew that on the way back we had to skirt around a minefield, and we knew also that there was probably a shore-based Exocet, removed from a destroyer in the Buenos Aires area, flown to the Falklands by Hercules and installed on some sort of farm wagon. We believed this was in the vicinity of Pembroke Point, and so we had a large red circle drawn on our chart representing the extreme range of this missile.

Captain Carlos B. Castro Madero
Weapons Officer, 5-Inch Anti-Aircraft Batteries,
Warship Belgrano

As well as the five AM Exocet missiles, we also had the MM-38 missiles. One was sent to the Malvinas and was fired from the shore and hit Glamorgan. Argentine engineers did a good job fixing that up.

Commander Ian Inskip
HMS Glamorgan

I saw a blip on 020 at eight miles, and I knew in my heart of hearts it was an Exocet. It wasn't there on the second or third sweeps of the radar, but there much closer on the fourth – but just painting. On the fifth sweep there was a firm echo, so I ordered, 'Starboard three-five.' I knew it was an Exocet.

Captain Michael Ernest Barrow
HMS Glamorgan

It was, therefore, with some alarm that shortly after 0630, whilst proceeding at twenty-four knots towards the carrier, skirting around the edge of the red ring, my operations officer noted what looked like yet another round from a 155mm howitzer coming in my direction. We'd been seeing these on the radar, so it was no surprise, but at the same moment the officer of the watch, my navigating officer Commander Inskip noticed a flare coming from the same direction.

Commander Ian Inskip
HMS Glamorgan

I asked the ops room if they'd got the contact, but they said it was a helicopter. I said it was too fast, but they insisted. I was making snap decisions. If they'd been right, I'd have turned in the wrong direction. It was fifteen degrees off the threat bearing, from Eliza Cove and not Pembroke Point. The helmsman immediately responded and put the rudder over in the direction for an aircraft attack, so although I caught it, we lost a few seconds turning back the other way. I gave the ops room a countdown as it closed. We'd just stood down after seven hours at action stations.

Captain Michael Ernest Barrow
HMS Glamorgan

A 155mm round doesn't have a flare, so it was quite obvious this was something else, and that in the next ten seconds, which was the time of flight of this missile, we would have to do something about it. The navigating officer, of his own volition and quite correctly, turned the ship away from the oncoming Exocet missile, as there was no doubt what it was. This was the correct tactic for an approaching Exocet, which at that stage is searching with its radar head for a returning echo.

Commander Ian Inskip
HMS Glamorgan

It was the ops room's job to fire chaff, and the officer of the watch should have called 'Brace, Brace, Brace'. I failed to tell them to do this. The net result was that people who shouldn't have been killed were killed. But you can only get some things right. I take it very personally, that I had it within my gift to have saved those people – but I didn't. On the other hand, if I hadn't done what I did do, the missile would have exploded in our Sea Slug main magazine, leaving perhaps a handful of survivors out of our ship's company of four hundred and fifty. That doesn't make it any easier to live with, but that is the price that has to be paid. We are the people who do the politicians' dirty work, and the buck had to stop somewhere – and it stops with me.

I lost the missile in the ground wave at about two miles, then I heard a scrabbling noise as the captain put on his command open-line headset and said: 'Where is it, pilot, where is it, where is it?' There was a dull thud and night was transformed into day. I said: 'There it is sir, about the hangar. Navigator off.'

Captain Michael Ernest Barrow
HMS *Glamorgan*

We were hit by the Exocet at 0636, and we were under helm, which is fortunate as instead of hitting us on the waterline as it is designed to do, it hit us at the turn of the upper deck and the ship's side, port side aft, abreast of the ship's hangar. The immediate result was a large explosion from the missile, followed by a second explosion, which was our refuelled helicopter in its hangar.

Commander Ian Inskip
HMS *Glamorgan*

Bells were ringing on the bridge. I remembered the *Bismarck* being hit with lots of rudder on. The first thing I said was 'Midships', so that as the steering motors ran down, they could be centralising the rudder. I then ordered 'Revolutions One Hundred' to slow us down and reduce the strain on the ship. I selected the alternate steering system, reset the alarm, and the bells stopped. I realised our luck was in as we could still steer. I spoke to the steam turbine room and we were all right for power, but had lost the gas room, so I steadied the ship on one-eighty at twelve knots. I then asked the sub lieutenant to get a sitrep from the hangar, but then decided someone with experience had to go, and went myself.

Captain Michael Ernest Barrow
HMS *Glamorgan*

I was in the operations room, and my first reaction was to slow the ship down. It was quite clear we'd been hit down aft. I knew there was a fire down there. I felt until I had got some kind of a report as to the damage, it was important to reduce the wind over the deck. But the ship had slowed anyway, because the vacuum from the Exocet blast had killed three out of the four gas turbines we were using to give us extra speed, so we slowed down whether we liked it or not.

Commander Ian Inskip
HMS *Glamorgan*

There were flames a hundred feet high, beyond the top of the mast, spread halfway up the port waist, lapping around the port Sea Cat director. There was a huge hole in the deck with smoke billowing out, and people were wandering around like headless chickens. I should have realised that when there is a big bang, people's brains switch off, but no one had told me that, so I was actually quite rude to them. But I did manage to kick-start people into action and we got firefighting going. But the flight deck was another matter.

Captain Michael Ernest Barrow
HMS Glamorgan
We spent the next four and a half hours fighting the fires, and shortly before eleven o'clock they were all out. We had to keep clear of the land and the threat of further enemy attack, particularly from the air, and to keep the ship afloat obviously, whilst putting out the fires; and not, in the process, damaging equipment that hadn't already been damaged.

Commander Ian Inskip
HMS Glamorgan
The port Sea Cat launcher had been blown over the side and was hanging in the flight deck netting. The rotor head of the helicopter was the only recognisable bit, and the hangar door was smashed like junk. Ammunition was exploding, but I felt I might be able to take cover behind the rotor head. As a ship's diver I'd organised the placement of various diving sets around the ship to augment the breathing apparatus. Wearing one of these sets, I was able to get behind the rotor head with flames three sides of me, to attack the base of the fire. Then after a few minutes, I received a blast of cold South Atlantic into the back of my woolly pully. People were shouting warnings about ammunition exploding, but I was more worried that the helicopter had got a Mark II depth charge loaded, which would have made a real mess exploding. I was angry and just got stuck in.

Captain Michael Ernest Barrow
HMS Glamorgan
The firefighting parties had to stop when we developed a very serious list, due to taking in enormous amounts of firefighting water, and until we'd pumped out and drained down we had to stop fighting the fire.

Commander Ian Inskip
HMS Glamorgan
We used timber to divert water round the hole, but we tipped over to about twelve to thirteen degrees, which for a six-thousand-ton ship is a lot of water.

I did notice our speed coming up, so I knew the battle was being won down below. Lying half in, half out of the hangar door was a dead petty officer, who seemed to be grinning. I remember thinking angrily: 'What the hell have you got to grin about? You're dead.'

When the helicopter fire died down, I asked a leading hand to get in and put the remainder of the fire out, which with some hesitation he did. I then stepped over the junk and this body, to get into the hangar office, whereupon this chief petty officer said: 'Give me a hand.' I thought he'd come in through the escape hatch or fallen down, and hadn't realised he was the body that had been there all the time. He must have thought me a right cold-hearted so-and-so when I said: 'Hang on chief, I'll just put out this fire.' I stepped over him, climbed up on a pile of bodies and put the hose through a shrapnel hole into the fire in the next compartment. At the time this didn't bother me at all. I knew I was using bodies as a convenient way of getting at the fire.

I succeeded in filling the hangar office with more smoke as I put out the fire, which didn't help the chief too much, and I retired coughing and spluttering. We'd been hit at 0637, achieved boundary cooling in fifteen minutes, and the fires were out by about 1010. I was absolutely knackered. My arms were hanging off, I had smoke inhalation and a splitting headache, and the captain told me to turn in so I could be fit for my proper duties. I awoke some hours later to find the ship tidied up. The bodies were wrapped in strips of canvas along the port waste, and we retired north-east to the task force.

When the *Sir Galahad* had been hit earlier, our Chinese laundrymen had wanted to go home, coming continually to the flight deck with their suitcases. The flight deck officer would tell them 'no more helicopters until tomorrow so go and get some scran', and they'd disappear below. When we were hit, the Chinese laundrymen were fast asleep in the tumble dryer. The laundry filled with smoke, so they got out of the hatch on to the launch deck to be confronted by this monumental fire. Someone told the ops room the fire was getting near to the Sea Slug, so the ops room pushed the buttons and fired them off. On the flight deck, the noise of the missiles taking off is incredible, four wrap-round boosts, going from nought to Mach 2 in 0.5 seconds . . . It took some considerable time to communicate with Number One Boy, and when two days later his hearing recovered, after being told how Number Two Boy was, he told the Laundry Officer: 'Silly flucker, sah. Wasn't wearing his anti-frash.'

Captain Michael Ernest Barrow
HMS Glamorgan
Within an hour of putting out the fires, we'd worked the speed up again to

HMS *Glamorgan*'s crew clearing the damage to the port side and helicopter hangar, caused by a land-based MM.38 Exocet missile on June 12, 1982.

twenty knots and at 1230 that morning rejoined the task group. The good news was that we were still afloat – and we are still the only ship to have been hit by an Exocet and survived.

The bad news was that thirteen members of the ship's company had been killed or died subsequently as a result of the hit and the fires. We'd also lost the helicopter, the use of one Sea Cat missile and ammunition, and the ability to track our Sea Slug missile, due to damage to the wiring of the missile's radar. Otherwise, the ship was operational. We were able to make twenty-seven knots by the time we got back to the task group, we still had our surface weapons system and air direction capabilities, and could fire Sea Cat and Sea Slug missiles.

Captain Chris Brown
148 Commando Forward Observation Unit, Royal Artillery

Being an older ship and more sturdily built, Glamorgan wasn't sunk. Our liaison officer on board that night was a great friend, and he'd also been on board HMS Ardent when she'd been sunk earlier. The word had gone round the fleet that when Captain Bob Harmes came on to your ship you were on a hiding to get attacked, so he wasn't exactly being welcomed with open arms. Indeed, right at the end, nobody wanted him on Canberra – which was taking us home. We reckoned there would be one Argentine submarine out there, which hadn't been told that the war was over, waiting until Canberra put its nose outside Port Stanley . . .

So we took Two Sisters with 45 Commando, consolidated our position on top, and were reassured that the Argentinians hadn't been able to coordinate their artillery to fire at us as we attacked. Their artillery observation team had left behind binoculars and maps with their gun batteries marked on, which was very useful. It was only after we'd dug in and built rock shelters, that they began firing at us, which, although sporadic, was frightening. There was a huge difference between their light artillery, which was the same calibre as ours, and their medium 155mm artillery. Their 105mm light guns could land shells twenty or thirty yards away, and so long as you'd got your head down in the rocks, there'd be a loud bang and a flash, and it did no harm. But the medium 155mm artillery shook the ground, threw up rocks all over the place, and did a lot of damage. But thankfully, we were not subjected to too much of that.

Commander Ian Inskip
HMS Glamorgan

Thirteen had died and another died later of his wounds. The most horrific injuries were in the galley, where the Formica scythed around like carving knives. One leading cook had three limbs cut off. I saw him being carried out by stretcher to *Invincible*, and they returned his body later that day for burial. A twenty-stone chief cook was standing in the passage very close to where the Exocet came through. He got blown twenty feet along the port passage through the swing doors, and was blinded for three days. Some people were lucky; others were not.

Lieutenant Commander Graham John Edmonds
Operations Officer and Squadron Warfare Officer, HMS Broadsword
Glamorgan had cut the corner of the Exocet danger zone while returning to the task force, which the other ships *Avenger*, *Yarmouth* and the *Arrow* refused to do – and then *Glamorgan* was hit. I listened to a very vitriolic radio conversation between various captains the next day. *Glamorgan* had probably become over-confident.

Captain Adrian Robert Freer
3 Para
The final assault took place on the night of June 10/11, and for some reason became a bit of a rush and was not done particularly well. The CO delivered well-prepared orders down at Estancia House, but by the time our company commander, Dave Collet, had hacked all the way back up to our position, there wasn't much time left. During our O Group we were being shelled by 155mm artillery, which was a fairly interesting experience.

Pat Whitney
Green Patch, East Falkland
I had no doubt that the attacks would be successful, but I had no foresight . . . the odds were against them, but we had no doubts about it. Nobody had explained the battle plan to us, just what we had to do. We knew they were being given orders, but we had to work it out for ourselves. I just hadn't realised how serious the whole thing was. It all caught up with me later, just how dangerous it all was for everybody. I was a bit of a greenhorn I think.

Neil Watson
Long Island, East Falkland
There were three companies of the paras, and I was with B Company. The day was pretty quiet, but in the afternoon we went up onto the ridge with this company, and a number of things stick in my mind . . . It was tragic really. I

had to get fuelled up before I left the Estancia, and there were two engineers from 9 Para Squadron – Scotty Wilson and his friend. They jumped in with me, and we motored them and their kit up the mountain. I'll always remember Scotty was as cheerful as heck, saying to me: 'Neil, we'll be in Stanley in two days' time, then away home.' But the other guy said to me: 'Or dead. . .' He was a bit morbid about it, whereas Scotty was very positive, keen to get going.

Trudi McPhee
Brookfields, North Camp
The night they took Mount Longdon, Huw Pike came with me in my Rover, and made a joke about wanting a bit of female company on his last night. I called him 'general' and wished him luck, to which he said, 'You should join the Army, Trudi. You'd go far.' We dropped him and everyone else off, then returned to the Estancia where the 2ic, Roger Patton, told us it was getting serious, and that we should write a letter to our next of kin and leave it at the Estancia in case we didn't come back. The waiting was the hardest bit.

Neil Watson
Long Island, East Falkland
We stayed up on Estancia Ridge, sitting around with these guys, brewing up and waiting to get on with the attack. Honestly, this was one of my worst days . . . I was looking in their eyes . . . you don't know what to talk about. I knew that some of these guys I was talking to were going to be dead in the morning and I felt really bad, bad inside about it . . . trying to be cheerful, sharing mugs of tea and trying to make conversation. I had been in the IDF before SLRs and GPMGs, and knew about the old Bren guns; I'd been a Bren gunner, so that was something to talk about.

Ailsa Heathman
Estancia Farm, North Camp
Most of the troops moved out on the night of June 11. The quartermaster, George Brown, and the B echelon stayed in the sheds, and suddenly the place was empty.

Tony had been very keen to go with them on the attack, but they persuaded him that with a wife, a farm and a baby he shouldn't do it. He's regretted it ever since. People here did a lot that night and got a long way forward. Although I was relieved at the time that he didn't go, I don't think he ever got over the regret of it, particularly more recently. I do feel guilty about the loss of life and people suffering, but that's what happens in war and you can't expect to come out of it unaffected.

Neil Watson
Long Island, East Falkland
So come the dusk, they moved off towards the Murrell River, and the rest of us with the Land Rovers lined up, about nine Rovers and a couple of tractors, loaded with ammunition. Some of the tractors had pretty bad bog-ins, so luckily we had a couple of BVs with us too, which pulled them straight out, no problem.

Captain Adrian Robert Freer
3 Para
We had a five-kilometre walk to the start line, then B Company carried out the first attack, with A Company coming round to the northern flank while C Company were held in reserve. The attack was what we call 'silent but noisy on contact', with us infiltrating the enemy positions with no pre-artillery fire. A lot of people questioned the wisdom of that, but I suppose it was to do with getting artillery ammunition to the guns, the huge amounts required by pre-arranged fire plans, and the need to retain enough ammunition to deal with the unexpected. We also had naval gunfire support, which proved crucial.

Pat Whitney
Green Patch, East Falkland
The night they went into Mount Longdon, we were on the top of Estancia Mountain, which was very noisy. The British mortars were at the top of the Estancia Valley firing over the top of us, and the Argentinians were shelling and mortaring. All this fire came over the top of us. We took some medics forward to Murrell Bridge, and one Rover got bogged in. All the medics piled into my Rover, and I somehow got there. We were carrying ammunition to the forward mortar line, which was halfway between Murrrell Brook and Mount Longdon – about a mile and a half from the top of Longdon. We could see the whole battle taking place.

Captain Adrian Robert Freer
3 Para
B Company bore the brunt of it, taking most of the battalion's casualties. A Company was to advance forward in a box formation from the northern flank, but the formation went to pot and we got split up. We were at the bottom of a concave slope with two platoons forward, being fired upon from the mountain and had to find cover in a peat bog. One of the signallers, Corporal Hope, and a man from one of the platoons were shot dead through the head, and it

became clear that further advance up this slope would be suicidal. We retraced our steps, but in putting down covering fire to get ourselves out, were firing into B Company at right angles, so we had to stop. While doing a small doubling back on ourselves, we came through a minefield, then moved up through a saddle about a third of the way down Mount Longdon.

Pat Whitney
Green Patch, East Falkland

After taking some medics forward, I went back to the Estancia and took a pile of mortar ammunition forward, from a bogged-in Land Rover that had been overloaded. An officer there said he wanted it all moving – 'Now!' There was far too much of it for one Rover. I knew it was better to be sure of delivering half, rather than not getting there at all with the whole lot. I told him I'd take half now and return for the rest, but he wanted it all taking, 'Right now.' I don't think this officer was used to being spoken to the way I spoke to him. I drove off with half, and haven't a clue what happened to the rest of it.

Captain Adrian Robert Freer
3 Para

B Company suffered quite heavy casualties killed and wounded, and were no longer effective as a fighting company. We came through them and took over. We'd taken about twelve hours, all in the darkness, very much proving the importance of artillery fire support. The naval guns, with their heavier shell and rapid firing, were very skilfully used by the naval gunfire team led by Captain Willie McCracken who was the senior forward observation officer, getting fire moving down the ridgeline in front of us as we cleared the rest of the mountain. He helped us greatly.

Trudi McPhee
Brookfields, North Camp

We had fourteen BVs and six civilian tractors, and after moving six hundred paras up the mountain, I thought it was dodgy for us to be standing there in the basin where any aircraft coming in from the west could make a real mess of us. The 2ic asked for a local guide to walk in front of our convoy. I was the only woman and was conscious that if I bogged a Rover I'd delay things and slow them down, so I volunteered. I walked one side of the Rover and a medic walked on the other. Pat Whitney drove the first Rover so he followed my backside into war! Then the other Rovers and tractors all followed in a big long line. There's a very bad ditch halfway between Estancia and the Murrrell

Bridge and a lot of the vehicles got bogged in. The 2ic was keen to keep going: 'You've got ten minutes. The ones you can't get out can bloody well stay.'

I said, 'Fine by me.'

That reduced the numbers of vehicles, but we pushed on, carrying the paramedics. Then as we were getting down to the Murrell Bridge, we came under fire from Mount Longdon. The drill was to get out of the vehicles and scatter. One of the drivers got a bit of a fright and shot up over the hill, and as a Shimuli flare went off, his windscreen reflected light so he could be seen, which worried us quite a bit. But we had to carry on as they said there were wounded at the other end. We were told that from now on there were landmines and booby traps, and Pat Whitney offered to walk so I could drive, but I said: 'No, it's OK.' At Murrell Bridge there were two people standing there and we thought, 'Oh no, what's this,' but they were British, so that was a relief.

Captain Adrian Robert Freer
3 Para

Longdon is about one kilometre long, a rocky outcrop like a spine, which falls steeply away to the northern side, in which the Argentines had used wire, angle irons and rocks to build sangars that would keep out small arms fire. They were very well positioned and took some getting out. The engagements took place at about fifty metres' range, then closed to the use of grenades and bayonets.

Pat Whitney
Green Patch, East Falkland

We'd left some Rovers beside a ditch, which we couldn't cross. A snowcat had pulled some of us through it, and we'd continued. Those vehicles on the other side of the ditch allowed us to get people back if we lost the snowcats. But even though it was still dark, the helicopters were coming in fairly close to take the casualties out directly, landing in one of the valleys.

Captain Adrian Robert Freer
3 Para

I was commanding a company fire support team, six of us with two machine guns. To operate a machine gun properly, using link ammunition, you need somebody to feed in the ammunition plus a third person as gun controller to direct the fire. The actual firer gets tunnel vision at night, and can't see anything apart from what he's shooting at. We were firing initially at about twenty-five to thirty metres, at positions as the platoons went in to attack them. After a while, the ranges became a little more, but not much. The rifle platoons were in close-quarter battle – gutter fighting. I was directing fire at muzzle flashes in the darkness, with the occasional stab of light from exploding artillery, which revealed the people we were firing at.

Pat Whitney
Green Patch, East Falkland
Driving over that terrain at night with no lights, you had to be really on the ball and work hard to keep on top. We could only go at walking pace, following the 2ic of 3 Para and Trudi walking out in front. There was snow on the ground with a very hard frost, which was a saviour for the troops as it helped keep their feet dry.

Trudi McPhee
Brookfields, North Camp
From what I saw that night, I was amazed anyone could come out of those mountains alive. The Shimuli flares and artillery illuminating shells burn forever, and it looked as though somebody was pouring bucket after bucket of red-hot coals down the mountain. The navy were firing over from Berkeley Sound in the north, about three miles away from here, but I don't remember the noise of it as much as the buckets of coal effect. They'd lob a couple of mortars at us; you'd hear them coming over, but they'd plop into the peat and were lost. We had someone looking after us – there's no doubt about that.

Ailsa Heathman
Estancia Farm, North Camp
We were in and out of the shed listening to the HQ's crackly radios and passing on the news to everybody in the house. We saw a lot of fireworks, but then for a day and a half we didn't hear anything at all.

Trudi McPhee
Brookfields, North Camp
The moon had come up enough so the drivers could look out of the side window. We followed the peat banks from the Murrell River around to the bottom of Longdon where we dropped off the paramedics. Me, Roddy McKay and Mike Carey were then told to go a thousand metres back and set up some torches for the helicopters so they could come in and pick up wounded. The first guy was brought in shot in the stomach. He was six foot four and was just

hanging on. He kept trying to tell me something but I couldn't understand him. They put him in a helicopter, but he died by the time he got to Teal Inlet. We stayed there all night putting people into helicopters, then at five o'clock we went back to Longdon where the paras had their OP. The 3 Para 2ic, Roger, turned to me and said: 'Good heavens, Trudi, you don't want to stay around here. Come dawn they're going to shoot the hell out of anything west of here.'

Neil Watson
Long Island, East Falkland
We ended up in the darkness somewhere near the Murrell Bridge, and sat there. There was a perfect view of the firefights on the Two Sisters; we could virtually follow the battle: the Royal Marines' fire going in, and the counter-fire coming back down – red tracer. I'd guess one position was an Argentine point five machine gun, which opened up; the marines would stop, call in naval gunfire, and the whole place would be lit up with star shell, then the navy 4.5-inch guns would pound the area. You'd think that would winkle the guy out, but no . . . it took two or three goes, and a long time. On occasions tracer came at us; it comes slowly at first, then speeds up at the last second and you duck your head.

Pat Whitney
Green Patch, East Falkland
It was confusing and very noisy, a lot of whistlings with explosions. If you heard the whistle you knew you were safe as the shell had gone by you ... looking away over to the far right on the side of the Two Sisters, it looked as though somebody with a big giant shovel was throwing coals at the side of the mountain, as all the shells exploded into it. I wasn't frightened at all; we were too busy.

Neil Watson
Long Island, East Falkland
Casualties were to be carried from Mount Longdon down to us, which was over a mile, then we'd drive them back to the Estancia. That was another thing I was dreading; that I'd have injured, maimed men in my Land Rover over that rough country. It was a clear night, so the Teeny Weenie helicopters and navy Wessex were flying overhead the whole time, getting right in there to the foot of Mount Longdon, casevacing the wounded directly to Estancia.

Pat Whitney
Green Patch, East Falkland

There was a moon, and at times it was clear, so the Argentines could see us. We came over a hill and were shelled. We took cover, and after a bit, as soon as we returned to the Rovers, they opened fire on us again and we took cover again. I said to the 2ic: 'The next time I go to my Rover, I'm driving on out of here.' They were playing cat and mouse with us, and sooner or later were going to score lucky. But the next time we went back to the vehicles, they didn't open up on us, but we didn't know if they were watching and would open fire again.

Even though we were driving in the dark, we could follow the BV's tracks through snow, which had fallen earlier. But we couldn't actually drive *in* their tracks, as the BVs were squashing the peat down, breaking through the frost and bringing all the water up, making it impossible for a Land Rover. At one stage we were underneath this big rock and I told Trudi I was going to have a cigarette. She said: 'Forget the cigarette. I'm getting the hell out of here!'

Trudi McPhee
Brookfields, North Camp

As we were going round the peat banks on our way back, the mortars seemed to be getting closer. Pat Whitney said: 'Would you like a cigarette,' and I said: 'No, thank you. Let's get the hell out of here instead.' It was now June 12 – my mum's birthday.

Pat Whitney
Green Patch, East Falkland

We'd gone in earlier than we were supposed to have done, and on the way back, we noticed shell holes in the track we'd just come along. It looked like it could have been quite nasty. We'd left a tractor and a trailer with a lot of ammo, and a sergeant was guarding it. As we moved back, I left him some of my rations as he'd run out. A shell had landed nearby, which he reckoned had lifted the trailer about a foot above him.

22

Fire Power

*I watched 2 Para walking past us on their march to Mount Kent
before their attack on Wireless Ridge. They looked in a much worse state
than the Argentines. But it was their spirit that counted, rather than
what they looked like, or the kit they had.*

Company Sergeant Major Peter John Richens
B Company, 2 Para
After a short helicopter lift from Fitzroy into a forming-up point on the back
of Mount Kent, we did a very hard battalion approach march across to the
start of our attack on Wireless Ridge. It was night and there were grass
tussocks, bogs, and heavy artillery harassing fire from the Port Stanley area.
Luckily, many explosions were absorbed by the peat.

Lieutenant Colonel David Robert Chaundler
Replacement Commanding Officer, 2 Para
The attack was due that night, June 10. We moved out at midnight using the
well-practised procedure we paratroopers understand; different coloured
marker lights are put out earlier, and the companies get up and head for their
own coloured marker, then form a line and start moving. It was a long night's
march over terrible terrain, at no more than one mile an hour. We tripped
over great tufts of grass, sinking through the frozen crust of the peat into mire,
feet soaking and freezing, scrambling across rock runs.

Staff Sergeant Richard James Elliott
REME, 3 Commando Brigade Air Squadron
We'd moved our helicopter base from Port San Carlos to the base of Mount

Kent behind one of the gun batteries. The Argentine prisoners didn't look too bad really – nothing like as dishevelled as we'd imagined they would. They had lots of kit, and were wandering round with dry feet wearing wellington boots. Quite a few big ones didn't look defeated at all – marines or special forces, probably.

I watched 2 Para walking past us on their march to Mount Kent before their attack on Wireless Ridge. They looked in a much worse state than the Argentines. But it was their spirit that counted, rather than what they looked like, or the kit they had.

David Cooper
Chaplain, 2 Para
It was terribly cold, and soldiers were continually falling out with acute diarrhoea, having to relieve themselves very frequently. Some of the soldiers who'd been brought in from the echelon were finding it very hard to keep up. One Catering Corps soldier fell out completely, so we carried his bergan for him. At the other end, we lay down in a scrape in the ground and simply froze. It was the coldest I've ever known. Then the cloud base dropped and it snowed. Helicopters continued flying by creeping forward literally one foot above the ground, lifting up over fences, dropping down then creeping forward again.

Staff Sergeant Richard James Elliott
REME, 3 Commando Brigade Air Squadron
We sat out and watched an RAF high-level Vulcan bombing raid from where we were on Mount Kent. We knew what time it was due, in the early hours of the morning. You could see the flash and shockwave from the bombs as they exploded, then all the lights from missiles trying to hit the aircraft, and the triangle of the Vulcan and her exhausts on afterburner in the distance as she was climbing out afterwards. Even though they missed the runway, these raids were sending a serious message – that we could hit Buenos Aires if we wanted to; and the Argentines had nothing similar. The pressure wave from these bombs would burst your eardrums if you were closer.

Lieutenant Colonel David Robert Chaundler
Replacement Commanding Officer, 2 Para
I had my radio tuned into 45 Commando's attack on Twin Sisters, so I could follow what was going on directly in front of us. The Argentine artillery was firing into the area, but in a rather unimaginative manner so we could snake

British troops advancing through the mountains towards Stanley in the final phase of military operations. Winter snowstorms were now a regular occurrence.

around their DFs. We crossed over the Murrrell Bridge then ran into a Royal Marine corporal who said there was a minefield up ahead, which deflected us even further to the north.

My orders were to link up with 3 Paras' patrol company in Furze Bush Pass, which was behind and slightly north of Longdon. By first light the whole battalion was out in the open and I still hadn't got to my RV. I talked to Julian Thompson on the radio: 'We're new here on the northern flank and I don't know what's to our north. It's going to take us a few more hours to get to the RV. Are you happy for us to continue north in daylight?' He said: 'Yes,' so we continued.

We got to Furze Bush Pass about midday, having been on our feet for twelve hours, and I went up to join Johnny Crosland at the head of the column. We lay for twenty minutes looking down into the deep valley that constituted Furze Bush Pass. We could see into the valley itself and Argentine artillery lining the ridge on the other side. We identified an area on the reverse slope where we would be safe from artillery fire. The rest of the battalion trickled in over the next few hours.

David Cooper
Chaplain, 2 Para

We could hear the attack on Twin Sisters. When we moved forward again, the weather cleared so we could see 3 Paras' attack on Mount Longdon – a very spectacular fireworks display. We were just short of Longdon by dawn, and turned left by the Murrell Bridge to avoid some shelling. It was interesting to see the people who hadn't experienced this at Goose Green jumping into ditches at the first sound of artillery shells. They soon got used to it.

The battalion then stopped at Furze Bush Pass, but we were very spread out and the RAP was isolated, so I liaised with the nearby sapper troop to decide defensive arcs and sentry positions. There was a risk of Argentine patrols so we doubled the number of sentries for that night. With no sleeping bags or groundsheets, we lay together in the bitter cold, and froze.

Captain Adrian Robert Freer
3 Para

On Longdon, while we were fighting, no quarter was given. Once the fighting was over, we felt no more aggression against the Argentines. There were a lot of enemy wounded, which we looked after as well as we looked after our own. The Argentines that stayed and fought were extremely brave and one cannot help but admire them. They inflicted twenty killed and forty-plus wounded on us, putting the better part of a rifle company out of action that night, which was very much a testimony to their courage. The only thing they didn't do was counter-attacking us. You are always at your weakest when you've taken an objective, but by that time they'd all disappeared toward Stanley.

Pat Whitney
Green Patch, East Falkland
We pulled back to the Estancia just before daybreak, which was deserted – as so many men had moved forward the night before.

Trudi McPhee
Brookfields, North Camp
When we reached the Estancia I jumped into another Land Rover and drove back over to Green Patch and spent the day of her birthday with my mum.

Ailsa Heathman
Estancia Farm, North Camp
We'd gone to Green Patch on June 12, where we'd heard that three civilian women had been killed in Stanley, then when we got back to Estancia sixty SAS had arrived. As I pulled up in the Land Rover, Roger Edwards opened the door and kissed me. I wondered what had me for a minute! I was very anxious to find out about my parents who'd been deported to Fox Bay.

Brigadier Julian Howard Thompson
Commander, 3 Commando Brigade
42 Commando had perhaps the most successful attack, on Mount Harriet, which was the southernmost objective. They had room to make a very wide swing south, recce'd by Sergeant Collins over a series of nights, before attacking into the middle and rear of the feature. This was the strongest objective and was taken completely by surprise at the cost of two dead and thirteen wounded. It was an absolutely classic attack; inflicting the maximum damage to the enemy whilst suffering a minimum ourselves.

My brigade was now very exposed under Argentine 105mm and 155mm artillery fire, taking casualties. It was vital to keep going, but our artillery gun lines, which had been stocked to five hundred rounds per gun before the attacks, because of the intensity of our artillery fire, were down to just a few rounds per gun and needed resupply. Then the commander of 5 Infantry Brigade asked for a twenty-four-hour delay on his attacks so his units could have a look at the ground.

Captain Adrian Robert Freer
3 Para

We then had a rather bloody forty-eight hours. Tumbledown overlooked us and should have been taken on the same night but for some reason wasn't. The Argentines on Tumbledown could see the south face of Mount Longdon and brought artillery fire on to us. We could see into Stanley and their gun positions. We were under pretty heavy fire at times, losing another eight killed and wounded.

Neil Watson
Long Island, East Falkland

We got back to the Estancia, and saw the body bags down by the creek. They took them to Estancia before they took them to San Carlos. There was nothing more we could do. Sad, but inevitable. I'd known the night before at the forming-up point that I was talking to dead men . . . Inside the house Ailsa was sitting by the stove during all the red alerts, feeding her baby, ignoring the air raids, the casualties coming in and out, and everything going on around her. Their front room was a little hospital, where the wounded guys went . . . there was nothing more we could do after that. Mount Longdon, Two Sisters and Mount Harriet had been won.

Brigadier Julian Howard Thompson
Commander, 3 Commando Brigade

After Goose Green we knew our training was superior to theirs, so our commanders would restore order from the chaos much faster than theirs, therefore we would always be inside their decision and reaction loop and be able to defeat them. We'd learned from Goose Green that moving on this open terrain in daylight meant being exposed for long periods to the fire of their heavy machine guns, which outranged everything we had apart from the Scorpions and Scimitars. I'd therefore decided to do all my attacks at night, even though this engendered great problems of command and control. I was, therefore, extremely relieved that we'd achieved all our objectives by dawn.

Lieutenant Colonel David Robert Chaundler
Replacement Commanding Officer, 2 Para

I kept asking 3 Commando Brigade for orders, but none came until six o'clock that evening, two hours before last light. A helicopter arrived bringing an old friend, Hector Gullan, 3 Commando Brigade's liaison officer. He ran towards

A Scorpion CVRT armoured car of the Blues and Royals, with its very useful 76mm gun, at San Carlos, entertaining a Falkland boy before driving east across the island. These initially underrated vehicles were eventually used to great effect as light tanks, providing highly mobile fire support, particularly at night using their night vision systems.

me waving his map, and shouted: 'Wireless Ridge tonight, chaps,' which must be the shortest set of orders ever.

I'd left my mortars and Blowpipe back on Mount Kent as they were too heavy to carry with enough ammunition to be viable. I did have artillery, and I also had the Blues and Royals' CVRTs, which in this type of warfare operate as light tanks. 3 Commando Brigade didn't know what to do with the CVRTs, so eight days earlier they'd been sent over to 5 Brigade at Bluff Cove, arriving in the middle of the night, splitting the water supply pipe, and drawing the attention of Argentine artillery on to us. I was cross and told the senior troop commander to push off, but before we went north to join 3 Commando Brigade it seemed sensible to take light tanks with us, so I asked the troop commander: 'Do you want to see the war?' 'Oh, yes please!' 'Be at this grid reference at this time tomorrow on this radio frequency and we'll call you forward to where we need you.' It was a long march for them back over the mountain, and they had to change a gearbox, but, needless to say, they were at the RV.

Two hours before darkness, I hastily made a plan, got the company commanders together and gave orders. But halfway through orders, a radio message from brigade changed the boundaries of my attack, then by the time I got to 'Any questions?', the message came through that our attack was cancelled. I was relieved, as time for preparation had been desperately short. I flew back to 3 Commando Brigade headquarters, to be told: 'No, it hasn't been cancelled, but postponed twenty-four hours.'

So I went back to 2 Para, for the coldest night of my life. We'd left our sleeping bags on Mount Kent and it was bitterly, bitterly cold – lasting fourteen hours. Men were doing PT, running up hills and even double sentry duty to keep warm.

David Cooper
Chaplain, 2 Para
We were called forward for an O Group, and only realised how far behind everyone else we were when we were late and received a bollocking. The CO, David Chaundler, gave orders, and looking at the map we could see the RAP was to be on a forward slope in direct view of the enemy. We had to use lights to treat casualties, so it was inevitable we'd be fired upon. Steve Hughes and I didn't know what to do, so we told 2ic Chris Keeble. Then the attack was postponed for twenty-four hours, the plan was changed, and the RAP given a new position on a reverse slope.

Major John Harry Crosland
B Company Commander, 2 Para

Other battalions weren't ready, so we waited twenty-four hours in a very exposed position over-flown by Argentine air force attacks. The delay allowed us to look over the ground, iron out a more definitive plan of attack and change the orders. We had terrific fire support, plus two troops of light armoured vehicles. Goose Green had been a 'come-as-you-are' party, whereas this was a much more deliberate night attack.

Major Philip Neame
D Company Commander, 2 Para

I had hoped we could stay as reserve, but it seemed likely that we would have to fight again. We bypassed 3 Para on Longdon, and exploited beyond them on to Wireless Ridge – with a very sparse set of orders telling us to get cracking. Fortunately, it was delayed twenty-four hours; the Guards weren't ready in the south, and as the Tumbledown and Wireless Ridge features dominated each other, the two attacks had to go in together.

Lieutenant Colonel David Robert Chaundler
Commanding Officer, 2 Para

I got my mortars flown to us, to add to our firepower. The other commando brigade units had been looking at their objectives for ten days and had patrolled them, so knew their terrain pretty well. Tony Rice and I wanted to fly up to Mount Longdon to look at the ground we were going to have to attack. But as we arrived to meet the helicopter, a mortar bomb took out a stretcher-bearing team coming down the mountain, so our helicopter flew off to pick up the casualties. Mount Longdon was under heavy artillery fire all that day. But eventually we got a helicopter, and were met on Longdon by 3 Paras' CO, Huw Pike – another friend. We realised the intelligence locations of the Argentine positions was inaccurate, so my plan needed a major revamp. Unfortunately, I had no communications back to 2 Para.

Six Skyhawks flew underneath us, wheeled round, and disappeared behind Mount Kent where we heard them bombing the brigade headquarters. It's always good for morale when the higher headquarters gets bombed. Happily, there were no casualties and 3 Commando Brigade moved out pretty rapidly. But this meant all helicopter flying was cancelled, leaving me stuck on Mount Longdon for six hours, which was very frustrating.

A Wessex 5 helicopter delivering ammunition in an underslung net to a gun battery position of 29 Commando Regiment, Royal Artillery.

The tactical headquarters of 3 Commando Brigade on the reverse slopes of Mount Kent.

(James) Robert Fox
BBC correspondent
After Two Sisters, before Tumbledown, I tried in a rather desultory way to get back to the ships to record these latest actions. A whole group of us were waiting to get on to a helicopter, reading letters, trying to scrounge some breakfast from Thompson's headquarters, when suddenly we were attacked. We'd been ashore for three weeks, and had become incredibly blasé about air raid warnings. I saw the underside of the two A4 Skyhawks, releasing bombs. The bombs had little parachutes to slow them down. They went crunching into the peat. I saw them going off. Nobody was hurt except the brigade aviation officer who was shaving and suffered a bust eardrum.

Thompson was furious. The brigade air squadron had parked their helicopters too close to the headquarters and communication tents, and it was a very clear, wintry, sunny Falklands day. The Argentine pilots could see the sun glinting off the canopies of the helicopters, which made a good opportunity target for them. They came round twice and we were very close to being hit.

Brigadier Julian Howard Thompson
Commander, 3 Commando Brigade
They'd found us using radio direction finding; we'd been transmitting from that location for too long. The HQ was well camouflaged, but they saw two helicopters carelessly parked too close with sun glinting from their canopies, and dropped seven thousand-pound bombs in two passes, firing cannon as well. I felt so helpless while this was going on; not frightened, even though I thought I was about to die, and was thinking in slow motion about all the things I'd wanted to do in life, but hadn't. I hurled myself behind a rock the size of a typewriter, which was the only cover nearby, making myself as small as possible. The explosions were contained by the peat, creating holes the size of a small room, but not one man was killed, even though the tent I was going to give orders in was pepper-potted by shrapnel, with the aluminium tubular legs of the chairs sliced off. It was sheer luck that all my COs and other key people weren't in it. The bombs had landed about forty metres away.

Neil Watson
Long Island, East Falkland
On hearing the air raid warning red for this attack, we drove our Land Rovers away from the Estancia as fast as we could. There were great piles of ammunition stacked beside the wool sheds, Milan missiles . . . you name it. If one hit,

there was going to be one awful mess. We snuck up behind a little peat bank to watch. The Skyhawks came in from the east. They'd done a circuit from Stanley direction, along the big stone run, then peeled off to the left, and we could see the bombs as they dropped. We were close enough to see them falling through the air, retard bombs with a parachute on the back, and we couldn't think what on earth they were going after.

At the Estancia, all the paras opened up at these aircraft, with machine guns, SLRs and everything, on the off chance they might hit something. Then one of the Skyhawks turned away and came towards us, and we realised that there was a good chance of us getting hit by friendly fire, so we ran round to the other side of this peat bank and crouched down. The Skyhawk kept coming towards us, really low, and then we saw something drop off it . . . which we thought was a bomb. It didn't explode, and the Skyhawk vanished over the top of us. I think it was in trouble, as it turned off in a different direction to the others. One of them crashed, and various people saw it trailing black smoke out of the back. Only weeks afterwards, when Tony Hickman actually found it, did we realise this had been a fuel tank and not a bomb.

(James) Robert Fox
BBC *correspondent*
It was probably battle stress again, but after transmitting some copy, I sat on board *Fearless* all day and read a detective novel by one of my Oxford friends, Simon Brett – paying no attention to anything going on around me.

Major Philip Neame
D Company Commander, 2 Para
That extra twenty-four hours gave us the chance to get our fire support together and adjust all the artillery targets – at least we thought they'd been adjusted. This contrasted with Goose Green, where we'd gone in blind. We were now prepared for what was probably the only genuine all-arms attack of the campaign, with no question of surprise, going in having blitzed the place already, with oodles of firepower, and plenty of time to get organised.

Lieutenant Colonel David Robert Chaundler
Commanding Officer, 2 Para
The first decision I had to make was the time of H-Hour: I needed enough darkness to capture all the objectives, but I also needed enough time to get us all to the start lines. I decided midnight, which gave ten hours to capture the objectives. The next decision was how to use the artillery. Until now,

the previous attacks had relied on secrecy, so objectives were not shelled beforehand, and then only once contact had been made. The Argentines knew they were going to be attacked, but not the direction or when; so we would have the advantages of shelling them comprehensively beforehand without giving anything away. My battery commander had two artillery batteries and a frigate, and later a second frigate, plus we had my mortars and those of 3 Para, the four light tanks and my own machine guns platoon – a considerable amount of firepower.

We had four different positions to attack, and I decided to attack each from a different direction so they wouldn't know where we were coming from next. We were up against their 7th Infantry Regiment, numerically stronger then us, so we had to concentrate available firepower resources on to one point, then when it was captured, switch all the firepower to the next point. My orders were never written down, lasted about ten minutes, and it says a great deal about the battalion that such a complicated attack should have succeeded with orders that brief.

Brigadier Julian Howard Thompson
Commander, 3 Commando Brigade
2 Para were hooking around the top of Mount Longdon to attack Wireless Ridge from the north. This was a good approach for 2 Para, as the Argentines' Wireless Ridge positions were located to support their unit on Mount Longdon, and so were much harder to attack from the south. 2 Para were going to use the Scorpions and Scimitars for intimate support, as the ground was rolling rather than vicious steep hills with rocks on top. But they were up against the entire Argentine 7th Infantry Regiment.

Private Domingo Morel
Argentine Infantry Regiment
We had entered into combat on Friday June 11 at eight o'clock at night until midday on the Saturday. We then moved to the position of B Company of the 7th Regiment to reinforce a sector that had been taken by the English but we couldn't recover it. When we arrived, B Company had gone. We couldn't reinforce anything because we were groups of only fourteen blokes, you see. B Company had withdrawn, leaving us with practically nothing, and no back-up. The sub-officer had no idea what to do because he was going under the orders of the second chief of the regiment who also knew nothing. We were left in *babia* [unable to do anything].

Private Jose Omar Ojeda
Compania Comando Servicios, 3rd Brigade
When my young girl heard I was in Malvinas, she asked my family if they knew anything of me, and she wrote me a letter. It was the only letter I received. It would be a lovely memory to have it, but sadly in a bad moment I tore it up. I will never forget this girl, what she wrote to me, the things she wrote to me about. It encouraged me, it gave me the energy to carry on and continue living . . . But what I sent to her, what I wrote was hard. At that time I felt anger, I wanted to kill. During that period, you put the blame on people who have nothing to do with it when you shouldn't. But I wrote very nasty, stupid things that have nothing to do with anything, nonsense, things that afterwards I regretted. She was ill for a long time, in a mess . . .

David Cooper
Chaplain, 2 Para
One soldier came to see me that night before our attack on Wireless Ridge. He said: 'I'm not superstitious, but tomorrow is the first anniversary of my wife's death from cancer.' For him, a night attack on the eve of this anniversary was something he needed to talk about, which he probably felt he couldn't talk about with his fellows or his platoon officer.

Private Jose Omar Ojeda
Compania Comando Servicios, 3rd Brigade
From the Puerto we could see the battles in the hills further out, up to twenty kilometres. You feel bad as well, useless because you are there and your company is fighting further ahead and you cannot do anything. If we had been able to go we would have gone, but we were not permitted. That's the problem, you were not responsible for your own decisions, you had to do what they told you and even though you know that all those in your company were already dying and needed help, you can't go. Everything was totally under orders, and whether it's good or bad, they screw it up. That's the pity of military laws.

Lieutenant Colonel David Robert Chaundler
Commanding Officer, 2 Para
We moved out at last light. The artillery forward observation officer on Mount Longdon had been wounded and our targets had not been adjusted, so as we were moving into position, the artillery adjusted all our targets in the dark, a remarkable achievement – and they got it right. We moved up behind a low ridge, and the Argentinians, knowing they were going to be attacked,

shelled our likely forming-up positions. At the same time as registering our artillery targets, we were also shelling and mortaring their artillery positions.

This was our third night without sleep; two nights before we were moving forward on foot, and the previous night had been too cold to sleep. We hadn't seen a ration pack for seventy-two hours, eating only what we'd stuffed into our pockets before leaving Mount Kent, and we fought all night between blinding flurries of snow showers.

2 Para was the only battalion that fought two battles in that campaign. The first time round, they'd seen their friends killed and maimed, so this time they knew exactly what was out there in front of them. I had the greatest admiration for my soldiers.

David Cooper
Chaplain, 2 Para

We were due a ration resupply, but ours were taken to A Company by mistake. I went to A Company but they'd already been distributed. Their company commander, Dare Farrar-Hockley, went round personally to get the rations back from his men, and came himself to the RAP to explain that he hadn't been able to get the chocolate back. That's the way things go sometimes. We had to move slowly over very difficult peaty ground. We arrived at our position just short of the start line and dug in.

Major Philip Neame
D Company Commander, 2 Para

Initially we were going to do a straight attack from the south on to the main ridgeline; but this additional position needed a preliminary operation by my company, then a sweeping round by me at the end of the day, to roll up this final ridgeline from west to east. The other two companies each did attacks on specific positions, using two batteries and a gun ship.

Lieutenant Colonel David Robert Chaundler
Commanding Officer, 2 Para

H-Hour was delayed when my main headquarters radioed for me to come back to their location, where they had something I needed to see. Chris Keeble was very insistent about this, so I walked back through the various battalion positions singing *Land of Hope and Glory* as I can never remember passwords, to find that my HQ had received a captured Argentine map from brigade headquarters, which showed a minefield straight across our main axis of attack.

It was far too late to do much about this if we were to capture our objectives that night. In moments like this, one often has quite irrelevant thoughts going through one's mind; I remembered being taught statistics at the Royal Military College of Science, when the lecturer had said the chances of standing on a mine when walking through a minefield were very remote. It was too late to change the plans, so I returned to my Tac HQ on a small knoll in line with the start lines. Johnny Crosland was there so I said to him: 'Johnny, we've got a minefield out there.' We just looked at each other and shrugged, and he went back to his company and we carried on. I subsequently told the lecturer this story, and he said: 'My God, if I'd have known somebody was going to put the theory to the test, I'd never have used that example.'

Company Sergeant Major Peter John Richens
B Company, 2 Para
The assault was in two phases, and we had lots of support. The weather was a little better and we had the sort of artillery support we should have had at Goose Green.

As we crossed the start line, Major Crosland turned to me and said: 'Pete, I haven't told anybody, but we're just about to cross a minefield.' I gave him a very hard stare, to which he said: 'If I'd told the lads, that would only have been another problem for them to come to terms with.'

Major John Harry Crosland
B Company Commander, 2 Para
We were severely shelled on the start line, and I'd had to kick my two signallers out from under my feet like puppies in order to grovel in the peat myself. Then just as we crossed the start line, the new CO told me there was a minefield right across our path. There was no point in telling the blokes about this; if we came to the traditional markings of a minefield of wire and markers and were not under fire, we could attempt to negotiate it, or, as shown by the Israelis in recent conflicts, just run, getting through the obstacle as fast as possible, accepting the casualties. I only had four sappers with me, equipped with metal prodders, so clearing a path through would take hours and wasn't on the cards. Whether there was actually a minefield there, I don't know.

Once across the start line, we moved in an extended line with A Company, which, according to 3 Para friends looking on from Mount Longdon, looked like a football crowd. The Scimitars on our flank were laying down terrific firepower, using night-vision goggles, on to the positions we were assaulting, lifting their fire at the very last moment, just as we moved onto the positions. It was a long, hard move across difficult country.

Lieutenant Colonel David Robert Chaundler
Replacement Commanding Officer, 2 Para
The first phase was D Company doing a right hook. I gave them two phases in this attack, because I'd been told at Goose Green they hadn't had a very prominent role. In fact I'd been advised erroneously. They launched and we put down a considerable amount of artillery, machine guns and light tank fire on to their position, which 3 Para had listed as one of their own. I was convinced they'd got their map reading wrong. By the time we started the attack, this had not been confirmed, but as we'd shelled it comprehensively and 3 Para hadn't complained, we went in anyway.

Company Sergeant Major Peter John Richens
B Company, 2 Para
We had Scorpion support which was a tremendous sight to see firing tracer; quite a morale booster for us. Our attack was largely unopposed. We went firm on the ridge to shelter from the wind, then came under fire from the Argentine artillery.

Lieutenant Colonel David Robert Chaundler
Replacement Commanding Officer, 2 Para
I gave the attacking company one battery of artillery in direct support, while the second battery was laying down fire on another Argentine position so they wouldn't interfere. The frigate was firing all along the final ridgeline to keep the two Argentine companies there quiet, and one platoon of mortars was firing illumination while the other fired on the fourth Argentine position. D Company's attack went remarkably smoothly. They found Argentinians who during the artillery firing had got down in their trenches with sleeping bags over their heads – a 'back to the womb' reaction to the noise and stress becoming too much to bear.

Major Philip Neame
D Company Commander, 2 Para
By the time we closed on the ridgeline position there was no opposition, just injured and dead Argentinians – and a few surrendering. The rest had fled, which is a good thing to achieve as a fleeing enemy upsets the others. There was no serious fighting through this position, but as we started to mop it up, we came under heavy Argentine shellfire, so I moved us forward a hundred yards to reorganise, leaving the Argentines' own fire to mop it up for us. A and B Companies then attacked the enemy headquarters, and I moved round ready to roll up the final ridgeline.

Lieutenant Colonel David Robert Chaundler
Replacement Commanding Officer, 2 Para

D Company reorganised on the captured position – which is one of the things you never do, and were fired upon by the Argentine artillery, so decamped at great speed down into the valley beyond. The Argentines were firing 155mm airburst, a quantum leap up from the 105mm the battalion had already experienced at Goose Green.

Major John Harry Crosland
B Company Commander, 2 Para

One of my heavily laden gunners fell into a river and got exposure, but he carried on. Being fairly small in stature myself, I had difficulty seeing where we were, but the actual attack went well. We fought through the positions against limited opposition, but the opposition switched their artillery fire on to the positions they'd just lost, and A Company were hit and suffered casualties.

David Cooper
Chaplain, 2 Para

It was a rather inactive battle for us, but we did have the undivided attention of the Argentine artillery for part of it. The casualties came in a trickle, with the largest contingent from the mortars. With the ground being so soft, at a very critical time in the attack the crews had decided to ensure accuracy by supporting the base plate with their feet, inevitably breaking ankles, and we received five of these. The company's casualties were being picked up by helicopter and taken direct to the field hospital at Teal Inlet.

Lieutenant Colonel David Robert Chaundler
Commanding Officer, 2 Para

In the second phase, A and B Companies in line attacked the Argentine main position of two companies and a regimental headquarters. We subsequently found maps bearing out this intelligence. I didn't need to provide flanking fire as we were in a long, deep valley. I accompanied this attack. The light tanks and machine guns gave direct fire overhead, plus both artillery batteries. I'd allocated such a lot of firepower to this part of the attack deliberately, for psychological reasons. Being shelled is a profoundly unpleasant and frustrating experience as you can't do anything about it. You just have to lie there in the dark and mud, and take it. The Argentines were not first-rate troops, and I believed that by comprehensively shelling them, they were liable

Argentine dead after British attacks on defensive positions in the mountains overlooking Port Stanley.

to crack, panic and start running away. I considered an Argentine running away was better than a dead one, striking fear into those behind, setting up a momentum – and you always have to have momentum. As a commander, you must always try to take your objectives with minimum casualties to yourself, and I was using firepower to achieve this.

David Cooper
Chaplain, 2 Para
It took an hour to carry a casualty one kilometre across that ground. Our stretcher-bearers were exhausted. Our MO, Steve Hughes, was suffering from an ankle injury he'd taken on the landing, and was now unable to walk himself.

Lieutenant Colonel David Robert Chaundler
Commanding Officer, 2 Para
We didn't have to do much fighting on the second objective. There was a pause to regroup my patrols with the assault engineers, to take out a small platoon position to the north, and to bring the tanks and machine guns on to the second phase objective, to fire in support of D Company, which was attacking in a long, wide, flanking movement along the final ridgeline of Wireless Ridge. The patrols and assault engineers had heard weapons being cocked and found warm boots, but the Argentines had made a hasty departure – the firepower having done its job before they arrived.

Captain Christopher Charles Brown
148 Commando Forward Observation Unit, Royal Artillery
Having fought through Two Sisters with 45 Commando, we'd then been told to do the whole thing all over again and join the Scots Guards for their attack on Mount Tumbledown. We'd already decided we were going to engage targets before we were attacked, but in the event we were unable to do so. The Scots Guards had quite a hard time and we fired a considerable amount of naval gunfire for them as they struggled their way up the mountain.

Commander Ian Inskip
HMS Glamorgan
It was a beautiful evening and we buried our dead at sunset. It was a very moving ceremony. Everybody came on to the flight deck in their best uniforms, and in the naval tradition, wrote messages on the canvas wrapping the bodies. Some of the bodies were recognisable; others had to be shovelled

into the canvas in bits. I was glad I didn't have to do it myself, as I'd been turned in when they did it.

I just remember the splash, splash, splash, splash . . . as the bodies were tipped over the side. We didn't have enough ensigns to cover each body and had to borrow more from other ships. We marked the burial position on the chart, then later made copies to give to the relatives, along with the ensigns.

We then sailed north-east to be repaired by the *Stena Seaspread*, whose engineer teams used scrap metal from South Georgia to mend the hole in our deck, melting down the wardroom's silver spoons as welding flux. But one of the most depressing realisations was that while we were fighting the fire, the tailors' shop had been looted. The ship's company were told to leave the loot in bin bags on the mess deck tables, no questions asked. We recovered fifteen dustbin bags full. The same thing happened in other ships. I don't understand it; if the ship goes down, you can't take it with you; and if the ship doesn't go down, the proverbial is going to hit the fan. What's the point? Maybe it's some people's way of coming to terms psychologically with being hit, or going on board another ship that's been hit?

Captain Alan John Warsap
Regimental Medical Officer, 2nd Battalion Scots Guards
One always wonders, when one teaches first aid to people like bandsmen and pipers, whether they'll be able to do it in battle. Piper Rogers actually played his pipes during the battle, but had to stop when casualties started coming in.

Brigadier Julian Thompson
Commander, 3 Commando Brigade
I remember standing, on what was to be the second last day of the war, a cold but lovely sunny morning, thinking that I didn't actually own anything other than what I stood up in and the few belongings in my rucksack, but that was all I needed. What really matters to me is to be surrounded by all these people who are my friends and comrades. I didn't know if I was going to survive the war, but I knew it was comradeship and not material things that really matter. It's who you're with, and not what you have, that counts. Obviously the longer you are away from that environment, the more material things begin to impinge back on you, but it does me good to remember this.

Captain Alan John Warsap
Regimental Medical Officer, 2nd Battalion Scots Guards
The Scots Guards forming-up position was at the west end of Goat Ridge, and

we dug in as some artillery fire was coming in from Port Stanley. It was novel to realise that the RAP was the furthermost unit of the British Army at that time. We were ideally situated, but this was a false sense of security, for later after the companies moved past me at night, I became unable to do much for the casualties as they occurred in a part of the battlefield over which I had no control medically.

Linda Kitson
Official war artist
From having been innocent, the sights of death and bodies very quickly became normal, walking past body bags and people's belongings left at Echelon. Dead bodies became objects of curiosity, I think as one imagines what it might be like to be lying there yourself.

The men looked so bizarre, with a wild-eyed expression as if ready for anything. The smallest hit can mean a lifetime of disablement, and people with hideous injuries still having to keep marching to reach safety. I found the sight of them with all their equipment, cam cream and combat gear, leaving for battle quite terrifying, and they were all buoyed up ready for it.

Captain Alan John Warsap
Regimental Medical Officer, 2nd Battalion Scots Guards
Major Bethel put in a diversionary attack using a scratch force of about platoon strength, along the more obvious approach from the south-west. They killed large numbers of Argentinians and took the position, having been undetected until the last minute. This was not what had been intended, and they were forced into a life or death struggle in the middle of the Argentine position, from which they then retreated. People also stood on mines whilst evacuating the wounded. Their casualties were not part of my evacuation chain and I think were dealt with by either the RAP of the commandos, or of the Welsh Guards – I'm not sure which.

Linda Kitson
Official war artist
The noise of the battle from a mile or so away was enormous. The sound of the artillery fire flying over your head was loud, and they all talked about it. It's all sights and smells that they will never forget. The Welsh Guards will never forget the smell of burning skin – the intangibles that keep it all in your mind.

Guardsman Jim Mitchell
Scots Guards
We came under fire, and there's an old military saying, always expect the unexpected – well, this was unexpected. You cannae really describe it. Nobody could describe it if they've not been there.

Linda Kitson
Official war artist
Being a woman wasn't a problem. The men were always helping me, despite me insisting that they shouldn't distract themselves from what they should be doing. Dealing with the menstrual cycle in the midst of such a barbaric environment wasn't a problem either. The feeling sick is nothing compared to the nausea, illness and sickness caused by fear, never mind the lack of sleep.

Captain Alan John Warsap
Regimental Medical Officer, 2nd Battalion Scots Guards
The main action of the night was with left and right flank companies, which had the unenviable task of taking the remaining eight-tenths of Tumbledown Ridge, occupied by regular troops of the 5th Marine Battalion. They held up our attack all night with heavy fire, and attempts by stretcher bearers to evacuate casualties were mortared and machine gunned, so all conventional casualty evacuation ceased. The enemy also had night sights and sealed off the approaches to the mountain. But even if you could get the wounded clear to a place where it was safe to stand up, carrying a stretcher across that ground was impossibly difficult. The parties became broken up and disorganised. Few came back through the RAP that night. People hit by aimed Argentine fire probably died on the spot. The only man who died, who might have been saved, was hit in both thighs and abdomen, and couldn't be reached until it was too late.

Guardsman Jim Mitchell
Scots Guards
There was no question of us losing this battle. It's drummed into us, that we're not a regiment to get beat.

Major John Harry Crosland
B Company Commander, 2 Para
I was becoming worried about whether the Scots Guards would take Tumbledown – next door, on our right. If they failed, come the dawn, we

would be overlooked in very open country. So once we'd secured our objectives I told my toms I wanted them to dig in and be below ground, out of sight by dawn. The shells coming down made it unnecessary to tell them to do a proper job.

Lieutenant Colonel David Robert Chaundler
Commanding Officer, 2 Para

D Company then set out on a long flanking attack down Wireless Ridge. I was reluctant to commit more than one company to this because it was overlooked by Tumbledown on the other side of the Moody Brook valley. We had no communications with 5 Brigade, and if the Scots Guards failed to capture it, we'd have our soldiers forward, overlooked by the Argentines. I'd have to withdraw them, and it would be much easier to do this with one company than two, with B Company earmarked to reinforce them.

D Company took the first positions very quickly as the Argentines had pushed off. They were now aiming to attack the second position, where the Argentines appeared captivated by the firepower demonstration we were putting on, at ninety degrees to D Company's flanking approach. The light tanks [CVRTs] in particular were terribly successful, with their machine guns, 30mm cannons and 76mm guns. The light tanks also had second-generation night sights and could see very much better than we could, so my machine gunners were instructed to fire on the same positions as the tanks.

Major Philip Neame
D Company Commander, 2 Para

It all seemed to take a very long time. We sat freezing on our start line waiting until the fire support was in position. The light tanks had to be brought on to A and B Companies' positions, but eventually we received the order to go. The ridgeline divides into two sections, each some eight hundred metres long. We were checking through enemy positions obviously abandoned in haste, following a rolling barrage of artillery fire.

Then we got to a low col overlooking the final ridge, and got the FOO to call up the last target, but he called up the wrong target number. He was only a signals sergeant from another battery, as there were insufficient FOOs. I'd already established that this character couldn't really read a map, but I was relying on him to at least be able to read off the correct target numbers – which proved a miscalculation. The number he chose was where were sitting, so we received five rounds air burst, fifty feet over our heads.

Lieutenant Colonel David Robert Chaundler
Commanding Officer, 2 Para
As D Company were about to launch their attack, the company commander called down artillery fire, which fell on to him, his company and his artillery FOO, who'd got the target numbers wrong. One soldier was killed, and it took them some time to get sorted out.

Major Philip Neame
D Company Commander, 2 Para
This 'friendly fire' killed one person and injured another – which was very, very lucky. We could easily have suffered two dozen injured or killed. Somehow I managed to refrain from shooting this FOO, and then got him to call up the final target number. This hadn't been adjusted, and the rounds landed near B Company.

Chaundler ordered all fire to cease as B Company were complaining, so we waited while the FOO went through the long rigmarole of adjusting the target.

I tried to urge the FOO to call up the previous target, which was us, and just add five hundred, which would have done the trick, but by then he'd lost his nerve. Eventually it was adjusted and we called down the fire and got ready to go – then the fire stopped. Apparently a gun had slid down in the peat and rounds were landing near C Company. I was tearing my hair out, and wanted C Company to get their heads down and ignore this fire so I could get on with it. The gunners were firing each gun one by one to identify the errant one, then Chaundler came on the radio demanding to know when I was going to attack. 'When I get the fire support you promised me,' and a shirty dialogue ensued.

While this saga was going on, the CVRTs were firing, drawing the Argentines' attention away from us in the west. Then, with Chaundler still berating me to get a move on, we got four out of six guns firing on the objective so I thought 'to hell with this' and we went in. Our momentum had well and truly gone, and it took a certain amount of encouragement to get everyone going again. Then one of our people let off an illum, and the enemy realised we were attacking from the west and not the north. Everyone hit the deck, and another crisis of momentum ensued, with nobody wanting to get up and moving again.

It boiled down to good, old-fashioned leadership at every level, with me and everybody else shouting their heads off – probably all gibberish, but it got the adrenalin going again, and off we went. I had only one signaller, and then

411

I lost him. I assumed he'd been shot. Fortunately I also had my personal company radio, but no link to the battalion, which was to cause a certain amount of aggravation later in the evening.

Our limit of exploitation was the ridgeline and a line of telegraph poles marking the edge of the SAS's area. We got to the telegraph wires and stopped, as this was our boundary. The Argentines saw we'd stopped, decided we'd run out of steam, and half an hour later put in a counter-attack.

Lieutenant Colonel David Robert Chaundler
Commanding Officer, 2 Para

I'd been given a rather restrictive left-hand boundary with the SAS, who were mounting a raid to blow up some oil tanks further along the peninsula, which I thought rather curious as we were within twenty-four hours of victory and would need that oil.

Major General (John) Jeremy Moore
Commander, British Land Forces

I had a heck of a lot of special forces. As we were getting to the end of their reconnaissance role, they were very keen to be doing things – and quite rightly so, as would any good troops. We concocted a plan for a raid on the northern side of Stanley at the same time as the final night battles, so that pressures were piling on to the Argentines.

Lieutenant Roger Edwards
RN Fleet Air Arm

We'd been flown on to Beagle Ridge for a diversionary raid north of Stanley and east of 2 Para. The defenders saw the SAS coming and their attack down on to Cortley Ridge was a total disaster. The Royal Marine raiding squadron boats, used to carry everybody across the entrance to the Murrell River, were riddled with holes and people were wounded. They had to be extricated under artillery gunfire provided by the naval gunfire forward observation team on Beagle Ridge, and withdrew back on to Beagle Ridge.

Lieutenant Colonel David Robert Chaundler
Commanding Officer, 2 Para

The SAS squadron were detected, blown out of the water and had to withdraw rapidly, and then requested that we bail them out. Julian Thompson rightly said no, we were too busy. But unknown to me, the SAS withdrew through my flank, which we spotted and were ready to fire the artillery on to them when one of my former SAS company commanders said he thought it was them. The lesson here is that once ground troops close up, the SAS, being strategic troops, should get off the real estate. Having SAS and conventional troops operating on the same terrain leads to disaster.

Major General (John) Jeremy Moore
Commander, British Land Forces

Possibly because there wasn't time, this SAS attack wasn't coordinated with 3 Commando Brigade's operations and hindered 2 Para. The SAS were not able to get through the enemy, but they did distract them. But 2 Para were also distracted from their attack by this operation on their flank, but fortunately not too much ... It wasn't helpful to them and was really my fault.

Major Philip Neame
D Company Commander, 2 Para

The NCO FOO had disappeared, so John Page, my platoon commander at the end of the ridge, called up a fire mission, which discouraged the Argentine counter-attack pretty quickly. I went back to the eastern end of the ridge to coordinate 10 and 11 Platoons defending south, towards Stanley. I'd despatched my runner, Hanley, to go back and get the platoon commanders together, but found he'd done the job for me – which was very encouraging – brilliant really. He was not a peacetime soldier, but a brilliant bloke in war.

While we reorganised, we were under a great deal of acute small arms and some artillery fire from Tumbledown, which the Scots Guards hadn't yet taken. Every time you tried to move, you were shot at, which made re-organising and keeping cool very difficult. It was quite a harrowing two hours.

Another counter-attack came in from the north, so I called in the artillery fire mission myself. Once the fire came down, their interest in counter-attacks very rapidly evaporated. Eventually we got into the enemy position, and they broke and ran along the eight-hundred-metre ridge. We cleared it literally at the trot, using grenades all over the place like confetti. It was a miracle we didn't suffer casualties from the grenades alone.

Guardsman Jim Mitchell
Scots Guards

We were behind some rocks and I saw a flash out of the corner of my eye, and the split second I moved there were a bang and my rifle was about ten yards away from me, so I musta threw it. But there was a blackness came over my head like a big sheet that just comes down and that was frightening. So I started screaming and the blackness went right over. I was hit in the right-hand side of my head and there was a lot of pain and a lot of blood.

I was on a stretcher and my mate was carrying my kit and started joking with me. Then sniper fire came down. I was dropped and the stretcher party ran off. So I got off the stretcher and took cover in the rocks. We couldn't see where the sniper was. Then another guardsman walked with me, holding my arm, back to our field ambulance.

Captain Alan John Warsap
Regimental Medical Officer, 2nd Battalion Scots Guards
We had a grandstand view. Straight lines of tracer from GPMGs were marching up the side of Wireless Ridge before fading out. Artillery rounds were arriving and throwing up mud, and when the snow flurries cleared for a few moments and the moon came out, we could see the side of Tumbledown illuminated in star shell, and the flashes of the rounds hitting the mountain. It was our artillery fire, brought in by the young artillery forward observation officers, which shook up the enemy and made it possible for our infantry to take their positions. As dawn was approaching, the enemy began to walk off the position and the companies reached the end of the Tumbledown feature.

Michael Thomas Nicholson
ITN correspondent
We were not allowed to know the plan for the final offensive on Port Stanley. We were allocated to go with the Gurkhas on Mount William, and spent the last night watching the 105mm field guns pounding the positions around Port Stanley. Fighting was taking place on Harriet and Tumbledown, in pitch black and snow. Bernard took his coat off and wrapped it round the camera so it didn't freeze. I did a David Dimbleby with my tape recorder, imagining what was going on in the darkness around us. But I hadn't imagined that there was hand-to-hand fighting, using bayonets and grenades.

Major Philip Neame
D Company Commander, 2 Para
As daylight came, things calmed down. I reunited with my company headquarters. My signaller hadn't been shot, but had fallen into a shell hole full of water. He was a black man from Liverpool, so there was no chance of finding him at night. He said Chaundler had been on the radio busting a gut, demanding to know what was going on. The Scots Guards got on to Tumbledown, and then we saw hundreds of Argentinians walking off the back

into Stanley, with equally large numbers walking out of Stanley, up on to Sapper Hill, which was obviously going to be their next defensive position. I couldn't get the artillery to fire on Sapper Hill, as it was allocated to other tasks – mainly with 5 Brigade. I was tearing my hair out, and tried to engage with machine guns, but received Argentine artillery fire so I stopped.

Chaundler did not believe what I was telling him, and when he came to see for himself, it had become an army in complete rout, with targets galore. 'Why don't you use your machine guns?' he raged. I was reluctant, but when I got one gun at the end of the line to fire and there was no artillery fire back, I felt a fool. But in the hour between the previous engagements and Chaundler coming up, things had moved on. We eventually got the artillery back and engaged targets, and Chaundler tasked Scout helicopters to engage the guns in the Stanley valley. But it was quite clear we were suddenly fighting an army that had totally collapsed. Brigade headquarters couldn't grasp the suddenness of this, and only when Chaundler persuaded Julian Thompson to come and see for himself were we allowed to exploit forward into Stanley.

Lieutenant Colonel David Robert Chaundler
Commanding Officer, 2 Para
At first light, I joined Phil Neame on Wireless Ridge, our final objective. Dawn took a very long time to come, but then we saw the extraordinary sight of what one can only describe as the Argentinian Army cracking. Below me, Argentine soldiers were walking back towards Port Stanley, a heads-down, dejected, defeated army – they weren't even running. This was a wonderful feeling of elation for us. We were seeing Port Stanley for the first time, and the Argentine army was routed and utterly defeated, withdrawing. We were in seventh heaven.

Private Domingo Morel
Argentine Infantry Regiment
On the Saturday we went into combat again from six in the evening, until it was Sunday, at two or three o'clock in the morning, when we withdrew back a little. Our units took it in turns to return to Puerto Argentino. We flanked the 12th I believe, and went the whole way around in order to return to Puerto Argentino, which we reached at dawn on Monday.

Captain Alan John Warsap
Regimental Medical Officer, 2nd Battalion Scots Guards
At first light I went forward in a naval Sea King helicopter with my Colour

Sergeant to where our wounded had been concentrated. We were fired upon accidentally by our own mortars, but although there were explosions and the aircraft was not damaged, the pilot seemed to have been unnerved and didn't take us all the way forward, which was a great sadness to me at the time. We returned with the Sea King to Tumbledown Mountain, but again the pilot felt unable to fly in to get our casualties. We then met Captain Drennan of the Army Air Corps at the RAP, who'd been a Scots Guard, and he volunteered to fly forward to get our wounded to surgery in time.

23

A Need for Honour

Argentine Military Code Article 751: 'A soldier will be condemned to prison for three to five years if, in combat with a foreign enemy, he surrenders without having exhausted his supply of ammunition or without having lost two-thirds of the men under his command.'

Brigadier Julian Howard Thompson
Commander, 3 Commando Brigade
By first light on June 14, 2 Para were overlooking Stanley from Wireless Ridge, the Scots Guards were finishing off on Tumbledown and the Gurkhas were just about to assault Mount William. I was summoned forward by General Moore to ground overlooking the next objectives, who said: 'The next lot's all yours,' so I continued round to Wireless Ridge.

Major General (John) Jeremy Moore
Commander, British Land Forces
By the morning of June 14, up in the hills with my two brigade commanders, I felt frustrated and disappointed that Menendez hadn't already surrendered and the fighting was continuing. It was only a matter of two or three hours later that we received the message that he wanted to talk about terms.

Major John Harry Crosland
B Company Commander, 2 Para
We could hear C-130s taking off from the Stanley airfield. Soon after first light, the last gunfire fell, and the Argentines seemed to be falling back. The Army Air Corps flew around firing missiles, rather like naughty boys scrumping apples. They'd pop up to fire, then duck away, leaving us to face all

the incoming shell fire directed at them. Great fun for the Air Corps, but tedious for us grovelling in our shell holes.

Lieutenant Colonel David Robert Chaundler
Commanding Officer, 2 Para

Scout helicopters firing SS.11 rockets replaced my cancelled air strike, but they drew too much fire back on to our own positions. The light tanks and machine guns were firing down into Moody Brook valley, and the battery commander had got a regimental fire mission on the way, when suddenly I realised we couldn't do this any more. We were now in danger of slaughtering people for no good cause. I ordered a ceasefire, six hours in advance of the official ceasefire, and in fact we never fired another shot.

Private Jose Omar Ojeda
Compania Comando Servicios, 3rd Brigade

They attacked from behind, from in front, from all flanks, from above; they attacked with everything they had and we couldn't do anything. We were totally surrounded. It was murder, to get people killed without necessity. There was no way to sustain the fighting. We needed help from our aviation section. If we had been given a daily aerial attack we would not have surrendered. But we were left without support, I don't know why. Maybe it was an agreement they had between the forces. Sadly we lost, because everything we did on the ground was on the basis that we had aerial strength. We were lucky because although many died, only three died from our group of twenty. When they attacked us from all sides, that's when they gave us orders to surrender and we had to surrender. They could have killed us all.

John Fowler
Superintendent of Education, Stanley

Then followed a period when the Brits were still in the hills and nobody was in control. Argentine soldiers were in a very unhappy mood, having come from the hills to discover the streets lined with containers full of food, and were setting fire to things in a very unpleasant way. We got all able-bodied men on to the hospital roof to mount a fire watch, as there was a good chance the entire town would go up. People moved out of the west end of town into the hospital, and by the end we had an impressive community, including a group of Argentine military policemen, who ate in our kitchen, and stopped a bunch of diehards from setting up a machine gun nest on the roof.

Lieutenant Colonel David Robert Chaundler
Commanding Officer, 2 Para

My next realisation was that the town was for there the taking right now. History is full of examples of what you could take today with a platoon, you need a division to take tomorrow. But with Mount Longdon in the way, communications with 3 Commando Brigade were no good. I had to relay everything through my headquarters, saying: 'It's over, they're finished, they're withdrawing.' I was getting messages back like: 'How many Argentinians can you see?' and I was replying: 'I can see thousands of them!'

Brigadier Julian Howard Thompson
Commander, 3 Commando Brigade

I remember standing on the Wireless Ridge skyline with one of my staff officers, looking down towards Stanley with my binoculars, when a 2 Para sergeant major bellowed: 'Get down off the skyline you idle people.' I thought how unhelpful and unpopular it was to be standing around on somebody else's skyline and flung myself down behind cover, feeling very chastened.

Lieutenant Colonel David Robert Chaundler
Commanding Officer, 2 Para

I got B Company moving forward on to the final ridgeline of Wireless Ridge and I was about to order them down into the valley when Julian Thompson arrived by helicopter. I was standing out on the forward slope wearing my red beret, feeling pretty pleased with life. He wouldn't have been fully aware of the tactical situation, so he crawled up the ridge behind a rock. Seeing me standing out there in the open and thinking he was about to lose another commanding officer of 2 Para, he rushed out and rugger tackled me! I said: 'It's all right brigadier, it's all over. We've got to get into Port Stanley.' He said: 'Yup, you're right.'

Brigadier Julian Howard Thompson
Commander, 3 Commando Brigade

I told David Chaundler: 'Go nearer to the town while I get the rest of the brigade moving.' I didn't want 2 Para dashing off into the town, becoming surrounded by Argentines and having a big battle in the town unsupported. I jumped into my helicopter, but my radio went dead until we landed. I'd just told my brigade major to move the brigade forward and occupy Sapper Hill, when division told us the Argentines were officially surrendering and there was a ceasefire.

Captain Christopher Charles Brown
148 Commando Forward Observation Unit, Royal Artillery

By around first light we'd captured Mount Tumbledown, and almost immediately were told to get across to 45 Commando for the attack on Stanley. I'd served with 45 on a previous posting, so it was a good feeling to know that if we were to fight our way into Stanley, it would be with people we knew. But as we pulled off Mount Tumbledown and met up with 45 Commando, the word came through that Argentinians were surrendering. Minutes later, we emerged on the front side of Tumbledown and could see Port Stanley and people streaming eastwards with lots of white flags. 45 Commando was then told to take Sapper Hill, which dominates Port Stanley, so that if the Argentines decided to go back on their decision to surrender, we'd be in a position to do something about it. We moved on to Sapper Hill and sat tight.

(James) Robert Fox
BBC correspondent

45 Commando had been ordered to move at the rush into Stanley, possibly to fight for the town. Although the war wasn't over, everything was very jolly – but it did seem to take ages. The young sappers were out in front prodding for mines along the line of advance, firing purple flares and taping the mined areas in absolute copybook style. Everyone had put on their berets. Wars and earthquakes are always full of fire and smoke where things have broken down. Stanley looked like a Nash wartime painting, with plumes of smoke going up.

John Fowler
Superintendent of Education, Stanley

From the windows of the hospital maternity ward in the west of Stanley, we watched as the Argentines' sporadic attempts to regroup petered out and became a retreat. Armoured cars and scattered groups of soldiers were moving back into the town, sad bunches of guys carrying wounded and dead comrades, in groundsheets and on makeshift stretchers; a trickle first thing in the morning, becoming a flood.

Major General (John) Jeremy Moore
Commander, British Land Forces

We'd tried from early on to make contact with the enemy. We'd sent radio messages asking an Argentine officer from their headquarters to talk with us, ostensibly about humanitarian issues. But what we then wanted to do was imply that they might start thinking about talking about terms... We believed that these messages would end up being passed on to much higher levels. That ploy worked for a while and the level did go up, but suddenly they stopped answering us. We carried on broadcasting and asking to speak, which we subsequently discovered they were taping and playing to themselves, but they didn't answer again until they wanted to talk terms.

We were very fortunate in having a chap called Roddy Bell whom I knew well, a Royal Marine officer who had been born and spent all his youth in South America and so spoke South American Spanish and understood South American attitudes. I remember, when he arrived to start his officer training at Lympstone, that he didn't speak English very well – it was obviously not his first language. He was a most invaluable chap.

Captain Barry Melbourne Hussey
Administrator of Health, Social Services and Education, Islas Malvinas
On June 13, Menendez and his staff were waiting for the end to come. It was on June 14 when the British made the transmission to us. I was with Mrs Eileen Vidal who managed the telephone system, and I sat with her until I got Menendez's authorisation to speak back. The one who was talking was a Captain Bell and he was sitting with Rose*. I wrote down the message, which said: 'You are surrounded, you have no way out, we don't want to kill you, you have no options. You're outgunned and we want to sit down and talk.' It was psychologically very well expressed. Rose must have written that without any doubt. So I went to Menendez and explained it to him. He phoned the continent and spoke to General Garcia, who was our commander but stayed at his headquarters in Comodoro Rivadavia. Galtieri did not want us to speak to the British, but Garcia understood the problem and said: 'Go ahead, speak. You know what to do.'

Menendez told me to contact Bell again: 'All right, tell them to come,' and so in the afternoon Rose came in a helicopter with Bell. They landed in the wrong place, between the hospital and Government House, so they had to jump a wire fence. Rose said: 'Now I understand why you said to land in the other place.' But it was because we knew our troops were already marching into town.

Colonel Manuel Dorrego
Head of Public Works Department, Islas Malvinas
When the operations were about to finish and the English were coming, some

---

*Michael Rose, Commanding Officer of the SAS, and terrorist negotiator soldiers threw personnel mines loose to protect themselves, but it is also true that these mines are easier to lift up; they are in sight, are not buried, and a specialist can with care lift those quickly. But there were also foot soldiers from the infantry, who installed booby trap bombs that were a brutality. I am ashamed there were people who worked in this way.

Company Sergeant Major Peter John Richens
B Company, 2 Para
We unloaded our weapons and replaced helmets with our red berets. Brigadier Thompson ordered my company commander to take us down to the racecourse, then stop, go firm and let 45 Commando go through us into the town. This was quite annoying to us. I waited until he'd gone, then said to my company commander: 'Look boss, we don't particularly want to go firm at the racecourse.'

He said: 'Don't worry about it.'

I said: 'We've come all this way, and don't want to stop at the racecourse on the outskirts of the town. We want to go straight in.'

Brigadier Julian Howard Thompson
Commander, 3 Commando Brigade
After completing arrangements with my brigade major, I flew back to 2 Para and walked into Stanley with them, with 3 Para behind. 45 Commando were moving on the high ground to take Sapper Hill, with 42 Commando in the rear. 45 Commando arrived on Sapper Hill at the same time as the Scots Guards arrived by helicopter, as their commander Brigadier Wilson moved them forward without telling anybody else. There could have been a clash – but in the event there wasn't. The general didn't want us breasting up to the Argentines as they were withdrawing and risking an outbreak of shooting, so I was told to stop 2 Para at the old racecourse. They were all for racing on, but even though they were not answering radio messages, I eventually managed to stop them through my artillery man Mike Holroyd Smith, speaking to the Paras' battery commander, and then I went on myself with some of my staff. I'd been told General Moore had flown forward, and had the idea of joining him.

Company Sergeant Major Peter John Richens
B Company, 2 Para
We moved off down towards the old marine camp at Moody Brook, then up on to the high ground, while A Company followed along the road into

Stanley below us. When we reached the edge of the racecourse, I looked at the company commander, who said: 'We're going on.'

Major John Harry Crosland
B Company Commander, 2 Para

Max Hastings came with us as we walked into the outskirts of the town. A Company moved faster than us on the road, so we followed them into the town itself.

Major Philip Neame
D Company Commander, 2 Para

I was bringing up the rear, with the distinct feeling the war was over. There was a brief moment of people wondering whether they really needed to be carrying all this ammunition, lobbing away smoke grenades, and mild celebration. My company sergeant major, realising there could be an accident, shouted the familiar order: 'Endex, Make Safe,' so everyone unloaded their weapons. I wondered what he was playing at. The fervour with which people pulled off their helmets and put on red berets, and the general party atmosphere, could easily have led to someone being killed in an accident.

Lieutenant Colonel David Robert Chaundler
Commanding Officer, 2 Para

We were joined with great rapidity by C Company of 3 Para who'd come off Mount Longdon, who I think were trying to race us. We encountered some small arms fire, but I'd got the tanks and machine guns on the other side of the inlet ready with covering fire, and the artillery were silently marking targets as we proceeded, in case we got into trouble.

Captain Adrian Robert Freer
3 Para

The entry into Stanley was a hard tab up the road with 2 Para leading. We'd bombed up on Longdon, and were going into action again, but heard the surrender when we reached Moody Brook. We found some seriously wounded Argentines needing urgent treatment and flagged down a BV coming up the road behind us from B echelon. One of the senior NCOs, who'd not been on Mount Longdon during the fight but had been safe in the rear area, made some gratuitous remark about how they could look after themselves. I thought how very wrong he'd got this, and after some short, very sharp words with him, these wounded men were loaded into his vehicle and taken to the dressing station.

Company Sergeant Major Peter John Richens
B Company, 2 Para

We walked through the golf course and past Brigadier Thompson who wasn't annoyed – but he'd certainly wanted the Royal Marines to lead the way into Stanley to take the surrender. Well, it was red rag to the bull; we were the first ashore, the first into action and the first into Stanley, so that was the end of it.

Lieutenant Colonel David Robert Chaundler
Commanding Officer, 2 Para

We were told to stop at the Esro Buildings, on the start line for what would have been the final attack, but the battalion were hell-bent on taking the town, and were well past that point before I got the order. We were finally stopped beside the war memorial on the western suburbs of Stanley, to allow ceasefire negotiations to take place. Menendez's headquarters in Government House was within my area, so one of my platoon commanders and a couple of corporals went in and had a chat with him somewhat earlier than any of the more official approaches. I took up residence in the former Argentine air force house, where my war ended.

Major John Harry Crosland
B Company Commander, 2 Para

This was a very uneasy period: the truce hadn't been signed, thousands of Argentine troops were milling about, and the forward edge of the battle area was not clearly defined. We approached Government House, and then withdrew a bit.

I told my sergeant major, Pete Ritchens, to find a house made of bricks and not one of the usual prefab bungalows, so that if there was to be an Alamo episode, we could at least fight from a defendable area. We knew we'd be kicked out of Government House, but made our base in some other senior person's place. Later that evening, the headquarters of 3 Commando Brigade arrived and demanded we vacate so they could move in. This was negotiated in an amicable manner; in other words I wasn't going to move, but they were welcome to come in and share, as we'd got the fires going and had found a good supply of bottles of red wine.

Commander Timothy John Gedge
RN Fleet Air Arm

I spent the last twenty-four hours of the war in HMS *Fearless*, helping tasking the air attack missions. We were planning the final push on to Stanley, with missions against particular targets using specific weapons. But suddenly a voice called over the net that white flags had been seen – at about 1545 on June 14, and we called off the incoming air strike. Some confusion ensued, as not everybody surrendered at the same time.

Private Domingo Morel
Argentine Infantry Regiment
It was known it was finishing but we did not show the flag to surrender. From half past twelve until half past one we were without weapons because we had left all the weaponry on the flanks. Then at half past one, the main under officer told me we had to go back to get the weapons because nothing was happening. We didn't know if they had surrendered or if the ceasefire had finished. When I went back I was gripped with fear, because we were then surrounded by the English.

Michael Thomas Nicholson
ITN correspondent
A Gurkha major came out of his bunker and said: 'There's a white flag flying over Stanley. Bloody marvellous.' We weren't ready to film, so we got him to do it again only he mucked it up a few times. The Gurkhas themselves were very disappointed. So were we. We'd have seen some great fighting. But it all ended with lots of little white dots running away down the hillside.

John Fowler
Superintendent of Education, Stanley
The first British soldier I saw close-to was a para, a huge Jock with a lantern jaw, about eight feet tall, festooned with hand grenades. I said, 'What do you do in the paras?' He said: 'I'm a nurse.' Two of them had come down from the war memorial where the Brits had stopped, and being medics wanted to see how things were at the hospital. They stood in the kitchen talking to an admiring crowd of nurses and medical orderlies, while in the corner our two Argentine military policemen were furiously scoffing what they thought would be their last hot meal for some time.

Captain Adrian Robert Freer
3 Para
We occupied some houses along Ross Road West. There was supposed to be a Mexican stand-off, but curiosity got the better of me. I felt we needed a vehicle, so set off with Sergeant Major Docherty and 'borrowed' a jeep, then

got some fresh sheep carcasses from the cold storage further along the road. All along the sea front were containers full of food and equipment. The Argentines were running around all over the place, their discipline gone, offering bottles of booze in exchange for your beret. It was quite bizarre.

John Smith
Falkland Islander

While the surrender was being negotiated, they crapped all over the post office including a huge pile of mail that hadn't been distributed, over the walls and even the ceiling. Similar things were done in people's houses too. The Argentines seemed to be unused to sanitation, but this was vindictiveness.

Air Vice Commodore Carlos Bloomer-Reeve
Secretary General, Islas Malvinas

We had the visit from the Colonel Rose, Captain Bell and the radio operator. The surrender negotiations were made by Menendez, Rose and Bell. These men negotiated the capitulation directly with London. The contract was consolidated with London, not with Moore, everything negotiated and agreed by Rose.

The British were coming in next day, so we prepared beds for them, and the secretary. There were a lot of local people at the Upland Goose, including a lady who was very dear to me; she kissed me in a moment of emotion, and then I left. I think I said something like: 'You'll have the English here tomorrow; in two hours you will be free.' And she started crying.

Brigadier Julian Howard Thompson
Commander, 3 Commando Brigade

We went to the secretariat building, and realised it was very strange for us to be wandering around, surrounded by all these armed enemy soldiers. We were looking very dirty and our badges of rank were not particularly visible. An Argentine military policeman asked us what we were doing in very good English, so I asked him where General Moore was. He said there was no English general, just his own general plus two British officers, Captain Rod Bell and Colonel Rose, who were still negotiating the terms of the surrender. Bell spoke Spanish and Mike Rose was a very experienced terrorist negotiator and the last thing they'd want would be a gash brigadier destroying the rapport of the proceedings, so I turned on my heel and went back to 2 Para, which had established themselves in a house, where they allowed us to stay that night.

Major General (John) Jeremy Moore
Commander, British Land Forces
There was the question of the word 'unconditional' in the surrender. We'd discussed earlier whether it should be included. From my reading of the Second World War, and the possibility of prolonging this war, I had not wanted 'unconditional' in the document. My mission was 'Repossess the Falkland Islands'. What the heck any surrender document said seemed to me unimportant – irrelevant almost – as long as I regained the Falkland Islands. So if this might put Menendez off and make him feel his military honour was impugned, I thought: 'Better left out.' My chief of staff told me the British government was insisting on the word 'unconditional', so I said to him, 'All right, I will of course take the document with that word in. But you can tell them back home that if he jibs at it, I'm going to cross it out.' In the time available, nobody was going to be able to get back to me and say: 'You are not to do that.'

Air Vice Commodore Carlos Bloomer-Reeve
Secretary General, Islas Malvinas
Menendez called Galtieri and told him he was going to surrender the islands. Galtieri told him: 'Take the men from the foxholes and make them fight.' Menendez said: 'You do not understand this situation, General. This is my responsibility, the men are worn out, and they cannot fight any more. It's my responsibility for their lives and we are surrendering.'

(James) Robert Fox
BBC correspondent
It was surprising how much stuff the Argentines had; unbelievable amounts of food in containers. Beside the racecourse there were about forty upended 105mm howitzers and ammunition boxes strewn all over the place, some with unfired shells and big brass shell cases, broken-down lorries, food, and then we came to the Beaver aircraft hangar where we met up with Julian Thompson, and Lt Colonel Nick Vaux from 42 Commando, who were very friendly.

Major General (John) Jeremy Moore
Commander, British Land Forces
I'd had many discussions with Roddy Bell, and our intelligence staff, about Argentine attitudes, and what was needed to bring them to the point of packing it in. Once a soldier was defeated having behaved honourably, Argentine honour deemed it acceptable to surrender. I had hoped after the

end of the second night's fighting to have brought them to the point where their military honour was satisfied. But now, it really did seem that Menendez felt honour had been achieved.

Michael Thomas Nicholson
ITN correspondent
We saw Jeremy Moore getting into a Wessex helicopter to take the surrender in Port Stanley. I said: 'Can we come with you?' He said: 'No, no, no.' I said: 'But we've got to film it.' He said: 'No, I'm going on my own.' And this was the man who wanted his son to see how his father fought in the war!

Staff Sergeant Richard James Elliott
REME, 3 Commando Brigade Air Squadron
We flew General Moore into Stanley, over rows of Argentine dead laid out beside some Puma helicopters, which had been carrying their special forces for an attack. They'd flown near a Rapier battery which had been wary of firing as the RAF use Pumas; but when they also saw some Augusta helicopters, which we definitely do not have, they opened fire and killed the lot of them.

Major General (John) Jeremy Moore
Commander, British Land Forces
The typed-up surrender document arrived at last light. A Wessex flew forward from *Fearless* with the document, picked me up from my tactical headquarters and flew me into Stanley. After a long, bumpy helicopter ride in a snowstorm I landed close to the Government offices and met the negotiating team who'd been there during the day. I felt very exposed. It suddenly occurred to me: 'What happens if the enemy decide to change their minds now and aren't willing to go ahead with the surrender? The six of us have pistols and a few small arms, with ten thousand armed Argentinians all round us.' Supposing I say the wrong thing and upset Menendez, and he says: 'I'm not going to.' What then? In any case, was he going to surrender? Could he surrender just the forces around Stanley, or would he surrender them all? There was a lot of internal tension.

(James) Robert Fox
BBC correspondent
We went to the Upland Goose Hotel, and even though we must have looked like scarecrows, everyone there was very friendly. They said the surrender was

taking place in the secretarial building. I managed to barge in there but was thrown out, although I did interview Jeremy Moore afterwards. We then toured the town and I chucked some Argentine officers out of a house that they'd just set on fire. I wasn't having that, as the fire was getting near some fuel storage tanks.

Major General (John) Jeremy Moore
Commander, British Land Forces
I received Menendez, who was perfectly upright with proper behaviour. He was under considerable strain, of course, surrendering his command to a chap who's just defeated you with fewer troops than you've got.

Captain Barry Melbourne Hussey
Administrator of Health, Social Services and Education, Islas Malvinas
At the surrender, I thought Jeremy Moore was very normal, but I knew he was under pressure.

Major General (John) Jeremy Moore
Commander, British Land Forces
I began by telling Menendez of our respect for the way the Argentine officer corps had shown its bravery, using the air force pilots as the example, because I felt this would help him feel that his military honour was satisfied. When I put the surrender document in front of Menendez, he did indeed jib at the word 'unconditional'. So we crossed it out. He also wanted another word crossed out – 'Lafonia', which is part of East Falkland. By the time we'd signed, it was after midnight GMT so the date was also wrong. Because of the way it had been typed, it was too difficult to change, so I asked Menendez: 'Can we falsify the time by fifteen minutes so we can get it all on the one date?' We agreed that. Then we couldn't find one of the copies of the document, which caused a fuss. But it's not like the Treaty of Versailles with conditions, but merely formalised the fact that they'd surrendered. And he had surrendered, whether he put his mark on a bit of paper or not.

Michael Thomas Nicholson
ITN correspondent
The surrender wasn't filmed or recorded by anybody. General Moore even refused to let a Royal Navy official photographer film it, in case – can you believe this – General Menendez was upset! If *we* had lost, you wouldn't have been able to move for Argentinian camera crews. And yet Moore flinched at

the last minute. The man just didn't have the confidence one expected from a general; a disappointing man.

Private Jose Omar Ojeda
Compania Comando Servicios, 3rd Brigade

They didn't say anything about surrender at the end; we were already seeing it clearly for ourselves. We knew that we did not have any way of saving ourselves. The only way of staying alive was to surrender. Many people were not in agreement with Menendez, but what was there to do if there was no way to continue attacking? We had to surrender or they would have killed us all, and for what?

Captain Barry Melbourne Hussey
Administrator of Health, Social Services and Education, Islas Malvinas

We abandoned the house because there was no water, no heating. It was useless living there, so for the last two days we moved into the secretary's building. We had two offices and we slept there too. British officers were sleeping in the other wing.

Major General (John) Jeremy Moore
Commander, British Land Forces

I went with Robert Fox and one or two others into Stanley town, and walked up to West Store where a lot of the people of the town had been gathered. I suppose I wanted to say 'Hello'. I think this was driven as much by the press's desire to have something, as it was anything else.

Michael Thomas Nicholson
ITN correspondent

I hitched a helicopter ride back to San Carlos, took a dinghy which I found on the shore and motored out to the *Norland*, climbed the ladder up the side and went to the radio room to break the news about the end of the war. 'Sorry,' I was told. 'There's a blanket veto on everything. You can't broadcast.' Then in comes Kim Subedo for IRN, and Max Hastings for the *Evening Standard*. *News at Ten* was coming up in half an hour. We'd all got our scoops, but we couldn't send them. I understand that Mrs Thatcher ordered this, so she could be the one to break the news, not us.

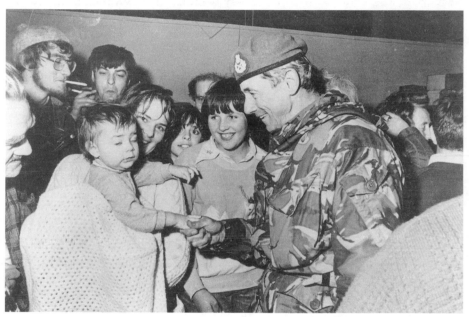

Major General Moore with islanders in the West Store, Port Stanley, after the surrender on June 14, 1982.

Pat Whitney
Green Patch, East Falkland

I went into Stanley on the Argentine motorbike I'd come by in the mountains. I got onto Two Sisters Flats, and met some marines who said it was all mined. I followed the tracks and caught up with a Snowcat, which stopped and a guy got out – I guess to tell me we were in a minefield. I'll never forget this ... he stepped on a mine. His foot was blown off. They put a flare up, whipped an injection into him, put his foot into a poly bag, a helicopter was flying round and landed in the Snowcat tracks, and two minutes after he'd stepped on the mine, he was on his way to hospital. He was in terrible pain. And he'd only got out to warn me about the mines.

The Snowcat, with me behind, continued following a track through the minefield, and we got down to the Two Sisters road and into town. The town was a mess. There were bodies covered in sheets of tin, my house had a shell through the roof, and two women had been killed six houses further along my road. Seeing twenty-six paras stretched out on the floor asleep, I decided to stay away until they'd found somewhere else.

John Fowler
Superintendent of Education, Stanley

On the night the surrender was signed, Dr Alison Bleanie came upon me in a hospital corridor, telling me in her no-nonsense Scots manner how she'd been twice to the secretariat to find out who was in charge: 'But there's nobody listening, John. I've got to go back and talk to those buggers again.' I volunteered to go with her, and we left via the Argentine part of the hospital. It was full of walking wounded waiting to be shipped off to the airport, many of them in a dreadful state of shock. I'd only been outside once before at night, and it was very strange to be walking through the curfew past Argentine soldiers, and then to see the secretariat absolutely ablaze with light. Just being out at night felt *illegal*!

Every single room of the secretariat was full of Argentine and British officers, all talking furiously, with an atmosphere in the building not unlike a cocktail party – professional people comparing notes. Alison and I felt really out of it, as if we were intruding. Whereas we were very emotionally tied up in all this, perhaps the military on either side were professionally, but not emotionally, involved? No one would admit to us who was in charge of the situation. I suppose the final details of the surrender were being hammered out right then, maybe in this building, so nobody was ready to get to grips with the new situation.

Major General (John) Jeremy Moore
Commander, British Land Forces
At somebody's suggestion I returned that night to Government House, in the no-man's-land bit between the two sides. I used the governor's bed and his things. Government House was my headquarters for about a fortnight, until the governor got back. We had to remove the Argentines' defensive sandbags, and the other mess they'd made. They did not look after accommodation properly – extremely badly trained and disciplined in that sense.

Captain Barry Melbourne Hussey
Administrator of Health, Social Services and Education, Islas Malvinas
I think that some have been very hard on Menendez, quoting things he was supposed to have said but did not say. Menendez is very special. He never had any ill feeling towards the people of the islands. The dining room at Government House was never altered. The Queen's picture was still hanging there. He never said why.

Captain Jeremy Larken
HMS Fearless
It was clear General Menendez had looked after things at Government House with almost loving care. Even the ornaments were still in their places. But once 3 Commando Brigade got in there and started using it as their headquarters, I think it suffered considerably. It's fair to say that the British were less careful with Port Stanley than had been the Argentine forces. I won't say our force ran amok, but there was considerable euphoria when the battle was over. In the early days, our control over our own people was not as good as it might have been. I won't say there was rape and pillage, but there was a great deal of acquisition of war materials. Mercedes jeeps were hot property. There was a generally acquisitive approach to liberating Argentine equipment. I was on the sidelines of all this, as we attempted to establish some kind of administration, and although I was more concerned with the maritime aspect, I was at all the meetings when this was discussed.

John Fowler
Superintendent of Education, Stanley
The water and electricity, which had been kept going quite marvellously by the public works department throughout the occupation, started failing, partly from damage during the fighting, but also because of the extra demands being made on it. It also became bloody freezing cold and there was snow.

Partially laid Argentine landmines along the coast, intended to obstruct a British landing from the sea.

Anybody with spare room offered it to British military folk, so nobody was on their own any more. By this stage, no more than three hundred civilians were living in Stanley. Once we'd been liberated, we felt inadequate; we were knackered, with very little sleep.

Major John Harry Crosland
B Company Commander, 2 Para

We set sentries on our building, and were told to keep away from an area of chaos further east where thousands of Argentines were milling about. The truce and surrender were negotiated and came into effect late that evening. We remained in our house, and recovered very quickly, faster than the other units, who'd just fought their first battle. But then we were put on standby to go to West Falkland, to sort out Argentine forces said to be considering continuing fighting. This threat did not materialise, so we remained in our house for the next three days.

David Cooper
Chaplain, 2 Para

That night, we heard a lot of noise in the Argentine half of the town and the electricity went off. It was clear they'd lost discipline. I walked into the centre of the town to find the vicar. We'd been told there would be no victory parade in Stanley, so I'd joked that the only reason we'd come all this way was so that I could hold a victory service in the cathedral, to which we would of course have to march. I found the dean, Harry Bagnall, who said we could do it tomorrow and we had a good turnout of islanders to cheer us on the way.

Captain Adrian Robert Freer
3 Para

We were filthy, needing to wash. Stanley's water and electricity system was on overload, and many of us developed dysentery. I'd drunk some pretty unpleasant water from a shell hole on Mount Longdon, which made me quite ill. I didn't recover until we got into Norland and I'd had a few days of decent water flush me through. Others were also ill, and it took time to get our bergans forward.

I was sent on a recce to the airfield to see if we could land aircraft to get rid of the prisoners, who eventually went back to Argentina on Canberra, guarded by C Company. This was urgent, as we didn't have the rations or infrastructure to look after them for very long. Some ships came into the harbour and we were able to go on board for a wash. There was an emotional church service in the cathedral.

Company Sergeant Major Peter John Richens
B Company, 2 Para

I was told to search a tug in the harbour. Its Argentine captain assured me it was a hospital ship, but we found a load of brand-new 9mm pistols and one hundred and fifty brand-new folding-butt FN rifles, which were all impounded and the crew arrested. They protested that they were medical personnel and shouldn't be treated like that. We handed them over to the military police.

Major John Harry Crosland
B Company Commander, 2 Para

The twelve thousand Argentines were in a desperate state, very frightened about what might happen to them. The island's economy couldn't even contain five thousand British troops, so we needed to get rid of them as fast as possible. We were living in private property, and very conscious that we needed to look after it. But according to my diary we hadn't washed for thirty-one days. We needed to get back home to our normal lives, and return the islanders to their normal way of existence as soon as possible. At this stage, we didn't know what was happening next ...

Captain Alan John Warsap
Regimental Medical Officer, 2nd Battalion Scots Guards

The Scots Guards didn't follow the general melee down into Stanley to enjoy the celebrations there, but held fast as last ordered, which was to take and hold Tumbledown Mountain. The battalion obeyed their orders to the letter, and stayed another night on the mountain before being relieved, and it was bitterly cold out there. My own section made use of an Argentine tent to keep off the ice particles. We stayed there until we were evacuated to the sheep sheds at Fitzroy, where we dealt with other casualties that revealed themselves.

Linda Kitson
Official war artist

When the Scots Guards returned to the sheep sheds from Tumbledown, I hadn't realised they'd just fought the battle. The commanding officer, Mike Scott, and his company commanders seemed very high, storming in, hot, dishevelled, triumphant and victorious. Their immediate talk was of the casualties, in what sounded like a First World War sort of battle, where they'd run out of ammunition at various stages and had to use their bayonets. The

Argentine prisoners of war after the surrender, passing lines of abandoned armoured cars in Stanley, on their way to Stanley airfield.

One of many piles of Argentine small arms in Port Stanley after the surrender.

close proximity of such bloodshed would stay with them for the rest of their lives. There wasn't enough room for everybody to lie down.

A sergeant brought one of his men to me. He was in terrible need of medical help but I was the nearest thing there was. He was so shocked as to be incoherent, unable to restrain himself. He fluctuated between telling me that the Scots Guards were the greatest, to how terrible the battle had been and how he wanted to be a decorator. The outpouring of his memories of the battle was really shocking.

The officers had their own part of the sheep shed, separated from everyone else by sheepskins hanging around. John Kisley, who had bayoneted two people, was extraordinarily composed, but maybe it hadn't yet come home to him. They all congregated and talked in a manic way, hard and fast, away from the responsibility, letting it all out to each other. They were mostly aged thirty and less. I had to leave them as I was feeling sick. Maybe I hadn't eaten.

I went into the other part with the men, six hundred of them all together, to draw them immediately as, they wrote letters home, worrying about the condition of their feet, being forced to clean their weapons to stop them blathering. Some were too animated to sit down. I had a technical problem with trying to draw all this, and the drawings are a long way from what I'd hoped. Maybe I should have stopped for a while. I was feeling sick, so I think I lay down. I was disappointed with those drawings, but there was only one chance, and they are valuable to the Scots Guards.

Captain Alan John Warsap
Regimental Medical Officer, 2nd Battalion Scots Guards
Many people suffered from trench foot, which we treated ourselves as there wasn't any more space left in the hospital ships. Everyone was so invigorated by surviving the experience of Tumbledown and being in action, there were no complaints or minor illnesses. Everyone was ennobled and strengthened by surviving this experience. I learned a lot about myself – we all did.

Linda Kitson
Official war artist
Sketching the wounded was the only way to record them and their experience. Taking photographs would have been unthinkable. I did eight or so sketches a day, but as I didn't understand what I was looking at, it was hard to simplify. The wounded are so quickly out of it, and feel guilty that they've failed, and they look appalling. These drawings required great effort.

Two British paratroopers in Stanley after the surrender.

Captain Alan John Warsap
Regimental Medical Officer, 2nd Battalion Scots Guards

All together we had forty-three wounded, and eight people were killed. Another man was missing from one of the stretcher parties, which had got split up. We'd given him up for dead and held a memorial service, with his name inscribed on a memorial on the mountain. He turned up seven weeks later, just as we were leaving on the *Norland*.

David Cooper
Chaplain, 2 Para

At the local civilian hospital I met the two doctors, Alison Bleanie and her husband, who asked if we had any coffins. I told them we only had body bags. He told me these two women had been killed, and seemed very bitter about it. It didn't upset me too much, but was the only time any of the islanders had seemed reproachful towards us. I understand that the Argentines had made it quite clear that this was the military end of town; and that the husband of one of these women had insisted on remaining in their own house. I'd buried too many of my soldiers to feel that two ladies who had elected to stay in a dangerous part of town deserved sympathy from me at that time, so he was talking to the wrong person. They didn't want to take up my body bag offer, but they got coffins from somewhere and I assume Harry Bagnell buried the ladies.

Captain Christopher Charles Brown
148 Commando Forward Observation Unit, Royal Artillery

The Argentine prisoners were held on the airfield, having handed in their weapons. Most were jovial, smiling, happy to be given food and that it was all over. I didn't think that the Argentines had been able to look after themselves particularly well. On a gun position immediately by the racecourse, to the west of Stanley, their gun crews had been living in shelters made from ammunition boxes and corrugated iron. They were under water, their sleeping bags drenched.

We were whisked away very sharply into *Intrepid*. There was still an Argentine garrison at South Thule, and we were going to send gunships with naval gunfire teams down there. Then there were rumours that we were to be pulled out, but eventually we came back in *Canberra*.

Trudi McPhee
Brookfields, North Camp

Ailsa's mum, Velma, who ran the Rose pub in town, had been taken off to Fox

Argentine prisoners with their discarded equipment in Port Stanley, being listed before being taken to the airfield.

Argentine soldiers under guard on Port Stanley jetty.

Bay by the Argies under lock and key, as she had very strong anti-Argentine views. Ailsa was worried as she didn't know where her mum was, and so wanted to get into Stanley as quickly as possible to find out what had happened. She asked me if I would look after the Estancia while they went into town, so I spent the next four days scrubbing and washing.

John Fowler
Superintendent of Education, Stanley

Having been shelled out of our house, even when it was repaired we had no desire to return there. We acquired another house and over the next two weeks we had most of 2 Para in for cups of tea, carrying their weapons and talking all the time. It was a form of mutual therapy, especially for the young guys who'd been at Goose Green. They had a great need to talk about what had happened to them, and only now were beginning to worry about what they'd done and what that meant about them.

David Cooper
Chaplain, 2 Para

At our church service, I asked our soldiers always to remember how they felt at this time, remembering themselves without any sort of veneer as they were facing death, remembering what they were really like and what really mattered to them. I urged them not to forget this when circumstances got better.

Brigadier Julian Howard Thompson
Commander, 3 Commando Brigade

The Argentine senior officers were gathered together and placed in HMS *Fearless* and one of the POW cages in Ajax Bay, as an insurance policy against the Argentine air force deciding they weren't going to surrender the Malvinas so easily. They were the only ones in a position to carry on, and could have made further attacks against our ships.

I was made responsible for disarming the Argentines in Stanley, and moving them off to the airfield. 42 Commando lined up on the isthmus and we made the Argentines march past, handing in weapons as they passed through. The only unit that maintained a soldierly demeanour was the Argentine marines, who marched past with their colours flying. Colonel Nick Vaux was standing there with his RSM and decided the colours would look good hanging in their mess, but this thought seemed to transfer itself telepathically to the Argentine marines, who stopped, removed the colours from the pikes and burned them before they could be seized – which is good. I'd have done the same.

My brigade major had requisitioned a civilian Land Rover he'd found with the keys in, which broke down. He then stopped a new Mercedes jeep being driven by an Argentine naval officer, ordering the officer to leave the keys and start walking to the airport. Suddenly everything had become public property, which was dangerous. Eight hundred people usually inhabited Stanley, but now there were some three thousand men who'd been fighting, and one pub. I read the riot act to my commanding officers, to ensure that discipline wouldn't break down. I put a curfew on us after last light, patrolled and imposed by our own people. Houses were crammed with our men as well as Falkland families.

John Fowler
Superintendent of Education, Stanley

We were seized by a collective madness for a while, everybody trying to bag a Mercedes, and I had my eye on a little Volkswagen jeep. For a while, the military and ourselves were just looting. The drill hall was found to be full of food, and as the military needed the space for accommodation, we were invited to empty it. The abattoir chiller room was full of carcasses, and I took a Land Rover full of best Argentine fillet steak and sirloin. It was liberating in one way, but couldn't be allowed to continue.

Michael Thomas Nicholson
ITN correspondent

It was very anti-climactic; I suppose most wars are. The mess in Stanley was dreadful, human excrement in the streets and the post office had been used as a lavatory. We had to wait ten days to leave, until the first Hercules could land at the airfield.

Major Simon Ewen Southby-Tailyour
Royal Marines

There was no great surprise about the victory, or sense of elation. It was quite obviously coming; I had a few glasses of port in my cabin, but then I always had a few glasses of port in my cabin. A most relaxed week followed, back to the way my life had been before the war, patrolling round the islands in ships.

Five Argentine Pucara propeller attack aircraft, abandoned at Port Stanley airport.

John Fowler
Superintendent of Education, Stanley
Our new house was big and central, and had been used by some important Argentine officer who'd left clean silk pyjamas in the main bedroom and a freezer full of very nice Argentine steak, maps and intelligence stuff on the walls, and a bunker out the back garden. A Parker Knoll sideboard had been defaced by the Argentines in some strange manner which we really couldn't understand, until a group of paras came in with rifles, and without a word, slotted them into this piece of furniture – the world's first Parker Knoll weapon rack.

Gerald Cheek
Director of Civil Aviation, Falkland Islands
In Fox Bay East on West Falkland, the Argentine major in charge came over at midnight that night, telling settlement manager Richard: 'You'd better get our flag down and put up the Union Jack – it's all over.' He was very happy and wanted to get home.

Company Sergeant Major Peter John Richens
B Company, 2 Para
The Falkland Islanders in Stanley were not used to a lot of people being around, and were starting to ask when we'd be leaving. We understood this attitude; we'd done our job, and were just as keen to be going.

Lieutenant Colonel David Robert Chaundler
Commanding Officer, 2 Para
I saw a great many very good troops on the airfield who'd not been involved, because the Argentine command thought we were going to attack Stanley head-on over the beaches. They'd been taught this by the US Marine Corps who rely on huge firepower to do things like that. There were minefields, barbed wire and defended beaches around Port Stanley, which they hadn't moved to cover the area we were coming from. This reinforced my feeling that had we delayed moving into Stanley by twenty-four hours, they would have redeployed these fresh troops to face us, and we'd have had to fight for the town.

Michael Thomas Nicholson
ITN correspondent
For some reason, during the Falklands War there was not the usual camaraderie among British journalists. At the end, we were in the Uplands

Goose Hotel at four p.m. one afternoon; it was already dark and candles lit the place. Somebody suggested that when we were all back in UK, we should get together, and Patrick Bishop said: 'I don't think we will, you know,' and we didn't. We got a bit drunk and various people came in for stick. One little Scot for some reason suddenly lunged at Max Hastings with a bayonet – they'd started collecting souvenirs. Derek Hudson from the *Yorkshire Post* grabbed him from behind, and said: 'This isn't the time or place to kill Max Hastings.' If death was to come at the hands of a hack, it was definitely time to go home.

David Cooper
Chaplain, 2 Para

We just wanted to go home, but the Argentine prisoners had to go first. Chris Keeble wanted a memorial at Goose Green, and had cajoled the settlement manager into making a stone cairn with a cross on it. We crammed a Chinook full of people and flew to Goose Green for a short service. We then flew back to Stanley and were dropped on to the racecourse, from where we walked across the road down to the waterfront and got into landing craft, which took us out to *Norland*, which set sail within hours. And that was the last I saw of the Falkland Islands.

Colonel Manuel Dorrego
Head of Public Works Department, Islas Malvinas

At the end we felt an enormous deception – and pain. In my own particular case I lost my son-in-law. He was at Mount Longdon and was one of the first to fall, a wonderful boy who had gone to Malvinas because I was over there; he asked to go there, and there he remains. So, well, all this . . . great pain. When the Gurkhas invaded Mount Longdon, I found out the next day. So everything that came afterwards, prison, the return . . . was very hard for me.

Neil Watson
Long Island, East Falkland

A few days after the surrender, it was Airborne Forces Day and they had a parade in Stanley with General Jeremy Moore on a dais taking the salute. Glenda and I saw a guy with leg injuries being pushed in a wheelchair who we recognised. I asked him: 'How's Scotty?' He broke up crying, then said: 'Scotty's dead.' After the attack on Mount Longdon, the next morning when they'd won the battle and captured the peak, Scotty was killed by Argentine artillery fire, and you'll see his name on the memorial . . . the other guy was wounded. I feel a bit of a Jonah; I took two guys up the mountain, and one of them's dead, the other wounded . . . yep.

Glenda Watson
Long Island, East Falkland
Two days after the surrender, my mother, who was about seventy-eight, had a stroke. She was very small and was the head of our whole family. Before she'd come out to us at Long Island, she'd physically stopped the Argentines from entering her house in Stanley. Neil went into Stanley on the Sea King helicopter taking her to the hospital, and that's where she stopped; she never got over it. She couldn't speak properly and died a year or so after. I'm afraid I've always blamed the Argentines for that.

Epilogue

Every year, come April and the winter, it all comes back to me: the body bags and things like that. At the end of big farm-working season when things slow down a bit, and the memories click in, it's always there.

Pat Whitney
Green Patch, East Falkland
Three nights after the battle, it all caught up with me. Right through the night I was waking up in a sweat, thinking there were mortar bombs exploding in the peat all around me. Thank God the flashbacks only happened for the one night – and never happened again to me.

Linda Kitson
Official war artist
People kept asking: 'When do we go home?' Home was six thousand miles and several weeks away. But first they had to bury the Argentine dead, as the Argentines didn't want them back, and clean everything up. One senior sergeant had to bury the Argentine he'd seen kill his oppo. He was so angry, and didn't want to touch the man who'd killed him. It was insufferable, living in this terrible place, memorial services *ad infinitum*, songs sung in sorrow, making goodbyes to friends. Many of the boys were wild and didn't believe in religion, but the padre didn't mind. He just gave the services anyway, and wasn't at all put off by dissension. The padre's role was inestimable.

Ten days after she was hit, *Galahad* was still burning, even in that terrible weather. The smoke was a terrible reminder to the men: still trying to find bodies, many not identified – their dog tags had melted; and people had left parts of their own bodies in that ship. The living felt guilty, and there was an endless trail of people who couldn't stay away, returning to the ship on pilgrimage.

At Fitzroy, where the Welsh Guards still lived weeks later, you couldn't escape from the war even though it was over; the battle mountains to the north, *Galahad* still in flames, beside where some of the men were living in a ship, or in the sheep shearing shed, surrounded in mud. The Argentine air force might keep fighting, and winter was coming on. It was snowing, and you couldn't afford to fall over as you might not be found.

I asked the Welsh Guards second in command if I should be drawing the burials. The way he looked at me I could have eaten my words. He knew every single body, and their being in those bags was more than he could bear, and I felt the same way. But that was a mistake. After the campaign he said I shouldn't have taken any notice of them: 'We wouldn't have stopped you; we were just shouting at everything. It's for my children that I wished you'd drawn those things.' A body bag isn't easy to depict, but it is the end of the line. I should have asked to be taken there. Long after the campaign, I remain haunted by this; and it was the same after the burned men asked me not to draw them when their blackened layers of skin were coming off. The nearer people have been to fighting, the more they want other people to know what it's really like, how terrible it can be.

There was one thing I couldn't draw but will never forget: the Welsh Guards travelling back on a wooden raft after a memorial service, and they were very sad. They had nowhere else to go but back to *Sir Tristram*, which was moored next to the *Sir Galahad*. The men on this raft wanted no longer to be on the face of this earth – such misery. I would have drawn it, but I couldn't. And when they saw me they tried to give me a wave. That was the one time when I tried to find somewhere I could weep; I just knelt face downwards in this bog, with people still endlessly walking past to look at the *Galahad* burning, and they knew what I was doing. I gave way to despair. Then after I'd mopped up, some of the guys returning from looking sat down with me and we had a cigarette. Most of the time I could hide behind the drawing equipment and sustain a great deal, but if I stopped my task, I was very vulnerable.

Captain Barry Melbourne Hussey
Administrator of Health, Social Services and Education, Islas Malvinas
My wife knew I was still alive through letters from the Red Cross. In San Carlos, we had no heat, no water, no nothing. Some of the British said: 'It's your fault because you sank the *Atlantic Conveyor*.' The troops had big boxes of all kinds of books and I read a lot of Shakespeare. Colonel Rose, who is a general now, talked with me, and the Welsh Guards that detained us were very, very nice people. One night I was invited to dinner on board ship. I was the senior prisoner, which gives you some honour, doesn't it?

Captain Jeremy Larken
HMS *Fearless*

General Menendez and entourage came on to *Fearless*. I thought I should make him comfortable in our own land commander's cabin, where he lived in his rather lonely and forlorn headquarters, working Spanish hours, and I daresay he had a siesta. In the evening I would drink some of the whisky with which I had so thoughtfully provided him, to enjoy some rather inconsequential conversations and what might pass as interrogation. Eventually a professional interrogation team came from the UK to look after him, led by a very mild soldier who probably wasn't any fiercer than I was.

Private Jose Omar Ojeda
Compania Comando Servicios, 3rd Brigade

One or two days after we surrendered, we embarked on the *Canberra*, where they treated us better than our own people; they bathed us, they cleaned us up, they fed us well and no problem at all.

Commodore Michael Verney Bradford
SS *Canberra*

The Red Cross came on board at Stanley and watched how we treated the prisoners, who were very dirty and bedraggled and in need of a good shower. Apart from some of the NCOs who appeared to be hostile, they were friendly – it was hard to believe that a few days ago ashore, they would have shot you. People were sleeping in cabins and on open decks all around the ships, and as we only had one company of paras on board, we hoped there'd be no trouble. I walked around with a 9mm pistol in my pocket for personal protection but they were very good and only too pleased to be out of it. They were fed the same as us.

We arrived at Puerto Madryn on the morning of June 19, met by one of their destroyers – the *Santissima Trinidad*, a British Type 22 frigate, which escorted us in. Three days before, she would have sunk us.

Federico Mirré (Argentine Ambassador, 2006)
Foreign Office, Buenos Aires

I was asked to go south to take care of the first batch of Argentine prisoners, coming in a cruise ship to Puerto Madryn. It was very cold. We had great difficulties getting the wounded down the side of the ship, some wounded being carried down piggyback. Others I could see had gangrene and their feet were badly affected by cold exposure. They didn't look in very good shape, but this was less than a week from the end of the battle. The general opinion of the prisoners, who were interviewed by the Red Cross, was that they had been very even-handedly treated by the British.

Captain Dennis John Scott-Masson
SS Canberra
We went alongside, and an Argentine general came on board and negotiated with our senior naval officer, Captain Burne. The Swiss representative of the Red Cross came on board and saw that fair play was done to the prisoners.

Federico Mirré (Argentine Ambassador, 2006)
Foreign Office, Buenos Aires
I was really furious with the high-ranking military officers. Nobody was taking charge of the whole thing, seeing whether people needed anything, like hot soup, drinks and so on. I grabbed some blankets and started throwing them to the soldiers as they stepped from the ship, as they were obviously very cold. These high-ranking military officers started to bark orders, and soon somebody else took care of the boys.

One of the high-ranking officers asked me if the Red Cross would mind if he shook hands with the prisoners as they stepped down. I said there could not be any objections; the prisoners were stepping *out* of a UK ship into Argentina so he could do as he liked. But I added: 'You are going to encounter some difficult moments with the people coming out of the ship.' His response was: 'Rubbish. I'm going to do this.' But when a major from an anti-aircraft battery came out, who I read later was a war hero, he responded to the senior officer's extended hand with some very harsh vocabulary indicating that he was not at all happy with the conduct of the operation.

Captain Dennis Scott-Masson
SS Canberra
The general and his acolytes lined up to shake the first ones by the hand as they stepped on to Argentine soil, but they soon got fed up with that. The troops disappeared into buses and trucks and were driven off into the night. There were no people there from Puerto Madryn, so we had no idea what sort of reception they were going to be given. They were all so grateful, clutching P&O menus and other memorabilia. We found many notes of thanks in English, tucked away under bunks, in drawers and beneath cushions. One Argentine lieutenant kissed Captain Burne on both cheeks, who was not terribly amused.

Argentine prisoners of war step down from SS *Canberra* at Puerto Madryn, to be greeted by Brigadier General Gariay of the Argentine Army.

Men of the Welsh Guards arriving at RAF Brize Norton, to be greeted by HRH The Prince of Wales.

Linda Kitson
Official war artist
I was sent to West Falklands for a rest with the Scots Guards, with instructions not to do any drawing. They had a party that night. One nineteen-year-old lad got totally pissed on his birthday and burned the company colours, so the next day he was having go through this court-martial with law books and military discipline. I thought they should just have let it go, as they were so miserable.

John Fowler
Superintendent of Education, Stanley
We left in the first batch of civilians to get out, travelling with the Welsh Guards in the ferry *St Edmund* – in August or September. They were in a hell of a state, not having been able to really do anything except get blown up on the *Galahad*.

Linda Kitson
Official war artist
My leaving was very different to the manner of my coming back, which I did with the Welsh Guards on a much smaller ferry – like a Dinky toy. The journey took two weeks. Everybody was terribly emotionally charged: they knew about the red-hot press investigation into who was responsible for what they were calling the Bluff Cove disaster, and the lads were out of hand at the thought of all the bereavement and funerals they were returning to.

John Fowler
Superintendent of Education, Stanley
The captain of the *St Edmund* decided that civilians shouldn't mix with the rude and licentious soldiery, so we were confined to messing with the officers and senior NCOs, spending more time than I would have liked in the company of Welsh Guards officers. It was like being back in a public school again. They were cordially disliked by their NCOs.

Linda Kitson
Official war artist
They all felt so guilty, having survived the burning of the *Galahad* and the incineration of their friends. The Welsh are an emotional people, and they felt guilty at remaining alive. Nobody had yet given way to tears and it was a very dangerous time. Their second in command, Major Joe Griffith Eaton,

said that every night they were stopping would-be suicide cases from jumping over the side – never less than four attempts every night.

John Fowler
Superintendent of Education, Stanley
The Welsh Guards soldiers and NCOs had huge resentment about the bombing at Fitzroy Roads, feeling that their officers had been safely ashore . . . [while] so many soldiers had been left on the ships. Their NCOs appeared to be an altogether tougher, soldierly bunch of people.

Linda Kitson
Official war artist
We landed to a strike-bound England with economic chaos, but having come from the wilderness of the Falklands, you land in a country of green fields, villages and hedges, an ancient country with its order and history showing topographically. You suddenly feel civilisation, coming from a barren rock, which was very moving.

I wanted to let the Welsh Guards off so they could meet the Prince of Wales, but I was ordered off the plane first. They hadn't wanted Prince Charles; their faith in religion, the government, the diplomats and all things human had gone. They were very rough men, but Prince Charles represented something upright and timeless, that helped them to make some kind of sense of it all. In the line, coming off the aircraft, the men began beaming, and I hadn't seen them smile for weeks.

John Smith
Falkland Islander
Many people were very badly affected. A sight, sound or smell can bring it all back very strongly. My generation and the next two generations are not going to be favourably disposed towards Argentina because they totally devastated our lives. A lot of people won't talk about it. The children were severely affected, particularly by the nightly bombardments. We didn't know what the Argentines might do.

Neil Watson
Long Island, East Falkland
Every year, come April and the winter, it all comes back to me: the body bags and things like that. At the end of a big farm-working season when things slow down a bit, and the memories click in, it's always there. Things happened here in my home. And then, over at the Estancia, I saw the real thing.

Glenda Watson
Long Island, East Falkland

Falklanders feel a sense of guilt about all the people who were bereaved because their loved ones came here to liberate us. Freda McKay, Ian McKay's* mother, came to our house and said: 'I can see how the Falklands has moved on, and that my son didn't die in vain.' We've always blamed ourselves, and when they come back, visit us, have a yarn about it, it takes away a bit of the guilt. They come back here as part of a healing process for them, but I think it's a healing process for us too.

Colonel Manuel Dorrego
Head of Public Works Department, Islas Malvinas

There is no reason, in my judgement, why today England should have left minefields that have not been cleared on the islands. If I were a 'kelper', I would make a demand, not on those who left them, but on England, to clear the mines, which would give them the peace of mind they need. The cost would signify absolutely nothing to England, if this brings peace of mind to the village that is there.

Air Vice Commodore Carlos Bloomer-Reeve
Secretary General, Islas Malvinas

We were relieved because there wouldn't be any more lives lost, but we feel failure. Without the war we were doing very well with the islands. Argentina is patient, but if we had gone on with what we were doing, in fifteen or thirty years the islands would have reached an agreement to have double nationality integration to the continent. I had a lot of friends there. We felt very friendly with no resentment against them. It's a pity I couldn't do more for them.

General Mario Benjamin Menendez
Military Governor, Islas Malvinas

The acknowledgement of Argentine sovereignty will remain with me until I die, and I think that my son, who was also in the Malvinas, and my grandchildren, will continue believing the same. After the acknowledgement of that sovereignty, we have to be very imaginative, very patient and very persistent with regard to the interests of the islanders – but their *interests* must not be confused with their *wishes*. The islanders have achieved some great advantages after the Malvinas. They are not going to thank the Argentines

---

*Sergeant Ian John McKay died on Mount Longdon and was awarded a posthumous Victoria Cross

Commander Tim Jones RN, the brother of Lt Colonel H Jones VC OBE, the Commanding Officer of 2 Para, at the British military cemetery, San Carlos.

for that, of course, but these may not last for ever. A repetition of war would not be wished, but who can give an assurance that something is not going to happen with the passing of the years?

Rear Admiral Anthony John Whetstone
Deputy Chief of Naval Staff (Operations), MoD Whitehall
Could we do the operation again today? Within months of the Falklands victory, the talk of defence cuts was starting again, and we've suffered a death of a thousand small cuts since. Quality of ships matters, but numbers matter too, and since 1982, we have considerably less ships, but rather more commitments.

Maria Fernada Canas (Head of Political Section, Argentine Embassy, 2006)
Argentine school teacher
I'm sure that we will have to come to a solution, which I hope I could see in my lifetime. It would be very sad to have this issue pending for so long, particularly between two countries which have so many things in common. The Argentine government are *obliged* by our constitution to take account of the islanders. I do understand the feeling of the islanders, but I think they could also understand our feelings, which are not so bizarre, even though they stem from something that happened in 1833.

I think that people in Great Britain don't feel as strongly about the Malvinas as we do. For British servicemen it was just one more job – and as a country you have much more fighting experience. For us, it was one experience in a century and with many conscripts doing the fighting. Maybe if both countries had taken the Malvinas issue more seriously, lives could have been saved.

Federico Mirré (Argentine Ambassador, 2006)
Foreign Office, Buenos Aires
Things have changed in Argentina. In 1983, one year after the Falklands/ Malvinas situation, we had a rebirth of democracy, and although we've had economic problems, we're progressing towards a more open and democratic society with less authoritarian ingredients. People know what they want now, and would not tolerate any return to old ways.

Gerald Cheek
Director of Civil Aviation, Falkland Islands
We hope we are now regarded as permanently British, with a sensible deterrent at Mount Pleasant airfield: four Tornados with air-to-air refuelling

capability, which can be reinforced in eighteen hours, plus good intelligence so we can't be invaded without plenty of warning, with helicopters to move troops quickly round the islands, an infantry company and guard ships here all the time. I'm content that the deterrent is effective. There is some uncertainty about the future and the British government's continuing commitment, complicated by the likelihood of oil being discovered here. There's also the likelihood of precious minerals being found on the land. We're progressing, people are more content, building twenty-five to thirty houses a year in Stanley, whereas when I was at school, one house might be built every five years. Hopefully, we'll continue progressing and won't have any more trouble with Argentina – but who knows?

Ailsa Heathman
Estancia Farm, North Camp

In some ways the Argies did us a favour, catapulting us into the twentieth century. The income from the fishing industry from 1986 onwards has given us a lifestyle that far outweighs our expectations, but the price of progress was very high. Our kids have grown up knowing only this good life, so they never knew what it was like before. I think they take it for granted. The most sickening part is that despite the loss of so many lives, we've still got the shadow hanging over us. Despite the geography we're still British – very British. The South American way of life is totally alien to our way of living I'm afraid. We were lucky first time round as they were silly enough to think they were coming to liberate us from colonialism and we'd be grateful. But now they know they're not welcome, I can't see us being so lucky a second time round. I hope it doesn't happen; they're on the bone of their arses, but since when has that stopped a country from going to war?

Federico Mirré (Argentine Ambassador, 2006)
Foreign Office, Buenos Aires

I've been very close to these territorial disputes for many years. The problem will not be solved for a very long time; and the fact that the war was fought and there were victims has made it all the more important. The war did not strengthen the UK's position, nor did it diminish the validity of Argentina's claim. I'm sure that at some time there will be a compromise solution. But I don't think that the current economic, political and military power of Britain can guarantee that it will prevail. In the nineteenth century, Argentina was far more prosperous. In the future, the prices of commodities like oil and soya beans will change, and problems like terrorism and immigration will evolve. Things could change enormously.

John Fowler
Superintendent of Education, Stanley

The invasion awakened the British government to their responsibility for us. Our prosperity now stems from the armed presence that is here now, which allows us to sell licences for the fishing zone. But whether that is worth all of what happened is another question – I don't know. We are very small, and sometimes I wonder what rights we have in the wider world. Quite regularly, disasters kill populations several times greater than all of us. I wouldn't like to have to stand in front of one of the widows from the *Galahad* or Mount Longdon and tell them that the sacrifice of their husband was worth it; equally I wouldn't like to tell her that his sacrifice wasn't worth it. We thought the Argentines would give up their claim and we wouldn't have to worry about it any more. But the dust had barely settled and they were back reiterating their claim in the United Nations, leaving us thinking, 'What the hell was it all for?'

Linda Kitson
Official war artist

The Falklands War taught me that there are always going to be wars. All the talking people like the Pope, the United Nations, Lord Soper on his box, peace movements, governments, NATO – they might just as well have stayed at home. Nothing could avert it, and yet it should have been a very easy war to stop. These things can't be resolved by talking. Until we evolve into a different species, these things won't change. People seem to enjoy it. The gentle voices are never heard.

Glossary

2ic – second in command

ATO – Ammunitions Technical Officer

AWO – Air Warfare Officer

battalion – body of troops, around 650 men in three rifle companies plus a support company and headquarters company, three of which may form a brigade

bergan – type of rucksack

Blowpipe – portable surface-to-air missile

brigade – a formation of three battalions, headquarters, an artillery regiment, engineer squadron, with signals logistics and other supporting units

Buzo Tactico – a unit of Argentine Navy Special Forces

BV – Bandvagn; a tracked, all-terrain vehicle

C-130s – Hercules transport aircraft

cam cream – camouflage cream

CAP pilots – Combat Air Patrol pilots

casevac – casualty evacuation

check-zeroing our rifles – firing to adjust the sights so that the rifle hits whatever the sights are aimed at

club-swinger – slang name for the PTI (Physical Training Instructor)

COMAW – Commodore Amphibious Warfare

commando – a battalion-sized unit of Royal Marines, with a commando artillery battery, troop of Royal Engineers and supporting sub-units; also one man, or type of warfare (i.e., commando-style raid)

CVRT – light reconnaissance armoured vehicle (Combat Vehicle Reconnaissance Tracked)

DF – referring to artillery, 'Defensive Fire', in which artillery fires at pre-registered targets on likely enemy routes and forming-up areas

DMS boots – Direct Moulded Sole boots

double sentry duty – Buckingham Palace drill, marching up and down, in pairs

DPR – Director, Public Relations

evolution – navy speak meaning everything that has to be done to some particular, and usually routine, end

EW – Electronic Warfare

EW team gollies – Electronic Warfare intelligence officers

FAL rifle – Fusil Automatique Leger, a light automatic rifle. 7.62mm like the British SLR, but also able to fire bursts of automatic fire

FIGAS – Falkland Islands Government Air Service

FOO – Forward Observation Officer

FUP – Forming-Up Place or Point

GPMGs – General-Purpose Machine Guns

GPMG SF kits – General-Purpose Machine Gun, Sustained Fire role, with the gun mounted on a tripod firing long belts of linked ammunition, with spare barrels for rapid replacements every few minutes to prevent melting from the intense heat

growlers – small icebergs

'hands to bathe' – a ships order permitting crew to swim in the sea

HE – High Explosives

H-Hour – the specific time at which an operation commences

IDF – Island Defence Force

illum – any sort of illuminating flare, rocket, mortar or artillery shell

LCU – landing craft (Landing Craft, Utility)

LCVP – Landing Craft Vehicle Personnel

lids – soldiers' steel helmets

L of C – Line of Communication

LPD – Landing Pad Dock: generic name for the commando assault ships *Fearless* and *Intrepid*

LSL – Landing Craft Logistic

MEXE – Military Engineering Experimental Establishment

MoD – Ministry of Defence

NCO – Non-Commissioned Officer, the collective description for all ranks from lance corporal to sergeant. Sergeants major are collectively described as warrant officers

NGSFO – Naval Gunfire Support Forward Observer

nutty – naval slang for chocolate and sweets (whether containing nuts or not)

O Group – Orders Group, when an officer gives orders for an operation

OP – Observation Post

Pan Am – Pan American Airlines, which ceased trading in 1991

PIN – Position Indicator

PJI – Parachute Jump Instructor

platoon – the basic unit of infantry; three sections of around eight men each, plus a small headquarters, commanded by a lieutenant

PNG – Passive Night (vision) Goggles

PWO – Principal Warfare Officer

RAP – Regiment Aid Post

RAS – Resupply At Sea

Red de Observadores del Aire – Argentine national organisation of airspace monitoring

REME – Royal Electrical & Mechanical Engineers

RFA – The Royal Fleet Auxiliary Service is a civilian manned fleet, owned by the Ministry of Defence. Its main task is to supply warships of the Royal Navy

Royal Marines – a corps of infantry troops, part of the Royal Navy, who are responsible for commando training and amphibious operations

RV – rendezvous

sangars – a protection structure created by soldiers in which they dig down, then build up walls round the edge of their hole, often of rocks in rocky terrain where digging a proper trench is impossible

SAS – Special Air Service

SBS – Special Boat Service, in 1982, often referred to as the 'Squadron', 'SB' or 'Special Boat Squadron'

SEAL – Sea Air Land: US Marines' SBS

Sea Wolf system – anti-aircraft missile system

Shimuli flare – hand-fired illumination flare

Ship's company – the crew of a ship

Sitrep – situation report

SLR – British 7.62mm self-loading rifle

Spring Train – the exercise which many of the task force ships were conducting, in the Med, before being sent to the South Atlantic

SS.11 rockets – anti-tank missiles

Swift scope – powerful monocular telescope made by Swift

tabbing (fit) – 'tactical advance to battle' – the Paras' term for very fast marching, carrying heavy loads over rough terrain

Tac – tactical headquarters; a small mobile group with radios, which usually deploys to command from the front line

Teeny Weenie helicopters (also Teeny Weenie Airlines) – Army Air Corps' helicopters

TEZ – Total Exclusion Zone

The Camp – refers to anywhere outside of Port Stanley. Probably derives from the Spanish word *campo*, countryside

The Flag – refers to the admiral, his office and his staff. Where they live and work is known as the flagship, as this ship is carrying 'the flag'

the white bellies – peacetime Harriers were painted white underneath

Toms – slang for Parachute Regiment soldiers (from 'Tommy Atkins')

TraLa – Tactical Recovery and Logistic Area

UHF – Ultra High Frequency radio sets: used by aircraft

Unifoxer – acoustic torpedo decoy

Index of Contributors

Number in brackets denotes IWM Sound Archive catalogue number. Page numbers in **bold** refer to photographs.

PM denotes Private Material supplied by the author

Thanks go to Graham Bound for permitting use of his personal collection

Transcriptions of Argentine material: Sonia Ollero Isidoro (Spanish) and Pauline Mitchell (Anglo-Argentine); Translations of Argentine material: Pauline Mitchell (Anglo-Argentine)

General Index

Note: page numbers in **bold** refer to photographs.